Frenchness and African Diaspora

Identity and Uprising in Contemporary France

Edited by Charles Tshimanga,
Didier Gondola,
and Peter J. Bloom

Indiana University Press
Bloomington and Indianapolis

This book is a publication of

Indiana University Press
601 North Morton Street
Bloomington, IN 47404-3797 USA

www.iupress.indiana.edu

Telephone orders	800-842-6796
Fax orders	812-855-7931
Orders by e-mail	iuporder@indiana.edu

⊛ The paper used in this publication meets the minimum requirements of the American
National Standard for Information Sciences—Permanence of Paper for Printed Library
Materials, ANSI Z39.48-1992.

Manufactured in the United States of America

Library of Congress Cataloging-in-Publication Data

Frenchness and the African diaspora : identity and uprising in contemporary France /
  edited by Charles Tshimanga, Didier Gondola, and Peter J. Bloom.
      p.   cm.
  Includes bibliographical references and index.
      ISBN 978-0-253-35375-7 (cloth : alk. paper) — ISBN 978-0-253-22131-5
  (pbk. : alk. paper)
      1. African diaspora—France. 2. National characteristics, French. 3. Africans—
  France—Social conditions. 4. Africans—France—Ethnic identity. 5. Africans—
  France—Attitudes. 6. Africans—France—Cultural assimilation. 7. Popular
  culture—France. 8. France—Race relations. 9. France—Civilization—African
  influences. I. Tshimanga, Charles. II. Gondola, Ch. Didier, date– III. Bloom,
  Peter J.
    DC34.5.A37F745   2009
    305.896'044—dc22

                                                  2009017102

1   2   3   4   5   14   13   12   11   10   09

CONTENTS

Acknowledgments   vii

Introduction: Examining Frenchness and the
African Diaspora   3

PART 1. *Auto da fé:* **Understanding the 2005 Riots**

1. Primitive Rebellion in the French *Banlieues:*
On the Fall 2005 Riots / **Didier Lapeyronnie**   21

2. The Republic and Its Beast: On the Riots
in the French *Banlieues* / **Achille Mbembe**   47

3. Figures of Multiplicity: Can France Reinvent
Its Identity? / **Achille Mbembe**   55

4. Outsiders in the French Melting Pot:
The Public Construction of Invisibility for
Visible Minorities / **Ahmed Boubeker**   70

PART 2. Colonization, Citizenship, and Containment

5. From Imperial Inclusion to Republican Exclusion?
France's Ambiguous Postwar Trajectory /
Frederick Cooper   91

6. Colonial Syndrome: French Modern and the
Deceptions of History / **Florence Bernault**   120

7. Transient Citizens: The Othering and
Indigenization of *Blacks* and *Beurs* within the
French Republic / **Didier Gondola**   146

8. The Law of February 23, 2005:
The Uses Made of the Revival of France's
"Colonial Grandeur" / **Nicolas Bancel**   167

PART 3. Visions and Tensions of Frenchness

9. A Conservative Revolution within Secularism:
The Ideological Premises and Social Effects of the
March 15, 2004, "Anti-Headscarf" Law /
Pierre Tévanian   187

10. Zidane: Portrait of the Artist as Political Avatar /
Nacira Guénif-Souilamas   205

11. The State of French Cultural Exceptionalism:
The 2005 Uprisings and the Politics of Visibility /
Peter J. Bloom   227

12. Let the Music Play: The African Diaspora,
Popular Culture, and National Identity in
Contemporary France / **Charles Tshimanga**   248

Appendix 1
A Call to Action: "We Are the Natives of the Republic!"   277

Glossary   283
Bibliography   293
List of Contributors   319
Index   323

ACKNOWLEDGMENTS

When we embarked upon this project, we had no way of knowing that so many people would lend their support and assist in all stages of the completion of this book. We would like to thank our contributors for their patience and willingness to create this collective intervention with us for the English reading community. Given the extended timetable for completing a university press publication in the United States, we appreciate their understanding, and have gained much from their perspective in our own ongoing research. We were also fortunate to find two excellent translators after encountering many difficulties along the way. Jane Marie Todd, a consummate professional of the highest caliber, has informed many of the texts that she has translated, and Naomi Baldinger, who completed her M.A. in comparative literature at UCLA, is clearly an emerging talent in translation but also in parsing and rearticulating critical arguments.

Assembling this volume has been a challenge, and Dee Mortensen, senior sponsoring editor at Indiana University Press, has been extremely supportive of the project since we first proposed it to her, and her enthusiasm has been critical to seeing it to completion. Laura MacLeod, assistant sponsoring editor at IU Press, has been extremely helpful in taking us through the production process, and freelance copyeditor Carol A. Kennedy has lent a careful eye to the whole manuscript. Finally, the suggestions of the readers, organized through the anonymous review process at IU Press, have greatly improved the final version of the manuscript.

We are grateful to friends and colleagues who generously contributed to the volume through informal conversations and email exchanges. Of these people we would especially like to acknowledge Fatou Biramah, Armelle Cressent, Frieda Ekotto, Maria Grosz-Ngate, Lachelle Hannickel, Bennetta Jules-Rosette, Trica Keaton, Alain Mabanckou, Corinne Mélis, Dominic Thomas, and Fatimata Wane. We would also like to thank

Houria Bouteldja for allowing us to translate the "L'Appel des Indigènes" manifesto and reproduce a signature image for the Indigènes de la République.

Our three institutions, Indiana University-Purdue University at Indianapolis (IUPUI), the University of California, Santa Barbara (UCSB), and the University of Nevada, Reno (UNR), have contributed their support to this project at various stages. Funding from IUPUI has been used to support the index for the publication as well as the research conducted by Didier Gondola in France that included a short documentary entitled *Transient Citizens* (prod. Didier Gondola, DVD, 50', 2006). At UCSB, Peter J. Bloom invited the co-editors to present a featured panel as part of the 7th Annual UC Irvine–UC Santa Barbara Graduate Student Conference in French and Francophone Studies in May 2006, allowing them to further develop the project at a crucial juncture. Research funding at UCSB has been used to support various failed and final translations included in the volume. Funding through the "Scholarly and Creative Activities Grant," sponsored by the College of Liberal Arts at UNR has contributed to several of the translations in our collection as well as various additional production costs. Research funding through the "Junior Faculty Research Grant" sponsored by UNR has been used to support research trips made to France by Charles Tshimanga. During these visits to France, he conducted interviews with French hip-hop performers, including Passi, Hamé, Ekoué, and Casey.

In conjunction with the collected articles for this volume, Charles Tshimanga has organized three panels entitled "The African Diaspora in France: Exploring the Notions of Identity, Culture, and Nation," at the 48th Annual Meeting of the African Studies Association (Washington, D.C., November 17–20, 2005); "Why Is Paris Burning? African Diaspora and Identity Issue in Contemporary France," at the 49th Annual Meeting of the African Studies Association (San Francisco, November 16–19, 2006); and "Frenchness and the African Diaspora," at the 50th Annual Congress of the African Studies Association (New York, October 18–21, 2007). Didier Gondola conducted a series of interviews with teenagers from the Seine-Saint Denis area, where the riots began, in November 2005. These panels and interviews have enriched the depth of reflection given to the theme of the African Diaspora in France.

Finally, this collection was a challenging collective endeavor for the co-editors, but has reinforced a sense of friendship and appreciation for one another's abilities and stake in seeing this project come to life. The volume has also been its very own process of coming to terms with our very different relationships to Frenchness, the African diaspora, and the 2005 uprisings.

Frenchness and the African Diaspora

Examining Frenchness and the African Diaspora

On October 27, 2005, a few days after the passing of Rosa Parks, one of the last iconic figures of the 1960s American civil rights movement, two youths of Mauritanian and Tunisian origin, Bouna Traoré (aged fifteen) and Zyed Benna (aged seventeen), died in Clichy-sous-Bois, a *banlieue*, located ten miles east of Paris.[1] Bouna, Zyed, and several others were returning to their *cité* (housing projects) after playing a game of soccer. Rushing home to break the Ramadan fast, they encountered a police patrol at the entrance of their *cité*. These teenagers then took off in different directions to avoid the prospect of police brutality; some managed to slip through the net of the patrol, while others looked for safety within an unlocked electrical substation.[2] Bouna, Zyed, and Muhittin Altun (a youth of Turkish origin) were among the latter group. After they spent approximately thirty minutes searching for a way out of the 10,000-volt substation, Muhittin's body was literally projected outside of the substation. He was severely scorched by an electrical charge, was later hospitalized, and has since recovered. Inside laid Bouna's and Zyed's corpses.

The subsequent uprisings throughout the country followed a well-rehearsed historical pattern, specific to France, in which social change is motivated by the paroxysms of collective unrest.[3] The dialectical tension between the notorious *bavure policière*, on the one hand, and youth rioting, on the other, has been well documented since the 1981 riots at the *cité* des Minguettes of Vénissieux, outside of Lyons.[4] Numerous commentators have interpreted these riots as a statement of rage and defiance against a discriminatory arsenal consisting of unemployment, ghettoization, and racial profiling that have become accepted features of social disenfranchisement (Beaud and Pialoux 2003). Although one could easily identify similarities between the 2005 events in Clichy-sous-Bois and previous *banlieue* riots, there are crucial differences. It was the gravity of these most recent uprisings, alternatively known as riots, as a historical continuity and a political rupture that has served as an impetus for organizing this edited volume.

The sheer magnitude of the three-week riots is one of the most salient features. Starting in Clichy-sous-Bois, the riots affected most major French cities and nearly all midsized ones in virtually every one of the ninety-five French metropolitan *départements.* There were 201 police casualties and 26 injured firemen; no less than 10,000 automobiles, 100 postal cars and trucks, 200 public buses, and several dozen police cars were either torched or stoned. Hundreds of public buildings (including schools, police stations, and city halls) were vandalized or burnt to the ground, and at least twenty religious centers (including mosques, churches, and synagogues) were seriously damaged. At the height of the riots, nearly 12,000 police and gendarmes were deployed to quell the nightly riots, whose operations resulted in 5,200 arrests. A report issued by the Renseignements Généraux (RG, the French equivalent of the FBI, with a secret service mandate) estimated the financial toll caused by these events at nearly $300 million (Mucchielli and Le Goaziou 2006: 9).

The aftermath turned out to be perhaps as momentous and revelatory as the riots themselves, especially in a post-9/11 world where cultural and ethnic difference of the underclass has been used to substantiate Samuel Huntington's distorted "clash-of-civilizations" paradigm, thus giving ammunition to a clinically paranoid but rhetorically efficient form of political communication that pits "us" against "them."[5] Dissent and subversion have become open-ended categories in the global war on terror such that the agentive power of minority populations is made synonymous with an international terror network justifying state repression.[6] With this call to order, an antagonistic Manichean rhetoric has reignited a climate of fear, condensed in arguments claiming that cultural differences finally function as obstacles to globalization. Former Interior minister, now president, Nicolas Sarkozy framed the riots within an ascendant politics of fear and innuendo, claiming that the racial underclass can be written off as an "organized intifada," a nondescript group of Islamic fundamentalists, a network of drug- and arms-dealing gangs, or diasporic polygamist tribes.[7]

These political arguments, intended to explain what Bernard Cassen has dubbed the "French Katrina," subliminally blame the riots on the irreconcilable cultural differences between the "French" (*us*) and the "Africans" (*them*) and on the atavistic inability of the latter to integrate.[8] Thus, these assertions have justified increasingly aggressive and defensive forms of state interventionism that not only stigmatize the *banlieues* as places of *non-droit* (lawlessness), where the laws as well as the values of the *République* are shunned, but as "sensitive neighborhoods" mostly populated by undesirable *immigrés* (immigrants).[9] Not only did Sarkozy refer to the rioters as "*la racaille*" (variously translated as rabble, trash, and scum), one-upping Jean-Marie Le Pen, he also blamed their parents for "[failing] to exercise authority [over their children]," and called upon the French Parliament to pass legislation depriving them of child support.[10] Yielding to appeals made by far right leader Marine Le Pen, daughter of Jean-Marie and heir apparent of the Front National, the French government decreed on November 8, 2005, a state of emergency by invoking the April 3, 1955, law used to suppress unrest in France during the Algerian War. When it was first enacted, this law legalized extrajudicial practices against Algerian nationalists and led to the infamous Paris Pogrom on October 17, 1961.[11] In its most recent form, it gave municipal authorities the right to declare curfews and exemplified, in the words of activist Mimouna Hadjam, a "colonial management of the [*banlieue*] crisis."[12]

Activating dormant colonial paradigms to deal with the immigrant population and their French offspring also suggests that diasporic issues in France exist within what Dominic Thomas has called a "transcolonial vector." Or a calculus of exclusion that no longer hinges on cultural superiority but rather on cultural difference, thus "deferring assimilation indefinitely." This is attributable to a pernicious situation in which "Africans in France remain the locus of colonial anxieties" (Thomas 2006: 8). Colonization thus becomes memorialized in rituals of *retournement* and *détournement* as part of a repressed master narrative motivating current events (Blanchard and Lemaire 2004). Mandating that nationwide secondary school curricula include the "positive role of a French overseas presence, especially in North Africa," is yet another example of what could only be described as the colonial unconscious made manifest.[13] The underlying message of article 4 of the February 23, 2005, law was to sanitize the colonial past by simply reaffirming the values of national sacrifice

associated with the *mission civilisatrice*. Yet, it was also an attempt to reinforce the postcolonial status quo by fingering the sons and daughters of
African immigrants for failing to assimilate. Victims remain in their place
so long as the materiality and rhetoric of oppression manage to invert
the roles of victim and oppressor, thus turning hegemony into progress
and the "purported" victim into a foil such that hegemonic agency can
masquerade in the victim's role.

The French government's approach to the riots has thus exposed
the paradoxical nature of the French postcolonial Republic in which
the universal values associated with Frenchness and citizenship function as part of a political discourse that masks the causes for inequality
and discontent. Accordingly, minority consciousness and activism are
perceived as a threat to France's long-proclaimed international humanitarianism precisely because they reveal racial inequalities in a country
that purports to be the standard bearer of the universal rights of man.
This explains the pervading myth that racism in France, as opposed to
Britain or Germany, functions in a vacuum, within a race-less society
where certain groups are unable to assimilate or embrace French cultural norms: it is yet another way of creating a climate of racial exclusionism, through the rhetoric of what Tyler Stovall and Sue Peabody
have called "racism without races" (Peabody and Stovall 2003: 1–11).

It is for this reason that the legacy of colonial stereotypes has served
as an important site for contestation. The African "other," who is in
fact French, has been variously positioned as the cause of violent confrontation because of a purported pathological condition, reviving
a social Darwinian order of being, and a series of political antidotes.
These social fictions resurfaced during the debates that ensued after the
riots. The political vocabulary of rebuke drew on a chain of oppositions,
beginning with an unabashed deployment of racial stereotypes whose
vanishing point refers to the perception of the immigrant as a threat to
national identity. An important component in this debate is the way in
which the New Right, associated with figures such as Alain Finkielkraut,
has asserted a new form of hostile social exclusionism.

Throughout the 1990s, the debates and court cases concerning
Vichy collaborationism have had a direct impact on notions of contemporary French identity.[14] On the one hand, the assimilationist sense
of Jewish identity has been celebrated as the embodiment of secular
French universalism, but this has also served to cover up how the pur-

ported model of French universalism shifts the nature of exclusionism to other populations and imputed social practices in a media apparatus that underscores *difference* as a source of conflict. The fight against anti-Semitism as adopted by the New Right has been transformed into yet another exclusionary regime that seeks to ignore difference in the name of universalism.

Admittedly, this is a complex dynamic of deferral that finally undermines the very foundations of French universalism. Though Frenchness might be paired with universalism, we are interested in addressing Frenchness as an ongoing site of contestation, through its interaction with the African diaspora. A significant theme that has emerged from this examination of the 2005 riots is the notion of the "event as rupture" that reveals a colonial legacy, such that the question of race cannot be seen, as in the psychoanalytic notion of scotomization—or an infantile, unrepressed wish that denies reality within the visible spectrum. This is why many of the authors in this volume examine the use of language that goes against the grain of French republican ideology. The use of the American term "black," as opposed to "*noir*," for example, by *banlieue* youth is discussed in a number of the contributions. Further, the relationship between affirmative action as defined in the United States and *discrimination positive* in France is yet another important source of debate. Several contributors underscore how the semantics of conservative French public discourse routinely camouflages racial difference.

In fact, this volume examines the contradiction between France's color-blind republican ideology and policies in relation to the "epidermalization" of French nationals of African origin. If the 2005 uprisings loom large in most of the chapters presented here and serve as a conduit for our discussions, it is because they have crystallized issues still confined to the recesses of republican principles bound up in unchallenged assumptions about the nature of Frenchness and Europeanness. They have given new urgency to a debate about the intersection and conflation of a discursive chain that includes race, class, citizenship, religion, violence, immigration, colonization, popular culture, police repression, and even slavery. The awakening of public consciousness on the nature of these social categories has also indirectly implicated the role of globalization, modernity, and *mémoire*. A crisis of identity associated with the 2005 riots has shattered the French idea of universalism and leads us to ask, following Pierre Laurent, whether French *banlieue* culture erves as a crucible for an inclusionary French social model of the future (Laurent 2005).

French studies scholars in the United States have only recently taken into account the changing demographics of metropolitan France and its social and racial implications. France has most often represented the instantiation of cultural prestige and value, such that disentangling the meanings of "True France" often took precedence over the more tumultuous, and even more tragic, "other France," or a "new France" in the making. Many American historians of France encountered the Hexagon through intellectual trajectories quite different from the approaches represented in this volume.[15] Just as the visibility of African Americans in France became an initial wedge in this discourse, important works on the history of French colonialism later culminating in the expanded discourse of postcolonial studies have been equally influential.[16] However, our intervention into the already rich reassessment of Frenchness has led us to see that some of the early works in North America reveal more about the conflicts associated with the civil rights movement and the Vietnam War that nurtured a hope for the revival of French universalism than an exploration of its exclusionary effects. France's purported color-blind society serves as a recurrent theme in works addressing the African American "presence and prestige" in France. Historian Arthur Barbeau, for instance, romanticizes the encounter between black American soldiers and Republican France during World War I and posits France as a locus of racial empowerment for African Americans without examining its relationship to colonial racism (Barbeau and Henri 1974). As part of a shifting trajectory represented by Tyler Stovall's *Paris Noir* and Leininger-Miller's *New Negro Artists in Paris,* works that focus on the embrace of a Parisianism that privileges difference distill a fascination with Frenchness and the Parisian reverie on the one hand, but complicate this story such that the very underpinnings of French national identity may be challenged. Stovall's examination of how the Left Bank intelligentsia's infatuation with African Americans through the lingering presence of French anti-Americanism inaugurates a line of inquiry regarding whether there is a direct structural relationship between the French celebration of African American exiles and the cultural denigration of African colonial subjects along with their postcolonial avatars. This trajectory has been joined with the adapted sociological tradition exploring the urban underclass in the work of Loïc Wacquant and Alec

Hargreaves. Further, Petrine Archer-Shaw's examination of interwar Negrophilia, or fascination with all forms of black and African cultural expression in France, decenters the all-knowing French avant-garde figures in favor of figures such as the American heiress and patron Nancy Cunard (Archer-Shaw 2004: 184).

In recent years, however, an emerging international generation of scholars working in North America have continued to explore the complex intersection of citizenship, race, and class in contemporary France and to explore another facet of France. The visibility of Islam, especially in a globalized post-9/11 world, looms large as a recurring theme in Trica Keaton's examination of how headscarved Muslim girls have been "fashioned as the quintessential other." Other studies have deliberately focused on a single group in an effort to illuminate tensions between national identity, on the one hand, and infranational and transnational belonging, on the other (Beriss 2004; Silverstein 2004). Taken together, these studies point to the emergence of postcolonial cultural patterns in France in which minority groups are more than merely dodging and subverting what Herman Lebovics calls the "straitjacket of [. . .] state-sanctioned identity," but are rearranging and rescripting narratives that structure the notion of Frenchness (Lebovics 1992: 196). For example, both Bennetta Jules-Rosette (1998) and Dominic Thomas (2006) have persuasively demonstrated how Paris has ultimately become an African metropolis, invested by African writers who have infused the ambient literary tradition with an Afro-Parisianism and outward-looking aesthetics of universalism. The same could be said of James Winders's *Paris Africain* (2006), exploring how African musical culture has shattered longstanding notions of French cultural hegemony and exceptionalism.

The essays gathered in this volume reflect these new orientations. Though diverse in their approaches to the notion of Frenchness, they explore a complex range of tensions that preside over the obliteration of "True France," and the emergence of a new, multicultural France. There is indeed an attempt, in all of these contributions, to reveal something about the cathartic process of coming to terms with the vestiges of the French colonial past in the *banlieue* geography of the postcolonial present, engaging in a process of *remue-mémoire,* or memory-work, in the name of reconciliation and against the rhetoric of social fracture, which cannot be set back into place.[17] This volume ties together original contributions from numerous scholars based in France whose work, for the most part, is unknown in North America. Thus, the volume primarily addresses international English-speaking and -reading communities in French and African studies, as well as in postcolonial and diaspora studies. Our focus on the African diaspora, which comprises the largest segment of the *banlieue* population, attempts to explore their trajectory from *indigènes* to *immigrés*, as Nicolas Bancel and Pascal Blanchard have suggested, unraveling the complex nature of Frenchness and republican assimilationism.[18] The recent surge of a *black* and *beur* consciousness in France can potentially recast assumptions still mired in colonial myths and reshape France's contemporary relationship to itself and Africa.

The first section of the volume, entitled "*Auto da fé:* Understanding the 2005 Riots," addresses the fall 2005 urban riots and the ways in which they have challenged and displaced the notion of Frenchness from its historical loci. Subtly refuting Samuel Huntington's theory (1996) that the post–Cold War period has been marked by a clash of civilizations, the essays in this section equally reject Alain Finkielkraut's claim that the 2005 uprisings were an expression of an ethno-religious movement.[19] The idea set forth by Nicolas Sarkozy and certain conservative members of Parliament that France is attacked from within by Islamic fundamentalists is similarly repudiated. Thus, the opening chapters deconstruct the binary opposition that proclaims Islam to be at odds with French culture and dismantles claims that the *banlieue* crisis is a result of French Muslims being unable to integrate into French culture. Instead, the contributors propose to look at the riots within France's broader revolutionary tradition of sedition, mutiny, riots, and disturbances initially suggested in Charles Tilly's 1986 groundbreaking study, *The Contentious French.*

The first section of this volume semantically associates the torching of automobiles as the most visible sign of the 2005 riots with the culpability of those accused. Didier Lapeyronnie's lead contribution rejects all romantic as well as simplistic approaches to the 2005 revolt, uncovering the rationale behind the rebellion while reexamining the revolt in light of the first urban riots of the early 1980s, within a social context fraught with social inequalities, discrimination, racism, police violence, and the emergence of ghettos. He argues that instead of being a form of criminality, the 2005 uprisings constituted a highly political collective action that articulated the demands of marginalized ethnic minorities. Lapeyronnie explains the logic of the rioter as an agent, emerging from the lower stratum of the marginalized, who directly opposes the ascendant destructive, cynical, and racializing political and social order. If rioting is a means of rational pressure against injustice, it is also a political act that reclaims the rights inscribed in the French Constitution.

Ahmed Boubeker, too, is concerned with the significance of the 2005 uprising. His essay offers an essential context that deconstructs the stereotypes that have stigmatized ethnic minorities over the last twenty-five years. Boubeker argues that France refuses to face the reality of its multiethnic population and treats ethnic minorities on the order of domestic foreigners. France's refusal to recognize the Other as a full-fledged integrated citizen breeds violence that feeds the tensions experienced in the *banlieues*. In addition, successive semantic changes bear witness to the construction of the Other, especially when one considers terms such as "mafia tendencies," "ethnic demands," and "communitarianism," and statements such as "France can no longer accommodate the destitute of the world." Boubeker shows the limits of the paradigm of assimilation (*intégration*) suggested by Gérard Noiriel (1988) in a France that has been exposed to globalization and new forms of cultural hybridity. He suggests that the institutions of the Republic have failed to integrate, but rather they discriminate.

Achille Mbembe's two articles were written in the aftermath of the 2005 riots and also offer insightful analyses of the rebellion. In the first article, Mbembe posits the riots as a response to state racism (embodied by Le Pen and more recently by Sarkozy), and refers to these unseen causes as the "shameful face" or "dark side" of a Republic that, in spite of recent events, has been a defining concept of contemporary world culture and civilization. Mbembe sees similarities between racially driven essentialist practices of categorization and control that were once practiced in the colonies, the treatment and humiliation of individuals deemed undesirable on French territory, and, finally, the denigration of French citizens of African descent. In his second short article, Mbembe reexamines the riots through the prism of "race." He highlights widespread practices of "racialization" that occur in everyday life, notably job discrimination, police profiling, unwarranted surveillance, school segregation, and a general lack of recognition and respect. He points out that since the 1980s, legislation applicable to foreigners derives from laws once applied to Jews and colonial subjects. He notes the contradiction between racializing practices on the one hand and the production of humanist and universalist discourse on the other. Mbembe is convinced that France can reinvent itself if the existing talent and energy can be fused together, as in the world of *le foot*—soccer.

In section two of the volume, "Colonization, Citizenship, and Containment," the four chapters address the status of French postcolonial citizenship through detailed analyses of the colonial legacy and the institution of French history. The nature of colonial geography in relation to citizenship is taken up in a nuanced and historically acute fashion in Frederick Cooper's article, "From Imperial Inclusion to Republican Exclusion?" Cooper persuasively argues that the transition from colonial to immigrant subject is complicated by a passage through the status of the imperial citizen. The competing arguments concerning the status of the imperial citizen, as both artifact of the colonial legacy and invention of decolonization, were not overdetermined by an exclusionary outcome, Cooper argues. In fact, he reveals that important distinctions between French citizenship and French national identity served as important claim-making constructs. Senghor's distinction between "nation" and "patrie," along with a layered approach to sovereignty, were influential to the post–World War II development of the *Union Française* as a potentially open-ended fraternity of French citizens. Cooper describes the legal terminology of "free circulation," which allowed for an influx of workers from North Africa into France during the 1950s on the one hand, but also allowed for French citizens to continue residing in the French colonies, on the other. Much of his discussion, that includes the *Français musulmans d'Algérie* as a category of French citizenship with particular rights, indicates the possibility of a more inclusive republican model that could have been instituted through this crucial passage from imperial subject to immigrant; it is a passage that might have allowed for equal access to all on the basis of French citizenship. In fact, he cites the short-lived decree of 16 *pluviôse* (February 4, 1794), which abolished slavery and further proclaimed that "all men, without distinction of color, resident in our colonies, are French citizens and enjoy all rights assured by the Constitution."

Cooper's rendering of citizenship rights as a site of possibility is addressed in relation to the themes of historical and political deception in the articles to follow in this section of the volume. Florence Bernault's chapter addresses intellectual responses to the current crisis, beginning with new initiatives taken in the early 2000s by French citizens of African descent to counter the ideological underpinnings of racial segregation, that she describes as the "Native's Promise." The creation of an array of organizations, including the Conseil Représentatif des Associations Noires (CRAN), and the Indigènes de la République, proposed a radical critique of hegemonic Republican discourse, and cut to the heart of a mounting conservative reaction among French historians and the institution of French history. Although historians were united in their opposition to the law of February 23, 2005, as Nicolas Bancel asserts in his contribution, Bernault shows how many among them reject colonial and postcolonial analyses of the crisis, for fear of "ethnicizing" the social question. For Bernault, the opportunity for intellectual strides offered by the 2005–2006 crisis, has been, so far, missed by most in the French academic establishment.

In Didier Gondola's intervention, "Transient Citizens," he examines how the theme of political complicity functions in contemporary France. Through the intersection of othering and indigenization, he describes a series of parables that connect political calculations of blatant exploitation on the African continent to the persistence of colonial relations between France and its population of African descent. In his discussion of the Elf oil scandal in the Congo, he describes the power of the company to buy off the kleptocratic elites who serve them, and points to how calls for democracy are negated by policies of postcolonial extraction and the purchase of militias to destabilize less-than-compliant politicians. Crucially, however, Gondola establishes a link between post-imperial relations organized through French corporate entities and state policies that serve to marginalize the French-born African population within the *métropole* itself. Through Gondola's comparative discussion of the African diaspora in France, the United Kingdom, and the United States, he finally addresses how the status of African immigrants in France is embodied by derisive colonial myths that lurk within, and are reinforced by, essentializing discourses that run the gamut from extreme right conservative politicians to progressive activists.

Nicolas Bancel's expanded discussion of the February 23, 2005, law picks up on some of the very same themes of political deception, as he describes how article 4 was used to court those repatriated to France from Algeria. The legislation itself, which proclaims the nation's duty to recognize the positive work of colonization, created a furor within the French community of historians. Through Bancel's detailed discussion of this affair, and the significance of the repatriated demographic, we come to see how it was the outcome of a ten-year-long process by which the colonial era was being repositioned in the politics of identity and the orchestration of denial. Contemporary polarizations and radicalizations have thus enabled the emergence of new organizations, such as the Indigènes and the CRAN, that have created a different context for debate about the uses of historical memory.

Finally, new visions and possibilities for reclaiming egalitarian and secular premises of the French *République* that unsettle established hegemonic narratives are addressed in the last section of the volume, entitled "Visions and Tensions of Frenchness." Through an examination of the headscarf affair and the contested terrain of popular culture, the contributors examine new discursive landscapes in which words taken as signs shape public opinion. As signifiers and semantic devices, revolutionary possibilities in creative thinking and social action are linked to the construction and dismantling of carefully crafted lexicons.

It is this kind of revolution, albeit a conservative one, that Pierre Tévanian examines. It is a revolution that deployed a secular lexicon over the seemingly innocuous issue of the headscarf to articulate deep-seated anxieties about post-imperial demographic and cultural changes taking place in the *métropole*. Tévanian's paper calls to mind Nacira Guénif-Souilamas's *Les féministes et le garçon arabe* (2004) as well as Keaton's *Muslim Girls and the Other France* (2006). These works analyze discourses and practices in late-twentieth-century France founded on cultural differences, which cast headscarved Muslim girls as "the quintessential other." Offering a unique approach based on fine-grained analyses, Tévanian explores the 2004 anti-headscarf legislation, which, he argues, served as a linchpin to a conservative revolution that attempted to lay claims to what many came to regard as forgotten French secularism. Although the majority of the population opposed legislation to ban religious sartorial displays at school, proponents of the law brandished the specter of Islamic fundamentalism—poised to undermine the French secular fabric, using headscarved school girls as a fifth column—thus turning secularism itself into a dogma and French public schools into contested spaces of secular fundamentalism. French secularism as an enshrined "neutral" frame intended to safeguard freedom, especially freedom of religion, and act as a great equalizer has morphed into what Tévanian calls "securitarian secularism." As an exclusionary ideology that would yield to no other claims and meanings, it serves as an ultimatum to Islam in France to become either secularized (i.e., accept state control) or confined to private performances and rituals.

The rise of this neo-secularism certainly accounted for the popularity of Zinédine Zidane, a multifaceted hero who became, following his exploits in the 1998 World soccer cup, an iconic figure and the embodiment of Frenchness. Contrary to headscarved teenagers, Zidane refused to wear his Islamic faith on his sleeve, nor has he used his visibility in the media to call attention to issues affecting ethnic minorities in France. This, to Guénif-Souilamas, owes much to the many "lives" of Zidane. His dual allegiance (French and Algerian) and uncanny ability to remain politically amorphous and inscrutable have turned him into a popular sensation, with several constituencies claiming his persona. Indeed, Zidane remains a paradoxical site for representations and contestations both on and off the field, invested first by none other than the state itself. Zidane's encapsulating lucrative image, intended for public consumption, enabled the state to create a lexical fiction, "*Black, Blanc, Beur*," later singularized and demoted to *l'Arabe* (the Arab), following Zidane's infamous head-butt in Berlin during the final France-Italy match. Zidane, the epitome of the model immigrant who rose from a blighted *banlieue* in Marseilles to the national pantheon and international fame, is reverted back into the figure of the Arab that has haunted French collective memory since Charles Martel.

In Peter J. Bloom's analysis of the gymnastic technique of *parkour*, and its presence in Luc Besson's blockbuster film *District B13* (2004), the body fulfills a similar function within narratives of escape from the confining spatiality of the *banlieue*. *Parkour* is known to the French *banlieue* youths under the term *Yamakasi*—which evokes the promise of Asian martial arts on the one hand, but is actually a Congolese Lingala term meaning "strong person." Bloom is interested in examining *parkour* as a global marketing vehicle promoted in the name of a multiethnic international *precariat* who are in the throes of confinement and in search of escape. Through an examination of its surface structure of commodification within a black American vernacular, he focuses on the mise-en-scène as an historical palimpsest of postwar French reconstruction. *Parkour* becomes a means by which to address the *banlieue* setting as synonymous with the history of La Muette in Drancy, which served as one of the most significant transit camps during the German occupation. Furthermore, Bloom picks up on the rhetoric of the "cultural exception" as a means of referring to a boundary unique to the position of French cultural creation in debates about globalization in cinema. He argues that these debates reveal an underlying structure of cultural and racial exclusionism in the name of universalism and the construction of the *auteur.*

Another arena of popular culture is examined by Charles Tshimanga, who shows how hip-hop aesthetics suggest new visions of Frenchness and rearrange the semantics of cultural identity. He, especially, demonstrates how rap discourse, notwithstanding its performativity and commodification, no longer operates just in the realm of contestation and subversion, but serves as a rhetorical strategy through which discernible, yet inchoate, possibilities are being negotiated. *Banlieue* rappers appear in Tshimanga's narrative to be the *griots* of silent, yet visible, minority youths who have no desire to retreat from Frenchness but want to partake in what looks more and more like Benedict Anderson's imagined community or, perhaps, a polity that transcends race, ethnicity, religion, and even class, *pace* Ernest Renan, in which Frenchness no longer figures as this singular, immutable category, impervious to global culture and demographic changes. Furthermore, through Tshimanga's interviews with some of the best-known French rappers, such as Passi, Hamé, Ekoué, and Casey, and his careful description of their engagement with contemporary political debates, he challenges French neo-reactionary rhetoric that claims "anti-white racism." His detailed analysis of Diam's 2006 release "Ma France à moi" and "Marine" puts into perspective how derisive stereotypes can be renegotiated through popular music and explains the crucial function of hip-hop idioms.

The four contributions in this third and final section of the volume address how the notion of secular affinities can position French multicultural society as a series of republican folds so long as Frenchness is understood by all as a *devenir* (becoming) or, as Tshimanga suggests, a borderless sense of belonging in perpetual flux.

Notes

1. French critics have juxtaposed the French *banlieue* crisis to the ghettoization of African Americans in the inner cities, comparing the 2005 French uprisings to the 1992 Los Angeles riots (Wacquant 2006). Clichy-sous-Bois has a population of 28,300 people and has long been part of what was dubbed Paris's "red belt" (*ceinture rouge*),

consisting of several working-class *banlieues* administered by elected officials affiliated with the French Communist Party. Half of its population is under twenty-five years of age, of which 25 percent are officially unemployed (Michel Delberghe, "Fuite des classes moyennes, chomage à 25%. Clichy-sous-Bois, radiographie d'une ville pauvre," *Le Monde,* November 6, 2005).

2. See Mohammed and Mucchielli 2006, for recent examples of police brutality against *banlieue* youths.

3. Lucienne Bui Trong, a French-Vietnamese criminologist and officer at the Renseignements Généraux (RG), has identified a total of 341 riots that erupted in the French *banlieues* between 1991 and 2000; see Trong 2003.

4. The *bavure policière* typically refers to a chain of events initiated by an identity-card check targeting young non-white men, who then resist, often leading to the instance of police brutality, later contributing to full-fledged rioting. As Michel Wieviorka suggests, this *bavure policière* cycle of violence witnessed in the *banlieues* of Lyon from Vénissieux (1981) to Vaulx-en-Velin (1990 and 1994) can also be attributed to the failure of political conflict resolution mechanisms or peaceful alternatives at the municipal level. At the national level, because successive governments have chosen to insist upon imposing law and order as a means of reinforcing the political status quo, their neglect of the root causes of the violence has made the recurrence of riots inevitable (see Wieviorka 1999: 210; Dubet and Lapeyronnie 1992).

5. *Le choc des civilisations* (Paris: Odile Jacob, 1997), the French version of Huntington's famed book, became the Bible of *intégristes de la République* and other *néo-réactionnaires* (neo-conservatives) in France.

6. Anne Giudicelli pertinently suggests that by appearing on CNN, French prime minister Dominique de Villepin felt compelled to dispel fears of an Islamic plot by "making a report" to the international community (*"rendre des comptes au monde"*); Giudicelli 2006: 23.

7. A report by the RG dated November 23, 2005, contradicted Sarkozy's assertion of an "organized intifada" and ruled out this conspiratorial rhetoric. Instead, the report stressed the spontaneous, leaderless nature of the riots, which erupted because of longstanding sentiments of "social exclusion" and "alienation" experienced by the youths of the *cités*. Sarkozy's branding of Zyed, Bouna, and Muhittin as delinquents involved in a robbery was also false. Instead, they did not have any prior police records, nor had they committed a crime on the day of the chase.

8. Bernard Cassen, director of *Le Monde Diplomatique,* and staunch "alter-globalization" proponent in France, has called for a "Marshall Plan" for the French *banlieues;* see Bernard Cassen, "El Katrina francés," *El Periódico,* November 8, 2005.

9. Pierre Laurent's passionate editorial entitled, "La banlieue, c'est la France" (2005), recasts the *banlieue* crisis as a defining moment in the struggle of the French labor movement. For a good overview detailing common misconceptions about the French *banlieue,* see Le Goaziou and Rojzman 2001.

10. For a comprehensive discussion of Sarkozy's rhetorical assaults, see Nasser Damiati, "Nicolas Sarkozy, ministre de l'Intérieur et pompier-pyromane," in Mucchielli and Le Goaziou 2006: 53–71.

11. On October 5, 1961, in keeping with the 1955 emergency law, Maurice Papon, then Paris Police prefect, ordered a curfew targeting only French Algerians. When more than 30,000 people bravely violated the curfew in a peaceful demonstration in Paris, the French police engaged in what Jean-Paul Sartre later called a "pogrom," murdering several hundred unarmed civilians on the banks of the Seine. Largely

suppressed by the state, the memory of these events has been well documented in Einaudi 1991, and Le Cour Grandmaison 2001. These events were treated in Leïla Sebbar's novel, *La Seine était rouge*, which has recently been translated and published as *The Seine Was Red* (Bloomington: Indiana University Press, 2008).

12. As many as twenty municipalities across France, including Paris, declared curfews shortly after the law was enacted. Before being reinstated in 2005, the 1955 law was reenacted only once, when President François Mitterrand used it in 1986 to quell separatist unrest in French New Caledonia, a remnant of the bygone French colonial empire. See Philippe Bernard, "Banlieues: la provocation coloniale," *Le Monde*, November 18, 2006.

13. Liauzu and Manceron (2005) have gathered some of the most stimulating critiques of article 4 in the 2005 law.

14. There are numerous sources that serve as the basis for this debate, culminating in the seventeen-year court case against Maurice Papon from 1981–1998. With the end of the investigation in 1994, a series of debates emerged in the French press reviving the history of French collaboration, and prosecution based on crimes against humanity. For further commentary on the collaboration of French police with the Gestapo, see Rajsfus 1995.

15. Downs and Gerson (2007).

16. There is an extensive array of works in English addressing French colonial history, including the history of the slave trade, Africans as spectacle on display in Europe, the legacy of the Tirailleurs Sénégalais, and, more recently, the reinvention of French studies through important contributions by Alec Hargreaves, Dominic Thomas, and Tyler Stovall, among others. In fact, these interventions related to France are only a subfield within the extensive array of approaches referred to as postcolonial studies.

17. According to Hajjat, the refusal to confront the past, even though this painful recollection process may produce conflicting and polarized *mémoires* (memories), precludes any serious discussion about immigration (Hajjat 2004). In a similar vein, Blanchard, Bancel and Lemaire (2005) argue against the determinism of the *fracture sociale* (class divide), to reveal instead colonial fault lines (*fracture colonial*) that traverse French postcolonial society. See also Hargreaves 2005.

18. Recent work has traced the untenable fallacy of *France terre de liberté* (France, land of liberty) back to the prerevolutionary epoch, when conflicting economic interests and moral principles pitted France's status as an imperial, slave-trading and -owning nation against the higher moral ground of abolitionism; see Bancel and Blancard 1998; Peabody 1996; Sala-Molins 1987; and Noël 2006.

19. Dismissing the 2005 riots as a "gigantic anti-Republican pogrom," Finkielkraut went on to argue that "the colonial project also sought to educate, to bring civilization to the savages"; see "What Sort of Frenchmen Are They?" Interview by Dror Mishani and Aurelia Smotriez, *Haaretz*, November 19, 2005. Finkielkraut is one of the most noted French philosophers of his generation and has become a self-proclaimed defender of the Republic, whose principles, he contends, have been threatened by right-wing extremists and neo-totalitarian leftists as well as by ethnic and religious communitarianists; see Finkielkraut 1989.

PART 1

Auto da fé:
Understanding
the 2005 Riots

Primitive Rebellion in the French *Banlieues:* On the Fall 2005 Riots

Didier Lapeyronnie
Translated by Jane Marie Todd

T he riots that followed the deaths of two teenagers in Clichy-sous-Bois on October 27, 2005, then spread throughout France over the next three weeks, transformed the political and social landscape of the country. These riots forced the French public to acknowledge, at least for a time, the presence of the *banlieues,* to which they had been largely indifferent. As with all the major uprisings in the *banlieues* over the last twenty-five years, the French media and French society "discovered" the "underlying issues": social inequality, unemployment, discrimination, racism, police brutality, and ghettoization. And as always, after the emotion of the event had died down and order had returned, after calls for civic action and for voter registration drives, the problem gradually faded from view, and society turned away from a recurrent problem that it can neither understand nor control. In spite of the large-scale engagement of intellectuals in the press and at colloquia, a few months later the public seems to be content with the absence of any significant measure, with the silence of politicians and of the government, with the return to order. Repression and silence seem to have been the only response, or absence of response, elicited by the riots.

Nevertheless, the magnitude of the events must be pointed out. On November 13, 2005, at the height of the troubles, 11,500 police officers and gendarmes were mobilized. Two hundred and seventeen were injured during the weeks of rioting. The Fédération Française des Sociétés d'Assurance (French Federation of Insurance Companies) estimated the overall cost of the destruction at about €200 million ($290 million in 2007 U.S. dollars), including €23 million ($33 million) for the ten thousand vehicles torched. Two hundred and thirty-three public and seventy-four private buildings were either defaced or burned. The Ministry of National Education counted 255 attacks on possessions or buildings, especially secondary schools, a confirmation that schools constituted special targets for the rioters. But gymnasiums, post offices, businesses, and places of worship were also assaulted. On the evening of November 30, 2005, according to the Ministry of the Interior, 4,770 people were questioned by police, of whom 4,402 were detained and 763 finally incarcerated.[1] What happened during these three weeks of violence? Not one investigation was completed during the riots. It is therefore only by adopting the method of a "disowning knowledge," to use Stanley Cavell's expression, based on the large quantity of information reported in the press, especially the statements of rioters, that we may be able to inquire into the nature of the riots, their construction, and their meaning. In fact, the rioters were much less silent than many commentators have claimed, even though they came from an environment where access to the public and political sphere is difficult if not impossible.[2] Rioting allowed them to express themselves, and their statements were conveyed in many news reports and interviews. But that mode of expression does not belong to the usual frameworks—instrumental and rational in particular—of the political system or of traditional militant action. The rioters' voices were largely ignored by media commentators, who in some sense "covered up" riotous speech. The riot was read in terms of the "situation" of unemployment and of banishment, which supposedly "determines" behaviors and explains revolt; rioters were seen to be somehow "reflecting" social mechanisms. It was also dismissed as nonsense or as stemming from instinctual drives or presocial motivations. Most of the readings combined the two interpretations, largely ignoring the rioters' words: "What has gotten into these young people's heads? . . . There is truly a language difficulty attached to the drives, and violent acts. . . . Unemployment and future prospects are central. . . . But there is a desocialization that it is important to take into account. These young minorities who engage in violent acts are self-centered, they are in a rage, and they combine despair and nihilism."[3] All these interpretations prevent the rioters from being heard; indeed, the interpreters refuse to hear them. Without turning the rioters into the vanguard of a social movement, without romanticizing them, we can begin with a favorable intuition. We can assume that their words have a meaning, rather than attempting to speculate on why the rioters made the choice of direct action and violence. Their words can shed light on the social meanings of such a choice.[4] That entails reading the riots as a form of collective and political action in order to then decipher its mechanisms and to provide an interpretation for it.

Rioting as Collective Action

On October 16, 2005, two young men riding a stolen scooter were trying to escape a special police unit (*brigade anti-criminelle,* or BAC) in the neighborhood of Mas du Taureau in Vaulx-en-Velin, an eastern *banlieue* of Lyons. They fell during the chase. One of them seriously injured his ankle and was hospitalized. A rumor began to circulate in the neighborhood that the police officers had put him in a coma. Fifteen years after Claudio Thomas died following a police chase in the very same neighborhood, riots erupted once again. Outraged young people clashed with police for several nights. According to observers, the 2005 riots in Vaulx-en-Velin were a sign of constant tensions between the institutions and the neighborhood population of the Lyons *banlieue,* an illustration of the "permanent duel with the police" in which young people were engaged. These riots elicited no emotional reaction and practically no political interest, unlike those in 1990, which had had a significant social impact.[5] In 2005 they were the latest event in the history of the French *banlieues* going back a quarter of a century, during which continued incidents and clashes with the police have multiplied and "urban violence" has become commonplace.

On April 1, 2005, a young man on a scooter in Aubervilliers, a northeastern *banlieue* of Paris, had been killed while trying to escape a BAC patrol. Rioting ensued for several nights. Cars and a commercial warehouse were burned, city property was destroyed, and young people clashed with police. On October 27, 2005, in the La Duchère area of

Lyons, ten cars were burned after an apartment building was demolished with the minister of social affairs and the mayor in attendance. According to the mayor, it "seem[ed] to be purely recreational, designed merely as a play for media attention." When two young teenagers died the same day trying to avoid a police checkpoint in Clichy-sous-Bois, the same chain of events unfolded—that evening, incidents erupted in the commune. A silent march was organized, and local authorities and families called for calm, respect, and dignity. Then the clashes and violence resumed for several days before subsiding. The usual pattern and sequence of events for such incidents were altered, however, when the riot gradually spread, first affecting the greater Paris area, then cities in the country as a whole, becoming a political event. The violence reached its height on the night of November 7, when 1,500 cars were burned and 274 communes throughout the country were affected. Peace was restored on November 17, after three weeks of incidents, clashes, and acts of violence.

Like any event, the fall 2005 riots had both familiar and new elements. The rioters' repertoire of acts and the sequence of events were obviously consistent with the rioting that has occurred in France over the last twenty-five years. In general, trouble with the police, often the death of someone in the neighborhood, sparks intense emotions that give rise to clashes between young people and the police, the torching of vehicles, damage to public buildings, and sometimes looting. In addition, silent demonstrations are organized, and the victim's family calls for calm and justice, without ever prevailing. Then, a few days later, emotions subside somewhat and peace is restored. Some of these riots regularly turn into "events" in the political sense of the term, stirring up emotion and debates that place the question of the *banlieues* in one form or another in the public arena. At least symbolically, the rioters are the center of attention, but without ever managing to be heard: the meaning of the riot becomes the object of a discussion or of political and ideological clashes among political leaders or intellectuals who have little connection to the *banlieues*. The riots of Les Minguettes in 1981, Vaulx-en-Velin in 1990, and Toulouse-Le Mirail in 1998 all became events. They gave rise to many political debates and interventions from leading personalities of all kinds, to voter registration drives, and to moral condemnation.

The particularity of the 2005 riots, then, lies not in how they initially unfolded, which was sadly commonplace all in all, nor in the fact that they became a political event, which had happened before, but in the spectacular way they expanded to almost three hundred cities across the country. It is precisely this expansion that made them an event and in a certain way changed their nature. The 2005 riots—and this may be their defining characteristic—were distinguished by their magnitude and ubiquity. They were not a local phenomenon. They were not limited to the most hard-core *banlieues,* but erupted in many "trouble-free" areas.[6] Whatever the reasons and whatever the rioters may have wanted to express, they did so in the same way in all the cities affected.

Rioting is therefore a collective action. It is not a consequence of ordinary delinquency or an extension of a culture of violence. Even when it is accompanied by violence, vandalism, and looting, even when it is "unconventional"—that is, when it unfolds outside the legitimate institutional mechanisms, in contrast to a workers' strike or a demonstration —it stems in the first place from an understanding of the social and political mechanisms that govern the formation and orientation of social and collective movements. In other words, rioting belongs to the normal repertoire of political action.[7] It therefore leads us to perceive "ordinary" behaviors in terms of rioting and not the reverse. Workers' strikes made it possible to understand the extent to which the "illegalities" of workers, such as work slowdowns or sabotage, could not be reduced to mere delinquency or more or less anomic behavior. On the contrary, these acts had to be understood more broadly as among the dimensions of class consciousness. The same is true for rioting: it sheds light on ordinary behaviors, individual or collective, and especially on violent or delinquent behaviors, which must also be understood in terms of rioting and not vice versa. From this standpoint, we must set aside the notion of "urban violence," which introduces a great deal of confusion by conflating very different kinds of behaviors, and above all leads one to read rioting in terms of deviance and social order, all ways of rendering it meaningless, of dismissing it as nonsensical or irrational (that has always been the reading of the opponents of rioting or the defenders of the social order, as Karl Marx already noted in 1848).[8]

In any case, as always in such matters, it is not obvious that there is any less irrationality or more meaning in the reactions of the authorities and ideologues of the social order. But because riots bear no clear meaning, are without leaders, and do not occur in any organized form, they give free rein to the most contradictory interpretations, usually overloaded with political and ideological reflections. Everyone sees rioting as a confirmation by events of what he already "knows" or "thought." There is nothing surprising about a riot or series of riots since, as some interpreters tell us, they are the sign of a situation of social despair that is growing ever more acute and that is fueled by neo-liberalism. Others, no more surprised, see riots as the consequence of a general anomie, the act of more or less mindless "barbarians," whose violence takes the place of language, or as the result of an absence of direction or a general lack of discipline. Rioting, in this view, is a "sign," the manifestation of a social or moral situation, the expression of the state of a society. Its meaning belongs not to the rioters but to their interpreters. From this standpoint, it very often looks much more like a pretext or a mere illustration. Hence it is hardly surprising that rioting elicits the most divergent and the most sharply divided interpretations. It is never anything but an issue, and often its indirect effects on the political sphere seem more important than its content itself. In other words, it is "instrumentalized" to serve ideological and political logics alien or external to it.[9]

Nevertheless, the riot has its own logic. It is the act of rioters, whose behaviors, to judge by their recurrence and regularity, are highly socialized. Rioters are also not particularly silent and can therefore not be reduced to "dangerous classes" threatening civilization. They also cannot be considered the unconscious reflection of a state of deprivation. In a now-classic work, the historian Eric Hobsbawm demonstrates that riots have long been an effective means for collective negotiation by poor populations denied access to conventional methods of political action. That was the case, for example, among workers prior to the advent of unions, in unrepresented urban populations, and in community movements in developing countries (Hobsbawm 1959). Rioting is the act of the "primitive rebel" in that it is a political act of protest by populations that the institutional system cannot or will not integrate. These primitive rebels make an appeal to the values of society against a social order they judge immoral and, at the same time, demand to become part of that order, to be acknowledged. Rioting is a "primitive" political movement lacking ideology and rules, because the populations that engage in it remain on the outside and erect their "us" against the institutions, but nevertheless intend to provoke an institutional reaction or bring about reforms. It is a strategy of exceeding the framework of the institutional system—

from above by its strong moral dimension and from below by its use of violence—and it is used by populations alienated from that system.

The Police, Injustice, and Moral Indignation

Rioting is defined in the first place by its anti-police dimension. It erupts following incidents with the police and is directed primarily against them. Such was the case in eighteenth-century France, when the arrests of beggars and the interventions of the constabulary frequently ended in unrest and even riots.[10] Most of the riots during the 1960s in the black ghettos of the United States broke out following incidents with police, including Watts in 1965 and Detroit in 1967. The same was true of Great Britain in the 1980s and 1990s. London's Notting Hill neighborhood saw a riot break out following an arrest in 1976. In Tottenham, a woman's death during a police search of her home sparked a riot in 1985. In 1992, the death of two young Bristol residents who were attempting to escape the police in a stolen car also unleashed a riot.

Over the past twenty years, rioting in France has been no exception to the rule. On December 18, 1997, twenty-four-year-old Fabrice Fernandez, a resident of La Duchère in Lyons, was shot to death by an officer at a police station. A few days later, his neighborhood held a silent demonstration in his memory. His mother "lectured" the young people present and asked them to stay calm, but she was unable to prevent further clashes with the police and violent incidents from erupting shortly thereafter. The mayor of the ninth arrondissement recounted:

> Dialogue was impossible. When we left, someone shouted: "Let's torch that heap of his!" We left the car in the parking lot. . . . The cops had cleared the entire center of La Duchère. We were trapped between gangs of young people. That was the hardest thing. The most responsible ones said there was no point discussing things that night: "We're going to avenge Fabrice, we've had it up to here." And the least responsible ones wanted to bash our faces in. I left a coat behind in the melee. Things got very hot. We stayed in the neighborhood all night long, just watching things . . . to at least tell the people we were with them. Things were hopping just about everywhere. . . . People realized the seriousness of the situation. The state is going to set a number of things in place. At Lyons city hall, it won't be like before.[11]

The course of the *banlieue* riots followed the usual pattern. At virtually the same time as the incidents in La Duchère, riots broke out in the Parisian *banlieue* of Dammarie-lès-Lys. A year later, in the Mirail area of Toulouse, violent riots followed the death of a seventeen-year-old male at the hands of police. The Clichy-sous-Bois riot of 2005 was set off by the same mechanisms: it was unleashed by the deaths of two young men trying to escape the police. The riot thus emerges from a problem of social control, and it is a protest or reaction against an institutional effort to repress or control behaviors that the informal social controls of society cannot handle.[12]

Nevertheless, the particular incident, which may be serious or relatively insignificant (sometimes merely an altercation with a traffic officer, as in Handsworth in 1985), is not sufficient in itself to incite a riot. In every case, rioting occurs as the culmination of a local or national history characterized by tension, violence, and antagonism between police and residents of the neighborhoods involved, rather than simply as the result of ordinary "urban violence." In both the United States in the 1960s and Great Britain in the 1980s, official commissions focused at length on that dimension. The deterioration of relations between police and neighborhood residents, young men in particular, was considered one of the essential factors in the rioting. The same was still true of France in 2005. The tensions and difficulties among youth in working-class neighborhoods, minority youth in particular, already have a long history that has profoundly shaped societal life in the *banlieues.* The death of two young Maghrebi boys in 1980 at the hands of the police in Strasbourg and Valenton sparked organized protests against excessive use of police force, as well as concerts. In 1983, the serious injury of a young man from Les Minguettes in Vénisseux gave rise to the March for Equality (Jazouli 1985). The long litany of incidents and deaths constitutes a sort of "community memory" for the neighborhoods, a memory of seriously impaired relations with police.

In addition, over a quarter of a century, the words of the young residents have been almost identical, expressing the same feeling of hostility toward the police and the same sense of injustice. "The cop arrests you, sometimes he disses you and breaks open your head, and afterward you're dragged before the judge, who finishes the job and has you locked up. If you ask me, they're all in it together, those guys, out to stick it to us more and more, to smother us."[13] In the housing projects of

Clichy-sous-Bois, graffiti is rampant and does not mince words: "Fuck the police"; "Cops Keep Out." The statements gathered by reporters are equally marked by hostility and rejection of the police. As one young mediator at the Clichy-sous-Bois town hall recounted, "The police provoke the mediators as well. They arrested me because I was running. I was running so I wouldn't get teargassed, and when I told them I was a mediator at town hall, their reply was, 'Shut your mouth, you've got nothing to say!' They made me lie on the ground. They patted me down. At no time did they ask me for my papers." Another resident of the projects told a reporter questioning him: "The BAC cops are always using strong-arm tactics. They say 'niggers,' 'fuck your race.' It's a new generation of police here. During a routine stop, they disrespect you on a daily basis. I was stopped on the *RER* train because I'd put my feet up on the seat. Okay, you're not supposed to put your feet on the seat. But just for that, the police officers called for backup. Three cars were waiting for me at the Raincy train station. The cops said: 'Why don't you stay in your filthy hole?'"[14] Whatever the reality and whoever holds responsibility for the way the incidents unfold, the rejection of the police and its methods, especially the ordeal of the more or less systematic identity checks, is one of the characteristics of life in the *banlieue*. The vast majority of neighborhood residents agree with that perception and share an understanding of the hostility toward the police, frequently accusing them of being more quick to stop and harass *banlieue* youth than to protect the population. "That violence surprised me, even though you can understand why young people support what happened in Clichy-sous-Bois. Here, they're systematically stopped for no reason. Even my son told me recently that if he saw a police checkpoint coming back from a game, he'd run away."[15]

Hostility between police and the working class is a long-standing and pervasive reality. Institutional restrictions on working-class forms of sociability are often accompanied by misunderstandings, but especially by acts of violence, and by a sense of identity deeply marked by energetic defiance of the police. The police, in turn, are convinced of the violent and illicit character of many popular practices.[16] In recent times, this hostility toward the police has been combined with an impression that, in addition to their desire to control working-class sociability, police are motivated by explicit racism: "They don't respect our children. I think it's because in this neighborhood everybody is black or

Arab. There's racism," explains the custodian of an apartment building in Chêne-Pointu, Clichy-sous-Bois.[17] The police directly discriminate against young Maghrebis and blacks living in the more volatile projects, a form of discrimination that fuels tensions and can lead to violence during police interventions.

The discrimination is exacerbated by the general impression that the police enjoy impunity, which, in the eyes of the young, allows officers to strip them of all rights and exert unrestricted power over them. "The cops disrespect us in the street and slap us around in the safety of their cars when they arrest us."[18] In the United States in the 1960s, the Kerner Commission pointed out the importance of the antagonism between police and young ghetto blacks, as well as the burden of racism. According to their report, incidents and clashes between police and young people appeared all the more likely in that police officers could count on the support of their fellow officers and enjoyed relative impunity, while the young people felt they were supported by their peers and, to a lesser extent, by neighborhood residents. Racism, harassment, and police pressure ultimately create a sort of collective "us" based on a common experience and on an opposition to a police "them." This "us," a negative feeling about the contempt, racism, and denial of rights they endure more than a positive identity, is much more closely attached to segregated urban areas, to housing projects, and to neighborhoods than to a popular culture to be defended. Although *banlieue* youth do not constitute a social or cultural category, they widely share the feeling that they suffer the same treatment, that in their lives they have a common experience at the hands of law enforcement.

Police practices of harassment and the institution's exteriority to the neighborhoods concerned, an exteriority that has been reinforced by the elimination of neighborhood policing in recent years, further consolidate this feeling of an iniquitous, and especially of a general and indiscriminate, treatment. "Now it's them against us!" declared a police officer in Clichy-sous-Bois.[19] The population as a whole, by virtue of its ethnic identity and location, feels directly impacted, the primary targets of a police force more quick to harass them than to apprehend the "real delinquents." Law enforcement is therefore perceived as an institution working against the population rather than for its benefit. As studies on American ghettos have shown, neighborhood residents accumulate so much experience and share the evidence of such a constant assault on their interests and honor that they have no reason not to perceive the police force as an institution of oppression.[20] "The police are not there to protect us. They provoke us all the time. We're called mongrels and niggers. It's only natural that young people hate them. The girls as well as the boys. . . . The other day, we were celebrating the children's birthdays with a friend. We were walking across the projects with them, and the cops jumped on us. They turned their cars around, stopped, then drove off again. It's intolerable."[21] Moreover, despite the residents' pursuit of very different social paths, a well-defined segmentation of social life in the volatile neighborhoods, and often tensions between apartment blocks, that shared "negative experience" generates an "us" that manifests itself as opposition to the police, or even as constant conflict with them.

This "us," constituted negatively through hostility to the police, is not meaningless. It is also structured in great part by a feeling of injustice, which the police embody. It is a sort of interpretive grid for the events and the situation; every incident, every problem comes to reinforce it. Conflicts thus legitimate the interpretation and perception of the victims, and by extension of the young, and weaken the dominant interpretation, that of the police and the authorities. "As soon as there's a problem with the police, they always say: 'The investigation has shown that you're to blame.'"[22] Not only does the conflict confirm the "us," it also reinforces the feeling of an absolute, deep-rooted injustice, one that violates the moral codes and fundamental principles of society and its institutions. Law becomes oppression, and legitimate methods of maintaining social order disintegrate (Janowitz 1968). An "injustice frame" thus replaces the "legitimating frame" and opens the possibility for action. The victims of injustice, the "us," suddenly have the capacity to prevail over the legitimate institutional authority responsible for their moral outrage.

The "us" also provides criteria for condemning the order. As Barrington Moore has shown at length in his study of the formation of the workers' movement in Germany, that shift and the constitution of an "injustice" identity make up the heart and origin of the action, as was also the case for many social movements and riots (Moore 1978). Hence this "*banlieue* youth," and the category of "*banlieue* youth" in general, are no longer "delinquents" or "dangerous classes" but victims of daily police harassment and racism, which are suddenly exposed by the incident.[23] In activating the "us" and undermining the legitimacy of the interpretive frames, the incident also renders the uprising both expected and legitimate. And it sets a very strong emotional tone for the revolt.

Mobilizing Emotion

The death of young people during police actions inevitably stirs up intense emotions at both the individual and collective levels and crystallizes the feeling of an "us" (victims of injustice) in opposition to a "them" (the iniquitous police force). During periods marked by frequent heavy tension, the incident precipitates rioting. After every encounter with the police, or sometimes with security guards, emotions generate rioting, an action directed against law enforcement in the first place. Historians, such as George Rudé, have long emphasized the significant role that emotions play in unleashing riots and determining their direction.[24] Emotions disintegrate the individual and unite the collectivity. According to Randall Collins, emotions are the social "glue," the thing that mobilizes the collectivity in the conflict, thus opening possibilities for action (Collins 1990: 28). Emotional reactions allow the individual to feel a direct attachment to the "us" and solidarity with those who share the same feelings, the same state of mind. The individual becomes charged with an energy that makes it possible to take action, a sort of electricity according to Émile Durkheim, an "emotional energy" in his view is also moral, because it is strongly linked to an attachment to life or to respect.[25] Very often, before or even during riots silent demonstrations take place, moments to gather and meditate, and symbols come to the fore: the parents of the victim, the mother especially, and sometimes religious and political authorities call for dignity and for overcoming sorrow through an increase in solidarity and respect in the face of the absurdity of violence.

The riots that followed the death of a young man killed by police at a roadblock in La Courneuve in July 1988 were accompanied by a silent march "to contain the anger," with the victim's family in attendance. In November 1995, the death of a young man at the hands of an officer at a police station unleashed a riot in Laval. It was followed by protests for "justice" in the city streets.[26] In December 1997, a silent march was held in Dammarie-lès-Lys during a wave of rioting, after a seventeen-year-old boy was killed by police.[27] A few days after the events at Clichy-sous-Bois, five hundred gathered for a silent march through the city: the parents of one of the victims led the procession, walking hand in hand, followed by the father of the other victim. Behind them were the two young men's friends, dressed in white T-shirts that read, "Senseless deaths." The mayor then addressed the crowd: "For the past few days, all eyes have been trained on our city. Let us show that, despite our pain and anger, we can remain dignified."[28] The group united not only around the feeling that they were the victims of injustice but also around the call for a moral superiority expressed as dignity and solidarity. The family, the shirts denouncing the absurdity of young deaths, and the pain and silence all stood in opposition not to institutions or social forces, but to the forces of death. As more or less incredulous reporters and political leaders have pointed out, the silent march puts the spotlight on the family, the mothers in particular, as in traditional community movements, just as rioting is carried out by young people and quite often by "children." As agents on the margins of the political system, often those most remote from political action and most confined to the private sphere, the mothers express an affirmation and a fundamental protest, that of life, which institutions, being more instrumental, are incapable of integrating or even understanding, and which they constantly dismiss as nonsense.[29]

Silent marches are in some sense both the flip side and the complement of riots. The strong symbolism of these marches inextricably links them to rioting: they are the emotional energy fueling the rioters, ensuring a certain group solidarity. "Sometimes the same people who were screaming their hatred at the police on Friday night now join hands, with vacant stares and grave expressions. As if the sorrow were finally managing to extinguish the anger." "We must be dignified. . . . We are not here to vandalize cars."[30] The silent marches reinforce the fundamental moral code of society and of the group, a code violated by the absurdity of police action, and thus establish the legitimacy of the anger: "I'm not a believer. We must not accept everything. I would just like to understand why the pigs did this."[31] The "us" constituted by the negative experience of the "them," the police, acquires a moral legitimacy that ultimately places that "us" in an antagonistic position to the social order in general, in addition to the forces of political repression. It is therefore as an individual that the rioter asserts a right to exist in the face of a deadly social order that negates him and prevents him from living. In the rioters' statements and declarations, moral protest and the demand for respect are often accompanied by a feeling that they are not being treated like human beings, that they are being reduced to a kind of animality. "We put up with identity checks and disrespect for no reason. They treat us like cattle," declares a young rioter from Sevran. "We're not dogs, but we react like animals," says another from Aubervilliers.[32] Still another rioter explains, "They took us down to the station and the insults flew. When I talked about my rights, they told me: 'Shut your trap!' They called me *tu*. We were treated worse than dogs."[33] There is no need to invoke a religious source of some kind or "control" of the riot by religious leaders. In fact, religious institutions have proven powerless to stop the violence or to channel it elsewhere, and they have remained silent.[34] Nevertheless, the emotion is strongly linked to a moral appeal for the rights of the individual and for the respect the individual is due.

Emotions and the sense of moral indignation, reinforced by group solidarity, give the riot its activist character and in large part explain its spread. In virtually all riots, rioters are not particularly delinquent, unemployed, or marginal. They are an integral part of their environment and fall into the average range of the population concerned, though they are younger than average.[35] The 2005 rioters were not especially known to police for their previous delinquent acts, and they too fell into the average range of young people; they were regular youngsters from the neighborhood.[36] In fact rioting, though it may sometimes be accompanied by looting, does not obey a logic of appropriation. In the 2005 incidents, rioters torched vehicles, warehouses, or schools. They did not seek to enrich themselves and did not follow any of the typical patterns of delinquent behavior. Through rioters' statements, it becomes clear that their actions were strongly motivated by emotion and indignation, for the rioters can almost never provide any rational explanation for their involvement and behavior. "When I saw the security police in the housing project, and also a helicopter flying over the block, I said to myself: They want war, they'll get war. So I put on my cap and scarf and went out";[37] "It's too bad, but we have no choice";[38] "I do it, that's all";[39] "We took action without really thinking about it much."[40] The rioters, when questioned by judges after being arrested, seemed unable to find a justification for their actions. Take the case of a young man from Bobigny named Mikaël, who according to judges and journalists did not seem predisposed to violence. When he was handed over for trial, he explained, "You don't fire on a mosque, a mosque is a thing of God!" and added that he "didn't think things through."[41] Anthony, tried in Nanterre for setting cars on fire, had little to add: "I ran into two friends at the bus stop, we talked about what was happening in the *banlieues*. . . . That day, I was really dumb."[42]

Because they are ordinary people, young rioters enjoy a great deal of understanding from their neighborhood population. "We condemn the violence, but we understand it."[43] The population shares the feeling of a general and indiscriminate oppression by the police and by society. "We have a state minister who said: 'You're all alike.' I say no, we all say no. But they repeat, 'you're all alike.' So that creates something in common."[44] But perhaps more fundamentally, the population feels a strong emotional solidarity with the young rioters. In the statements gathered by reporters, it is often repeated that these are children, "our children." The clash itself, the images of the riot, and its proximity also foster that emotional solidarity, which leads people to take action and accentuates the emotional dimension of the "us": "When the security police were in the housing project, I really wanted to go in, to go there myself. But my mother didn't want me to. I was at the window. I saw everything and couldn't do a thing. I was so outraged!"[45]

Because it was highly expressive and motivated by moral protest, the riot in Clichy-sous-Bois would probably have lost steam once the emotional energy had dissipated. But the repressive police action, and especially the setting off of a tear gas canister outside the Bilal Mosque in Clichy-sous-Bois on Sunday, October 30, combined with the declarations of the minister of the interior, who had denounced the "scum" and "hooligans" a few days earlier, provided the fuel necessary for the violence to spread. Riots are always propagated by emotion. They progress by diffusing the emotion and concentrating it on fixed points that allow for a more generalized revolt. Long before the invention of radio, television, or even newspapers, riots spread in the same way. Such was the case, for instance, in Sicily and Tuscany in February 1848 and during the Great Fear in France in 1789, to take two famous examples—not to mention the Jacquerie uprising of 1358.[46] Rioting spreads when it encounters favorable soil, when individuals and groups feel they share the same grievances, have the same experience and the same moral indignation.

The spread of rioting even leads to a certain pride. "There's no competition in the projects. It's all solidarity," declared a young rioter from

Aubervilliers.[47] Rioting does not spread by imitation or competition, or even by contagion; rather, it obeys a process of diffusion, which the modern media accelerate but do not cause. The attack on the mosque, along with the minister of the interior's insults, served in some sense to generalize the feeling of the "us" and its opposition to the "them" (both the police and society at large). These acts confirmed the sense of injustice and intensified emotions generally, because their agents in some sense embraced the moral outrage, affirmed that they were cynically violating the fundamental values of society. "By attacking the mosque, they tampered with a place of worship. That we will not forgive. That's too much! And no one said anything! That means we're outcasts. All we ask is that they apologize."[48] Individual experience is thus transformed into the experience of a collective domination, the shared experience of being the object of contempt or of insulting behavior that directly attacks the person. "It's not for their benefit that I'm acting out . . . it's just so they'll respect us. I blame the state for putting us in this situation!"[49] Rioters' declarations are unequivocal. They exemplify moral protest against police brutality and against the words that legitimate it. "You don't throw tear gas at the faithful while they're praying. They're slinging mud at our religion."[50] "They shouldn't have called us scum and sent in the police."[51] The demand for respect and an attention to dignity are traditional characteristics of marginalized and destitute populations. For the rioters, the minister of the interior's words and attitude distilled the humiliation they had experienced and activated the demand for respect. "There's more outrage than hatred. . . . Since we're scum, we'll give that racist something to hose down. Words hurt more than blows. Sarko must resign. So long as he does not apologize, we'll continue."[52]

Throughout the events, the minister of the interior crystallized the resentment. For the rioters, he embodied a system and an order that not only marginalizes them but humiliates them as well. "When Sarkozy calls young people scum, that doesn't surprise us. He already called young people hooligans without trying to understand what was happening. Sarkozy condemns rather than trying to solve the problems," said the leader of an association in the Hautepierre neighborhood of Strasbourg. "It's calm, but that's because it's Ramadan. After his words, some people are likely to get agitated. It's shameful for a prime minister to call people scum. We're French like everyone else. We pay taxes and have a hard time finding work. What he said, I call that an abuse of power. That guy magnifies the violence," added an unemployed young man from the same neighborhood.[53] Urban riots rarely expand beyond the local level. But in 2005, the emotional intensity of the reaction to the death of two very young men, combined with the assault on a symbolic site and the minister of the interior's insults, caused them to become widespread. "We were sick to death of the police and Sarko, they were provoking us too much."[54] From this standpoint, the minister and law enforcement played the role of political operators, allowing a local conflict to spread and unleashing a phenomenon of group identity formation and solidarity.

Rioting, highly expressive and motivated by indignation, is not meaningless. On the contrary, it seems to display a sort of overabundance of meaning: rioters oppose an order they consider deadly, and they embrace their own moral "us." Rioters do not consider their actions immoral in any way. On the contrary. That is also why rioting is embraced as such: "We're not vandals, we're rioters. We all get together to make our revolt heard."[55] The revolt is legitimate. It stands as the affirmation of a collective morality, conveyed by young people, adolescents taking risks, and fueled by the sorrow and the dignity of mothers, who enter the public sphere through the silent marches. It is the affirmation of a right to exist, a call for social solidarity and unity. But unlike a strike or a political demonstration, it is not directed at a social adversary and makes no negotiable demands. In other words, rioting moves beyond the frame of the social and political systems by its moral dimension and by the use of violence, to directly call into question an order that is lethal and cynical because it prevents people from living.

Violence and Rationality

Traditionally, social movements and collective protests call into question a balance of power or the distribution of resources. In democratic countries, they are organized within existing institutional channels; even conflicts marked by the use of relatively violent methods remain largely circumscribed and limited by the acceptance of conventional rules. Paradoxically, the initiation and elaboration of protests require access to the institutional channels that allow actions to be taken and demands formulated. Riots deviate somewhat from this pattern. Carried out by populations with meager resources and little access to political mechanisms, they call into question the civil and social order. But they are nevertheless a form of political action. As Frances F. Piven and Richard A. Cloward have noted, because the poor have a low rate of institutional participation, the only aspect of life in society they can interrupt (like a striker blocking a production line) is civil peace, by participating in riots. Violence and public unrest are their only possible and effective means of struggle (Piven and Cloward 1977). Even if riots result from a weakening of social control mechanisms or a sudden loss of legitimacy, they cannot be reduced to delinquency. In the absence of political mechanisms, rioters express their feelings about the social world and attempt to bring them into the public arena.

Destroying public and private property makes a clear statement, as Lee Rainwater has pointed out regarding American rioters in the 1960s: "The greater the damage in terms of the financial cost of looting and burning, the more effectively the point has been made."[56] For the participants, rioting is a way to enter the public arena or to impose their presence in it. Because they are deprived of access to that arena, and deprived of representation perhaps above all, violence becomes a way to "force entry," to exist. "It's the only way for us to be heard. But we know very well that not a single camera will be left once everything calms down. We won't exist anymore."[57] It is also the only way to achieve gains. In fact, for the population concerned, rioting cannot appear totally irrational: in addition to affording them access to the public arena and short-lived acknowledgment, it allows them to obtain some benefits. As William Gamson has shown in his study of the history of political violence in the United States, rioting ultimately led to substantial gains for the populations concerned and was a perfectly effective strategy of social protest (Gamson 1990).

To confine ourselves to the population in the housing projects of the French *banlieue*, the 1981 riots of Les Minguettes, as well as those of Vaulx-en-Velin, led to measures favoring disadvantaged neighborhoods, whether safety measures, programs to fight youth unemployment or renovate neighborhoods, or, later, changes in urban policy. The same was true at the local level. Violence often appears to be relatively effective in obtaining gains from various institutions, whether it takes the form of pressure on a social worker in daily life or of local unrest leading to the distribution of services and aid, even jobs, by the municipalities. "When people are afraid, politicians pay attention, they think things over and end up proposing solutions."[58] "People want to attract attention. They say to themselves: 'If we raise hell, then they won't forget us, they'll know we're a volatile area.'"[59] Just as there is an emotional rationality to rioting, there is also an instrumental rationality that is not negligible.

Unlike in conventional protest movements, alienation from the mechanisms of representation and conflict resolution keeps rioters from formulating a precise list of demands. Rioting violence thus stems from a demand for acknowledgment or citizenship, demands that are not open to negotiation. The gains achieved are never enough to check an inexhaustible demand, one that is constantly renewed in contact with the police and with a good number of institutions. Lived experience—marked by racism, unemployment, and poverty—fuels in large part that sensation and in turn provides justification for the revolt. In the nineteenth century, worker violence was particularly fierce because workers were unable to organize unions and thereby enter the political arena. Rioting tended to disappear as the forms of industrial democracy were gradually set in place and workers were recognized as social agents and allowed to organize.[60] Violent rioting by American ghetto dwellers in the 1960s was related in large part to their inability to gain access to the political system. Leaders of the civil rights movement had very little connection to these residents. The violence declined once access to the political system improved, making this population's actions more effective.[61]

In 2005 the French rioters also belonged to marginalized populations who were kept on the fringes of the political system. And like all such populations, these rioters ultimately stayed on the fringes, embracing their distance. Residents of volatile areas often display a profound lack of interest in political matters, even hostility toward politicians. They believe that the political system belongs to the very society that excludes and racializes them. They thus reject a system that denies them access and that they hold responsible for their situation. That explains the calls for voter registration drives after every riot and the minimal success of campaigns to promote civic activity. All in all, rioting is an extremely effective form of action: it does not require individuals to join a game and enter a world which they do not control, in which they are often humiliated, and which does not allow them to achieve obvious benefits. The failure of earlier generations to penetrate a closed system confirms and reinforces the mistrust, increases the maintenance of distance, and justifies the search for other modes of action (Masclet 2003). "You talk about moving forward, but it's useless. We've had papers for generations but we aren't French like everyone else."[62] Rioting is a kind of short circuit, making it possible to clear obstacles, to become recognized political agents, and at the same time to achieve gains, if only in a negative, short-lived, and illusory way, without being able to control, even less negotiate, the potential acknowledgment and benefits.

Generally speaking, it is institutions as a whole, not just the police and the political system, that are called into question, rejected as an alien world that marginalizes this population in the same way as unemployment and racism. Comments repeated about the schools illustrate this: "In any case, what else do you want us to do? Out of the hundred résumés I sent out, I got three interviews. Even when people pull strings for me, I'm still turned down. Schools are useless. That's why we burn them."[63] The life situation, more than the experience of domination, fuels solidarity and understanding among residents. "I don't necessarily agree with that, but at the same time, if I were in such a difficult social situation, I'd blow a fuse. When you've got no work, when you're crammed together in some hole of an apartment building, you don't think things through so much, you have less perspective on life."[64] Ultimately, the whole social system, like the police, is perceived as an instrument of banishment, exclusion, confinement, even political repression. "I'm twenty-five, and when I go out at night, my mother's scared. She tells me to be careful with the police. They talk about a sealed-off ghetto, but they do everything to keep us from getting out of it. We're stuck here."[65] But to an even greater extent perhaps, the social system, like the police, is experienced as something that keeps individuals from living, that destroys them. "If I could leave, I would, because I'm rotting here."[66] Violent rioting thus exists within a life situation dominated by distance from institutions, feelings of exclusion, and poor quality of life, which the rioter does not and cannot manage to translate into a list of demands.

But the legitimacy of the violence, especially with respect to schools, does not lie entirely in the life situation or in the fact that institutions of learning, like the police, betray their own values. The violence is also fueled by the population's dependence on these institutions. As with any impoverished population defined by their political powerlessness, the *banlieue* residents, and perhaps the young rioters in particular, feel a great dependence on forces and institutions that are external to them.

"We feel like we're locked up in here, and we're not the ones with the keys. They are."[67] "They" designates first and foremost the politicians, but also social service agencies and the school system. The term connotes a dual feeling of powerlessness, resulting from the combination of poverty and exclusion. "In our ghetto, we're poor people!"[68] In other words, ghetto dwellers feel they lack the resources and strength necessary to manage their own problems or to find solutions. They are dependent in their daily lives and in their personal plans.

They are also politically dependent: they can cause a reaction in the political arena, but they do not have the ability to control its direction. They wait for the political realm to act on their behalf, while they themselves are unable, or feel too "insignificant," to act. It is also this dependence on the political realm that explains in large part why they focus on politicians (on a negative leader in this case) and want to elicit a reaction from them. "Maybe this will make people in the government understand."[69] For the rioters, as for the landless peasants in France analyzed by Karl Marx, or the "common people" of Paris at the time of the Revolution, the use of violence and rioting turns out to be both a perfectly rational strategy of exerting pressure and the result of a lack of autonomous agency, of a strong dependence on a system to which they are denied access.[70] Rioters are thus defined both by their marginality and by their dependence. They are "outsiders," victims of a system that rejects them, discriminates against them, and ultimately "prevents them from living." Yet they are also the "poor," the "insignificant," who feel heavily dependent, especially in political terms, on this same system and this same society.[71]

All in all, there seem to be four determining factors governing the logic of rioting: absence of legitimacy, coupled with high dependence; absence of a political role; low quality of life; and the segmentation of the population by discrimination or racism. Rioting is not simply the product of a social situation of poverty. It is not merely the result of unemployment. In fact, the rioters, most of them very young, were not unemployed. They were more often coping with school, or with expulsion from school, than with the labor market. Schools were vandalized and burned much more often than businesses or warehouses. As always, "it is the daily experience of people that . . . points out the targets of their anger" (Piven and Cloward 1977: 21). And it was obviously the police, but also the school system, that were the main objects of the rioters' animosity. Rioting is also not merely the product of racial exclusion. Although urban segregation and discrimination reinforce the isolation of the population and greatly foster the constitution of an "us," rioters did not place forms of ethnic, religious, or racial identification in the forefront. It seems rather that the combination of powerlessness, linked to the low quality of life, and the absence of personal prospects, linked to exclusion, were the cause of the rioting. In the views expressed by the rioters, the sense of "being unable to live one's life" because of a lack of resources and an institutional system that marginalizes them appears omnipresent. It is especially prominent among young men, who are more affected by the lack of prospects than the older generations, and who may certainly find an "excitement" or "vital intensity" in the direct action of rioting, which somewhat makes up for their negative feelings. Adding to the powerlessness and exclusion is dependence: rioters are dependent on institutional systems to which they do not have access. It is for this reason that they so often seem "speechless." They seek to obtain benefits without being able to formulate a list of demands: they exert a violence whose results will lie beyond their control, in the "good-will" of institutions or in the capacity of political agents to instrumentalize the violence.

Conclusion

Rioting, as described by the rioters, thus falls short of the institutional and political system, while simultaneously exceeding its boundaries. Rioting is very clearly infrapolitical, marked by the incapacity of an impoverished, marginal population to gain access to the political system, and by dependence on that system. Violence is both a rational and effective means of applying pressure and a means of protesting an "unlivable" situation. But rioting is also very clearly suprapolitical. It appeals to the fundamental values of society: it is supported by the assertion of moral superiority by an "us," victim of injustice, and also by the rejection of a system that is deadly, because it keeps the "us" from living. Rioting is in some ways an attempt to exceed the limits of the system from above and from below, an attempt fueled by an emotional energy that rapidly runs out, and it is founded on the demand for the rights of the individual. Rioters are not revolutionaries or militants. They are not agents of a social movement. But they are also not individuals driven by their barbarous instincts, or mere reflections of a situation of anomie or unemployment. Rioters also speak. They act. Their actions are not irrational and meaningless, as those opposed to them claim. They do not threaten "civilized society," and, in large measure, they know what they are doing. Very often, they have a greater understanding of what they are saying than many commentators, who do not take into account the social and political meaning of their interpretations.[72] Paradoxically, the rioters have spoken much more than the political world, which has remained extremely silent, with the exception of calls from the Right to restore order and the denunciation of rioters as "maladjusted" from the Far Left.[73] Rioters seek to escape the emptiness of the ghetto that is destroying their individual lives and from the political vacuum to which they are confined, one that keeps them from acting in a coherent, integrated way. They therefore oscillate between the moral affirmation of their right to exist, their right to live, and the use of a destructive but rational violence from which they hope to gain entry to or acknowledgment from the system. They swing between a moral appeal to the "us" and solidarity—an appeal that seeks to encompass society as a whole— and rage against that same society. They are not social agents but, to borrow Eric Hobsbawm's expression, "primitive rebels" in both senses of the word "primitive": in the "crudeness" and directness of their motivation, namely, the defense of their right to exist as individuals, and in the "rudimentary" quality of their modes of action. But they are also "primitive rebels" because their moral protest and their situation cannot be expressed as a list of demands, given the closed nature of a supposedly republican political system. The system remains stubbornly hostile to them and confines them to marginality and to a relationship with the norm, preventing them from being agents.

Notes

1. *Le Monde*, December 2, 2005.
2. "The events are associated with the actions of very young men, actions that are very violent and meaningless in themselves. But we may wonder whether the term 'nihilism' is appropriate for designating the current movement. To be sure, nihilism is characterized by the absence of speech and itself stems from an environment that makes speaking out difficult. In some sense, violent acts are replacing speaking out (*prise de parole*), the reverse situation of May 1968. There is no speaking out, except through songs and rap." Pierre Rosanvallon, *Libération*, November 21, 2005.
3. Jean-Pierre Le Goff, *Libération*, November 21, 2005.

4. Aviad Kleinberg explains that "the question of why an individual chooses" to act in one way or another is different from the "social meaning" of his choice and action. In fact, he adds, "no one knows the precise combination of factors that impels people to act." See Kleinberg 2005: 112–13, 117.

5. Richard Schittly, "Situation précaire et tension permanente dans les banlieues lyonnaises," *Le Monde*, November 2, 2005. A police officer told a reporter for *Le Monde*, "Many neighborhoods are at the breaking point. As soon as there's a problem with a state institution, it explodes, you see flare-ups that are a bit anarchical. At any moment a serious incident can set things ablaze."

6. In the Paris region, the towns of Sèvres, Suresnes, Antony, and Villeneuve-la-Garenne were the site of incidents. See "Violences urbaines: Les villes sans histoires contaminées," *Le Parisien*, November 4, 2005.

7. See George Rudé's classic study of rioting during the French Revolution (Rudé 1959).

8. See Karl Marx 1964 and, on the notion of urban violence, see Bui Trong 2003.

9. Interpreters construct their interpretations against those of their adversaries, usually by anticipating their interlocutors' arguments. The media play a very useful role in this process: an instrument of stigmatization for some, they are the best huckster of "good intentions" and "sociological excuses" for others. According to some people, "sociologists" are responsible for the riot: "The expression of what is essentially a cultural problem, the revolt in the *banlieues,* of which meaninglessness seems to be the principal characteristic and hatred the driving force, can be explained primarily by the nihilism to which a certain political culture has led, inspired by a certain sociology rather than by philosophy." (See Redecker 2006: 37). The 2005 riots gave rise to an extensive body of literature and many statements of positions in the public sphere. (See for example Moulier-Boutang 2006, and Belaïd et al. 2006.)

10. The historian Jean Nicolas has counted 494 skirmishes and riots over the course of the century following the arrests of beggars. See Nicolas 2002: 354.

11. Gérard Collomb, at the time Socialist mayor of the ninth arrondissement of Lyons, in *Lyon-Capitale,* January 23, 1998. Collomb was later elected mayor of the city as a whole.

12. On this theme and on the American ghettos, see Lee Rainwater, "Open Letter on White Justice and the Riots," in Rossi 1970.

13. Quoted in Jazouli 1985. On this question, see also Marlière 2005: 238, and Kokoreff 2004.

14. *Libération,* November 5, 2005.

15. Aissa Diawara, director of the women's organization Relais de la Cité des 3000 (Community Liaisons for the Cité des 3000) in Aulnay-sous-Bois, quoted in *Libération,* November 3, 2005.

16. On this theme, see Gary T. Marx 1967. For a historical view, see Muchembled 1978, and his more recent work, Muchembled 1998.

17. *Le Monde,* October 29, 2005.

18. Aziz, age twenty, in *Le Figaro,* November 14, 2005. In its 2004 report, the Commission Nationale de Déontologie de la Sécurité (National Commission on Ethics in Law Enforcement) also points out that the sense of impunity is one of the causes of "police slipups."

19. *L'humanité,* November 5, 2005.

20. See Hannerz 1969: 165. Along the same lines, see Clark 1965: 45.

21. Statements by young women from Montfermeil, in *Libération,* November 12, 2005.

22. Sahra, Montfermeil, *Le Monde,* November 12, 2005.

23. An "injustice frame" is defined as "an interpretation of what is happening that supports the conclusion that the authority system is violating the shared moral principles of the participants. An alternative to a 'legitimating frame' it provides a reason for non-compliance." See Gamson, Fyreman, and Rytina 1982: 123.

24. In French, the term *émotions populaires* means "rioting."

25. For a recent discussion of these aspects based on Durkheim's sociological theory, see Collins 2004.

26. *L'humanité,* November 3, 1995.

27. *Le Monde,* July 19, 1988, and December 25, 1997.

28. See *Le Monde,* October 29, 2005, and *L'humanité,* October 31, 2005.

29. This is a traditional characteristic of movements of the poor or of community movements, especially in Latin America. On this point, see Castells 1983, and Touraine 1988.

30. "Le Chêne-Pointu entre rage et recueillement," *Le Monde,* October 29, 2005.

31. *Le Monde,* October 29, 2005.

32. *Le Parisien,* November 4, 2005; *Le Monde,* November 8, 2005.

33. Fahmi, age seventeen, La Courneuve, in *Jeune Africain Intelligent,* no. 2340, November 13, 2005.

34. "Quand les 'frères musulmans' tentent de ramener le calme," *Le Monde,* November 2, 2005.

35. On the revolutionary riots, see Rudé 1959. The American and English riots were also the acts of ordinary people and not especially of fringe elements. See Oberschall 1973.

36. *Le Monde,* November 26, 2005. "These are . . . young people from the neighborhood coping with relatively fewer family problems and possessing a higher level of education. The majority of them are enrolled in vocational programs, often in apprenticeships."

37. Aziz, age twenty, Bobigny, in *Le Figaro,* November 14, 2005.

38. Rachid, rioter in Aubervilliers, in *Le Monde,* November 8, 2005.

39. Dramam, age seventeen, rioter, Aulnay, in *Le Parisien,* November 5, 2005.

40. Momo, age sixteen, La Courneuve, *Le Figaro,* November 14, 2005.

41. *Le Parisien,* November 5, 2005.

42. *La Croix,* November 9, 2005.

43. *Le Monde,* October 29, 2005.

44. Eric, age thirty-four, Montfermeil, *Libération,* November 5, 2005.

45. Sabrina, age seventeen, Les Bosquets, Montfermeil, *Libération,* November 12, 2005.

46. On the rural and urban riots in Europe and their spread at the end of the Middle Ages, see Mollat and Wolff 1970. On the American riots, see Janowitz 1968.

47. *Le Monde,* November 8, 2005. On the spread of rioting, see Oberschall 1973: 298. For an analysis of the minister of the interior's declarations, see Le Goaziou and Mucchielli 2006: 53ff.

48. Rachid, young rioter, Clichy-sous-Bois, *Libération,* November 5, 2005.

49. *Le Monde,* October 29, 2005.

50. Youssef, age twenty-five, Aubervilliers, in *Le Monde,* November 8, 2005.

51. *Le Monde,* November 4, 2005.

52. *Libération,* November 3, 2005.

53. Ibid.

54. Kays, Bobigny, young rioter, *Le Figaro,* November 14, 2005.

55. Youssef, Aubervilliers, *Le Monde,* November 8, 2005. On this aspect during the American riots, see Hannerz 1969:172.

56. Rainwater, "Open Letter," in Rossi 1970: 124.

57. Draman, age seventeen, Aulnay, *Le Parisien,* November 5, 2005.

58. Farid, Aubervilliers, *Le Figaro,* November 14, 2005.

59. Eric, age thirty-four, Montfermeil, *Libération,* November 5, 2005.

60. For the case of England and the shift from dangerous classes to toiling masses, particularly through strikes following riots, see Jones 1971.

61. For further discussion see Oberschall 1973 and McAdam 1982.

62. Resident of Clichy, age forty, *Le Monde,* November 2, 2005.

63. Nadir, age twenty-four, Aubervilliers, *Le Monde,* November 8, 2005.

64. Julien, age twenty-two, Paris region, *Libération,* November 5, 2005.

65. Mohammed, age twenty-five, Clichy-sous-Bois, *Le Figaro,* November 28, 2005.

66. Mamadou, Saint-Denis, rioter, *Le Figaro,* November 14, 2005.

67. Skarj, Clichy-sous-Bois, *L'humanité,* November 5, 2005.

68. Young rioter from Sevran, *Le Parisien,* November 5, 2005.

69. Young rioter, Aulnay, *Le Monde,* November 4, 2005. For an analysis of the relationship of dependency between the ghetto population and the political realm in the United States of the 1950s, see Gans 1962.

70. See Karl Marx 1963 and Cobb 1970. Robert Blauner makes similar observations concerning the uprising in the American ghettos in the 1960s; see Blauner 1969.

71. On that dialectic of exclusion and poverty in the popular movements of Latin America, see Dubet et al. 1989.

72. For example, see Alain Lecourieux and Christophe Ramaux, "La République à jeter ou à achever," *Libération,* November 15, 2005. And for remarks on the hostile stance taken against the rioters in the name of the Republic, see Moulier-Boutang 2006. In 1848, Marx had pointed out that French politicians and intellectuals were "steeped in republican ideology to such an extent that . . . they were stupefied by the gunpowder smoke in which their fantastic republic dissolved" (Karl Marx 1964: 57).

73. On this theme, and especially on the silence of the Left and Far Left, see Véronique Le Gouaziou, "La classe politique française et les émeutes: Une victoire de plus pour l'extrême-droite," in Le Goaziou and Mucchielli 2006.

CHAPTER TWO

The Republic and Its Beast: On the Riots in the French *Banlieues*

Achille Mbembe
Translated by Jane Marie Todd

The two short chapters to follow by Achille Mbembe are translations of previously published articles that were written in the heat of the moment following the urban uprisings of October–November 2005. As one of the best-known intellectual figures associated with francophone post-colonial criticism in the United States and beyond, Mbembe has been able to articulate the aspirations of the dispossessed while also bring-ing to bear a theoretical and intellectual appreciation for the principles of justice, humanitarianism, and universalism associated with French republicanism. We have translated two crucial essays as "The Republic and Its Beast: On the Riots in the French Banlieues*" (first published in the Douala-based Cameroonian journal* Le Messager, *issue no. 2002, November 8, 2005: 7. Most recently it has been available in French on the Toulon section of* Les Droits de l'Homme *website: http://www.ldh-toulon .net/spip.php?article971 [accessed on August 3, 2008]), and "Figures of Multiplicity: Can France Reinvent Its Identity?"(first published in* Le Messager, *issue no. 2006, November 15, 2005: 6–7. It appeared under the title, "Les figures du multiple: La France peut-elle réinventer son iden-tité?" It is also available in French on the Toulon section of* Les Droits de l'Homme *website: http://www.ldh-toulon.net/spip.php?article2221 [accessed on August 3, 2008]). Paradoxically, these two texts emphasize* *the significance of the humanitarian impulse associated with French thought and culture on the one hand, but also probe the dark side of contemporary France, on the other. They also examine the difficulty the French republic has had in dealing calmly with the race question, constituting what Mbembe describes as the shameful face of French democracy. Finally, we have chosen to include these essays because they are documents of political intervention, evoking the nature of France's colonial past and calling on France, as a multi-faceted republican identity, to finally come to terms with decolonization and reinvent itself in the name of values most critical to French identity that include democracy, tolerance, and fraternity. —Eds.*

France is an old country, proud of its traditions and of its history. Without its contribution to philosophy, culture, art, and aesthetics, our world would undoubtedly be poorer in spirit and in humanity. That is the limpid, almost crystalline side of its identity.

The Beast and Its Nocturnal Face

Unfortunately, old age in itself does not necessarily make peoples or states more reasonable. Every old culture conceals, behind the mask of reason and civility, a nocturnal face, a vast store of obscure drives that, given the opportunity, can turn lethal.

In the West, that nocturnal face and those drives have always been fixated on race, the Beast whose existence the French republic, in its sometimes blind concern for universality, has always refused (not always wrongly) to admit. The Jewish philosopher Hannah Arendt, speaking precisely of race, was right to proclaim that it represented the final frontier beyond which the political in the strict sense no longer had any meaning. Had she not seen how Germany built concentration camps in the 1930s and 1940s, in order to be done once and for all with "the Jewish question"? Fortunately, France has not come to that.

That said, the evasive strategy it has continually used with the Beast since the early 1980s may soon blow up in its face. Perhaps more than other European countries, France is now experiencing two crises—of immigration (represented by the figure of the "alien") and of citizenship —which are now fueling each other. As a result of these crises, the nocturnal aspect of the republic, stirred up in great part by "Le Penism" and relayed by "Sarkozyism," is gradually revealing itself. We see it in the way state racism, which has always constituted the shameful, and for that reason carefully veiled, side of French democracy, has now become commonplace. The Beast, which demagoguery deployed by preference against foreigners, is now turning against the political body itself, threatening to divide it between the "French of pure stock" and those French who are "not quite like the others."

As always in times of emergency, people bow to the imperatives of "presentism" and tend to forget the deep causes. The relationship between France and the black and Arab nations of Africa has long served as an outlet for that state racism: paternalist and accommodating in its postcolonial version, monstrous when necessary, as during the Algerian War. Lurking in the shadows was always the Beast. For a time, it could be seen clearly only by the light of France's African policy, conducted with perfect continuity by successive administrations since 1960.

One may wonder what the riots in the *banlieues* (outlying regions) of Paris have to do with Africa. It must not be forgotten that the policy France conducted on that continent for several years is in great part responsible for the twin crises of the "alien" and of the citizen, which has found expression in the current flare-up of violence in the urban neighborhoods. After all, the phenomenon of so many French citizens of African descent packed into the ghettoes is a direct result of the colonization of parts of sub-Saharan Africa and the Maghreb in the nineteenth century. Before colonization, there was the slave trade: hence the existence in these neighborhoods of West Indians, Guadeloupans, and many others. The acceleration in migratory movements toward France is also the direct product of that long history. More decisively, the flow of illegal immigrants from the countries of the former French colonies is one of the consequences of the multifarious support the government of France has continued to offer predatory indigenous elites who run countries they have not ceased to pillage and impoverish since the achievement of independence.

In large measure, France is reaping at home what it believed it could sow elsewhere, irresponsibly. That has created a moment when the Republic is being asked to take seriously the question of the plurality of memory. Relatively belated efforts have been made to symbolically assume responsibility for slavery and its abolition. As for the "colonial fracture," it is still gaping wide. Since no one wants to hear about affirmative action policies, the restoration of public order in the *banlieues* will necessarily be achieved by white police officers pursuing young people of color in the streets. In the meantime, a legislative bill celebrating the "civilizing" and colonial enterprise has been passed by Parliament.

It is a good thing to confront the United States when it tramples underfoot an international law, which, in any case, very few nations were respecting. In addition, however, we must set an example in our own relationship with the weakest, the most vulnerable, the most dependent members of society. From that standpoint, France's conduct toward its minorities is comparable to its conduct in Africa since the end of direct colonization: anything but ethical. Since 1960, France's African policy has radically contradicted everything the country claims to represent and the idea it has formed of itself, its history, and its fate in the world.

No mutual attraction exists any longer between France and Africa. Execration and rejection now seem to characterize that old relationship, judged on both sides to be more abusive than ever.

The Geography of Infamy

In francophone Africa especially, the hostility, even seething hatred, of the younger generations toward France and what it represents is only getting worse. In all the major cities, tempers flare at every incident, however insignificant. The paradox is that anti-France sentiment is thriving at a time when there are increasing signs, if not of a real dis-engagement, then at least of widespread indifference on the part of the former colonial power toward its former protectorate.

Of the many roots of that tension, two in particular risk leading in short order to a huge morass. The first has to do with immigration policy and the treatment inflicted on refugees and other Africans living in France illegally. The second, a corollary of the first, concerns the "pacification" policy in the *banlieues,* inhabited for the most part by French persons of African descent or descendants of African slaves who, by force of circumstance, have also become French citizens.

We are all well aware of the hard line now being taken. It has recently been expressed in the proliferation of sweeps taking place on urban sidewalks, in the high schools, and at metro stops. There has been news of evictions. Families, students, and single people are offered only a few nights in a hotel, then thrown out onto the street. Every day throughout France, thousands of people of color are systematically stopped by police for no apparent reason. In some cases, the structure of power relations and the constant harassment have resulted in deaths. We are also aware of the spread of camps designed to isolate aliens whose status is irregular, then to force them back to their countries of origin, often by military means. Then too, there is the outsourcing—exportation outside the boundaries of the European Union—and subcontracting to developing countries of the management and protection of refugees, in exchange for an increase in "development aid."

Border camps are located near airports, seaports, and international train stations—whether they are called "waiting zones," local "detention" centers, or "warehouses" for aliens, the nomenclature hardly matters. Judges have remarked that the prefectures send them aliens every day, asking that their detention be extended, even when there is no longer any room at the centers. Metropolitan France as a whole is now covered by a geographical web of infamy, from Bordeaux to Calais-Coquelle; from Strasbourg to Hendaye; from Lille, Lyons, Marseilles, and Nantes, to Nice, Bobigny, and Le Mesnil-Amelot; from Roissy, Nanterre, Versailles, and Vincennes to Rivesaltes, Rouen, Sète, and Toulouse; from Dunkerque, Lyon-Saint Exupéry, and Saint-Nazaire to La Rochelle and Toulon; and on and on.

Across the Atlantic, everyone is aware of the humiliations many Africans face on a daily basis as they seek to obtain visas for France in the African consulates (with the exception of the South African bureaus). The arbitrary methods used in the consulates are directly related to those that colonization employed, at a time when every "little king of the bush" was in the habit of doing as he pleased.

The threefold system of identity checks, screening, and expulsion, then, with its procession of brutal acts, of physical violence and psychological warfare, is being inflicted once again, as under slavery, on the black body, the difference being that instead of the slave ship, the privileged instrument is now the charter flight.

Palestinization

This treatment and these forms of humiliation, which were once tolerated only in the colonies, are now resurfacing in the metropolis itself, where, during sweeps and raids in the *banlieues,* they are applied not only to aliens—illegal immigrants and refugees—but increasingly to French citizens of African descent or the descendants of former African slaves.

In other words, a conflation is occurring between colonial modes of control, treatment, and segregation, the treatment in metropolitan France of men and women judged undesirable, and the treatment of citizens considered to be second-class simply because they are not "French of pure stock" or "of the white race."

It is not by accident that we have come to this conjuncture. Over the last ten years, not only have representations of the "alien," the migrant, and the refugee been fabricated to make them appear a threat to national security, but laws have been enacted that, in their obvious violation of common law, are in many respects inspired by the Code de l'Indigénat (Native Code) of colonial times. Through the byway of the fight against the right to asylum, illegal immigration, and terrorism, the sphere of rights has been invaded by legal conceptions relating to war. These conceptions have in turn provoked a clear resurgence of state racism, which as we know was one of the cornerstones of the colonial order.

The law is now being used not as a tool for rendering justice and guaranteeing freedom but as the stratagem that, if it does not authorize extreme violence, at least exposes the most vulnerable and deprived populations to extraordinary methods of repression. The great advantage of these methods is that they can be used rapidly, arbitrarily, almost irresponsibly. To control immigration, a segmenting of the administration of justice has come about.

As during the colonial period, the law itself is now fragmented. In France we find laws that apply only to certain "human species." These laws prescribe offenses specific to the "human species" they target even as they grant the authorities charged with their application extraordinary powers deviating from common law. The crimes detailed in these laws can be invoked only against these particular "human species." The system of sanctions applied is also exceptional because it has been placed outside the realm of common law.

The Code de l'Indigénat was elaborated to govern the colonies. By its very nature, this was a government of extraordinary powers based on state racism. Here the function of the law was precisely to multiply, spread, then universalize situations of illegality and to extend them to all spheres of daily life for people of races judged inferior. The legal philosophy underlying the Code de l'Indigénat—and of its corollary, state racism—is now being brought back to metropolitan France. That philosophy is being deployed in the struggle against categories of persons in France judged undesirable (illegal immigrants, undocumented aliens, refugees).

It is well known that for several years the French population has been led to believe that the *banlieues* constitute a direct threat to their lifestyle and to their most cherished values. Both the Left and the Right wish to believe that the social bond cannot be reestablished in these neighborhoods unless problems of immigration and integration are transformed into problems of national security, and secularism is enlisted to police both religion and what is disdainfully called "communitarianism."

But as soon as the *banlieue* is defined as a place inhabited not by full-fledged moral subjects but by an undifferentiated mass that can be summarily discredited (as little savages, scum, hooligans, delinquents, gangstas running the parallel economy)—as soon as it is constructed as the domestic front of a new planetary war (cultural, religious, and military all at once), where the very identity of the Republic is being played out—there is a great temptation to want to apply colonial methods drawn from the lessons of the race wars to the most vulnerable categories of French society.

All things considered, the images of hundreds of armed white police officers pursuing or arresting young "people of color" in urban neighborhoods of the twenty-first century cannot fail to recall what happened in the ghettoes of the northern United States, and especially in the American South, more than forty years ago. The same images remind us of events that occurred more recently, in the townships of South Africa in the 1970s. But more than the American South and the northern ghettoes, more than the townships of South Africa, stone-throwing and acts of arson in the *banlieues* of Paris subliminally echo the flames and smoke rising from the Palestinian refugee camps.

Moreover, the vocabulary used by some members of Parliament and by very high government officials, who talk of "hosing down" the *banlieues* or going on "hooligan hunts," only encourages such comparisons. If we are not careful, the structure of power relations, pushed to the limit, may easily lead to a "Palestinization" of the *banlieue*, directly related to the colonial ideology of race wars. In substance, that is the grave danger threatening French society and its democracy—and beyond it, twenty-first century Europe, once more in the grip of its Beast. It is the problem of race, to which the problem of religion has been added. From the standpoint of the law, "Palestinization," as we have seen elsewhere, generally tends to make the exception into the norm, even while claiming to establish or impose order and justice by means of terror. In so doing, that system ultimately makes law the instrument of a semblance of "order" and of a pseudo-justice characteristic of the "state vested with extraordinary powers," that is, making the most vulnerable synonymous with a state of illegality and fostering a state of disorder and general insecurity for all.

Is that truly the direction this old country wants to take, a country that has contributed so much to the world in the fields of philosophy, culture, the arts, and aesthetics and that, in so doing, has so enriched its spirit?

CHAPTER THREE

Figures of Multiplicity: Can France Reinvent Its Identity?

Achille Mbembe
Translated by Jane Marie Todd

The root cause of the crisis in the *banlieues* is the way France has historically tried to dodge the question of race even while engaging in multiple practices of "racialization" at every level of daily life. This crisis exposes the impasse that has resulted from the country's refusal to undertake its own decolonization. If France still wants to exert minimal influence on the contemporary imagination, it must quickly come to realize the urgency of the situation.

Never in any country has civil peace and public order, let alone the social contract, been established through political repression alone. This is particularly the case for postcolonial societies, a category to which almost all European democracies once possessing a colonial empire belong.

The *banlieues* of France will prove no exception to that rule, despite the police questioning and mass arrests, the assembly-line trials and convictions, and, lurking in the background, the exhumation of colonialism and slavery. These old cadavers, as we have been told repeatedly in the last ten years, were never properly laid to rest: the past refuses to pass away.

It is now clear that the major victim of recent events is French democracy, its credibility and respectability in the world. If France still wants to exert minimal influence on the contemporary imagination, it must quickly come to realize the urgency of the situation. That urgency lies not in the resurrection of old colonial laws that date from the Algerian War and that have granted extraordinary powers to the state—in metropolitan France itself and in the twenty-first century—but in the slow patient work by which the country will forge a new identity for itself in the era of globalization.

We must hope that once a semblance of order has been restored, France will quickly display the courage needed to treat the structural causes of a problem that, far from being accidental, exposes the impasse that has resulted from the country's refusal to undertake its own decolonization.

It has not been repeated often enough that the root cause of the crisis is the way France has historically tried to dodge the race question even while engaging in multiple practices of "racialization" at every level of daily life.

What is new is that "aliens" are no longer the sole targets of these practices, which are increasingly applied to the most vulnerable French citizens and to those most marked and stigmatized by their ethnicity. Through the recent riots, then, France is paying the price for the double exaction it has never ceased to demand of these sectors of the population: that of "class" and that of "race."

Beneath the real social problems raised by life in the *banlieues*, the race question constitutes the substratum of the "insurrection of the invisible" we have just witnessed. As we see clearly in the extraordinary measures currently being imposed in certain of these areas, "race" also lies at the foundation of the mechanisms aimed at repressing that "revolt of the *sans-parts*," whom we have, in a brilliant display of unanimity, rapidly criminalized.[1] No longer content to show itself only underground, in the unconscious, the Beast has suddenly leapt out into the open, corrupting along the way rights, law, and justice, and creating a situation that will long leave indelible scars on the skin and face of the nation itself.

Self-Inflicted Disaster

The reason that the self-inflicted disaster has been so spectacular, and in many respects so comic, is that France, after so many years of arrogance and bad faith, has finally fallen into the trap of its own hypocrisy. Having tried to deny responsibility for its history, and therefore at a loss as to how to heal its wounds—though in large part it had the means at hand—it now finds that the past has suddenly caught up with it. At the intellectual level, the tragedy (or should we say the farce?) is particularly serious because France has long refused to equip itself with the conceptual tools that would allow it to analyze properly what is happening.

How are we to explain, for example, the hostility and contempt of right-minded elites in regard to "postcolonial studies" or "critical race theory," two paradigms whose limitations are well known but that in other countries have greatly contributed toward a deeper understanding of citizenship and alterity? Long ago, the elites and intelligentsia of France chose to bathe exclusively in the waters of narcissism and the "cultural exception." Unbeknownst to them, the world was even then broadening its horizons, as these French elites spent their time loudly proclaiming an anachronistic version of universalism too beautiful to be true.

As a result, they have not understood that, in the wake of the collapse of the colonial empires, and more recently, of communism, the major challenge of European democracies—which, moreover, are exposed to the pressures of globalization—is the political and symbolic negotiation of racial and religious differences. Once the specter of communism was destroyed, the explicit recognition of religious, racial, and cultural pluralism born of the colonial encounter became a prerequisite for inventing new national identities.

Every nation is now transnational and diasporic. The crucible in which the nation is being forged is as much outside its territorial borders as inside. The distant, the elsewhere, and the here-at-home meet. Because of that dislocation, it no longer makes much sense to raise the problem of that new identity in terms of "integration." If we wish to move beyond the new fractures that have resulted from the entanglement over the long term of different histories, we must make the transition to cosmopolitanism. In France over the last ten years, have not the fantasies and hysteria surrounding Islam and "communitarianism" had the effect of muddling the terms of that discussion and of putting off the moment when we finally face reality?

France, lacking adequate concepts to analyze what is happening, has dug in its heels. In so doing, it has revealed the enormous cultural handicap from which it suffers, and which makes it unable to understand that the implosion in prime time of its *banlieues* discredits at the international level its discourse on social integration, while further eroding the already weak appeal that its models of citizenship and democracy exert on the contemporary imagination.

The causes of that cultural handicap are too numerous to be examined at length here. Let us merely indicate that, for the most part, they lie in the epistemic obstruction ultimately constituted by the ideology of secular republicanism in France. Originally revolutionary, that ideology was unfortunately transformed into a sort of religion without scripture and without theology—like all forms of fundamentalism. Of course, there is no question here of reconsidering the separation of church and state, a principle that, in any event, has always concealed (and continues to conceal) what is sometimes a very useful collusion between the two.

But given the scope of the failure, how can we not be astonished that a country of such education, filled with so many brilliant minds, displays such an inability to understand that the abstract concept of radical equality can paradoxically serve as a veil to conceal state racism?

Could French society as a whole be so blind that it cannot see the danger represented for its democracy, its political system, and its aura, by the use of "aliens" as scapegoats for a "national sovereignty" now out of the nation's hands and undermined by both Europeanization and neoliberal globalization?

Is it really so complicated as all that to understand that the "social problem" cannot be reduced solely to class differences and inequalities? Or that the horizon opened up by the Republic—namely, radical social equality—also entails recognition and dignity, and requires taking the question of race as seriously as that of gender?

Symptom and Repression

The power of denial runs just as deep. Many French people refuse to acknowledge that most of the rioters were born in France—they are of French nationality. Many as well judge that these "children of immigrants" contribute nothing to the nation: they may enjoy "French nationality" but they are not truly "French citizens" in the same sense we are. Pushed to extremes, we might tolerate their presence among us. But in any event, they are obviously not our kind. What difference does it make that most of them have never set foot in Algeria, Morocco, Senegal, Mali, or Guinea? What really counts are their parents' and grandparents' origins, race, and religion. Those are the primordial marks of their deep-seated identity, what distinguishes them from *us*.

That is how, floundering in the nets of psychological repression, the French debate on democracy and citizenship has ultimately been rendered meaningless. It is now dominated by considerations of autochthony and allochthony. As a result, the discourse on what in France has for several years been called "communitarianism" appears in its true light. Far from designating an objective reality, that discourse is above all the manifestation of drives and fears, themselves fed at the root by an unconscious for which "race" serves as the obscure symptom.

It should hardly be surprising that the symptom took on such substance, such life, and such density in the wake of the cold war, and more recently, in the context of the "fear factories" of globalization, Europeanization, and the war on terror. For several years, have not the French been led to believe that, after the religious wars and the revolutionary wars of the past, the country is now on the brink of a new civil war? That war supposedly pits the "autochthonous" (those from here) against the "allogenous" (those living here but from somewhere else). Since these people-from-somewhere-else have a skin color different from our own, occasionally speak languages we do not understand, and worship gods unfamiliar to us, the new civil war is supposed to be all at once a race war, a war of languages, and a religious war.

Class analysis alone cannot account for passions so obscure and fantasies so deeply rooted in popular culture. Of course, what is happening in the *banlieues* has a very strong social dimension. Is not unemployment endemic? "Out of the hundred résumés I sent out, I got three interviews," you often hear. Marginality and financial insecurity are the lot of many. Likewise failure at school and what now amounts to the imprisonment of the urban environment and of the drab high-rises, the absence of recreation, the drop in life expectancy. But tackling the material conditions of those living in the projects will not be enough to end the turmoil.

In an act of collective repression, the public, the media, and the government prefer to speak of "urban violence," even though race is a central dimension of the riots. In fact, they are directly related to the events in the American ghettoes of the north since the mid-twentieth century, in the poor neighborhoods of England in the 1970s and 1980s, and in the South African townships during the struggle against apartheid.

The Manufacture of Race and the Appearance of the *Sans-Parts*

In each of these cases, segregation in housing and confinement to the urban areas, along with discrimination in hiring, in and of themselves constituted structuring factors in the manufacture of race. Far from being accidental, state racism became a machine for producing inequalities. And in every case, the production of inequalities went hand in hand with the infliction of significant psychic wounds on the victims of racism.

Every time they speak up to describe their burned-out lives, the young rioters from the French housing projects observe more or less the same thing: discrimination in schooling, the absence of recognition and respect, constant police harassment, widespread surveillance, discriminatory hiring practices based on race (work, when it can be found, is undervalued, repetitive, insecure, and low-paying), boredom in the shadow of the drab high-rises, a state of mental and physical siege—in short, hell on earth. Anyone taking an interest in their cultural products will find they have constantly repeated the same anthem since the 1980s, in rap or hip-hop, poetry or song.

It is altogether significant that in these accounts, a central place is granted to stops by the police. "We don't have the words to express what we feel," one of them says. "Today I was stopped twice," says another. "The cops had me spread-eagle on the ground, they stuck a flash-ball gun in my face and disrespected me."[2]

From the many descriptions given by young people, it emerges clearly that police violence is not merely physical. Because it has to do with the race of those subjected to it, that violence ends up causing its victims deep psychic wounds every time it is used. In the vocabulary of the young, that is the particular connotation of the term "disrespect."

It would be wrong to underestimate the anger fueled in the projects by the daily bullying and police violence. The French police, like many sectors of law enforcement (prefectures), the various organs of democratic rule (municipalities, regional councils, Parliament, political parties), and even entire swathes of public life (the print media, television, advertising) and academic institutions, are overwhelmingly white.

As during the segregationist past of the United States, racial minorities are visible only in sports (especially soccer, boxing, and track and field). And as in South Africa under apartheid, the repression of the recent riots has been carried out for the most part by white officers pursuing children of color, arresting them, and sending them into a totally white judicial system that will sentence them to prison terms. They will serve their sentences in prisons whose guards are also nearly all white.

Some will object that in spite of all that, the *banlieues* of France bear little resemblance to the American ghettoes and the South African townships. No doubt. State racism *à la française* has always expressed itself in very original forms. A brief chronology of its many ages will allow us to distinguish four moments, sometimes superimposed, sometimes overlapping, and sometimes distinct.

The first era was a very long period that included both the slave trade (the Code Noir, or Black Code) and European anti-Semitism. During that era, the Other was considered either "property," an object to do with as one pleased, or simply a "castoff." That era ended, on one hand, with the major slave revolts and insurrections (in Saint-Domingue, for example) and, on the other, with Jewish ghettoes and pogroms, the emancipation of the Jews, and, soon after citizenship was achieved, round-ups of innocent people and the establishment of concentration camps.

The second era is typical of colonial imperialism and was played out under a system of selective inclusion, or tokenism, characterized by the opposition between the citizen and the "native." This was the time of the Codes de l'Indigénat (Native Codes), the segmentation and hierarchization of laws, segregation in housing, and the establishment of boundaries establishing differences between persons as a function of their skin color or level of "assimilation."

This was also when the law, as applied to the indigenous people, ceased to be the expression of a universal ethics and became a form of primal violence. As a result of the growing interpenetration between penal and administrative institutions, the law became a way of continuing, by other means and within society itself, the processes of subjugation inaugurated by the wars of conquest and the so-called pacification operations.

The third era of state racism *à la française* began with the repatriation of the Algerian *colons,* and, beginning in 1973, with an accelerated rate of migration around the Mediterranean basin. It was a period of functional, semi-clandestine, almost invisible racism, marked here and there by a few outbreaks. During this period, control mechanisms were gradually set in place whose discriminatory effects specifically targeted those then called "immigrant workers." These effects were not limited to the labor market. In fact, they pointed the way to the social apartheid system of which the *banlieues* are now the most obvious expression.

The fourth era—that of globalization—coincided with the appearance of the "alien" in the sphere of fantasy. It can also be characterized as the age of resentment. "Le Penism" is its most vulgar expression. (The radical right covers more surface area of electoral politics in France than in nearly any other European democracy.)

It is helpful to consider at length that new phase of state racism, because it allows us to understand what is happening today. By the 1980s, France had inexorably returned to a climate of cultural violence and resentment toward the "alien," presented even at that time as a social problem insoluble by its very nature. From then on, in response to resentment toward subalterns, a series of laws was enacted with the aim of making the life of migrants in France intolerable. These laws were intended to weaken the migrants as much as possible, to constantly harass them, to humiliate them whenever possible, and to place them in a financially precarious situation of a structural nature as soon as possible.

It is very significant that, since 1980, the two principal sources of French law regarding aliens are the laws applied to the Jews before their emancipation and those targeting the indigenous peoples of the colonies under the empire. The Republic thus drew from its own "archives of shame" for the laws enacted against aliens in the last quarter of the twentieth century. It set in place techniques for governing aliens, techniques whose objective was to strip them of all rights, precisely though the enactment of laws whose function was to abrogate those rights and assure extraterritorialization.

We therefore find ourselves facing the paradox of a democratic system that by the light of day claims to assure justice, security, and liberty, but under cover of night operates through the derogative suspension of rights and constant recourse to the colonial techniques of jurisdiction, monitoring, and punishment. This is a democracy that, having instituted a segmentation of rights, easily makes its peace with extraordinary legal measures.

The major shift at the beginning of this century has been to extend to nonwhite French citizens the disgraceful treatment previously inflicted on colonial subjects and, in our own time, on migrants, refugees, and those called simply "aliens." As in South Africa under apartheid, the idea is to exacerbate class antagonisms by transforming into scapegoats a class of "intruders" or *sans-parts* whom one wishes to cast out of the human community.

In reality, more than a quarter century ago, the *banlieue* was turned into a new penal colony. Now, by virtue of segregation in housing, extraordinary legal measures have been imposed on citizens already long since interned. That explains the systematic limitation of freedoms—beginning with freedom of movement—the proliferation of identity checks and pat-downs, the interference with family life, the stratagem of confinement to the high-rises, and the quasi-institutional discrimination on the labor market even for the most qualified individuals. The requirement that citizens in these areas always carry a document on their person recalls in many respects the South African pass (the work documents under apartheid) or the procedures used at Israeli checkpoints. The racial ghetto was thus invented and actively produced. It did not come about spontaneously.

Looking beyond Race

Must we recall that the struggle for recognition, equality, and dignity took different forms in each of the eras I have briefly described above? Think, for example, of the struggles during the years of Negritude. From 1920 on, a generation of radical black thinkers elaborated in France a critique of republican citizenship, revealing the impasses of the ideology of integration, which at the time was developed in terms of "assimilation."

They demonstrated, for example, that universal citizenship and radical equality cannot coexist with the practice of state racism. In so doing, they stripped bare the contradiction that has been at the core of the French civic ideal since the Revolution. That contradiction took a unique form, they claimed, given that French nationalism (in the last instance, a certain idea of race and ethnicity) decked itself out in all the frippery of liberty, equality, and fraternity to better mask its violence toward the colonized peoples. In other words, France either had to make its colonial subjects French citizens pure and simple or restore their sovereignty to them.

The thinkers of Negritude, exemplified by Léopold Senghor, Aimé Césaire, and later Édouard Glissant, complemented their political critique of democracy and citizenship with the insight that universality consists primarily of sharing differences. That sharing is total: according to Senghor, for example, it has a biological and a cultural component, which results in the intermixing of different races.

Glissant speaks rather of "Creolity." Nevertheless, beyond the differences in emphasis, the Negritude thinkers of the time showed it was possible for a form of critical humanism to emerge from the encounter between France and distant peoples, a humanism in which a concern for self is inseparable from the concern for the other and for the world in general.

Everything clearly indicates that the Republic could be revitalized and that France could forge a new culture and identity by conceiving of itself as the country whose particularity it is to unite the different facets of the world into a single whole. Among all these thinkers, migration, even colonization, are the object of a transfiguration. The excluded become in some sense the *felix culpa* thanks to which "the encounter between giving and receiving" becomes possible, even as the utopian horizon of the "civilization of the universal" finally opens for the first time in human history.

Hence the thinkers of Negritude opened the way for a shift toward cosmopolitanism in France. At the start of the twentieth century, they offered the country the intellectual tools for taking responsibility for its postcolonial condition. They proposed that France transfigure a violent memory, a violent past, into a new concern for the Other and for the world—a way of enriching its own revolutionary heritage and of achieving the idea of a wise and reasonable universalism, one capable of negotiating difference and of celebrating the unity of the human race in the multiplicity of the figures of humankind.

The Republic would not listen to them. On the contrary, it applied a model of integration stemming directly from its Jacobin ideology. As we now see, that model rests on an unconscious shaped by fear of the Other and by an old fount of religious intolerance. That is in part what explains the migrants' strike against racism in 1973, the emergence of the SOS-Racisme movement in the 1980s, and even the *Beur* movement and the struggles of undocumented aliens in the 1990s.

We must therefore place the question of race at the center of the production of democracy and of the reflection on French citizenship. This time, to be credible, the project of radical equality must be aware of its contingency. It cannot be a matter of numbers, of arithmetical or geometrical progression. Race, coupled with poverty and unemployment, ultimately creates a class of *sans-parts,* that is, of pseudocitizens who, because of their race, not only are excluded from the mechanisms of distribution but also are refused recognition, dignity, and respect. The recent riots allow us to put an end to the false certainty that French democracy is given once and for all and that the presence of nonwhite European citizens on European soil is temporary.

How to Forge a New Identity

In the early 1980s, a new phase of state racism began within the context of globalization, the establishment of the European Union, and above all the war on terror. In that context, the risk is that the *banlieues* will become one of the designated targets of authoritarian populist movements, whose increasing power in the last quarter of the twentieth century has been observed in all European democracies.

The strategy of these populist movements is to exacerbate the fear of an imaginary enemy in the hope of relegitimating state violence, especially toward the most vulnerable. In inventing an enemy from whole cloth and making fear of that enemy the cornerstone of daily life and culture, they seek to legitimate the role of government authority as the purveyor of protection and security. That protection and security are obtained in exchange for an abdication of independent critical thought. Blind obedience to the figure of the Father thereby becomes the very foundation of patriotism.

We have seen it in the United States. As Josep Ramoneda, editorialist for the Spanish daily *El País,* aptly reminds us, for the most deprived portions of the population, and especially for disadvantaged racial minorities, that means a shift from "the social state to the penal state." It is not out of the question that, on the pretext of opposing "public assistance," masked behind a discourse on individual duties, obligations, and responsibilities, proposals will soon appear whose objective is to dismantle the French "social safety net," which has heretofore allowed a few people not to fall into utter destitution. As in the United States, the conflation of extreme poverty and delinquency, and then of delinquency and threats to security, makes it possible to criminalize an entire part of the population and to "racialize" social problems, which can then be presented as insoluble except through penal institutions. That explains, moreover, the disproportion of racial minorities in U.S. prisons.

In that context, the French government is faced with two choices.

The first is to radicalize police and penal repression in the directions I have just sketched, combining them with forms of economic sanction applied by preference to racial minorities.

The second is to embrace politically the multicultural, multiracial, and multireligious character of the nation and to open the way for a truly cosmopolitan society that defines itself explicitly as such and that seeks to translate that ideal into its institutions, policies, and culture.

More than half a century after the attempt on European soil to exterminate the Jews, France and Europe as a whole need to take another qualitative leap forward, to embrace the democratic idea and realize the ideals of the Enlightenment, by negotiating the mutual assimilation of peoples, religions, and races set in motion by slavery, the colonial encounter, and globalization.

But to build a harmonious nation, symbol of a true "universal city," we must put an end to the crisis of nonrepresentation that has affected all the institutions of French public life (political parties, national and municipal governing bodies, the police, the army, law enforcement, academia). The same applies to the institutions of civil society.

This effort also requires that an intelligent affirmative action program be set in place, one that does not espouse a policy of quotas pure and simple and is no longer applied exclusively on the basis of race. Such a program should be limited in time and should target areas as varied as access to home ownership, education, and recreation. It ought also to establish economic development zones offering tax advantages to businesses that agree to locate themselves there.

Even though it is vulnerable to manipulation for politico-ideological ends, the question of order and security in the *banlieues* is real. As we have seen elsewhere, poverty and criminality go hand in hand, especially when deep inequalities separate those who have nothing to lose from those who have everything to protect. The struggle against delinquency entails at once punishment, prevention, and the fight against inequality. Things are the way they are today because the French state has failed in its task to create the conditions for relatively equal opportunity. In several respects, the forms its presence has taken in the *banlieues* have only exacerbated the problems rather than solving them.

The return to civility and the creation of a culture of harmony thus entails other forms of government presence. It also requires the support of a dense network of local associations, especially in the arts, sports, music, and culture generally. It calls for the actions of a police force that the residents themselves will support because the police have learned how to win the population's respect and not only because they inspire terror, fear, and dread. At that level, the inclusion of blacks and *Beurs* in law enforcement will not suffice. France needs a well-educated, well-trained, disciplined police force aware of the ravages of racism and deeply committed to respect for fundamental human rights. It also needs an ethnically and racially diversified elite—which is hardly the situation at present.

Finally, we cannot underestimate the capacity of the media, advertising, and market forces to transform a society's imaginary. In South Africa, whose racist legacy profoundly marked attitudes, behaviors, and the psyche generally, we now see what can be accomplished when the major cultural industries make racial crossover the cornerstone of their commercial practices and business ethic. In the absence of major private foundations in France—which in the United States, for instance, often effectively compensate for the shortcomings of the state, especially in the area of social innovation—the capitalist class must take the lead and demonstrate more social responsibility than it currently does.

For the rioters, the choice of violence is obviously a dead end. It partakes in an ideology of nihilism whose ravages we have seen elsewhere. It only reinforces the vicious cycle of poverty and self-destruction, while too easily vindicating those who wish to keep the people concerned from enjoying the benefits of citizenship.

That said, long years of neglect and state racism have shown that citizenship is never bestowed. It is obtained through civil struggle. But in a democracy, a rage that responds to no watchword, no organization, and that uses only the language of fire is not tenable. The symbolism of nocturnal acts of arson large and small must therefore be replaced by a properly political approach.

On that road, Islamism and Afrocentrism will be of no great help. The approach requires the development of social practices in the *banlieues* focused on a new ethics—that of individual responsibility. The privileged place for applying that ethics of individual responsibility is the schools. As the Jewish example has already shown and as the recent Asian immigrants to the United States are currently demonstrating, education is the most effective means for minorities to amass social capital, even in circumstances of deep-rooted hostility.

In a situation where the state has fallen short, the ethics of individual responsibility is one of the essential conditions for rebuilding the social bond. It has been seen in many countries of Africa. No longer able to expect help from a tutelary and benevolent government, people have taken responsibility for their own fate, a resolve that has translated into a new social creativity. Such is the significance of the many associations and other networks, religious and communitarian, that dot the urban landscape in many of these countries.

The same strategy could be followed in the *banlieues* of France. The associative life of these areas needs to be reactivated by the residents, who must learn to draw from the reservoir of experiences provided by the societies where their parents and grandparents originated. The many practices developed in Africa, East and Southeast Asia, and Latin America with respect to autonomous organization, self-financing, and the establishment of networks of mutual aid and support can be creatively adapted to the circumstances.

The new struggles for citizenship will also have to include cultural innovation. In the eyes of the world, French society will be culturally impoverished so long as it has not integrated the cultural practices of the millions of its citizens that came to it by way of immigration. We see this in the United States: what would the cultural globalization that country has spearheaded be without the creative works of African Americans or the technical ingenuity of Asians? What would contemporary English-language literature be without Salman Rushdie, Zadie Smith, and other postcolonial immigrants? In almost all areas, the new age of French culture will emerge from the fusion between genres and styles created in the urban neighborhoods on one hand, and the old French fount stripped of its smugness and pointless arrogance on the other.

This presupposes the rise of a generation of French intellectuals of all races that will reconsider French culture in terms of its margins (the *banlieue*, the overseas territories, the former colonies, francophonia). The standoffish discourse of "the cultural exception" hardly allows us to deal with the hegemony of the English-speaking world. In order to truly face it, we need a real cultural renaissance, one based on a mode of thought and on artistic and cultural practices ready to embrace France as—in Glissant's expression—the "Tout-Monde" (Whole-World) in miniature. The kind of racial fusion observed on the soccer field ought to extend to every other field of culture and the arts. This implies that the French intellectual and artistic scene, along with the media, must find the equivalent of what we already see in Great Britain, with the sociologist Paul Gilroy, the cultural theorist Stuart Hall, the photographer and filmmaker Isaac Julien, the postcolonialist theorist Homi Bhabha, the artist Yinka Shonibare, and so on.

But none of what has been said here can come about without the acquisition and exercise of the right to vote. If the people of the *banlieue* do not vote, they do not count politically. So long as that population does not take its civic duties seriously, shady politicians will be able to manipulate resentment toward French subalterns without risk. The youth in the *banlieues* must therefore register to vote and then vote.

If none of what has been proposed here works out, then we will have to do battle with an obviously hidebound republic by using the ideals that inspired the two great revolutions of the twentieth century: the nonviolent struggle against racial segregation in the United States and the struggle against apartheid in South Africa.

We must do so not by copying these two models, but by adapting the spirit that animated them, and that has made them examples not for a particular race but for humanity in general, to the conditions of contemporary France.

We will have to create a new civil rights movement in France able to regenerate that old society and to spur on that old culture, which once contributed so much to the world but is now rambling incoherently, staggering about, giving the impression that it is about to collapse from a stroke.

Notes

1. *Sans-parts:* Jacques Rancière's term for those who do not share in the benefits of society and thus have no stake in it.
2. A flash-ball gun is a handheld weapon that fires rubber bullets.

CHAPTER FOUR

Outsiders in the French Melting Pot: The Public Construction of Invisibility for Visible Minorities

Ahmed Boubeker
Translated by Jane Marie Todd

The French *banlieues* are not yet Watts or L.A., but a quarter century of social opprobrium has already lit the fuse on that powder keg of poverty and resentment. And for just as long, the enfants terribles of the housing projects have been pilloried by the public uproar. Heirs to the legacy of immigration from the former colonies, most are French, but their experience proves that, in the country of Voltaire and Jean-Jacques Rousseau, the outsider is no longer just someone who comes from somewhere else. From a state of otherness—the other. The immigration of the "invisible man" (Ellison 1952) has resulted in the *banlieues* of visible minorities. That construction of a sudden visibility, far from being real recognition, has dressed up the anonymity of individuals in the latest frippery of the social question. No one knows their number—10 percent, 12 percent of the French population?—or even what to call them: "young immigrants," "*Beurs,*" "little savages," "scum"?[1] No stable designation, no mental framework, for judging the situation of these new "outsiders within." They mark the end of politics as the power to give names and a context to events, to situate the same and the other in a common space. The eternal return of urban violence to the public arena has thus drawn the new internal borders of French society as a socioethnic partition of metropolitan France, a radical break between fully recognized and second-class citizens, sounding the death knell of republican universalism *à la française* and its sacrosanct integration model.

But the "scum" is striking back. These nameless young people refuse to be consigned to some phantasmal house arrest in the rubbish heap of French history. They butt their heads against the security walls of a society that prefers to close its eyes to its visible minorities so as to preserve its simplicity and its nostalgia for grandeur. In the face of an enduring crisis that reawakens the old demons of racism even within the political class, denial of the ethnic question and the escalation of "closed discourse"—in Herbert Marcuse's expression—have been the only constants of public action over the last twenty-five years. If words were made of stone, the concrete poured into the walls of all the French *banlieues* would be practically weightless compared to the verbal outflow shaping the official assumptions and watchwords concerning these housing projects on the city's outskirts. Immigration is ensnared by words, and the *banlieue* of political slogans does not correspond to the *banlieues* of the native population. The paradox of invisibility for those living in these neighborhoods is that they are still subject to total public visibility. The paradox assumes an existential dimension for the heirs to immigration in the media spotlight: poor kids acculturated in the early 1980s, victims of economic and social disaster a decade later, and now cast as dangerous members of the deviant sect of "communitarianism," an Islamist, sexist Mafia—in short, as the bogeymen in a monstrous figuration of the ghetto American style.

But how is the unthinkable ethnic question resurfacing today behind the smoke and mirrors of a republican rhetoric that has allowed French democracy to gradually become accustomed to its internal fractures and borders? And in the first place, what led up to the current reality, to the public construction of the French immigrant paradox—the invisibility of visible minorities?

Behind the Headlines

France is proud of its social model, by virtue of which identities are conceived as positions in a class society structured by labor. That "figuration of the social" (Rosanvallon 1998), founded on the protection of the wage earner and the defense of social cohesion, has long made it possible to exorcise the specter of a worker uprising and to manage conflicts in the social relations of production. Group interests and group representation have been guaranteed by the welfare state. Let us specify that these are established groups, since in the history of France the vagabonds of the *Lumpenproletariat*—immigrants in particular—have never been anything but the supernumeraries of the social question. By dint of singing overmuch the praises of the welfare state and the great family of workers, we have forgotten that the social rights of immigrants have long been eroding. We have forgotten that they were never anything but resident aliens, prohibited from moving about freely, prisoners to the factory, subject to bureaucratic harassment of every sort, stripped of all rights, trapped between asylum and expulsion. We have forgotten that they were only the poor relations, if not the black sheep, of the great family of workers. Do we need to recall that in the early twentieth century, in certain bastions of the workers' movement, anti-immigrant strikes were more common than those against management?

It is therefore painfully ironic to reduce the fate of immigrants to the social condition of workers. Of course, in the French imaginary, the immigrant is in the first place the immigrant worker. Has not the antiracist education of schoolchildren relied for decades on the Épinal image of those brawny garbage collectors of metropolitan France? It is France that invented the European model of the "guest worker program"; before the early 1980s, the Maghrebi, Africans, and other whipping boys were never perceived as immigrants who had come to stay. Despite the gradual establishment of their families in France, they were still perceived as lone workers, guests of wage-earning society. In return, work was the justification for any plan to migrate. It was in the name of work that millions of men agreed to uproot themselves and to live as undocumented aliens, confined to social invisibility. But the most recent waves of migration ran aground on the shores of industrial society, as is now clearly established well beyond the borders of metropolitan France. Shaken by globalization, even the national foundations of societies are crumbling. The primacy of financial issues, the development of new technologies, the widespread flexibility and individuation of labor relations are all factors in the decline of the old social order. The drive for higher productivity actually results in a drop in the number of jobs. When work becomes scarce, it is the pillar of a representation of the social world that gives way. Immigrants, invisible so long as they were reduced to their labor power, burst onto the public scene in the early

1980s. Even today, it is in the defense of the labor market that discourses on controlling migration find their justification. Even so, immigrant families are the first victims of the crisis (Boubeker 1999). How many successors of the old laborers have broken off from the collectivities, living by their wits on odd jobs, cut off from the circuits of production and from social recognition? In a postindustrial society marked by unemployment, exclusion, and the loss of the old points of reference, the interpretive grid of the social question proves to be inadequate for understanding the proliferation of breakdowns and fractures, the dynamics governing the reestablishment of the social bond, and the new alliances at work.

Yet it is that obsolete interpretive grid that has been imposed by force on the experience of the new visible minorities over the last quarter century. Everything constituting the lived experience of the heirs to immigration is analyzed solely through the prism of the "social problem." Even the urban riots, which attest to the possibility of revolt, are said to presage nothing but a social vacuum, unlike the workers' movement, supposedly a source of social cohesion. The ethnic question is thus placed under the rubric of social welfare, even in its state of decay. For when long-established social protections are scaled back, a corresponding rise in suspicion makes the "welfare cheats" and other scheming immigrants responsible for the social security deficit. The Front National, which has portrayed the immigrant as in competition with the downwardly mobile worker, is thus reaping the electoral bounty of France's nostalgia for its social model.

The Primal Scene of the Great Misunderstanding

Les Minguettes, in the *banlieue* of Lyons, exemplifies the lost illusions of a housing project that nearly marked a turning point in interethnic relations in the France of the 1980s. There, in a dismal setting of asphalt and concrete—nine thousand housing units thrown up in the 1960s—French society experienced its first urban riots in summer 1981. It was the summer of the first "rodeo riots."[2] That event, which according to President François Mitterrand "threatened to tear the social fabric to threads," sounded the alarm about the problem of the *banlieues*, stripping the "second generation" of its anonymity. For a long time, these young people had remained "negative images" in their parents' shadow, invisible hostages of public discourses, caught between the threat of expulsion and compassion, between cops and social workers. The intrusion of the youth of Les Minguettes on the public scene appears to have marked the end of a mutual exclusion between French society and the high-rise cities of exile. From the rodeo riots to hunger strikes to the media apotheosis of the March for Equality in 1983, which brought out 100,000 demonstrators, the "Minguettes generation" was in the limelight, asserting its right to a civil status beyond the immigration pool. The press invoked the young immigrants' French nationality with the term *Beurs,* and the government decreed the urgency of renovating the Republic's forgotten housing projects. These beginnings of public recognition looked like the dawn of a new era, in which French society could at last purge an abscess of its history. For the time of a brief flirtation, the *Beurs* were seen as the "heralds of a multicultural future for metropolitan France" (Beau and Boubeker 1986).

But very quickly, the clocks were set back to the time of an eternal France of assimilation. It was said that publicly raising the ethnic question would call into question the universality of the republican model, since only the Far Right spoke that language of infamy. By 1986, the *Beurs* were returning to oblivion, for it was now urgent, precisely, to thwart the rise of Jean-Marie Le Pen, who made immigration his stock-in-trade. That moment marked the beginning of the great misunderstanding at the heart of the recurring politico-media fascination with the high-rise cities of exile for the heirs to immigration. That public misunderstanding, which reduces the "unrest in the *banlieues*" to an acute manifestation of the social question, passes over in silence the profound changes in French society. It was then the Far Right that seized on the identity question and became, paradoxically, the only place where the growing visibility of ethnic minorities was represented, as in a funhouse mirror. Under the auspices of these xenophobic crusades, a public imaginary was constructed that enacted the clichés of collective memory, a return to a world of "hovels, wogs, and black whores," as Albert Londres ironically described it. A return as well to intense public fears of urban violence and the threat of invasion by hordes of swarthy delinquents, sons of the fellaghas of French Algeria. To invoke publicly the new internal borders on which these barbarians of the security hysteria were encamped was to think in terms of unprovoked assaults, violence, vandalism, all symptoms of a chronic illness that would have to be contained—the choice was between amputation and shock treatment—to avoid infecting the social body as a whole.

At the start of the 1980s, the socialist Left, itself torn apart by the fear of losing power, bungled a historic opportunity to initiate a major public debate on the new multiethnic and multicultural dimension of French society. In the absence of debate, outdated palliatives: the celebration of the cause of human rights in opposition to racist aberrations and the grandiloquent proclamation of the old republican schema to reaffirm common values. "Words of state," to borrow the expression of Abdelmalek Sayad, illustrated that policy drift toward a publicity campaign. These words forestalled all debate, all discussion, and held some up for public opprobrium without possibility of appeal. An event by the mere fact of their articulation, they were the words of a sorcerer's apprentice that, through the secret spells of reason of state, brought to life the phenomena they designated. Words like "thresholds of tolerance"[3] and "social mixing." Words like "undocumented," which would make it possible to distinguish between "good" and "bad" immigrants. The politico-media management of the unrest in the *banlieues* foundered in "closed-world discourse" (Marcuse 1964). Words of state become a cliché when meaning is, so to speak, held captive by the word. And they avoid all contradiction when contradiction is, in fact, contained within the word. So it is with the paradox of the injunction to integrate issued to the third and fourth generations of the heirs to immigration. And so it is with biting formulations, such as this "bon mot" from a prime minister, Michel Rocard: "We cannot welcome all the wretchedness of the world!" (January 7, 1990). A bon mot, in fact, bearing the stench of the "banality of evil" (Arendt 1964), since it is supposedly in the name of political realism, and even of the fight against racism, that the excess aliens are to be expelled.

It was very much in an antiracist language that the *banlieue* of the 1980s found expression. Political questions were reduced to moral universals and the great encompassing love of humankind. From that standpoint, to palliate the return of public fears and of racism, it would be incumbent to implement a policy of consensus in the name of political realism, choosing the lesser evil to avoid catastrophe. For anyone allying himself with that moral coalition of the "community of citizens" (Schnapper 1994), it becomes impossible to understand the *banlieue* uprising in political terms. By contrast, for anyone who rejects the rules of the game, the Republic has no clothes. The government's impotence is expressed in its inability to name the people living in the *banlieue* and to prevail. For even in these neighborhoods, there is no disciplinary society under the domination of Big Brother. The state has lost so much of its supremacy that the immigrant *banlieues* are the last bone assuaging its appetite for grandeur. The poor, white state jealously guarding the bad subject of its nightmares. It is as if immigration, in its very marginality, had become a central fiction of public discourses, crystallizing the verbal upheavals in the general movement of French society. A strange tale, that trompe l'oeil actuality. A tale of mirrors and bids for recognition that seem to have left things in their former state. A tale of misunderstandings and smokescreens. The tale of a society grappling with the pressing demands of its historical moment and periodically banishing present reality to the secret dungeons of its memory.

From the Society of Exclusion to the Eternal Return of the "Dangerous Classes"

In the early 1990s, the rhetorical taking in hand of the unrest in the *banlieues* led to further urban riots in Vaulx-en-Velin, also in the Lyons metropolitan area. The problem was becoming endemic. The public programs set in place seemed to be rooted in "counterproductivity," in Ivan Illich's sense of the word. In terms of social achievements, years of renovation policy costing several hundred million francs culminated in nothing, or very nearly so. Access to employment, housing, and social recognition remains a mirage for the second-class citizens of the *banlieues*, perpetual trainees, the chronic unemployed, or periodic inmates in penal institutions.

For a time, the notion of exclusion made it possible to believe that new perspectives were opening, beyond the classic model of the social question. But the unbridled use of the notion assumed the dimensions of an ideological catchall in which the youth of the *banlieue*, welfare recipients, and other hope-deprived were all thrown together. In addition, the social movement of 1995 led to a return to the hard social question as a defense of wages and social gains. The theme of exclusion was then minimized, particularly since the inability to effectively combat the social roots of unrest in the outlying housing projects led to radicalization of a moralistic nature: public suspicion of immigrant families, held responsible for their condition, a suspicion of duplicity or of the community's insularity. Such is the theme of the deviant ethnic, Islamic, communitarian mafia of the neighborhoods, a new version of the "dangerous classes" in Louis Chevalier's expression, which would be in league against the Republic and the sacrosanct community of citizens. The political Right's return to power at the start of the 1990s marked a passing of the batons in the projects, and police control became the panacea. The Left itself aspired to forget its rosy outlook on this security issue, and a political consensus tended to reduce the unrest in the *banlieues* to a problem of public order caused by a few delinquent minorities.

The riots of November 2005 did not change that new configuration. In their wake, a series of news items promoted the new figure of a public monster held up to media obloquy: Youssef Fofana, the brains behind the "gang of barbarians" involved in a sordid crime, a deadly hostage taking in March 2006. That sorry specimen of humanity brings to mind Bigger, Richard Wright's "native son." He would in fact be damned without confession, the ideal perpetrator decked out in the frippery of the human beast as it appears in the nightmares of humble folk on both shores of the Atlantic. Yet, according to James Baldwin, who also wrote on the American racial question, Bigger's black soul is only the mirror of white society's dishonesty. That monstrous character in Wright's protest novel reassures the prim and proper, since he has only to be evoked to induce a true shudder of virtue. In the same line, the Fofanas of the media world lead us to believe that some men could be less human than others. They are nothing more nor less than caricatures of a sham alienness that reinforce an unhealthy taste for the sensational even while appeasing the conscience. With no place of recognition to hang their hats, these new barbarians in the news do not even have the extenuating circumstance of being the offspring of generations of poverty and oppression. For under the state of emergency of monstrosity or subhuman barbarism, they are emptied of all social meaning, deprived of any experience proper to them. In the image of Bigger, the eternal outsider to his own life, is not Fofana the quintessence of the perpetual immigrant whose every trace vanishes in the limelight? The scapegoat of French exceptionalism, that ideal perpetrator conceals the vast mob of his ilk, the other resident aliens within, "native sons," those who ultimately resemble everyone else and whom, above all, one ought not to resemble. He makes it possible to banish their experience to a no-man's-land of radical alterity.

The New Dimensions of a Fracture in Representation

France in decline has returned as a leitmotif in public discourse: the homeland in danger, threatened with internal collapse by the obsolescence of its representations. But strangely, most of these critical reports are elaborated in terms of the prestige of France and the safeguarding of its universalist legacy, as if the grandiloquent evocation of the past glory of the "Republic, one and indivisible," could resuscitate it. For that eternal France of republican nostalgia is truly dead and gone. How can one denounce the obsolescence of representations and at the same time prop oneself up against an abstract universalism that long ago veered toward French provincialism? It is precisely that annoyance of a nostalgia for grandeur, of "the imposture of an unreal France"—as Emmanuel Berl phrased it long ago—that exacerbates the malaise. The French malaise, the crisis of a political paradigm founded on a single form of rationality and universality, which gives rise to another sort of malaise, the unrest in the *banlieues,* through its rejection of the other as component of the same, as condition for self-identity. Hence, the heirs to immigration are once again designated outsiders within. That escalation of symbolic violence within a language increasingly stripped of any real content seems to be leading to the definitive eclipse of the question of ethnicity. France refuses to face the ethnic dimension of social inequalities, which translates into problems of urban segregation, racial discrimination, and the denial of recognition.

Nonetheless, behind the protectionism of the republican model can be detected internal rents in the fabric, fractures in representation that raise questions.

The Urban Question and Segregation

For a long time, French cities mirrored the social question in their division between the outlying working-class districts—later replaced by "communist-voting *banlieues*"—*and* the bourgeois neighborhoods of the city center. It would seem there are no ghettos in France, only "sensitive areas." Even so, history and current events attest the opposite.

Has it been so quickly forgotten that, in times past, the Maghrebi of France found refuge only in the shantytowns on the fringes of the cities, in no-man's-lands, places that officially did not exist. The shantytown, or *bidonville*—city of *bidons*, of trash barrels—rubbish heaps of history in the glory days between 1946 and 1976, an invisible city behind the city, a place to dump the waste from the banquet of French democracy. The *bidonville* was built on the borderline between the disposal of refuse and the assumption of responsibility for immigrant worker housing by slumlords. No one saw the shantytowns growing, not government leaders and not employers, who were only too happy to keep the workforce in its place. Underground labor within the purview of the public gaze at a time when illegal immigration was informal. It would take a generation for the shantytowns to be assimilated. Then came the time of transitional housing, then the *banlieues*.

Workers, civil servants, middle managers: the *banlieue* pioneers came from every walk of life. And that social mixing lay at the very foundation of urban planning. In the minds of the architects of the large housing complexes, candidates for public housing bliss, in cutting themselves off from their respective affiliations, represented the vanguard of a new modernity. For the grand design of these "shining cities" was to create new forms of sociability on the ruins of the working-class districts: finally, the social classes would be reconciled, communities of origin forgotten, working-class mentalities reformed, thanks to public amenities giving instruction in collective life and in a civilization of leisure. Never in metropolitan France was the mania for dividing up space as a means of managing the social question pushed so far. And never did urban utopianism culminate in such failure. For the history of the *banlieues* is a veil woven of lost illusions. Very quickly, the image cracked. The promised group amenities remained in the planning stage. Complaints succeeded hopes. The pioneer families packed their bags and landlords became less finicky about the qualifications for occupancy, in order to turn a profit on their public housing projects. The shining cities gradually metamorphosed into refuges for "problem populations." The deterioration of the apartment blocks and the growing presence of immigrants then raised the specter of a "ghetto *à la française*."

From the dream of shining cities to dread of the ghetto, public discourses on the housing projects are diametrically opposed. Everything seems to have been said about the unrest in the *banlieues*, that chronic illness in need of containment to avoid the gangrene of the social body. The public policies implemented to "wipe out the ghetto" make reference to affirmative action but are actually in line with classic social reallocation policies, far removed from a new plan of social justice for all. Hence, the question of housing access for immigrant families is still marked by discrimination. The government's priority remains to check the flow of new applicants for public housing. That screening for low-cost housing consists of slowing the rate of arrival of immigrant families and of investing in urban marketing schemes to attract mythic middle classes in the name of public action watchwords: "social mixing," "restoration of the neighborhoods' social balance." The troubles in the *banlieues* are ascribed to the concentration of immigrant populations. No scientific method, however, allows us to verify these assumptions. By contrast, studies reveal the perverse effects of the procedures that are designed to fight inequality, but that actually contribute to reinforcing the process of ethnic segregation in public housing projects (Grémion 1996). What do the mayors care? Such would be the price of the war of images. Restoration of the luster of communes marred by recent events in the urban areas is now a government priority. That is the justification for sacrificing homeless families in the name of the municipal dream of a return to modern public housing populated by virtual middle classes. The *banlieue* still dreams of the ideal city. But that dream is now restricted to illustrating moral and political issues in a desert of social prospects. A Big Brother dream of a low-rent district for an ideal city stripped of any whiff of human exuberance. But that dream of stone also aspires to be the last bastion against the incipient nightmare of the ghetto American style. The war of images in the *banlieue* has thus become a war of dreams.

Yet the subtext remains the same: fear and rejection of the other, denial of reality.

Even so, the city is a heterogeneous environment where the management of diversity cannot be reduced to ideology. When we consider the life stories of the heirs to immigration, we always end up leaving the confinement of public housing. Not only do "those people" excel at breaking down barriers, but their lines of sight outside the walls of the *banlieues* participate in a new urban dynamics, in the construction of way stations, points of convergence, gateways, hubs between the local and the global. Some "ethnobusiness" neighborhoods thus constitute crossroads for mobility through a "globalization from below" (Tarrius

2004). What eludes the paltry understanding of the urban crisis is precisely that capacity of the heirs to immigration to cross boundaries, to wager on the miracle of a pathway, to perpetuate a nomadism that builds doors and bridges between fragmented universes. Linking the world, metropolitan France, the city, and the neighborhoods are new territories of mobility, trajectories leading from exile to networks where people, commodities, and information circulate, far, far away from the social question.

The Question of the Nation and Discrimination

The urban question is constantly being folded back on the social question, but it involves more—in a nutshell, the decline of the old social reference points and the rise of the question of the nation. For at issue is truly the republican model on which the French political imaginary and national identity rest, and which has not managed to block the rise of ethnic discrimination. French society is paralyzed by a calling into doubt of its national categories of political understanding. How to explain otherwise the silence of civil society after the riots in fall 2005?[4]

Unlike "equal opportunity" American style, the French model is founded on a leveling of the playing field designed to encourage individuals to recognize themselves as alike, beyond their original affiliations. With the crisis of the welfare state, that model, based on social reallocation policies, has come up against its limits. In the case of the most recent guests of French democracy, then, talk of an "integration problem" better obscures the historical failure of public and institutional springboards to equality. Not only have the schools, trade unions, and businesses not played their integrative role, they have even become centers for reproducing inequalities and discrimination. In fact, far from abolishing differences in the public arena, the social equalization model has managed only to lock the heirs to immigration into a stigmatized identity. Since the early 1980s, when populations from the old colonial empire burst onto the media scene, the golden legend of our national integration model seems to have been faltering. Banished to the secret dungeons of national history, immigration has returned through the prism of current events, so much so that it can now be glimpsed in the modes of articulating national identity. That shows how blurred the boundaries have become between the other and the same, the other having become the same and the same the other, an outsider to its own history. It is as if everything that French exceptionalism had not wished to know about immigration revealed precisely what it did not know about itself—and about the golden legend of the "French melting pot" (Noiriel 1988).

According to that old story of the French melting pot, time and the contribution of many waves of immigration established the unity of the great French family. The immigration of lone workers was an essential factor in the smooth functioning of the employment system: the cannon fodder of social controls, guinea pigs of flexibility, undocumented workers in the growth years made it possible to circumvent the rigidity of the work world without undermining the social gains of the traditional working class. No country in the world has had such a large influx of foreign labor since the beginning of the twentieth century. But France, unlike the United States, never saw itself as a nation of immigrants. The ethnic and linguistic unification of metropolitan France had long been considered complete when that flood of new populations occurred: in these migrations, populating France was not at issue, and no one foresaw citizenship for these nomads of capitalism, a subproletariat subject to monitoring of every sort, condemned to the dirtiest jobs, assigned the status of temporary workers for the time needed to build an industrial France that had been snubbed by rural France. That explains the national amnesia about the contribution of generations of migrant workers. These auxiliaries to the working class were the exception to the universality of the republican model, doomed to invisibility by their original exclusion from collective memory and French history. A strange fate for immigrants who for ages have not been outsiders to French society. The history of these invisible men was not integrated into the national patrimony: no monument in the realms of metropolitan France's memory symbolizes the presence of Maghrebi immigrants throughout the twentieth century, of those who, unlike the others, did not vanish into the melting pot. The integration model has thus accommodated itself to processes of ethnic discrimination, and behind the showcase of French exceptionalism lies banishment from the nation's grand designs.

The children of these pioneers are subjected to a different invisibility. Deprived of individual access to social positions of recognition, they are also refused any form of collective expression, which is perceived as a communitarian aberration. Invisible in the sites of representation of French democracy, they are accused of destroying republican equality when they demand a place at the table. It is in order to escape that paradoxical injunction for invisibility—invisible both as victims and as successes—that the visible minorities are now demanding "equal opportunity." When more than 30 percent of *banlieue* youth are jobless and homeless, there is reason to wonder about the integration policy mess. So the lawmakers have decreed the urgency of setting up a program to fight discrimination. But in actuality, we remain at the stage of declarations of intent, as if the escalation of public discourses made it possible to forgo dealing with the situation. Hence the public condemnation of affirmative action by fanatical patriots of the French republic. What does it matter if no political majority has implemented that reform and if some citizens are in fact less equal than others? For these ideologues, the threat of calling into question the abstract universalism of republican egalitarianism is intolerable in its very abstraction! As for the rest, it seems that Charles de Gaulle's expression still has currency: "L'intendance suivra."[5]

Yet no headway will be made against the government's immobility if we cling to a French conception of formal rights that makes principles prevail over objectives and entails no demand for results. No legal system permits us to definitively restrict interethnic relations to a tribunal of egalitarian norms; for in so doing, we obscure the reality of the many circumstances and historical events in which the discriminatory processes are grounded. Formal rights are thus powerless because society in its practices preexists the law. As a result, because there is no use made of agents at work in the field—and in the first place in the *banlieue* associations, groups composed of the heirs to immigration—which would allow the "forgotten of equal opportunity" (Sabeg and Méhaignerie 2004) to constitute themselves as legal subjects, it remains a risky undertaking even to arrive at a legal definition of discriminatory acts.

Moreover, the battle will remain in doubt without a broad public debate around the question of the nation. For in a French society that aspires to economic equality but that dreams only of individual privileges, it is in the first place corporatism, nepotism, personal favors, forms of insularity, and police misconduct that provide the rich soil for ethnic discrimination.

The Question of Identity and Recognition

Must we sound the death knell of French exceptionalism? The historian Pierre Nora points out the broad scope of the metamorphoses in French society, the shift within a few years from a "unified national consciousness to a patrimonial consciousness" (Nora 1977)—memory as the last bastion. Hence the incantatory invocation of the model of collective assimilation through individual and cultural integration in the name of the Republic's universal values, which would remain eternally valid because they have been declared the patrimony of all humanity in the heaven of ideas: first, second, or third generation, we are all the children of immigrants! The exile, suffering, and persecution of generations of the destitute proscribed from the history of France would now contribute to the prestige of the nation-state. Such is the irony of collective memory: all the genealogies of invisible men are reintegrated into an uninterrupted series of precedents to the integration model, a golden legend celebrating the uneclipsed glory of the French melting pot. All the misfortunes of the past find their meaning in a justification of the present, and France is populated with memories and ancestors whose existence it had never suspected. What does lived history matter? At stake is the eternal return of a single interpretive grid within a history of uniformity, versus the singularity of the experience of the outsiders within. That "patrimonial drift of the Republic" (Noudelmann 2006), that whitewashed universalist genealogy in its patrimonial version, is invoked by Milan Kundera in his most recent novel, *Ignorance:* "The French, you know, they don't need experience. For them, judgments precede experience. They were not interested in what we thought, they were interested in us as living proof of what *they* thought" (Kundera 2005: 194). The history of immigration in its most republican version is thus assimilated to the golden legend of the French integration model. And the Republic holds on to the myth of a French exceptionalism that embraces all without distinction of origin and race.

Were there never any races in the country of Jacobin universalism? The Republic, all the same, possesses a shameful memory. By Friedrich Engels's own admission, was not the concept of "class struggle" inspired by the French historians' notion of "race war"? The racial problematic was defended by Joseph-Arthur de Gobineau, Maurice Barrès, and Georges

Vacher de Lapouge, and by the ethnologists of colonial thought. And, in the twentieth century, a biological theory of the alien also inspired the demographers who devised immigration policy. Nevertheless, in France today, there are no "minority studies," no "race relations studies." Unlike in the English-speaking countries, where the neologism "ethnicity" has made it possible to replace a racial vocabulary, in metropolitan France that term has only gradually acquired a conceptual dimension in the language of the social sciences, given the reservations of an academic institution that identifies the term as an ideological weapon for implementing racial theories or at least as a localized concept within the context of intergroup relations in the United States. More broadly, in the world of research, immigration remains a shameful subject, like a black hole in the French tradition of the social sciences, a victim of "universalist chauvinism" in Pierre Bourdieu's phrase. But in that field, it undoubtedly expresses an inability to envision the very existence of the immigrant as a constituent dimension of the national body. The media's depiction of the unrest in the *banlieues* and the current reality of Islam in France have thus served as a platform for intellectuals committed to the legacy of French universality and Enlightenment humanism— against the obscurantism of outsiders to that European patrimony! A strange scientific rhetoric, that repetition of already-thought thoughts, in a public ritual worthy of a new quarrel of universals that would consist of bandying about words like magic formulas to exorcise the language of society.

As it happens, the society in question, at least the component of it that is heir to immigration, refuses to be satisfied with the "denial of recognition" (Honneth 1992), refuses to live with the identity assigned by the grand designs or dreads of eternal France and its scholars. That assignment is the negation of the individual's right to an ambiguous identity—the right to be from here and from somewhere else, with no obligation to choose among different allegiances. It is a glaring absence of respect in the Kantian sense of the term. It is the confinement to invisibility. One word sums up that tragedy of visible minorities: "scum." One word, a single word too many, pronounced by Nicolas Sarkozy sparked the crisis in November 2005.

For *banlieue* youth, "scum" is a form of recognition by means of self-derision, but in the interior minister's mouth it became the most perfidious expression of social opprobrium. Because "police" is also the name for the symbolic violence of the institution of language, the ensnarement of words mentioned previously. A snare the subject can escape when his experience comes to be conveyed in discourse. Therein lies all the power of the symbolization practices implemented by dominated groups against the omnipotence of the wordmasters. To escape the contamination of linguistic labels, the back-slang Verlaines of the accursed projects respond with the magic of secrecy or the obscenity of the cliché. Behind the hidebound formulas, they recover a voice drowned out by the uproar of others. These manners of speaking amount to explorations of language, verbal creations in the name of the capacity to choose, to answer for one's convictions, to construct and assess one's own identity while forgetting the stigma and overtalkativeness of others. New words but also twists on "words of state." This always involves opening up the space within the word. Opening up words to go beyond words and to prevail over the sedimentation of language. To prevail over homonymy on its own territory. To prevail over stereotypes. "To excavate within language a foreign language"—style, according to Gilles Deleuze. To articulate difference and repetition to the breaking point of language in order to bring forth a second figuration of already-spoken words. Secret words behind the words, unspeakable codes of an interpretive community that involve a feeling together. A figurative meaning. Only the force of the symbol feeds the impulse to break out of the prison-house of meaning by the power of a metaphorical redescription of reality.

But though the symbol is envisioned as a return to the birthplace of language, it is not a question of losing one's way amid the origins—forever lost—in quest of the purest meaning of the words of the tribe. On the contrary, as Paul Ricœur points out, a mediation on figures always starts from the fullness of language and from preexisting meaning: at issue is an actualization, a recharging of language. Hence the legacy of immigration is the reference to a "we," an identity that can be invoked by different sign systems embodied in specific figures in these sites of irruption that are the "worlds of ethnicity" (Boubeker 2003): figures therefore, figures of narrative authority, figures of the thing narrated, figures of the resistance of a tenacious narrative. Figures as cultural base, as demand for meaning and quest for expression. Figures of the imaginary of the worlds of ethnicity, with pioneers, heroes, victims, or schemers, individual and collective destinies—jumbled together in popular imagery but symbolizing as well whole worlds of meanings—a communitarian ethos and fractures between generations, modes of expression and communication with other worlds of French society. Beyond the diversity of life paths, it is truly a narrative in several voices that is being articulated, putting into play individual stories and collective reference points. A self-told tale of immigration or of the *banlieues*, a story different from that of the golden legend of the French melting pot.

Conclusion

It will likely not happen right away, but could ethnicity in France, seen as a mode for constructing the experience of the heirs to immigration, be articulated with other modes of social classification and become a constitutive dimension of the organizational principles of French society? The question remains polemical, giving rise to controversies between the proponents of pluralism and the unyielding defenders of the French integration model. Even so, though the old refrains of public discourse might suggest that nothing changes for the eternal dupes of immigration—the colonial workers of yesteryear, then immigrant workers, and now *banlieue* youth—the "ritornellos" (Deleuze and Guattari 1980) of ethnicity, for their part, are grounded in a dialogical framework. For despite the snare of words, immigration is still a series of encounters.

Encounters at the crossroads of reinterpreted values, of meanings twisted by generational conflicts and interactions with French society as a whole. Encounters where tension is played out between traditions and innovations. Between nostalgia for origins, the laments of the uprooted, and the ballads of the pioneers working their new land. Where the official data see only integration problems, anomie, the spleen of the ghetto, or the stigma of exclusion, we need to rediscover the living subject, the swarming mass of humanity that eludes categorization by little republican schemas. No one can deny the precarious condition that makes the heirs to immigration the supernumeraries of the social question. Poverty, of course! Lousy jobs, of course! Squalid housing, of course! How do those poor people manage to survive? Of course! But also, how do they reinvent the world in a black hole of public prospects? How is their individual and collective existence constructed in encounters, alliances, conflicts, in the relation between memory and forgetting, individual choices and collective movements? How do these individuals and groups become the subjects of their own lives and their own history, without being confined within public clichés?

That narrative of the supernumeraries of the French melting pot could open new vistas on the Republic's values. Is not the last word of Ellison's invisible man, "Who knows but that, on the lower frequencies, I speak for you?"

Notes

1. Until the early 1980s, the children of Maghrebi immigrants were lumped together with their parents and called "young immigrants." After the first urban riots in the Lyons metropolitan area in 1981, the public discovered that most of these young people were born in France: they were then renamed the "second generation," then *Beurs.* The latter term comes from back slang for the Arabic word for "Arab." That form of self-designation by *banlieue* youth is merely a way to bestow on themselves one name among others ("cousins," *rhors, rebeux*), but its success in the media after the March for Equality and against Racism in 1983 allowed it to enter French-language dictionaries. Increasingly corrupted by the media, the term *Beurs* is taking on pejorative connotations for the young people in the *banlieue,* who prefer new terms: *zupiens* [from ZUP, *zone à urbaniser en priorité,* priority development zones—trans.], *cailleras, rebeux* [back slang for *racaille,* "scum," and *Beurs,* respectively —trans.]. Public discourses usually speak of "youth," but some interior ministers responsible for the *banlieues* provide their own semantic precisions in response to the political contexts. Hence the Socialist Jean-Pierre Chevènement spoke of "little savages" in 1998, in a context marked by the rise of a preoccupation with security. And Nicolas Sarkozy co-opted the term *racaille*—another ironic self-designation by *banlieue* youth—to make populist and political use of it in November 2005.

2. [During the so-called rodeo riots, young people from the *banlieues* stole automobiles, went joyriding through the city, and then set the cars ablaze. —trans.]

3. Used by politicians from François Mitterrand to Jean-Marie Le Pen, that notion of the "thresholds of tolerance" beyond which the coexistence of immigrants and native French in the neighborhoods would become contentious is not based on any sociological reality. It appeared in the early 1970s. On October 5, 1973, a circular from the construction department of the Ministry of Development specified that the proportion of immigrant families in public housing ought not to exceed 15 percent. It at first went unnoticed. But beginning in the 1980s, it became the social panacea for landlords and municipalities united under the anti-ghetto banner. Even today, that notion of thresholds of tolerance lies behind the watchwords "restoration of the social balance" or "social mixing" in government programs.

4. Rather than a silence among leftist intellectuals, we would probably need to speak of a swing toward security issues. Since the start of the 1990s, and even more after September 11, 2001, media figures such as Alain Finkelkraut and Régis Debray have rediscovered the republican virtues of law and order. For the failure to demonstrate one's authority and the surpassing of the limits of tolerance—that road paved with the best of intentions—has supposedly led to the hell of a social vacuum, to an abdication by parents and educators in a postmodern aura of irresponsibility.

5. [Roughly, "the logistics will take care of themselves." —trans.]

PART 2

Colonization,
Citizenship,
and Containment

From Imperial Inclusion to Republican Exclusion? France's Ambiguous Postwar Trajectory

Frederick Cooper

When one opens a French newspaper or listens to television news today, the word "republican" appears again and again. The suburban disorder of 2005, to critics of the status quo, represents the incapacity of the republican model of governance to integrate fully recent waves of immigrants into French society. The same phenomenon, to others, reveals the incapacity of immigrants, particularly Muslim immigrants, to adapt to a republican order.

Both sides of such debates assume a basic core of republican ideology: a one-to-one relationship of individual citizen and state, stripped of mediating social affiliations, be they the "estates" of the eighteenth century (nobility, clergy, third estate) or race, religion, gender, or ethnicity in the twenty-first. The citizenry elects its representatives by universal suffrage, and the state, in turn, guarantees them equal rights and duties along with equal access to state institutions, independent of any social affiliations or markings. To many French people brought up in the republican ambiance, any deviation from such principles would be destructive not only of the state, but of individuals' aspirations for equality. To others, the republican edifice is built on foundations of hypocrisy, for it has always been juxtaposed with colonialism, the negation of any principle of equality. The present situation is a continuation of the colonial past—prejudice, discrimination, and exclusion directed at French citizens and residents who were born in North or sub-Saharan Africa or whose parents or grandparents came from once-colonized regions—leading to despair and anger.[1]

Both the insistence on a singular, unitary vision of French republicanism and the exposé of the continued colonial nature of French society rely on two different readings of the last two hundred years of French history. One points to a continuing republican tradition emerging from the French revolution. The other sees a French nation exploiting "others," from the slaves taken from Africa to the colonies of the West Indies to Africans exploited on their own territory. These two readings are mirror images of one another; they posit a very French France exploiting a very African Africa. The virtue or the evil of "France" is that of a singular nation moving through time and acting for or against other societies. France's "others"—yesterday's colonized people, today's "immigrants"—lie outside this France, either the innocent victims of French racism and exploitation or else aliens whose own culture makes them difficult to assimilate to French society.

But might not both readings of history represent backward projections of a "national" France whose historical depth is in fact much less than either story allows? Might not the claim that France has been, is, and must be governed by a set of republican principles miss out on the much more varied and contested course of republicanism in France? And might not the story of a colonial France, accurate as it is in revealing the dark side of French history, miss out on something important too: that colonial rule wasn't such a solid, implacable edifice, that political action on the part of Africans and others among the "colonized" had their effects, that struggle wasn't always in vain, that French political institutions and ideologies weren't givens that one either accepted, rejected, or stood outside?

Historical analysis will not settle policy debates over such questions as whether affirmative action is a good policy or a bad approach to remedying inequality and discrimination or what the range of practices of marriage or gender relations in a republic should be. But historical analysis can respond to attempts to *exclude* certain possibilities from consideration at the outset—on the grounds that such possibilities aren't "French" or aren't "republican." It can show that the spectrum of political possibility in the past was wider than people in the present— projecting backward their own positions—allow it to be. Perhaps a less closed past could help us at least to recognize the possibility of a more open future.

Let us look briefly at the relationship of national and imperial France since the 1789 revolution, then in detail at the openings and closures of the two decades after World War II.

Revolutionary Citizenship: National or Imperial?

To whom the principles of the Declaration of the Rights of Man and of the Citizen applied was not so clear. To some, the French "nation" was a bounded entity. Citizenship applied to people within its borders, and the plantation colonies of the Caribbean were its dependencies, not constituent parts of the polity. Slaves could not be citizens. To others, colonial conquest and slavery were violations of the principles of Enlightenment, whether at home or overseas (Muthu 2003). But the boundedness of the revolutionary "nation" was thrown open by events in the empire.[2]

In the plantation colony of Saint-Domingue, in the midst of the revolution, French planters, then property-owning people of mixed origins, and finally the slaves—revolting in 1791—evoked citizenship discourse in order to claim their part in a revolutionary society. The freeing of slaves in Saint-Domingue in 1793 and in other French colonies in 1794 reflected both the inclusive version of citizenship and the state's need for new categories of citizens to defend the Revolution against royalists and rival empires seeking to take over the colony. The revolution, like most successful social movements, brought together people across social categories in a struggle that—long before it aimed at seceding from France—sought to make France into a different sort of polity, an empire of free citizens. Its famous leader Toussaint L'Ouverture was for a time a commissioner of the revolutionary government. Just what citizenship would entail—and how much ex-slaves would have to be trained and disciplined to function as free laborers and free citizens—was contested in Saint-Domingue and other plantation islands, among ex-slave leaders as well as between them and European Frenchmen.

The revolutionaries of Saint-Domingue were arguing that principles laid out in Paris applied equally to them. As Michel-Rolph Trouillot has pointed out, many African-born slaves had no more desire to be ruled by French republicans than by planters and monarchists. They constituted a "revolt within the revolt," although it isn't clear what sort of polity might have emerged had their version of the revolution succeeded (Trouillot 1995: 31–69). But it did not. Napoleon tried to repress the revolution and reestablish slavery. In most of the French plantation islands, he succeeded, but not in Saint-Domingue. The revolution turned from a struggle for freedom within the empire to a successful struggle to get out of the empire, ending in the creation of the Republic of Haiti in 1804. For a time, however, two separate questions had been opened up: could a republican government in France accept that its principles be generalized to people outside of European France, including people of African descent? Could republican leaders—including those from the colonies—accept as fellow citizens people who did not live according to the principles of the republic? Such questions were on the revolutionary table in the 1790s. They were still there in 1945.

Republican Citizens and Colonial Subjects

Under monarchical or republican government, the line between a national France and an imperial France was frequently contested. In 1848, the definitive abolition of slavery in French colonies brought an entire category of people, of mainly African descent, into the realm of citizenship rather than into an intermediate category. In the oldest African colonies, the Quatre Communes, or Four Communes, of Senegal, as well as in the enclave colonies of India, the original inhabitants (*originaires*) were recognized, also in 1848, as having the rights of French citizens, including the right to vote. There was an important difference between the two versions of citizenship. Unlike their Caribbean compatriots, whose personal lives were regulated under the French civil code, the *originaires* of the Quatre Communes could exercise these rights but still come under Islamic law in civil affairs, notably marriage and inheritance. Such affairs were handled by Islamic courts under the authority of the French state. These arrangements became known as *citoyenneté dans le statut* (Diouf 1998: 671–96).

But the Quatre Communes were the exception, and an increasingly marginal one. Most likely, it was the enclave nature of the Quatre Communes within an as yet unconquered African sea that led officials to accept the plural nature of the society they ruled; an inclusive version of citizenship would keep as many people as possible on the French "side."

The new citizens of the Caribbean—having been stripped of attachment to ancestral land, custom, and law by the slave trade—had no alternative to the nationality and the civil code that the French government imposed on them.

In Algeria, conquered beginning in 1830, things took the opposite course from Senegal. The original terms of French acquisition—in which France promised to respect Algerians' status under Islamic law—was interpreted to exclude them from French citizenship. A series of judicial decisions clarified what this meant: Muslim Algerians—and Jews too until 1870—were French subjects and French nationals, but not French citizens. A ruling of 1865 made clear that they could become citizens only by renouncing their personal status under Islamic law and satisfying officials of their assimilation into French civilization. Few wanted to make such a move; far fewer were accepted.

The juridical reasoning behind these provisions stressed personal status. Indeed, in European France, women were excluded from the most important right of the citizen—to vote—until 1944, on the grounds that they were not independent actors but dependent on the male head of the household. That a person was subject to Islamic or Mosaic law was similarly an impediment to the full autonomy of the citizen. The cultural dimension of the story shines through: the Muslim Algerian was too different, not least in regard to conceptions of marriage and family. The specter of a man voting, influencing perhaps the government's family policy, and then going home to his four wives was for many French political actors difficult to swallow (Blévis 2004 and Saada 2007).

As French colonization extended into sub-Saharan Africa in the last third of the nineteenth century, Africans became French nationals and French subjects but not French citizens. The Third Republic's progressive image of itself was satisfied by leaving the door open to Africans who renounced their status under "customary" law, accepted the French civil code, and convinced officials that they had acquired the French way of life. It was a door through which very few people passed throughout the history of French Africa (Conklin 1997).

None of this was as neat as it appears at first glance, nor was it entirely persuasive to French legislators themselves. During the 1880s and after World War I, some deputies tried, unsuccessfully, to eliminate juridical distinction among different kinds of French people. The issue was practical as well as principled: when France had greater need for "its" people to serve in the military, inclusionary rhetoric became stronger, only to be pulled back when veterans and others made claims to fuller rights on the basis of having paid the "blood tax" (Conklin 1997).

In Senegal, *citoyenneté dans le statut* came under attack by some European Frenchmen, officials and others, for conveying too many rights to Africans by virtue of their category—*originaires*—rather than by their having met certain criteria as individuals. World War I gave Senegal's leading African politician, Blaise Diagne, the opportunity to firm up his constituents' rights. He campaigned for the *originaires* to be subject to the same military regulations as all other French citizens, including conscription and service in regular regiments; as a quid pro quo, the French legislature reaffirmed in 1916 the rights of the *originaires* to their special citizenship regime (Johnson 1971; Conklin 1997).

There were attempts after the war—in response to the claims of those who had paid the blood tax—to make the citizenship system less exclusionary. But proposals for significant change failed. With the exception of the Quatre Communes and the small number of individuals who passed all the obstacles to become citizens, citizenship was something French Africans knew about but couldn't have.

Toward an Empire of Citizens?

Colonialism was a moving target, something that complicates efforts to attribute contemporary problems to a "legacy" of colonialism—it isn't always clear which colonialism is being assigned causal power.[3] After World War II, European powers—deeply weakened by war, the taken-for-granted quality of racial discrimination undermined by the mobilization against Hitler, facing activism in many colonies and revolution in Vietnam—knew that things would have to change, but sought to reinvigorate and relegitimate empire rather than abandon it. France made use of military power, torture, collective punishment of communities, and surveillance and detention of suspected rebels to keep the empire together: the massacres of Sétif (1945) and Madagascar (1947), the bloody and vain wars in Vietnam (1946–54) and Algeria (1954–62), the police violence inflicted on Algerians in Paris (1961). Yet keeping the empire together also entailed an effort to give people a stake in its institutions; just how far France could swing toward either the repressive or the incorporative pole was very much in question during the 1940s.

The change of direction reflected the shock of war. Hitler gave racism a bad name. Japan had conquered most of Southeast Asia, forcing France, the Netherlands, and Britain, after the war, to try to reconquer former colonies, not just defend them. A newly empowered United States seemed to favor open markets over closed empires, and the USSR thought it could lead once-colonized peoples against capitalist powers. Britain and France had built up a large debt, financial and moral, toward their colonies, which made the level of repression that would have been required to maintain a colonial posture very difficult to afford. And the change had a great deal to do with the different forms of political mobilization that took place in colonial situations.

The new imperialism of the postwar era, like the old, would balance incorporation into a polity with differentiation within it, centralized control granting colonial elites an incentive to cooperate with the system. The sincerity of French officials and legislators is not the most relevant question; more important is that the new politics of egalitarian imperialism gave African leaders institutional and ideological mechanisms to make claims against the French state. The possibilities of mobilization —from revolutionary internationalism to imperial reformism—were more varied than the desire for independent nation-states, and the future shape of a world order hard to predict.

The most uncertain moment of all was right after the war, through the debates over the constitution of a new, Fourth, Republic. As committees met to plan a postwar future, one was appointed in 1944, chaired by a leading Gaullist, René Pleven, to consider the "just place of the colonies in the new French Constitution." Its report backed away from the expression "France and its colonies"—which implied "a juridical relation of possession"—and instead sought a new vision of France, from Caribbean to Pacific, in Europe, Africa, and the Indian Ocean, as "an ensemble," a "French community . . . as indivisible as a living organism." Beyond its pious words, the committee wrestled with how different members of this community should be represented. Most members were talking about a federal France, capable of recognizing distinct and varied parts of the polity, yet still French. That Africans should sit in legislative bodies was more widely accepted than how power would be divided between territories and the French federation as a whole: should Europeans retain a decisive voice in running overseas territories and should Africans have any voice in policies affecting France as a whole, including its European component?[4]

The upshot of the initial deliberations was that the next step, the writing of the constitution, included African voices (and voices from other overseas territories), but not in proportion to population. Minority representation proved extremely important. Certain aspects of colonial rule could not stand the exposure given them by African delegations. Forced labor and the separate system of justice, the *indigénat*, were abolished by the first postwar legislature. Legislative leaders realized that if colonial deputies refused to go along with the constitutional process, the provisions on the overseas territories would have no legitimacy.

The African territories' electorates who voted for members of the Assemblée Nationale Constituante were divided into two colleges, one for "citizens," dominated by residents of European origin except in the case of Senegal, where the majority of citizens were African, and one for "subjects," mainly Africans. The Africans' presence changed the tone and substance of debate over citizenship and the constitution as soon as it began in the Assemblée.

But what were African deputies bringing to the debate? Senghor— Senegalese, but not from the Quatre Communes—had experienced *citoyenneté dans le statut* from the outside; born a subject, he had become a citizen individually, by asserting his educational qualifications and coming under the French civil code. In 1945, he published an article in which he told his fellow Africans, "assimilate, do not be assimilated."[5] They should critically examine what French culture had to offer and incorporate it in their conceptual universe—but not give up what he continued to call their "negro-african" heritage. Although Senghor did not accept the pretenses of those French intellectuals who equated their own cultural heritage to universalism, he did not respond to these claims with a radical communitarian perspective. Instead, he sought a wider conception of the universal, including multiple particularisms interacting and influencing each other.

Elected to the Assemblée Nationale Constituante, made a member of its Constitutional Commission, Senghor applied his conception to the practical problem of writing a text that would shape the place of colonial peoples in a broad conception of French identity. It was a propitious moment: leading political figures imagined a Greater France of 110 million Frenchmen instead of a (European) France of 40 million. The minister of overseas France opened discussion of the relevant section of the constitution by declaring, "Nowhere beneath our flag should people under its protection have the sentiment of being citizens of an inferior race."[6] From the earliest drafts of the constitutional provisions on the French Union, as the Empire had been renamed, the deputies seemed to agree that all subjects should acquire the "qualities" of French citizens, with all rights connected to that status. And they should have these rights without having to give up their personal status.

In a report for the Assembly, Senghor developed a systematic argument for generalized citizenship with diverse civil regimes. He evoked the revolutionary heritage, citing the decree of 16 pluviôse an II abolishing slavery and further specifying: "all men, without distinction of color, resident in our colonies, are French citizens and enjoy all the rights assured by the Constitution." He condemned the decree of Napoleon—"the dictator"—reestablishing slavery, and he lauded the revolutionary government of 1848, which had definitively made slaves in the colonies into citizens. Now, after World War II, came "the necessity to free the overseas people from the modern slavery of the indigénat and occupation." That is why all "nationals and inhabitants [*ressortissants*]" of the metropole and overseas territories had to have the political rights and qualities of the citizen.

Senghor recognized that the two questions put on the table in the Saint-Domingue revolution—the place of colonized people in the French republic and the place of difference among French citizens—were still around, but that their significance had changed. In 1798 and 1848, "the Jacobin tradition was vital." The only possible political stance was that of assimilation. But since 1848, there had been progress in sociology and "especially ethnology." France had discovered "the brilliant Arab civilization," the metaphysics of India, and the social humanism of China and Indochina, as well as the "collectivist and artistic humanism of black Africa." The vigor of these civilizations and their importance within the French Empire "went against a brutal integration that risked breaking a French equilibrium and the equilibrium of these new worlds."

To codify a France that respected difference and equality simultaneously meant a compromise between federal and unitary visions of government. His report proposed that all French subjects be defined as "simply citizens without specifying whether they are 'French citizens' or 'citizens of the French Union.' Usage will decide the label, which in any event, is of secondary importance." All overseas citizens would be represented in the federal parliament, but not in large numbers; at the same time, the territorial assemblies would be given stronger powers than those of regional councils in the metropole.[7]

The draft constitution that emerged was vague on the powers of different assemblies and modes of elections. But all seemed to agree that all inhabitants of overseas territories should be citizens and participate in some manner in governing themselves, compromising between a homogenizing Frenchness and dichotomous difference. As the centrist deputy Paul Coste-Floret put it, "We are today partisans of a pluralist democracy, that is a democracy of groups." An Algerian deputy wanted a France that would guarantee Muslim Algerians the right to keep their personal status, allow them a future right to independence, and meanwhile encourage "the flourishing of their culture, their language, their civilization and their spiritual life."[8] In extending the qualities of citizen to all in the overseas territories without requiring them to give up the application of Islamic or "customary" law, unless they so chose, the draft seemed to embody Senghorian principles.[9]

Fearing that the draft constitution might be defeated in the referendum on its approval scheduled for May 5, 1946, Lamine Guèye asked the assembly to put in the form of law the constitution's provisions on citizenship. The bill passed unanimously.[10] The proposed constitution was in fact voted down in a referendum in which only people who were citizens under the previous constitution had the right to vote—leaving out most Africans. The defeat stemmed more from domestic conflicts than from colonial questions, but it led to new elections and a more conservative Constituante.

Over the summer, defenders of old-style colonialism mobilized, attacking the extension of citizenship except on an individual basis.[11] As the debate resumed in the second Assemblée Nationale Constituante, an influential deputy, Edouard Herriot, warned that if one took literally the notion of all citizens participating equally in electoral institutions and if one looked at population figures, then France could become "the colony of its former colonies." At this, Senghor jumped up to reply, "This is racism!"[12]

But Herriot's point had been made before and would be made again—including by Senghor himself. A unitary conception of French politics—one citizen, one vote—would indeed make the deputies of European France a minority, but Senghor and his colleagues had made clear that what they wanted was a pluralist, federal France, in which each component, European France included, would exercise power over its own affairs and express its own "personality," while a federal government would oversee common matters. The summer's debate certainly witnessed expressions of hostility toward African participation in French political life, but it also opened up a serious debate over how the coherence of a French polity and the multiplicity of the people who made it up could be reconciled.

When the governing party tried to dilute the citizenship provision of the original draft, overseas deputies, including Senghor, Lamine Guèye, Gaston Monnerville, and Ferhat Abbas, formed an "intergroup" to defend the disappearing consensus. They briefly walked out of the assembly, and the government backed down.[13] The citizenship provision came back with studied ambiguity: all inhabitants of French territory would be citizens, but it was not entirely clear what they were citizens of. The final version stated (article 80) that "All inhabitants of overseas territories have the quality of citizen, on the same basis as French nationals of the metropole or of the overseas territories. Specific laws will establish the conditions under which they will exercise their rights as citizens."

The right of citizens "who do not have French civil status" to keep their status unless they renounced it—and still have all rights and liberties attached to their "quality as French citizen"—was guaranteed by article 82. Together, these clauses allowed the French Overseas Ministry to claim that "the legislature wanted to mark the perfect equality of all in public life, but not the perfect identity of the French of the metropole and the overseas French."[14]

The institutions of the Fourth Republic did not live up to such an ideal. They were a peculiar hybrid of federal and unitary systems, with ultimate power residing in a National Assembly, which remained "national" but was no longer so metropolitan. It had representatives of the overseas territories and Algeria (but not Associated States), but not in proportion to population. The federal idea was honored by the Assembly of the French Union, half of whose members represented overseas France, half metropolitan. But this assembly had a consultative role only. While the president of the Union—the president of the Republic, wearing a different hat—represented federal executive authority, he had no federal cabinet or ministries. Those powers resided in the prime minister, but he was responsible only to the Assemblée Nationale, not the Federal Assembly. It was an odd structure.

Federal France? Unitary France?

Some current historians do not think that the citizenship provisions of the French Union represented much of a gain for Africans (Coquery-Vidrovitch 2001; Genova 2004; and Dimier 2004). But Lamine Guèye and Senghor regarded them as a triumph—one for which they had to fight very hard within the constitutional assembly. The case against the provisions is strongest in regard to elections and representative institutions. Just as the sanctifying of the French citizen in the Revolution of 1789 did not bring with it universal suffrage until 1944—when women got the vote—the Fourth Republic's generalization of citizenship did not result in universal suffrage until 1956. It kept in place the two-college system in Algeria and most of Africa, a decision that all but doomed Algeria to violent struggle, but that was terminated peacefully in sub-Saharan Africa in 1956. The territorial assemblies, which were to have been where each of the diverse components of greater France expressed its "personality," had few powers.

But the dismissive argument misses a key dimension of the citizenship concept. What citizenship is has less importance than how it is used. Citizenship's particular power lies in the fact that it weaves together obligations and rights, so a state that wants to enforce obligations cannot easily dismiss claims to rights made in the same terms in which state hegemony is being expressed. West African political and social movements appreciated the claim-making power of citizenship quite well. They kept up steady pressure in the late 1940s and early 1950s to remedy the defects of the constitution: to give the federal assembly real power over issues affecting overseas France, to give territorial assemblies real power over issues affecting the territory, to eliminate the double college and reduce disparities of voting strength, and to institute universal suffrage throughout overseas France.

The mobilizing effort entailed developing the social and economic dimensions of citizenship, not just the political ones. Social citizenship meant a great deal more in European France after the war than it did before, as social entitlements were expanded and consolidated into a welfare state. Africans could claim—as I have argued elsewhere—that social legislation applied to them as much as any other citizen, and they argued strongly for equal wages, equal benefits, equal education, and equal access to medical care (Cooper 1996).

The political and social dimensions of citizenship posed a dilemma for government leaders. The logic of equivalence implied that the standard of living of African France had to be leveled upward, with no obvious place to stop other than a continental French standard of living. By 1956, the government was willing to concede key political demands in the hope that it could distance itself from the social ones. Suffrage became universal, and elections in each territory predictably put in place governments elected by an African majority. The territorial assemblies were given strong budgetary authority, while the institutions that exercised important functions for all the territories of French West Africa, heretofore an instrument of administrative centralization, were stripped of most of their power and were soon abandoned. Now, French leaders hoped, African leaders elected by African taxpayers in each territory would have to pay the bills for social entitlements. Well aware that increased autonomy for territories meant less of a claim on resources of the French Republic, African leaders sought to exercise the power that the new law conferred on them. Senghor saw more clearly than most how high the price was: Africa was being "balkanized," cut into fragments too small to be economically or politically effective. The possibilities for a federal France seemed to be disappearing. Africans might be getting more of a chance to govern themselves, but less of a basis on which to claim equality with other citizens of the French Union (Cooper 1996: 407–31).

Meanwhile, the French government was having a hard time coming to grips with the constitutional provision that allowed for multiple civil regimes. Officials knew that they needed to specify rules by which marriages, births, and inheritance could be recorded under different regimes of personal status, and they realized that the constitutional provision that allowed people to renounce their personal status and come under the civil law had to be spelled out in the form of a law. But the government, until the end of French rule, couldn't manage to enact a definitive legislative text on these subjects.[15] Civil status was not supposed to matter in regard to political rights, but politically it did as long as the two-college system for elections was in place (which it was for a decade). Government reluctance to define rules for change of status reflects a lingering belief that the civil code represented a French culture that had to be protected against people attached to local customs "such as polygamy." So admission to French civil status would have to be regulated, demanding evidence of conformity to the French way of life.[16]

The inability to provide a juridical basis for a multicultural citizenry brings us back to ambivalence over the basic object among the rulers of European France. The constitution of 1946 was, formally, egalitarian and multicultural, but few government leaders thought that French culture was simply one among many. Officials feared both that a French social order would be compromised by admitting unworthy people into it and that the indigenous societies of Africa would be undermined by weakening the social relations that each contained.[17]

At the same time as leaders of European France tried to save the Empire by making it less colonial, they deeply believed that France had a special mission to elevate the people of the overseas territories. Leaders of African France were using the development concept too, making claims on Union-wide resources needed to lift impoverished, poorly educated populations to the level of European France. The idea of federal France, in which people would be different but equal, did not eliminate inequalities of resources or—for many involved—beliefs in a developmental scale on which Africans placed lower than Europeans.[18]

This unstable situation was being pushed in different directions. Senghor and many of his colleagues kept trying to strengthen imperial federalism: to bring together different West African territories into a "primary federation" based on the older structure of French West Africa that would in turn be part of a greater France. Félix Houphouët-Boigny led a faction that rejected the African federation but wanted to preserve a French one, with each territory participating in French institutions. Student and youth groups were, by the mid-1950s, beginning to claim total independence from France.[19] Among leaders of European France in most of the center and left of the political spectrum, attempts to lower the burdens of social citizenship across the Union went along with a desire to retain some form of a wider community that would in some sense be France and in which they, as representatives of "France," would exercise a degree of authority.

Within that part of the spectrum, the concession of considerable power to African political leaders within the French Union was acceptable. A right-wing anticolonialism was also surfacing in the mid-1950s, an argument that colonies—especially given the escalating demands for development assistance and social expenditures—were costing France more than they were bringing in, and should be allowed to go their own way if they so chose.[20] Clearly, different definitions of France were in play, as were different definitions of Africa, some more "national" than others.

Nationality—French and African—in Question

Following such debates across the 1950s, to the independence of African states in 1960, is too complicated a task for this chapter. Instead, I will take up a particularly revealing moment in the history of pluralist or unitary conceptions of French nationality.

The context was shaped by the war in Algeria, the crisis in French politics, de Gaulle's coming to power, and the advent of the Fifth Republic. After October 1958, the French Union became the French Community—another attempt to reconfigure a France that was wider than the hexagon. This constitution retained the central feature that concerns us in the 1946 version: the people in the overseas territories were French citizens, with all the rights accorded someone of that status independent of personal status regime (article 75).[21] The relation of territories to the French Community, however, was quite different. Overseas territories became "Member States" of the Community; any such state had the right to leave the Community and become independent. Member States were self-governing except in regard to foreign affairs, defense, monetary policy, and a few other designated areas. Representatives of Member States no longer sat in the National Assembly, but heads of each government met regularly with the French president and prime minister in the Executive Council.

The 1958 Constitution stated explicitly that there was only one citizenship and that was "of the French Republic and of the Community." All citizens could exercise their rights in the territory of any Member State. But the constitution said nothing about nationality.

At the February 1959 meeting of the Executive Council, a decision was taken that there was only one nationality in the Community. It appears that de Gaulle and his prime minister, Michel Debré, gave the other heads of state little chance to debate the issue in any depth.[22] But the African leaders were not happy with the decision, and at the July meeting they insisted on further consideration of the question of single or multiple nationalities within the French Community. The council accepted "the need to respect, on the one hand, the existence of growing national sentiment in each state, and on the other hand, the unity of all members of the Community in relation to the exterior."[23]

French leaders saw nationality as implying a political entity whose personality was recognized by the community of already existing nations; overseas territories had no such status except through the French state. African leaders thought of nationality as coming not from without but from within, as a sense of collective purpose and action. Senghor distinguished "nation" from "patrie," the latter a given attribute of language and common customs, the former a construction coming out of a common project. "State," on the other hand, was a mechanism, a means by which nationality shaped itself and through which nationality was projected.[24]

In such terms, the insistence that France had nationality while African Member States did not was demeaning. French leaders, including Prime Minister Debré, got the point and backed off from the position that there was only a single, French, nationality within the Community. A committee of "experts" was called in to come up with a new synthesis. They advanced the idea of a "superposed" nationality. Each Member State would have its own nationality; it would write its own nationality legislation and decide whom to consider a national. The nationality conferred by an individual state would automatically confer nationality *and* citizenship at the level of the Community. Inside the Community, there would be many nationalities, but the outside world would see only one, that of "The French Republic and of the Community." The committee's version of superposed nationality was accepted by the Conseil Exécutif in December 1959.[25] Here we see a remarkable admission on the part of the French government of how far it would go to preserve the French Community: accepting that African officials in Abidjan or Dakar could decide who had nationality of the Community and could therefore exercise the rights of the citizen—in European France as much as anywhere else.

But African leaders did not agree among themselves whether there was a single African nationality or multiple ones corresponding to each territory. Senghor and his Senegalese political colleague Mamadou Dia had for some time argued for an African rather than a Senegalese focus and for francophone African territories to form an inclusive, federal state. As Dia put it, "It is necessary in the final analysis that the imperialist conception of the nation-state give way to the modern conception of the multinational state." This desire for a layered sovereignty—territorial, pan-African, and Franco-African—was in part practical: the territories were too small and too poor to be the instruments of human progress; interdependence was a necessity. And it was in part cultural, focused on people whom Senghor termed the "négro-africains de l'Union Française."[26] The territories of French West Africa, with their common experience, were a vanguard that might one day bring together all of Africa.

Houphouët-Boigny did not agree, preferring a direct relationship between Côte d'Ivoire and the French Community, and other African heads of state were sensitive to the reality of their territorial electoral base and their territorial power, however much they were attracted to the idea of African unity. Time was not on Senghor's side, for the reality of territorial power was bringing leaders to invoke a territorialized vision of the nation. In Côte d'Ivoire, riots against *non-ivoirien* Africans date to the late 1950s.[27] For a time it looked as if Upper Volta, Dahomey, and Niger would join Senegal and Sudan in trying to overcome these structural obstacles and create an African federation that would, as a single collectivity, participate in a renovated French Community. But in the end only Sudan and Senegal went forward to found the Mali Federation. It was Mali that began in early 1960 the process of negotiating with France for the status of international sovereignty, that is for independence.[28]

All this was happening in the shadow of the Algerian war. The brutality with which the French government attempted to suppress the FLN and keep Algeria French has in recent years emerged from the shadows of a consciously obscured history.[29] In deeper shadows still is the other side of the attempt to keep Algeria part of France. Todd Shepard has recently called attention to the de Gaulle government's program of *promotion musulmane*, what Americans would call affirmative action, directed at a specific category of French citizen—*Français musulmans d'Algérie*. I will turn to this subject shortly.[30]

When these factors are taken together, one sees the importance that the French government attached to holding together in some way the Community—successor to Empire and Union—certainly as an effort to preserve French power and influence in the world, but not simply in an intransigent defense of a colonial status quo. French officials were well aware that in the conjuncture of the postwar years, France had to present a vision of inclusivity and acceptance of diversity to its former colonial subjects—and at least enough substance to obtain the contingent accommodation of political elites, trade union officers, and other influential leaders. But the government had already learned the financial consequences of bringing colonial populations into a developing welfare state. And the first generation of African politicians to exercise real authority over budgets and bureaucracies in African territories were eager to assert as much territorial power as they could. The route from colonial empire to federalism was far from clear.

Member states had the right under the constitution to demand independence when they so chose, and Mali exercised that right, while trying to negotiate a way to stay in the French Community in a new status. Independence would render the idea of a superposed Community nationality obsolete before it was implemented, for it would imply that Mali had its own nationality—in the sense of both Senghorian aspiration and conventions governing international relations. But the French government now changed its own rules to allow Member States becoming independent to remain in the French Community.

In the first few years of the Fifth Republic, the French government—under pressure from the war in Algeria and political and social movements in Africa—was willing to accept that the rights of citizenship would extend to people who neither came under the French civil code nor were exclusively attached to the French nationality. Moreover, it was willing that citizens from its overseas territories exercise those rights throughout the Community—including European France.

Africans in France:
Ambiguous Inclusion at the Time of Independence

Not the least of the effects of citizenship—but also of an expanding French economy and officials' interest in workers who were in some respects "French"—was the intensification of labor migration from North and sub-Saharan Africa to the metropole. Such migration was not new, but what was new was not only its growing extent, but the fact that migrants arrived as citizens. Before the war, local officials at points of origin exercised often arbitrary control over the movements of subjects. But after the war, an Algerian or a Senegalese had a legal right to go to France and seek work.[31]

In the mid-1960s, some three hundred thousand from North Africa alone were in France. The Labor Ministry pointed out that "North Africans working in the metropole should be assimilated to metropolitan workers and they should benefit in this regard from workers' protection and the normal action of institutions of social security."[32] Concerned nonetheless about the presence of workers from overseas—all the more after the outbreak of the Algerian war—the government wanted both the usual institutions governing workers and special institutions to keep an eye on them. As Alexis Spire points out, there is a difference between formal regulations and the way a bureaucracy acts, and the police, with many veterans of repressive action in Algeria, often acted as if any Muslim was a suspected terrorist. Other ministries had to remind the police that Algerians had the rights of citizens (Spire 2005).

The other side of police surveillance was "social assistance in favor of the Muslim population in the Metropole." The Interior Ministry—not wanting to leave everything to the Labor Ministry—insisted that the needs of Algerians in regard to housing, language instruction, professional training, and schooling needed special, integrated attention.[33] When de Gaulle came to power in 1958, the policy was clarified:

> [T]he new head of Government in the interest of marking the interest he brought personally to all questions relevant to the situation of Algeria and the relationship between the French of North African Origin [de souche Nord-Africaine] and the French of Metropolitan origin [de souche Métropolitaine], believes that social action in favor of French Muslims of Algeria resident in the Metropole should be significantly reinforced and more closely coordinated, under the authority of the President of the Council.[34]

The details of how policing and services mixed are beyond the scope of this chapter. The point is the existence of the category: Français musulman d'Algérie. From today's vantage point—especially the argument that a republican government cannot recognize ethnic distinctions among its people—the precedent is a striking one: the Fifth Republic recognized Algerian Muslims as a distinct category of citizen so that social programs could be directed to them. Under the Fifth Republic, *promotion musulmanne* entailed the setting aside places in both the metropolitan and Algerian civil service for "Français musulmans d'Algérie" (Shepard 2006).

Sub-Saharan immigrants were neither so numerous nor were they perceived as such a threat, and while the Ministry of Overseas France kept an eye on them (as it had before the war), it did not devote the same attention to surveillance and social support as was the case with Algerians. Hence, officials felt ignorant about what was happening among Africans in France.

With independence for French West Africa in 1960 and for Algeria in 1962, the question arose of modifying the policies of the past fifteen years of emphasizing the "Frenchness" of colonized people. French citizens had to be sorted into nationalities corresponding to the old metropole and new states, but the road to turning imperial citizens into "foreigners" or "immigrants" was not a straight one.

The place of ex-citizens in a postcolonial order came up first in the negotiations over the independence of Mali. Even having accepted that Mali would be independent and Malians would have their own nationality, French officials did not want to admit that they would be "foreigners to France." The government's position paper for the negotiations presumed that Malians wanted to gain a state but not lose a nationality. Many of them were "firmly attached" to France, especially "the most French part: métis, originaires of the Quatre Communes, civil servants in metropolitan administrations, soldiers, citizens who had given up their personal status. It is, in a way, the French human capital of these states that will be sterilized by the ambiguity of the situation in which they would be placed in regard to nationality." Forcing Malians to make a choice would be a dilemma for such people, leaving their loyalty "always suspect" in whatever nation they chose. Those who chose Malian nationality would most likely be the ones with the least attachment to France.

The solution, French negotiators thought, was double nationality: Malians would become Malian nationals but would not cease to be French nationals. Because Mali was becoming independent with the full consent of the French government, there would be no "secession." Officials noted that there were many double nationals living in France and that the British law of 1948 provided something analogous to Commonwealth citizens, who had citizenship rights in Canada or Australia and, as a consequence, in the British Commonwealth as a whole.[35]

From the perspective today of a France protective of its "national identity" and of its borders, the thinking of top officials in 1960 might appear surprising. Here we have a defense of an inclusive France, one capable of recognizing that Africans wanted their own states but almost pathetically hopeful that they would still want to remain French. French officials were perfectly aware that the position they advocated during negotiations would allow Malians who had been French citizens to come to European France, reside there, work there, go to school, and exercise all the rights of French nationals. Throughout the negotiations, it was clear that French officials were less worried about Malians coming to France than about French citizens losing their ability to reside in Mali.[36]

Malians were ambivalent and not in entire agreement among themselves. Senegalese leaders, after Senghor and Dia's long effort in favor of federation and confederation within the French Union and Community, were more desirous of preserving some form of Community citizenship, whereas the Sudanese were more eager to assert sovereignty in a complete way. As discussions dragged on, Malians and French negotiators became increasingly enmeshed in a bilateral process. In the end, much of what the Community was supposed to define through *membership* was preserved by treaty. France and Mali would have separate nationalities and separate citizenships, but each would extend reciprocal rights in the other state. Malian citizens could go to France, French citizens to Mali; they could reside there, work there, do business there. They would have rights to social services. It was on this basis that Mali became independent, and France changed its laws so that it could remain in the French Community in its quality as a sovereign state. These bilateral accords became the model for independence negotiations for the rest of French West and Equatorial Africa. Following the negotiations, one sees that Mali got most of what it wanted from France—so eager was the French government to maintain itself as something like a multinational polity.[37]

Algeria was a much more painful separation—renamed a "decolonization" only in retrospect, as Todd Shepard has argued, once France abandoned the myth that Algeria was an integral part of the French Republic (Shepard 2006). The Evian Accords that ended the war in 1962 gave "Algerians" and "French" people the right, within certain parameters, to opt for either nationality. But the French government's attitude differed from its formal commitments. This was made tragically clear in France's failure to help its Algerian supporters who had given most to the defense of the Republic, the *harkis,* resettle in France; thousands, remaining in Algeria, were marked as traitors by the revolutionary government and killed. Behind it lay something de Gaulle would not say in public, but did in private: "Arabs are Arabs, French are French" (Shepard 2006: 23–42, 77). Meanwhile, the sudden and unanticipated exodus of *pieds noirs* from Algeria in the summer of 1962 made clear how bitter the separation was, and also that the French government was willing to admit people who were identified as French, even if many of them had tried to sabotage de Gaulle's policy of disengagement.[38]

Although many of the large number of Muslim Algerians resident in metropolitan France during the war returned home to help build the new nation, the civil war that erupted almost immediately in Algeria produced a new wave of movement to France, and labor-hungry France was eager to have them. Some 263,000 Algerians came to France in 1963. Both the French and the Algerian governments, however, soon moved against the ambiguous middle ground of nationality. Algerian officials often destroyed migrants' French papers when they returned to Algeria to visit—giving them no option but Algerian nationality—and France negotiated with the Algerian government in 1964 to ensure that Algerians would be admitted to France only under Algerian identification documents, unless they had opted definitively for French nationality. Both states seemed intent on constructing their own nationalities, whatever the behavior and feelings of people who were moving back and forth between two states and two social milieus. It was harder for an Algerian of Muslim civil status than someone of French civil status to obtain French nationality, but at this time the possibility was still open, ambiguously located between the "naturalization" of a foreigner and an affirmation of a pre-existing French nationality.[39]

Algerians who served in the French civil service—at least some of them the products of the earlier *promotion musulmane* program—exemplified the ambivalent situation after the Algerian war. Those who served in Algeria were expected to stay there and serve the Algerian state; they could keep positions in the French civil service only if they moved to France and declared French nationality, and only on condition "that their comportment toward France justifies it." Algerians serving in metropolitan France, however, could continue to do so without declaring French nationality. Those serving elsewhere in the Community had to declare French nationality to stay in the French civil service.[40]

France in the early 1960s was not quite ready to think of itself as a nation-state—one people in one territory with one state. For all the bad blood between France and Algeria, Paris accepted—not without self-interest—the principle of "free circulation" of people between the two. The immigration of Algerian workers was "not regulated" and constituted a "considerable influx." The government was interested in negotiating with Algeria agreements that would regulate numbers consistent with both states' manpower needs and would provide for medical controls and training.[41]

The approach was similar to that in regard to sub-Saharan African workers—a regime of "free circulation." Officials by 1963 were expressing anxieties that would become familiar over the years—poorly educated migrants, not necessarily with skills adapted to the French labor market, living in bad conditions, under no surveillance—possibly leading to "an unassimilable subproletariat of African origin."[42] But there was not much to be done, given the nature of the independence treaties and relations of France with its former colonies: "for obvious political reasons, it would not be possible, in the absence of agreements, to proceed to massive repatriations of people who, by virtue of the dispositions in effect, are simply required to present a passport or a national identity card to be admitted to France" and who are not required to have a "carte de séjour."[43] Bilateral agreements with African countries—who presumably didn't want to see their countries drained of manpower—was again the route. Police complained that given the regime of free entry, they lacked the means to follow and observe "immigrants." They didn't even know how many of them there were but presumed they were numerous: "In the street or, here, in the metro, they are visible." But however much they appeared ill prepared to live in a European country, the African migrants were supposed to be "treated in this regard as if they were French citizens in regard to labor legislation."[44]

So in the years immediately following the end of French colonial rule in Algeria and sub-Saharan Africa, the boundary between a truly national France and a more inclusive France—of former subjects who had in 1946 acquired the rights of citizens—had still not hardened.

Becoming National

In the middle of 1960, both France and Mali backed into much more "national" positions than either had wanted in the last fifteen years. The collapse of the Mali Federation and of the French Community were closely related, for one of the main reasons Africans like Senghor were interested in the Community was so they could build an African federation under its umbrella. When Africans could not agree on the latter, the former became less interesting. French officials were willing to accept the Mali Federation because its willingness to stay in the Community would set a precedent that might keep the Community together. But Mali's rejection of Community citizenship—and its insistence that other community institutions be consultative only—weakened whatever substance the Community had. Both Mali and France, as negotiations proceeded in March 1960, found that what they really wanted could be had by bilateral negotiations rather than Community institutions.[45] Other African states, following Mali toward independence, saw things the same way. With it went the possibilities of layered sovereignty that had been on the table since 1946: France, like the new African states emerging from its authority, would be a conventional nation-state.

The Mali Federation did not last; it broke up largely over fears by the leaders of Senegal and the Sudan that their own political bases would be undermined by its partner.[46] Senegal and Sudan (which kept the name of Mali for itself) became separate states and soon passed their own nationality acts (Decottignies and Biéville 1963). France revised its own nationality act, thinking first it wanted to keep the option of retaining French nationality open to its former citizens overseas and hoping especially that French-educated elites now governing African states would act more favorably to French interests if they had double nationality. It then moved in a more conventional national direction by allowing only former colonial citizens who resided within the current boundaries of the French Republic to claim their French nationality, then setting a time limit on when such a move could be made.[47]

The independence of Algeria in 1962 was a further step toward making France more national at the same time that Algeria acquired its own nationality. With Algerian independence, Muslim Algerian deputies— who between 1958 and 1962 made up nearly 10 percent of the French National Assembly—left that body, turning a once diverse legislative body into the kind of Franco-French institution it has been ever since (Shepard 2006: 14). Political separation made it harder for a middle ground between Algerian and French nationalities to remain open.

With the tightening of immigration rules in 1974 and the increase of anti-African and anti-Maghrebian xenophobia in the 1980s, the idea of a clearly defined French nation defending itself and its republican values against outsiders became a staple of French political discourse. Others defended a more open France, more adoptive of diverse peoples, perhaps in need to atone for its sins in the colonies. Both views posited a very French France.

The history of the growing restrictions on immigration has been analyzed elsewhere, but my point is that the national conception of France that lay behind them was not an automatic consequence of France's being a republic or its having been a colonial power. France in the 1970s had to devise rules to reverse what it had done in the 1950s, when it tried to assert that Africans had a place within both overseas and European parts of the Union/Community, first as rights-bearing citizens, then, after 1960, as foreigners of a special—positive—sort, with rights of free circulation and the right to seek employment. French politicians who insisted in the late twentieth century that France could not tolerate communal distinctions among its citizens or forms of social regulation different from the civil code had to turn around a policy written into the constitutions of the Fourth and Fifth Republics that recognized different forms of personal status among citizens, and they had to reverse a pragmatic social policy that had marked a category of citizens—French Muslims of Algeria—for special treatment. France had to *make* itself more national.

One thus does not move directly from "colonial subject" to "immigrant," but rather passes through a phase in which Africans became imperial citizens, with all the ambiguity that phrase implies. For a few years after the formal separation of the national paths of France and its colonies, "free circulation" persisted. It took a lot of work before the French state moved systematically to bar entry to the children of people it had once tried to keep within a French polity.

Conclusion

The interest of this story does not lie in speculating whether a colonial situation could ever have been turned into a truly federal, multinational, egalitarian France—if only European French politicians had been willing to pay to bills to make aspirations to equality realistic, if only African politicians had not been so concerned to maintain their territorial political bases. The point is instead to recapture the sense of possibility in this moment of political mobilization and claim-making. It is to remind us that any assertion of what France truly is should be met with skepticism. That France is a nation of equivalent citizens and that France is a nation responsible for enslavement and colonization are parts of its history. But not the only parts—and never uncontested parts. There are precedents in recognition of different civil statuses and in past state policies for using distinctions among French citizens to integrate people into a composite whole and to remedy social ills. Whatever arguments can be made for or against such policies, the argument that anything other than a homogeneous citizenry isn't "French" is misleading. But the argument that a colonial France in and of itself gave rise to the prejudices and discriminations of present-day France is also insufficient: it lets the politicians of the 1970s and thereafter off the hook too easily, for they had a choice among alternative models of what France could be. That some of them opted for an exclusionary version of the French nation, with "its" inherently French values and institutions was not a necessity, not intrinsic in the genealogy of the French state or the necessities of republican government. Alternatives were considered, and some for a time were declared policies or became the subject of negotiations.

That an African could be a citizen of France and something else—an African elder, a Muslim patriarch, an African nationalist—was a central premise, arguably *the* central premise of a considerable spectrum of political actors in African and European France during a moment of uncertainty, conflict, and possibility in French and African history. People tried to figure out, unsuccessfully in the end, institutional mechanisms for the expression of distinct national personalities and destinies within a greater France that remained egalitarian. At certain moments during a colonial history that witnessed the routinized degradation of colonial subjects, possibilities existed in the political imaginary of those subjects of finding a different sort of France. The Franco-Haitian revolution of 1789–1804 raised at the very beginning of republican France the question of whether the boundaries of a rights-bearing citizenry would be a narrowly defined, European France or else an imperial France, with people of African origin inside it. Whether would-be citizens had to conform to the values of French civic life was a question that could be— and was—debated in regard to Senegal, Algeria, and other parts of the empire. In 1946, the relatively open Senegalese model of citizenship with different civil regimes became the constitutional norm for the French Union as a whole.

The failure of federalism, within Africa and between Africa and France, is explainable, but explainable does not mean that failure was inevitable and that the attempt is a minor detour along the path of history. The France that came into being after the independence of West Africa in 1960 and of Algeria in 1962 is a contingent France, not an essential France, and projecting backward the self-conscious nation-state that emerged from the failures of colonialism and of the attempts to build a more egalitarian multinational polity does not help us to see the uncertainties and possibilities of the past. Perhaps recognizing uncertainty and possibility in the past will help us to come to grips with the uncertainties and possibilities of building a France today that in new ways faces difficult questions of reconciling equality and diversity.

Notes

Abbreviations used in notes: ANF: Archives Nationales de France; AS: Archives du Sénégal.

1. For more on this question see Florence Bernault's contribution, "Colonial Syndrome: French Modern and the Deceptions of History," in this volume.

2. See James 1963, Dubois 2004a, and Dubois 2004b.

3. Herein lies the major flaw in Mahmood Mamdani's influential 1996 book *Citizen and Subject: Contemporary Africa and the Legacy of Late Colonialism*. For a critical analysis of this and other interpretive problems in the history of colonialism and decolonization, see my *Colonialism in Question: Theory, Knowledge, History* (Cooper 2005).

4. Commission chargée de l'étude des mesures propres à assurer aux Colonies leur juste place dans la nouvelle constitution française, Report, July–August 1944, and transcript of sessions of May 1 and 9, 1944, papers of Gaston Monnerville, Fondation Nationale des Sciences Politiques, GM 26.

5. Léopold Sédar Senghor, "Vues sur l'Afrique Noire, ou assimiler, non être assimilés," in Lemaignen, Senghor, and Youtévong 1945.

6. Testimony before Commission de la France d'Outre-Mer, December 12, 45, C//15293, ANF.

7. Assemblée Nationale Constituante, Rapport Supplementaire of Commission de la constitution on Union Française, Léopold Senghor, reporter, April 5, 1946, in Assemblée Nationale Constituante, *Documents*, Report #885.

8. Coste-Floret, Assemblée Nationale Constituante, *Débats*, April 9, 1946, 1640; Mohamed Bendjelloul, Assemblée Nationale Constituante, *Débats*, March 7, 1946, 646.

9. Commission de la Constitution, Assemblée Nationale Constituante, *Comptes Rendus Analytiques*: statement of Marius Moutet, head of committee on overseas territories, January 25, 1946; presentation by Gabriel d'Arboussier of draft of Article 1 by committee on overseas territories, January 25, 1946, 259, 261, 264, 328.

10. Minister, Circular letter to High Commissioners, June 14, 1946, AP 3655, Archives d'Outre-Mer, Aix-en-Provence.

11. Conclusion of meeting of les Etats Généraux de la Colonisation, *Le Monde,* August 25–26, 1946. On the conservative drift in government thinking, see Lewis 1998.

12. Assemblée Nationale Constituante, *Débats,* August 27, 1946, 3334.

13. *Libération,* September 21, 1946; see Guèye 1966: 161–62.

14. AOF, Directeur Général des Affaires Politiques, Administratives et Sociales (Berlan), note, July 46, 17G 152, AS. The preamble to the constitution stated, "France forms, with the overseas peoples, a Union founded on equality of rights and duties, without distinction of race or religion. The French Union is composed of nations and people who make common and coordinate their resources and their efforts to develop their respective civilizations, to improve their well being and assure their security."

15. There is much data on the importance and the shortcomings of the *état-civil* in Senegal during the 1950s in the series 11D1 in the Senegalese national archives.

16. Minister, circular to High Commissioners, June 13, 1947, F60/1401, ANF.

17. See for example Governor, Senegal, to Haut Commissaire, May 31, 1952, 23G 96, AS.

18. The development concept was a two-edged sword, a basis for a colonial state's claiming legitimacy and for African social and political movements to make demands and, in the end, to argue that they could better represent African's social and economic needs than could a colonial government. See my "Modernizing Bureaucrats, Backward Africans, and the Development Concept," in Cooper and Packard 1997: 64–92.

19. One of the best places to follow these vigorous debates is the pages of *Afrique Nouvelle.*

20. See Raymond Cartier, "En France Noire avec Raymond Cartier." *Paris-Match* 383 (August 11, 1956): 38–41; 384 (August 18, 1946): 34–37; and 386 (September 1, 1956): 39–41.

21. See Norbert Rouland, "Les statuts personnels et les droits coutumiers dans le droit constituionnel français," in Le Pourhiet 1999: 145–226.

22. There is a handwritten, not entirely legible, account of the meeting, more or less verbatim, taken by Jacques Foccart in his papers, FPR 105, ANF.

23. Communique of Conseil Exécutif, *Afrique Nouvelle,* September 18, 1959.

24. Senghor, speech as president of the Assemblée Fédérale du Mali, to that assembly, Dakar, April 6, 1959, copy in FPR 238, ANF.

25. Conseil Exécutif de la Communauté, Comité des experts chargés de l'étude des problèmes de la nationalité et de la citoyenneté," transcript of meetings of November 16 and 18, 1959, FPU 215, ANF. The committee included representatives from Senegal-Sudan and other overseas territories. For the approval of this report, see Conseil Exécutif de la Communauté, December 11–12, 1959, "Relève des décisions qui resultent de l'approbation du rapport sur la nationalité et la citoyenneté par le Conseil Exécutif," ibid.

26. *La Condition Humaine,* November 29, 1951, May 31, 1956; Senghor, "Rapport sur le méthode du Parti," in report on congress of the Bloc Démocratic Sénégalais, ibid., April 26, 1949; Mamadou Dia, "L'Afrique Noire devant la nouveau destin de l'Union Francaise," ibid., August 29, 1955; Senghor, ibid., July 11, 1948.

27. *Afrique Nouvelle,* October 31, 1958. Dahomeans and Togolese working in Côte d'Ivoire were the first victims of this early manifestation of xenophobia.

28. For background, see Foltz 1965.

29. Key texts for opening up this past include Branche 2001 and Stora 1998.

30. See Shepard 2006: 50–51, and Spire 2003: 48–66.

31. The government refers in 1948 to the "current regime of freedom of passage." Government Général d'Algérie au Ministre du Travail, 3 June 1948, F/1a/5046. There were some differences in status and formalities depending on whether one was from a Territoire d'Outre-Mer (most of Africa), Algeria, or an Associated State (Morocco, Tunisia), but all had the legal right to be in France. For further discussion see Spire 2005; on sub-Saharan migrants, see Manchuelle 1997.

32. Ministère de Travail, 1954, cited in Ministère de l'Intérieur, Note pour M. le Ministre, April 4, 1956, F/1a/5044, ANF.

33. Ministre de l'Intérieur à M. le Secretaire d'état au Travail, June 1, 1956, F/1a/5044, ANF. Spire (203) brings out the differing views of surveillance.

34. Le Préfet, chef du service des Affaires Musulmanes et de l'Action Sociale, Ministère de l'Intérieur, Note à l'attention de M. le Ministre, Feb. 25, 1959, F/1a/5045, ANF.

35. Note relative à la nationalité, Jan. 9, 1960, FPU 218. On Britain, see Paul 1997.

36. "Note, projet de convention franco-malienne d'établissement," March 24, 1960, and Prime Minister Michel Debré to President de Gaulle, March 19, 1960, FPR 106, ANF; see also Spire 2005: 208.

37. Debré to de Gaulle, March 19, 1960, FPR 239, ANF; papers in the file "citoyenneté: négociations Mali 10–15 Mars 1960," in FPU 201, ANF, including draft of the bilateral agreeement, dated March 15, and Secretariat General of Community, "Accord de Communauté relatif à la citoyenneté de la Communauté et aux nationalités dans la Communauté," n.d. [March 1960].

38. See Jean-Jacques Jordi, "The Creation of the Pieds-Noirs: Arrival and Settlement in Marseilles, 1962, " in Smith 2003: 61–74.

39. Ministre de l'Intérieur, Circular letter to prefects, October 26, 1963, FA/1a/5048. See Spire 2005: 213–14.

40. Le Secrétaire Général du Gouvernement au Ministre de l'Intérieur, December 26, 1963, F/1a/5045, ANF.

41. Ministre de l'Intérieur, circular to Prefets, April 23, 1964, F/1a/5048, ANF.

42. Ministre de la Cooperation to Prefet de la Seine, Feb. 15, 1962, F/1a/5136, ANF.

43. Ministre de l'Intérieur, Note pour M. le Directeur Général des Affaires Politiques et de l'Administration du Terrritoires, Services des Affaires Musulmanes, April 9, 1963, F/1a/5136, ANF.

44. Statement of Le Prefet Mamassoure, representing Ministère de l'Intérieur, to meeting of Conseil Economique et Social, Section du développement économique et social des pays autres que la France et de la cooperation technique, meeting of Feb. 6, 1964, F/1a/5136, ANF.

45. One of the Malian leading negotiators, Madeira Keita, later put it this way: "Mali intended to be tied only by bilateral accords that it freely negotiated with France, because the Malian delegation negotiated in the name of an absolutely independent state." Address to meeting of Union Soudanaise, May 28–31, 1960, FPU 1677, ANF.

46. The best narrative up to this point is *From French West Africa to the Mali Federation* (Foltz 1965), but the recent opening of archives of the Federation, housed at the Archives du Sénégal (Fonds FM), and of the papers of Jacques Foccart at the Archives Nationales Françaises (Fonds FPU and FPR), allow for a deeper examination of this history. The present author is exploring aspects of this topic.

47. The post-independence shifts on nationality legislation can be traced in dossier FPU 557, ANF. More generally, see Weil 2002.

CHAPTER SIX

Colonial Syndrome: French Modern and the Deceptions of History

Florence Bernault

The 2005 riots in France are the hallmark of a triple failure: a failure to assimilate, a failure to integrate, and a failure to globalize.

—OUSMAN KOBO

It is not terribly demanding to ask historians of Europe to acknowledge that colonies mattered. It is another thing to ask them to rethink the narrative of the nation-state.

—FREDERICK COOPER

The 2005 riots against discrimination and racism have uncovered a ferocious war of representation going on about France's past and present, a war with multiple fronts and numerous combat zones. As the French social body is slowly imploding over the fate of citizens of color, the aftermath of the riots has unearthed considerable cracks and fault lines in France's republican ideals, such that new realities no longer fit into dominant social scientific conceptual models. Indeed, the depth of the crisis recalls, fifty years after Georges Balandier coined it, the metaphor of colonial assaults "revealing" African societies' weakest points (Balandier 1955: 6).

The parallel is not coincidental. Since 2005, unprecedented portions of the social body have come to grips with France's colonial past. Political commentators increasingly refer to imperial legacies to talk about current racial discrimination.[1] On the media front, colonialism has become a mine for filmmakers and talk shows. In academia, the analytical power of colonial studies has become amplified, ending a long marginalization in French universities. These engagements shed light on three major changes at work: (1) the thinning and wearing of classic intellectual tools and the crafting of original categories of analysis, (2) the coming of age of a new "cultural" turn, where culture and identity emerge as central battlegrounds for social critique and political action, and (3) the unfolding of new forces and alternative fronts in France's social and political fabric, particularly among citizens of color and immigrant origin.

The volatile combining of these dynamics explains why the colonial paradigm has proved disturbing to the point of becoming, in France, a veritable syndrome. In 2005, when the new colonial studies landed on French shores, their edges had been well worn out and softened.[2] Yet they came to *affect* academia with a ferocity that contrasts with the ways in which, in the United States, colonial and postcolonial studies' capacity of intellectual disturbance ranges from the moderately exciting to the painfully predictable. A consistent engagement with grassroots actors quickly grounded the disputes amidst deeper social and political currents. At the university, the anchoring of the paradigm quickly started to make established methodologies and scholarly fields overlap, stretch, and burst beyond recognition.

This chapter proposes a roadmap of these battles, by tracing first the long impotence of the colonial question from the 1980s to the early 2000s. Then, to delineate and understand the ideological camps that crystallized around its new irruption in the 2000s, I focus on two initiatives taken by Frenchwo/men of color in the wake of the 2005 riots, the CRAN (Conseil Représentatif des Associations Noires) and the Indigènes de la République. Against these associations and their scholarly supporters, a conglomerate of academics rose up in arms. Dismissing the amplitude of social turbulences (Bertrand 2006b: 206), these scholars, including prominent specialists in area and colonial studies, deny that colonial models of social analysis can shed productive light on France's racial and political fissures. The chapter thus returns in conclusion to the academic terrain and explores current opposition to the analytical valence of colonial and postcolonial studies.

The 2005 Watershed

Although scholarly engagements with the colonial past formed in France long before the 2005 riots, no lasting articulation between political doctrines, research venues, and forms of social mobilization had successfully emerged around the colonial question. Colonial studies remained shadowed by anticolonial, third-world, and neo-Marxist propositions, failing to spill over into mainstream high school and university curricula or engage with enduring social initiatives.

In the 1970s, at the twilight of anticolonial struggles, scholarly interest in dependency theory and the rise of the third world led to the formation of a leading research laboratory at the University of Paris 7, the Laboratoire Tiers-Monde Afrique (Laboratory for Third-World and African Studies), where a single curriculum combined African, Asian, and Latin American studies. By the late 1980s, however, the influence of the Paris 7 initiative remained limited. Outside of Paris 7, specialists of Africa, Latin America, and Asia remained entrenched in geographical and analytical niches. Among *Tiers-Mondistes* themselves, a rather outdated anti-imperialist and dependency narrative continued to reign unscathed, deflecting attention from alternative theories emerging at the time, from subaltern to postcolonial and new colonial studies.

Meanwhile, in the larger public, the French-Algeria conflict—and its flip side, anticolonial movements in the 1950s and 1960s (Ferro 2003)—worked as a metonymic decoy, hiding the tremendous complexity of France's colonial past. Many Frenchmen still do not know much about colonial violence beyond torture during the Algerian war, about racial and ethnic engineering beyond citizenship in colonial Algeria (as well as the four communes of Senegal),[3] or about the history of the modern African diaspora beyond the case of North African immigrants in France. The same reduction is visible in the political field. When, in the early 1980s, the rise of the extreme-right Front National party sparked a new awareness of the endurance of white supremacist ideas in the aftermath of Algerian independence, the commotion failed to prompt inquiries into France's *other* colonial legacies. Thus in the 1990s, when Africanist and colonial historians started to move away from Marxist and dependency theories and look into the imaginary and cultural fabric of colonialism, including its legacies in metropolitan France, they were met with indifference or skepticism.

By the mid-1990s, the colonial question at large remained hardly visible in French academia. While a few were fighting, in what seemed a lost battle, to improve the currency of colonial/postcolonial studies (Coquery-Vidrovitch 1999; Mbembe 2000; Bernault 2001; Dulucq and Zytnicki 2003), a group of scholars started to work on domestic imperial legacies. Not yet inserted in the academic establishment, these young historians organized in an association, ACHAC (Association pour la connaissance de l'histoire contemporaine). In 1992–93, ACHAC organized two high-profile conferences in Paris and Marseilles, and published a groundbreaking volume on colonial visuality, followed by several volumes on the French colonial past/present (Blanchard and Chatelier 1993; Bancel, Blanchard, and Francis 1997; Bancel and Blanchard 1998). By the late 1990s, the success of ACHAC had become the target of mounting suspicion among specialists of African and colonial studies, who described the association as a group of mavericks eager to spin the theme of colonial continuities to serve personal ambitions.[4] In the early 2000s, with the publication of *Zoos humains* (Bancel et al. 2002) and *La fracture coloniale* (Blanchard, Bancel, and Lemaire 2005), the group had become the most influential player in the field of new colonial studies, as no alternative project had organized to contest or complement their intellectual propositions, with the exception of a group of scholars aggressively concerned with rehabilitating French colonialism (Lefeuvre 2006).

On the social front, until the early 2000s, *immigrés* and Frenchwo/men of color did not mobilize around analyses of France's colonial past and postcolonial tactics. Instead, movements against discrimination and racism (SOS-Racisme, Mouvement-Immigration-Banlieues in Paris, DiverCité in Lyon), followed a classic antiracist and leftist republican tradition (Battegay and Boubeker 1993; Wihtol de Wenden 1997; Bouamama 1994b and 2006). Most of the *immigrés'* political allies at the time (Mouvement national contre le racisme, Ligue des droits de l'homme, Parti Socialiste) inserted such a fight into a republican narrative of minority rights, aiming for *immigrés'* complete absorption into a preexisting "Nation" and an undisturbed "Frenchness." Indeed, the dominant school of immigration studies in France, developed most forcefully in Gérard Noiriel's monograph, *The French Melting Pot* (1988), suggests that French strategies of assimilation, from the nineteenth century on, have amounted to a "grand model" of integration comparable to, but diverging from, the American melting pot. Instead, *le creuset français* endeavors to "make migrants French" by eroding inherited cultural particularities (Noiriel 1988; Weil 1991: 299-301, 310–31). For Noiriel and his followers, the French assimilation policies that have taken in southern and eastern Europeans since the eighteenth century will prevail in absorbing migrants of North and sub-Saharan African origin (Laurence and Vaisse 2006: 270).

The proposition seldom envisions that integration policies can reproduce and reinforce, rather than erase, racial and cultural traits; and it is often unaware of the ways in which assimilationism fuels racial animosity. Nor does it examine how the promise of the melting pot, and the interpretative power of the model at large, might be compromised by a diminishing faith in the attraction of a universal "Frenchness." Last but not least, immigration scholars have paid little attention to the colonial genealogy of such assimilationist strategies. Studies of immigration published before 2006 deflect a sustained engagement with the history of colonialism and colonial legacies (Noiriel 1988, 2001, 2007; Weil 1991, 2002; Green 2002). Gérard Noiriel's latest volume, for instance, hardly examines the legacies of colonial policies of identity and citizenship after 1962, as if what he calls "the decolonizing of colonial emigration" had suddenly stopped them from shaping French views of immigrants of color (Noiriel 2007: 542–47 especially). The adjacent field of minority studies tends to dismiss colonial history and the French empire (Wieviorka 1993, 2001; Lapeyronnie 1993). To be sure, this is a widespread pattern. A decade after Pierre Nora notoriously ignored the colonial, recent histories on the nation, the Republic, and the construction of French citizenship have still absorbed little or none of France's colonial past (Nora 1983–1993; Schnapper 1994; Duchesne 1997; Le Pors 1997; for a recent exception: Duclert and Prochasson 2002). A recent 527-page scholarly history of contemporary France, for instance, offers a grand total of five pages on colonial issues, all limited to Algeria (Sirinelli 2005: 390–95).

The 2005 series of acute legislative, judiciary, and social incidents broke this configuration, forcing greater engagement with France's colonial past. After the much-publicized controversy over the law of February 23, 2005, and article 4, which asserts the "positive aspects of French presence overseas,"[5] a lesser-known debate on slavery and colonialism prompted historians to question their responsibility in interpreting France's past.[6] Both episodes coincided with major museological and commemorative projects on the colonial past that include the newly opened Cité nationale pour l'histoire de l'immigration, the Musée du Quai Branly, and the Mémoriaux de la France outre-mer. While a few *pieds-noirs* associations became more vocal in celebrating France's colonial past, the idea of France's "colonial debt" spread among African migrants and Frenchwo/men of color (McGaffey and Bazenguissa-Ganga 2000: 81; "Cité dans le texte" 2005). When Jacques Chirac's government responded to the 2005 riots by reenacting a state-of-emergency law used during the Algerian war, outcries on the enduring colonial nature of the French state took center stage.[7]

In sharp contrast to the pattern of fast dilution discernible in the 1980s and 1990s, a lasting debate on the colonial paradigm has finally emerged. The involvement of Frenchwo/men of color is a remarkable feature in this transition. By the end of the riots in November 2005, associative groups recruiting among citizens of color and of *immigrée* origin, staged the (post)colonial question as central to national politics. On January 19, 2005, Le Mouvement des Indigènes de la République launched an online petition drawing direct relationships between French colonial and postcolonial policies, after which time they formed as a permanent association (Robine 2006). On November 26, 2005, closing a year of demonstrations and meetings, the CRAN coalesced as a lobbying organization that represents the rights and visibility of black Frenchwo/men .

The Native's Promise

In the summer of 2004, following a media frenzy against Muslim youth accused of harassing a Jewish woman, a young feminist militant, Houria Bouteldja, decided that the term *Indigènes,* borrowed from the imperial repertoire, best captured the legacy of negative images applied to Frenchwo/men of color. This bold act of lexical reappropriation diffused rapidly among activist circles close to Houria Bouteldja (Robine 2006). *Indigènes'* catchy label derives its strength from reclaiming the stigma, an old strategy of resistance among the oppressed, and one that seems particularly fitting for individuals who are, in France, constrained to assert their cultural and religious identity defensively (Bouamama and Tévanian 2005: 247–49). In September 2004, Bouteldja organized an informal meeting of the Indigènes de la République among her friends, and across a constellation of militant groups.[8] In January 2005, the group published a national petition on line, "L'Appel 'Nous sommes les Indigènes de la République!,'" calling for a mass demonstration in Paris on May 8, 2005, and the formation of a Conference for Postcolonial Anti-Colonialism (*Assises de l'anti-colonialisme postcolonial*).[9] For Bouteldja and her friends, the date signaled the fiftieth anniversary of a high noon in the articulation of colonial and republican history: on May 8, 1945, the French government simultaneously celebrated the defeat of Nazism in metropolitan France and colonial massacres in Algeria.[10] (See appendix 1.)

According to the leaders of the movement, the *Appel* encountered immediate success among Frenchwo/men of *immigrée* origin, and collected a massive rush of signatures, with people saying: "The *Appel* speaks to our guts, it is our life, we did not have the words. . . . [It] came to give meaning to experiences of oppression that were deprived of a discursive vehicle" (Bouamama 2005). The *Indigènes'* first demonstration in May 2005 gathered about seven thousand people on the République-Bastille axis.[11] By then, the movement had started to demonstrate that it could capitalize on Frenchwo/men of color's disenchantment in the 1980s and 1990s—a period marred by economic crisis and the steady deterioration of social, urban, and educational hopes—and that it could offer a solution to these groups' enduring atomization (on immigrants' atomization see Beaud 2002; Beaud and Pialoux 2003; Beaud and Amrani 2004). By spring 2006, the consolidation of the movement progressed with the creation of a monthly journal, *L'Indigène,* and the posting of an intricate website, where essays and responses to critiques rapidly formed a rich political platform.[12]

The *Indigènes'* core conceptual move is grounded in the proposition that discrimination belongs in a structural system, modern history in a coherent narrative, and victims in a single social front. Aggregating ubiquitous experiences based on geographical location (as in the *banlieues*), gender, religion (as in attacks over Muslim headscarves), and nationality (as with migrants and *sans-papiers*), the *Appel* suggests that scattered acts of racism and discrimination do not occur at random, but are structurally produced by a coherent and enduring system, *la République coloniale,* identified as a singular enemy and a new horizon for political action. Present colonial ideologies in France, the *Indigènes* further argue, are part of emerging transnational and global beliefs in

the "clash of civilizations" (Huntington 1996). Reenacting older reper-
toires of otherness (barbarity, savagery, fundamentalism), this global
matrix is colonial in origin and in nature. It allows a new distancing of
Arab, Muslim, and black *immigrés*, among other cultural minorities in
the West. In response, only the merging of a wide range of progressive
forces across the racial divide can fight for the decolonization of the
French republic and the world at large.[13]

Yet, the Indigènes de la République insist that they work within
France's political tradition and engage with republican ideals, albeit
in a critical way. In an important text, sociologists Nacira Guénif-
Souilamas and Christine Delphy explain how the movement is made up
of "Indigènes-who-do-not-want-to-be-treated-as-Indigènes," demanding due recognition as citizens and asking that "this country of ours
should now act upon the promises engraved on the facade of our city
halls" (Delphy and Guénif-Souilamas 2006). The genitive form *de* in
Indigènes de la République thus carries two meanings. It denounces
the term *Indigène* as an ascribed status produced *by* (*de*) the French
republic's enduring colonial matrix, but also signals a genuine claim for
belonging in (*de*) the Republic.

Although the Indigènes stress that their perspective is secular and
their agenda political, they have been frequently maligned as being
driven by hidden sympathies for Muslim fundamentalism, or by ethnic
and communitarian goals. These accusations, they argue, reveal how
colonial and postcolonial racist tactics confuse and counterfeit social
dynamics. In the words of Saïd Bouamama, "domination works precisely by overturning the order of causality . . . if communitarianism
exists in France today, it is first and foremost produced by social logics"
(Bouamama 2005, Indigènes 2005). Racist ideologies essentialize populations as if they exist in an unchanging and defensive state of being. In
doing so, they substitute cultural and racial explanations for a socially
engaged critical analysis, successfully disqualifying the claims of their
victims and potential challengers.

These nuances, large and small, proved lost on the media. In
February 2005, lumping the Indigènes together with the black humorist
Dieudonné's diatribe against Jews, the centrist journal *Le Monde* listed
the movement among the supporters of a rising "new anti-Semitism" in
France. The same month, the journal published an interview with the
president of the French League for Human Rights (Ligue des droits de

l'homme—LDH) who expressed concern about how the Indigènes produced confusing accounts of historical situations that ignored scholarly
studies on colonialism and immigration.[14] In December 2005, *Le Monde*
invoked the movement again as "a sign of the emergence of a double
movement of contraction [*repli*] on communitarianism and memory that
has gained momentum for some months" (Montvallon, 2005). On the
center right, *Le Figaro* criticized the "confusion" (*amalgame*) and "excess"
(*outrance*) on behalf of the Indigènes as part of an anticolonial repertoire
that was starting to gain public acceptance.[15] Other media outlets were
less restrained. *Le Nouvel Observateur,* a centrist magazine close to the
Socialist Party, condemned Indigènes as "The Damned of the Republic,"
and their manifesto as a "blurry [*fumeux*] cocktail of poujado-leftism,
cheap alter-mondialism, and post-Fanonnian radicalism."[16] To the left,
the journal *Respublica* shunned the movement as a "sect," a "mortiferous
alliance of islamo-fascists and communalist-Lefties," whose "ideologues
trash [*vomissent*] integration, the Republic, and secular values [*laïcité*]."[17]
At the center-right, the popular magazine *Marianne,* under the title "The
New Racists," explained that the Indigènes belonged to a "reactionary,
clerical, anti-secular, communitarian and ethnic constellation," and that
their *Appel* was "a paranoid . . . and at times insane text."[18] Reactions in
academic circles largely echoed media rhetoric.[19]

Meanwhile, in December 2005, a concurrent movement, the Conseil
Représentatif des Associations Noires (CRAN) was organized as a lobbying group to defend the rights of black French citizens. Patrick Lozès, a
pharmacist born in Benin and naturalized in the late 1970s, has been the
leader of the movement with Louis-George Tin (born in Martinique),
and Pap Ndiaye (of Senegalese origin). Tin and Ndiaye are both academics who were trained at the elite École Normale Supérieure in Paris.
By contrast with the considerable suspicion roused by the Indigènes, the
CRAN met with a general approval in the media and from the French
political class. Prominent academics applauded their initiative and
agreed to serve in the movement's Conseil scientifique (intellectual leadership). Promoting a discourse of race relations analogous to U.S. equal
opportunity and affirmative action agendas, the CRAN has asserted a
positive definition of race, while reinforcing a fundamental trust in the
republican promotion of minority rights. As a historically underrep-
resented group, black Frenchwo/men hope to achieve greater access to
shaping their own representation in the media, in the labor force, and

in politics. Such a political platform reaffirms a narrative of progress and equality that is ultimately submissive to established class hierarchies[20] and poses negligible risks to republican myths of belonging. It allows the concept of race to be absorbed in hegemonic discourses on the French nation as "one and indivisible." With respect to the malaise, palpable in popular and scholarly circles, that ideals about the nation (a human, territorial, and historical community) and the Republic (a political regime with foundational principles) are in crisis, and will undergo major reconfigurations in the years to come (Nora 2006b: 48; Citron 2006: 44), the CRAN responds in full support of the ascendant republican regime and France's grand narrative fictions (*le grand récit national*) (Citron 2006; Sibeud 2002; Bancel et al. 2002). This claim is seasoned with conventional nationalist formulas: for Patrick Lozès and Louis-Georges Tin, the CRAN is an "institutional lobby" engaged in "the labor of the Republic," that firmly stands "on the side of universalism." Proudly "bear[ing] the color of France," it wishes "to recruit an army, not against, but for France."[21]

By contrast, the Indigènes' deconstruction of race and critique of assimilation policies poses considerable threat to a wide range of republican myths. Whereas the CRAN validates racial identity and republican equality, the Indigènes see both constructs as historically produced fictions indispensable to the reproduction of a repressive order. For the Indigènes, race is not prior to, or distinct from, the project of modern nation-building, but has historically emerged as a state-sponsored tool of distancing and othering, while the French republican order, under the pretense of imposing universal civil rights over cultural and racial loyalties, has essentialized racial and cultural differences (Dirks 2002: ix–xi; Guénif-Souilamas 2006b: 128–30).

Thus the Indigènes take issue with mainstream policies for the integration/assimilation of migrants and Frenchwo/men of color. They argue that such policies, while prompting *immigrés* of color to abandon their cultural traits and national heritage, are unable to prevent the social and political body from constantly reinscribing cultural, religious, or ethnic markers on French citizens of foreign/colonial origin. It is a pattern visible in the enduring popular imaginary of Arabs as social pariahs (religious extremists, oppressive patriarchs, and delinquent young males), and black Africans as dysfunctional parents and vectors of uncontrolled sexuality (polygamists, vectors of the HIV-AIDS virus, and patriarchal barbarians imposing female excision).[22] By claiming that civic rights need not be prescribed on cultural conformity, and by promoting a new alliance among descendents of the colonized, based on a historicized reading of discrimination, the Indigènes address those citizens of color who "have few illusions about integration policies, and experience their hardships not as a transient situation, but as an enduring reality" (Battegay and Boubeker 1993: 184). Calling for a radical critique of republican ideals, national identity, Frenchness, and assimilation, this proposition has also exercised immense symbolic violence on a number of intellectual routines.

The Telos of the Nation: Primordialism and Evolutionism

Hostile reactions against the Indigènes, by contrast with the widespread support for the CRAN, derive from deep-seated imaginaries about race and Frenchness that remain barely articulated in academic circles. The French melting pot (*le creuset français*) and the perspective that the Republic historically managed, despite setbacks, to "make migrants French" (*rendre français*) (Noiriel 1988; Weil 1991, 2002 and 2005; Haut Conseil à l'intégration 1993) reflects a particular belief in the construct of the nation and the Republic where, as Alistair Davidson proposes, the primordial tie between individual citizens and the state exists in the form of a political contract, itself constitutive of an egalitarian public sphere (Davidson 1999). In this view, the public sphere should be left untouched by cultural difference and religious values, whose domain of action should be confined to the private sphere. This construct underplays scrutiny over social and cultural factors (class, race, gender, ethnicity, religion, historical origin), at the same time that it tends to predicate the regulation of the public sphere on state action, rather than on civic initiatives at the grass roots. In the same vein, dominant French immigration studies analyze integration processes from the top down, from the central viewpoint of governmental practice and ideology, rather than the multiple, bottom-up perspective of individuals' experiences and needs (Schnapper 1994: 73–222; by contrast, Sayad 1991 and 1999).[23] Otherness per se (i.e., not seen as a transient state) is acknowledged mostly as a trait to tame or repress, rather than a resource to promote.[24] The idea that a national project can actively encourage religious, ideological, or cultural divergence among its citizenry appears utterly foreign to this intellectual tradition, and is almost never envisioned as an alternative to the French melting pot.

Since the 1990s, a majority of scholars have used this silent ideology to paint the political initiatives of *immigrés*, especially those of African and Asian origin, as a threat to civic virtue, nation-building, and French identity. After the 2005 riots, an antiquated form of social Darwinism has been revived, drawing rudimentary oppositions between the particular (*ethnos*) and the universal (*res publica*), and demonizing race and culture as weapons threatening the public sphere. The result is an extraordinary amalgam of teleological and rationalist propositions, where the abundant use of normative formulas tries to hide the lack of empirical research and theoretical nuance (Hajjat 2005: 42).[25] A constellation of commentators multiplies primordialist and naturalizing views of the social that foster a mechanical opposition between "archaic" and "civilized" forms of political identity. Experts in immigration studies and specialists of African or Asian studies imply that ethnic, religious, racial, or cultural identities threaten the nation with dissolution. They seem unable to disentangle the current political context from anxieties over the rise of "communitarianism," religious extremism, and social regression.

From this vantage point, *identités* work along a kind of loose pyramid, starting at the level of an overarching, refined French "national identity" (Sarkozy 2007; Décret No. 2007–999 du 31 mai 2007), and disbanding into a myriad of centrifugal, sub-political identities (*mobilisations identitaires* and *communautarisme*). Within that structure, the most refined form of identity is supposedly acquired through universal reason, one's sublimation of inherited traits, and the respect of republican rules of authority and negotiation. At the bottom, other identities survive that, allegedly, derive from narrow interests and irrational faith, and engender perverse political reflexes. Such primordialist views imagine the state as a rational and normative entity, that is, as the central agent in regulating the public sphere, and a collective, single consciousness.[26] Any opposition to this credo is labeled as ethnic pride, religious fanaticism, or patriarchal dictatorship, and demonized as a sign of political regression and social disaster (Schnapper 1994: 116–19; Badie 1997: 5–7; Le Pors 1997: 33–39; Chrétien 2006: 193; Bertrand 2006a: 44–46).

In this perspective, the 2005 riots are no more than a "proto-political" episode produced by a downtrodden "sub-culture" (Mauger 2006: 131, 140, 145–48). The rise of minorities is seen as a "regression of citizenship" (Le Pors 1997: 33). The Indigènes' project is shunned as a conspiracy that tries to force divisive quests of origins on naïve people. According to their critics, the fact that the Indigènes talk of *immigrés'* common colonial past results in imagining "a kind of hereditary legacy of experienced oppression . . . that tends to ethnicize or confessionalize political conflicts, in its promotion of communitarianism" (Bensaïd, Joshua, and Vachetta 2005). Ethnic groups are seen as unable to express progressive political agendas, or to connect "indignation and emotion to rational political action" (Lapeyronnie 1993: 280). In a political land-scape supposedly overwhelmed by emotional passions, a new "horizon of victims" (Barbier and Mandonnet 2005), accompanied by a surge of "traumatic identities" (Pétré-Grenouilleau 2005: 93), threatens national bonds. Multiculturalism itself is interpreted as a suspicious "identity of compensation" (*une identité de consolation*) produced by globalization and the erosion of class consciousness (Amselle 1996: 169–72; Badie 1997: 5–7; Bordes-Benayoun and Schnapper 2006: 212–22).

Commentators and scholars vigorously opposed to the Indigènes and the analytic purchase of colonial studies are found mostly among historians and political scientists. Politist Jean-François Bayart, a special-ist of Africa, argues that "post-colonial studies are politically dangerous [. . .] In the current debate, they tend to ethnicize social issues and thus may work as a form of cultural engineering of political domina-tion" (Bayart 2007: 271). Among those opposed to the Indigènes, social evolutionism looms large, including dichotomous views of popular memories and professional history (Merle and Sibeud 2003; Boilley and Thioub 2004; Chrétien 2005; Meynier 2005; Boilley 2005; Dulucq et al. 2006; Lefeuvre 2006; Saada 2006a and 2006b). The *Études coloniales en France*, a website organized by Daniel Lefeuvre, is an important archive and network for these perspectives.[27]

A more moderate group includes people aware of the challenges of multiculturalism and globalization, yet confident in the French repub-lican model of integration. Some became active members of CRAN's Conseil scientifique, and in general, can be associated with the move-ment's softer approach to race, *intégration*, and republican values. History is the dominant discipline among them. A few come from area studies, such as Jean-Loup Amselle and Catherine Coquery-Vidrovitch, but most specialize in French history, as with Gérard Noiriel and Patrick Weil. Loosely grouped under the leadership of Gérard Noiriel and around the École des Hautes Études en Sciences sociales (Paris), many write in Noiriel's journal *Genèses,* and on the website of his association, the Comité de vigilance face aux usages publics de l'histoire (CVUH).[28]

The Dissidents

From the late 1970s to the 1990s, out of step with this doxa, dissenting studies on *intégration à la française* have accumulated. Inaugurated in France by Abdelmalek Sayad (1991 and 1999), Saïd Bouamama (1992 and 1993), and Ahmed Boubeker (1999, 2001, and 2003), these studies foster a critical vision of integration policies (Geisser 2006; Otayek 2000; Duclert and Prochasson 2002; Benbassa 2004; Guénif-Souilamas 2006b; Fassin and Fassin 2006). For these authors, the policies of *intégrationnisme,* or the ultimatum to integrate, are in fact conducive to social discrimination. They create two categories of citizens, "integrated" and "non-integrated," trapping immigrants in a cultural double-bind (Hajjat 2005).[29] Citizens of foreign origin are summoned to abandon their cultural values (religious, social, ethnic, national) in order to fully participate in the French nation (Sayad 1994; Hajjat 2005). Yet when they do so, French society (and the ideology of cultural determinism) constantly reinscribes cultural and racial markers on the immigrant's mind and body, forbidding h/er, in practice, to enjoy full civil rights (Guénif-Souilamas 2005: 200–202). The adoption of the recent law on religious insignia in public schools, silently targeting the wearing of Muslim headscarves, is a case in point (Bowen 2007: 1; Bouamama 2004; Bouamama and Tévanian 2005: 251).

For these authors, and for the proponents of the colonial paradigm, the process recalls the discriminatory forms of citizenship created in the French colonies, and can be compared to a partial recycling of prior *politiques indigénistes,* or nativist policies (Amselle 1996: 170). In the French empire, the language of *assimilation* (a precursor to metropolitan *intégration*) allowed white perceptions of cultural difference to crystallize in the form of *statuts personnels* restricting the civic rights of black citizens (Bernault 1996: 94–95; Coquery-Vidrovitch 2001; Cooper in this volume). The continuity had already been identified by sociologists in the early 1990s: "Colonialism [has] found its ultimate refuge in the integrationist proposition [. . .] in one case, factual differences used to deny equal rights are invoked, in another, factual differences in the name of equal rights are denied" (Sayad and Bourdieu as quoted in Hajjat 2005: 36). Indeed, several sociologists specializing in grassroots immigration studies have fostered the heuristic potential of colonial studies in order to understand modern France and minority politics.[30] Today, these important figures have nearly vanished in the public and media frenzy over immigration and citizenship. With the exception of Stéphane Beaud and Catherine Wihtol de Wenden, they teach and work in relatively marginal institutions, and no public intellectual figure has emerged among them. Next to them, the handful of historians who tried to push the colonial paradigm to the forefront of mainstream histori-cal studies have enjoyed little influence, and teach outside of the most prestigious institutions in France (Bancel and Blanchard 1998; Coquery-Vidrovitch 1999; Mbembe 2000; Bernault 2001; Vergès 2002; Stora 2005; Gondola 2007).

The Deceptions of History

Indeed, French historians, and among them specialists of area studies, have voiced some of the harshest critiques against the colo-nial paradigm, or the project of historicizing present discriminations from the vantage point of France's past colonial policies. A frequent critique is that of "continuism," that is, a forced connection between different historical contexts and processes, obscuring the originality of present dynamics (Saada 2006b). The argument, however, ignores that no proponents of the colonial paradigm argue that colonial legacies and continuities exhaust the interpretation of current conflicts. Another critique suggests that colonial scholars play the sorcerer's apprentice by encouraging old conflicts and particular grievances (i.e., ethnic or reli-gious) to surface in the social debate: "To everyone his own history, to everyone his own version of the past, his suffering, his status as victim. France has become a mosaic of wounded memories" (Askolovitch 2005: 14). The diagnosis stems from the belief that the neutrality of science should be separated from irrational popular ideologies, an argument oftentimes articulated around the concept of memory and history. Once an innovative field, the history of memory has contributed to a regres-sive reflex among historians, a transition in reverse that requires deeper investigation.

French historians, following the lead of sociologist Maurice Halbwachs (1925 and 1968) have published since the 1980s one of the most comprehensive bodies of work on the social construction of memory and the political use of the past (Nora 1983–93; Crubellier 1991; Rousso 1990, 1998, and 2001; Augé 1998; Ricœur 2000). Yet this conceptual breakthrough has recently boiled down to a crude opposition between memory, ideology, and history (Nora 2006b: 51; Rioux 2006: 165–82). In this perspective, partial "memories" emerge mostly in the private sphere, as a series of fragmentary and pre-ideologized narratives about the past. "Ideologies," in turn, crystallize at the intersection of the private and public sphere, providing larger groups with specific identities and a common political agenda. However, such ideological narratives are unable to transcend group interests and offer inclusive myths of national belonging, by contrast with professional history. At a higher level, historians see themselves as equipped with professional objectivity and sanctioned tools of research. They tend to think that history, therefore, is able to debunk archaic myths of identity and to encourage acceptable forms of civic glue. In this evolutionary schema, historians are mythologized as arbitrators of the political realm, and historical critique is painted as the building block of modern republican virtue. For French historians, not only are interpretations of the past and present not created equal, but this very proposition is overqualified by the predicament of truth. Even historians aware of critiques on the heuristic objectivity and social neutrality of their discipline discourage the disclosure of such critiques on the ground they would only deepen popular confusion between partial and impartial knowledge (Saada 2006a: viii).[31]

Since 2005, the rhetoric of fear and social crisis has contributed to exaggerate the opposition between impartial history and archaic "memories." For Jean-Pierre Rioux, a specialist of contemporary France, "In the name of atavism, [the politics of identity] could assign every person, human group, and people to their source of origin, and prevent them from identifying with a collective, shared, and secularized memory. It could push them into a cycle of civil violence and social, then racial or religious exclusion" (Rioux 2006: 170–71). Commenting on ACHAC publications, a specialist of ethnic strife in Africa complains that in France "everything seems to work as if the colonial relationship . . . becomes a new 'tale of origins' . . . explaining present disasters through past tragedies as part of a memorial quest, and by justifying political mobilizations around identity" (Chrétien 2006: 189). In other words, the colonial paradigm is poised to transform a somewhat stable French social scene (or so commentators believe) into a battlefield of racial hatred and ethnic massacres. Ironically, this means that colonial and postcolonial studies are less dreaded for their intellectual power than for their capacity to trigger social disturbance, an interesting testament to French scientists' long-standing illusions about the social import of scholarly discourse.

In this landscape of doom, colonial and postcolonial theorists loom as figures of betrayal and disaster, and are portrayed by critics as opportunists who seek to undermine the cautious craftsmanship of the classic historian (Boilley and Thioub 2004), or worse, as "good apostles of Saint-Repentance and Saint-Pluralism," force-feeding the public with "fantasies" (*fantasmes*) and "tranquillizers" (*neuroleptiques*) (Chrétien 2006; Rioux 2006: 156). High-brow commentators have joined ex-Marxists to bemoan the ways in which rioters and postcolonial intellectuals are blinded by rampant consumerism and sordid materialism (Debray 2005). Indeed, from the disinterested angle of the erudite elite, fractional "memories" too easily fall prey to material temptations (Nora 2006a: 23; Bertrand 2006b: 129). The Indigènes' leaders are thus denounced as a small clique of educated bourgeois obsessed with social visibility, and eager to misappropriate immigrants' political capital (Girard 2006; Robine 2006). ACHAC historians supposedly seek to "patrimonialize" the colonial past into a cheap, commodified cultural capital that they traffic around in order to grease ideological markets. A few critics have gone as far as comparing postcolonial scholars to "colonial propagandists" serving the continued oppression of the masses (Merle and Sibeud 2003). Such paternalist views of subaltern blindness and greed explain why French historians support a virtuous struggle against the debate for financial *réparations* or political *repentance* for colonial crimes (Barbier and Mandonnet 2005; Lefeuvre 2006).[32]

Didactic Narcissism and the Annales Complex

Moral stances and paternalist alarms, however, can conceal endless methodological traps. Those who denounce the dangers of the colonial paradigm often dismiss ongoing arguments and epistemological debates among colonial and postcolonial study groups. Moreover, they are sometimes unaware of the intricate history of social and cultural engineering in the colonies, or of the fact that concepts forged in the context of Colonial studies have contributed to global discussions over the formation of modern states, public power, and nation-building. In the colonies, European rule relied more on cultural technologies of power than on tools of economic or military domination. But these technologies, under the guise of "civilizing the natives" or building "modern nations," could be socially regressive, for instance when centralized colonial states forged and imposed neo-traditional identities—including race, gender, and ethnicity—upon local societies. Thus, in the colony, powerful regimes of subjectivation were also made of state-sponsored strategies to naturalize and primitivize the social fabric. Social categories were never impermeable or fixed. The racial divide itself, central to colonial domination, was the matter of constant negotiation and contention (Stoler 2002). This is the reason why determinist historical explanations, including the construction of ethnicity and race, and teleological views on social or stately progress have been long debunked by colonial scholars, at least outside of France.

Oblivious to or unaware of this scholarship, French historians also demonstrate a general lack of engagement with the question of subjectivity and subalternity, a significant methodological innovation in the field of area and colonial studies. To this day, the French history curriculum does not include any routine introduction to the ways in which analytic methods are produced and negotiated, how professional competence is socially achieved, and why critiques of subjective authorship are essential to the crafting of scientific expertise. African and colonial studies, including anthropology and sociology, seldom engage the analytical validity of subaltern voices. When they do, they mock subaltern studies as a naïve "discovery," a teleological "revelation" of the oppressed (Bertrand 2007: 282–84). Meanwhile, as the *mandarinat* system in France has remarkably survived the turbulence of May 1968, the production of sweeping theories and self-aggrandizing narratives remains a major preoccupation for the stars of the system. Teaching methods, even at the graduate level, are predicated on didactic authority, in the form of large or small lectures, allowing only minimal input from students. Unsurprisingly, histories from below (not just commanding views on "popular mentalities"), displaced subjectivities, and fragmented narratives have little or no bearing in the discipline. Paternalistic or universalizing discourses are barely challenged, and continue to dominate the writing of history.

In French universities, exposure to foreign methodologies and philosophies remains limited. The enduring marginality of world history in the French curriculum, coupled with the low visibility of non-Western area studies, has prompted little engagement with international debates and foreign schools of thought. Linguistic barriers do not entirely explain this pattern: scholars writing in French outside the Hexagon reach only a limited readership.[33] Among Africanists, a significant lack of engagement with plural or global dynamics, including diaspora studies, persists. The trend accounts for a large part of today's palpable irritation against the invasion of English new and (post)colonial studies in the intellectual market of the Hexagon. Having ignored it for many years, and failed to make significant contributions to it, mainstream French academics find themselves unsettled by the field's surging currency.[34]

Last but not least, the insularity of French historians has been nurtured by a curious "Annales complex" (pun intended). In the 1920s and 1930s, the Annales school grounded modern historical practice in a renewed attention to popular *mentalités* and grassroots actors. Heirs to this methodological revolution, French historians tend to see themselves as analysts of the lowly, a perspective that allows some to assume that they are preternaturally exonerated from ideological or social biases, a belief sustained well into the 1990s by the enduring influence of Marxism and neo-Marxism in academe. The recent success enjoyed by publishing ventures of "ego-history" has reinforced this pattern to the point of caricature.[35] The genre was inaugurated by Marc Bloch and pursued in quieter times and more conventional ways by Fernand Braudel (Bloch 1949; Braudel 1986). In the last twenty years, prominent French historians have felt compelled to emulate this model and to publish book-long narratives about their personal and professional trajectories (Nora 1987; Duby and Lardreau 1992; Le Goff 1996; Farge 1997b; Ariès 1999; Corbin 2001; Noiriel 2003). The fashion, virtually unheard of outside of France, is a savory paradox in a country that has once nurtured the sharpest critique of the autobiographical genre (Bourdieu 1986). In addition, and maybe to imitate the founding fathers of "total" history, another project invented by the Annales School, modern historians try to publish synthetic, wide-reaching monographs on the craft of history and the fate of France. The inward-looking perspective of *ego-histoire* coexists with overblown assertions about national history and catalogs of methodological "breakthroughs" little conducive to engagement with subjective criticism, or intellectual debates beyond the Hexagon (Veyne 1971; Le Goff 1988 and 2006; Prost 1996; Noiriel 1996 and 1998; Chartier 1998; Rioux 2004 and 2006). For the wannabe stars of French academia, these writing strategies function, today, as a rite of institutional passage.

Pliable Historians

Because French historians see their discipline as essential to the working of the Republic and the nation, they tend to imagine themselves as rational experts regulating, educating, and guiding the state's "duty of history" (*devoir d'histoire*) against the dangers involved in "partial" memories (Chrétien 2006: 141; Dulucq and Zytnicki 2005: 68). That history is a pure science and historians impartial gatherers of facts is the grandest illusion of all, one long denounced as socially barren and intellectually vacant (Bloch 1949). Yet the debate on the heuristic validity of the colonial/postcolonial paradigm has all but amplified this bias.

In 2005, leading historians launched two petitions against the Law of February 23, 2005, and against the legal attacks against historian Olivier Pétré-Grenouilleau, a specialist of the slave trade.[36] Two factions emerged from these initiatives, one led by Gérard Noiriel and his CVUH, the other by Pierre Nora, who underwrote the petition "Freedom for History" (*Liberté pour l'histoire*).[37] The former advocates a regulated dialogue between legislators and historians; the second champions the "liberty of history" and opposes any legal restrictions to the work of professional historians.[38] Underneath the divide, however, the petitions demonstrate that leading French historians believe in the power of their discipline to be the ultimate mediator of public discourse and debate. Both groups claim a place within the closed-door territory of political decision making. Critics would maybe challenge my interpretation by recalling how state legislation (the 2005 law) was the first to intrude into the field of history. But on myriad occasions, historians have sought the patronage of secular elites, and have maintained an interest in defining their objects of study as a supplement to various forms of political and institutional power.[39]

The desire to produce a discourse that counts, that holds currency in the public realm, has entertained considerable political pliability among historians, encouraged by French political elites' knack for instrumentalizing history. In the last few years, politicians have multiplied initiatives to take advantage of the rich symbolic and political resources associated with France's colonial past, from the Musée du Quai Branly (opened in 2006) and provincial Mémoriaux d'outre-mer, to the Cité nationale pour l'histoire de l'immigration (CNHI), located in the former Museum of the Colonies (2007).[40] A sizable number of social scientists have worked closely with local state officials in these projects, leading to institutional forms of collaboration.[41] This is a predictable pattern in a country where politicians casually patronize scholarly gatherings and conferences. In the fall of 2006, for instance, an interdisciplinary conference on the history of immigration, led by historian Nancy Green, was inaugurated by the political patron of the CNHI, European deputy and former mayor of Paris Jacques Toubon.[42] The series of scandals surrounding historians' involvement in the Mémoriaux de la France outre-mer, and the recent resignation of historians from the CNHI to protest President Sarkozy's creation of a Ministry for Immigration and National Identity, can also serve as negative proof for the enduring and problematic, if little scrutinized, interaction between French scholars and the state.[43]

This chapter started with a sweeping landscape of social upheaval, intellectual shifts, and political initiative. It closes on a powerful barrage of academic sanctions and reactionary ideologies. The basis for the colonial paradigm and new interpretations of the social have been dismissed by the dominant establishment of historians. As individuals, a corporation, and an ideological group, historians are not immune to political positioning and intellectual rigidity. Since 2005, immigration and race have become some of the most important and visible political issues in France. By the same token, conflicting interpretations of French colonialism, past and present, have entered the eye of the cyclone. Race and culture, as invisible in pre-2005 France as gender was in the US before the 1960s, have triggered a painful process of *dévoilement* among intellectuals and the larger public. Not that the issues did not exist, or were not talked about prior to 2005. But many found it expedient to funnel them back into the colonial past, the Algerian war, ethnic strife in Africa, or the soon-to-be-completed grand assimilation of migrants in eternal Frenchness. Today, the return of the colonial, and the return of the colonized, does not spare any terrain, from the political to the cultural, the academic, and the popular, and the land of imagined universals. Everywhere the colonial paradigm has proved, for better or worse, highly disruptive of established routines and polite discussions. Syndrome or convulsion, the freezing of the past has broken down, and a few deceptions with it. *L'ère des surprises commence.*

Notes

The first epigraph is from a personal communication. Ousman Kobo teaches African history and modern Islam at Ohio State University. The second epigraph is from Cooper 2002: 65.

1. Journalist Philippe Bernard explained how the inhabitants of the *banlieue* were not "natives lost on the French territories who can be flogged, Kärcher-cleaned, or expelled back to their native douar." "Banlieues: la provocation coloniale," *Le Monde,* November 18, 2005. A month later, the rhetoric reached new grounds when historian Pierre Nora protested against the cancelation of the commemoration of Napoleon's 1805 victory in a sarcastic "Pleading for the 'Natives' of Austerlitz" (Nora 2005). For later and increasing uses in the political realm, see "'Indigènes': demi-victoire ou grande récup?" posted on January 23, 2006, at www.indigenes-republique.org. Catherine Coroller, "Sans-papiers malgré un passé d'indigènes," *Libération,* November 23, 2006; Jean-Baptiste de Montvalon, "La République et la Nation l'emportent sur le communautarisme dans la campagne," *Le Monde,* December 16, 2006; Geneviève Brisac, "La malle coloniale du mépris misogyne," *Le Monde,* March 2, 2007; "À Madagascar, M. Chirac évoque le caractère 'inacceptable' des 'dérives du sys-tème colonial,'" unsigned article, *Le Monde,* March 27, 2007. Feature movies have been aired, most notably *Le malentendu colonial* (dir. Jean-Marie Téno, 2005), *Indigènes* (dir. Rachid Bouchareb, 2006), and *L'embrasement* (dir. Philippe Tréboit, 2007). Scholarly publications include special journal issues, "La question coloniale," *Hérodote* 120 (2006); "Passés coloniaux recomposés," *Politique africaine* 102 (2006); "Pour comprendre la pensée postcoloniale," *Esprit* (2006); "La colonie rapatriée," *Politix* 76 (2006).

2. At the onset of the 2005 crisis, historians outside France had long sought to explore the legacies of colonialism back into metropolitan cultures and societies (Lebovics 1992; Zantop 1997; Conklin 1997; Cooper and Stoler 1997; Ezra 2000; Hall 2002; Stoler 2002; Aldrich 2005). Mostly written in English, these studies investigated how native policies and racial imaginaries crafted in the colony continued to inform current representations of immigrants and citizens of color in Europe. They also contended that the construction of the French nation-state and the Republic could hardly be disentangled from the imperial context in which both had emerged.

3. For instance, see contents of special issue on "Sujets d'Empire," *Genèses* 53 (December 2003), edited by Emmanuelle Saada et al.

4. Based on personal conversations in Aix-en-Provence and Paris, 1989 to 1996.

5. Article 4: "Les programmes de recherche universitaires accordent à l'histoire de la présence française outre-mer, notamment en Afrique du Nord, la place qu'elle mérite. Les programmes scolaires reconnaissent en particulier le rôle positif de la

présence française outre-mer, en particulier en Afrique du Nord, et accordent à l'histoire et aux sacrifices des combattants de l'armée française issus de ces territoires la place éminente à laquelle ils ont droit." Assemblée nationale, loi n° 2005-158 du 23 février 2005 portant reconnaissance de la Nation et contribution nationale en faveur des Français rapatriés. (Translation of Article 4: University research programs should give the history of the French overseas presence, notably in North Africa, its rightful place. High school curricula should recognize the positive role of the French overseas presence, particularly in North Africa, and take into account the sacrifices endured by French army veterans from these [formerly colonized] territories and grant them the esteemed historical place to which they are entitled. National assembly, law number 2005-158 of February 23, 2005 Recognizing the Nation and National Contribution in Support of Repatriated Frenchmen). See Bancel in this volume.

6. In June 2005, historian Olivier Pétré-Grenouilleau (2004), criticized the Loi Taubira recognizing slavery as a crime against humanity. He suggested that the slave trade should not be compared to the Shoah, or a genocide (interview in *Journal du dimanche,* June 12, 2005). In October 2005, the Collectif DOM (Départements d'outre-mer) filed a judicial complaint against him, a move that provoked outcries among professional historians. Connecting the case to the Law of February 23, 2005, they argued that the lawsuit encouraged further attacks against historians' freedom of speech. Collectif DOM dropped the litigation in January 2006.

7. Signed by Prime Minister Dominique de Villepin on November 8, 2005, the state of emergency was established by the Decree n° 2005-1386, later extended for three months, on November 13, 2005, by the National Assembly. It was then lifted by President Chirac on January 4, 2006. The 2005-1386 decree reactivated the Law n° 55-385 of April 3, 1955, voted in during the Algerian war. This law was itself recycled from various decisions that served to establish an *État de siège* during the Franco-Prussian conflict in 1870, then during World War I and World War II. In 1955, President Edgar Faure changed the term *État de siège* to *État d'urgence,* arguing that "any allusion to a state of war with Algeria must be carefully avoided" (Houillon 2005).

8. These groups included (1) leftist associations such as the Collectif Les Mots sont Importants; (2) feminist groups: Les MotivEes, Ni Putes ni Soumises, Les Blédardes, ToutEsEgaux, Collectif féministe, Droit des femmes musulmanes de France; (3) minority and immigrant rights associations: Mouvement autonome de l'immigration du Nord, Collectif des Musulmans de France, Oumma.com, Groupe de Recherches Activistes sur l'Afrique, Fédération des Étudiants et Travailleurs Africains de France, Festival Permanent contre les lois racistes (Strasbourg), DiverCité (Lyon), and the Association des Travailleurs Maghrébins de France; (4) internationalist and anti-imperialist associations: Campagne civile internationale pour la protection du peuple palestinien (CCIPPP), Coordination des comités Palestine, Centre d'études et d'initiatives de solidarité internationale (CEDETIM). Many leftist or alter-mondialist militant groups, however, criticized Indigènes, including the Ligue communiste révolutionnaire (LCR), the Green party, ATTAC (Association pour la taxation des transactions pour l'aide aux citoyens), and various feminist groups and militants. See for instance Clémentine Autain (candidate for the French Communist Party in the municipal elections, Paris, 2001), "Pourquoi j'ai retiré ma signature," *Le Monde,* March 17, 2005.

9. Text originally published on the website ToutEsEgaux, www.toutesegaux.free. fr, under the title *Appel pour les Assises de l'anticolonialisme postcolonial* [Call for the Postcolonial Meeting against Colonialism]. The text was soon renamed "Appel des Indigènes de la République: 'Nous sommes les Indigènes de la République!'" Refined

by numerous texts and interviews posted on the Indigènes' website, www.indigenes-republique.org, the doctrine underlined in the *Appel* has not changed significantly since 2005.

10. French troops and settlers retaliated against nationalist demonstrations in Sétif and Guelma by organizing mass massacres of Algerian civilians (Rey-Goldzeiguer 2001).

11. Estimate from Indigènes. On February 16, 2005, the Indigènes gathered for the first Conference on Postcolonial Anti-Colonialism [*Assises de l'anti-colonialisme post-colonial*] at the Bourse du Travail, but were not authorized to use the place for their meeting.

12. Issue 6 of *L'indigène* appeared early April 2007. In the winter and spring of 2006, the Indigènes suffered several setbacks. In February, a group of early supporters seceded from the *Mouvement des Indigènes de la République,* and founded a distinctive initiative under the name Indigènes de la République. They complained that the movement's leadership engaged in "sectarianism," anti-democratic decision making, and dependence on political party politics. The dissident group seems to survive only as a discussion forum. See their website at www.indigenes.org. By May 8, 2006, attendance at the Indigènes Parisian demonstration declined precipitously, by their own estimates, to only four thousand.

13. The collapse of historical time, social experience, and geographic stasis ("France has been a colonial state . . . France remains a colonial state!") provides the Indigènes with a crucial rhetorical weapon, yet the movement is often tempered by cautionary statements claiming that discriminatory policies cannot be explained away by colonial continuities.

14. "Dieudonné et le nouvel anti-sémitisme," *Le Monde,* February 22, 2005. "Entretien avec Michel Tubiana," *Le Monde,* February 22, 2005. Indigènes sent a protest letter to *Le Monde* on February 25, 2005, entitled "Droit de réponse adressé au Monde par des signataires de l'appel 'Nous sommes les indigènes de la République,'" and available online at www.indigenes-republique.org/article.php3?id_article=32.

15. "Les 'indigènes' s'en prennent à la 'France coloniale,'" *Le Figaro,* February 25, 2005.

16. "Les damnés de la République," editorial by Jean Daniel, *Le Nouvel Observateur,* March 9, 2005. *Poujadisme* refers in France to movements characterized by narrow ideas and corporatist projects.

17. Evariste, "La lepénisation des esprits des Indigènes de la République," *Respublica, journal de la gauche républicaine,* February 15, 2007, www.gauche republicaine.org.

18. "Et maintenant les nouveaux racistes!" François Darras (pseud. for Jean-François Kahn), *Marianne,* December 21, 2005. See also dossier in journal *Politis* 847, April 14, 2005.

19. The few researchers who took the time to investigate the politics advocated by the Indigènes articulated significant discomfort with the movement's style and ideas. A long and detailed article published in the scholarly journal *Hérodote,* for instance, deplored the Indigènes' "slightly caricatural radicalism," and the fact that their manifesto's success was based on "a communitarian or ethnic dimension" (Robine 2006). I was aware of academic reactions through regular email exchanges and discussions with fellow historians at universities in Paris, Lyon, and Aix-en-Provence in the months preceding and following the 2005 crises. Catherine Coquery-Vidrovitch played a vital role in mediating these exchanges.

20. The institutional academic prestige of the CRAN membership is significantly

greater than that of the Indigènes, who have a more social activist orientation. While the former come from, and teach in, prestigious universities (École Normale Supérieure and École des Hautes Études en Sciences Sociales—EHESS), the latter work in second-tier institutions.

21. "*Nous voulons lever une armée pour la France et non contre la France.*" Louis-Georges Tin and Patrick Lozès, interview in "Les associations noires se fédèrent," *Le Monde,* November 29, 2005. "*La couleur politique de cette nouvelle fédération? Aux couleurs de la France répond Patrick Lozès [. . .] Nous sommes du côté de l'universel [. . .]."* Communiqué Agence France Presse, November 27, 2005. "*Nous voulons être un groupe de pression au sens classique, effectuer un travail républicain.*" Louis-George Tin, "Si on est conscient de son passé, on devient sujet de son avenir," interview in *Libération,* November 27, 2005.

22. See TV star Pascal Sevran's infamous comments on African fertility, in his 2007 book *Le privilège des jonquilles* (Sevran 2007: 214).

23. A striking example of this ideological construct is apparent in the title of Patrick Weil's seminal monograph on citizenship and immigration, *France and Her Aliens* (*La France et ses étrangers*) (1991).

24. As Frederick Cooper suggests in his contribution to this volume, the French colonies in the 1940s and 1950s were the only places where such a project existed.

25. I am following the insightful argument of Francine Hirsch's study of the Soviet colonizing and nationalizing of the Russian empire. Striking parallels indeed can be found between Soviet social primordialism and today's French social scientists' assumptions on how social units work in modern nations (Hirsch 2005).

26. See how proponents of the law against the wearing of religious symbols trust that only government action can counter what they see as dysfunctional religious pressure, and can protect victims of patriarchal diktats (for instance the wearing of headscarves being imposed upon young women by superstitious families).

27. For further information, see www.etudescoloniales.canalblog.com.

28. The group includes anthropologist Jean-Loup Amselle, historians Catherine Coquery-Vidrovitch and Patrick Weil, and sociologists Michel Wieviorka and Dominique Schnapper.

29. The double-bind is encapsulated in the recent slogan adopted by the Indigènes in April 2007, "*Va t'faire intégrer!*" (Go integrate yourself). The pun turns on the parallelism with the popular insult "*Va te faire foutre*" (literally: Go fuck yourself).

30. Many of these writers have contributed to the journal *Hommes et Migrations.* Contributors to the edited volumes by Guénif-Souilamas (2006) and Mucchielli and Le Goaziou (2006) give an accurate, if not exhaustive, idea of scholars close to the Indigènes, while the contributors to Blanchard, Bancel, and Lemaire 2005 (*La fracture coloniale*) reflect some of the core supporters of ACHAC.

31. As Emmanuelle Saada writes, "Interrogations on the capacity of history to produce a discourse of truth have recently developed. If these critiques are useful in the scientific debate, they also open the way to militant positions: if history is just a narrative among others, why not push all memories forward? As many of my colleagues have argued, I think we should defend the autonomy of history, which is a profession regulated by scientific and ethical rules: if history does not produce any absolute truth, it possesses objectifying procedures (*objectivation*) against the distortions of memory: the critique of sources, the cross-reading of documents" (Saada 2006a).

32. The lament over Frenchwo/men of color's naiveté and greed, in addition to legitimizing the accusers as disinterested experts, is an interesting postcolonial avatar of the old elitist view according to which "the dispossessed cannot but be possessed by the desire to possess" (Bourdieu 1994).

33. In Julliard and Winock's *Dictionnaire des intellectuels français* (2002) they devote only limited entries to Franz Fanon, Aimé Césaire, and Léopold Sédar Senghor, and make no mention of contemporary francophone authors such as Patrick Chamoiseau, Edouard Glissant, Valentin Mudimbe, Abdelmalek Sayad, Mohamed Arkoun, and Abdelkebir Khatibi. For contrast, see Murray 2004.

34. See Jean-François Bayart's recent critique of postcolonial studies as socially dangerous, intellectually worthless, and heuristically indigent. Contribution to the international conference organized by the Centre d'études et de recherches internationales (CERI), Paris, May 4–5, 2006, "Que faire des Postcolonial Studies?" and his chapter in Smouts 2007.

35. In French, *ego-histoire.* The term was coined by Nora (1987), in a volume featuring the memories of Maurice Agulhon, Pierre Chaunu, Georges Duby, Raoul Girardet, Jacques Le Goff, Michelle Perrot, and René Rémond. "Essay d'ego-histoire" serves today as a nickname for the biographical essay (official name: *synthèse*) required for historians submitting their candidacy for full professorship as part as the *habilitation* process, which also includes a *dossier de travaux* (equivalent to a second doctoral dissertation).

36. See the text of article 4 as reproduced in note 5.

37. Petition on the liberty of history, led by Pierre Nora, published in *Le Monde,* December 14, 2005. Petition against the Law of February 23, 2005 organized by the Comité de vigilance face aux usages publics de l'histoire (CVUH), led by Gérard Noiriel. See the website www.cvuh.free.fr.

38. In addition to the 1990 law against the negation of Shoah, and the 2000 law recognizing the genocide of Armenians, a 2001 law has claimed slavery to be a crime against humanity.

39. Nora's *Lieux de mémoire* is a case in point. See also the many "intellectual histories" of France, narrowly focused on elite circles, where French historians continue to envision secular sites of power as undisturbed grounds for higher intellectual thinking. A recent historical dictionary on French intellectuals, for instance, confines its investigation to privileged, elite Parisian institutions, from Bibliothèque Ste-Geneviève to the École normale supérieure (Julliard and Winock 2002).

40. The museum stands next to the park of Porte Dorée in Paris. The original building was erected during the 1931 Colonial Exposition, then transformed into the Museum of the Colonies. In 1965, André Malraux renamed it Musée des Arts Africains et Océaniens.

41. This assertion is based on a conversation with Daniel Lefeuvre on May 1, 2006, in Aix-en-Provence, where we discussed his participation in two projects, the Mémorial national de la France outre-mer in Marseilles and the Musée d'histoire de la France en Algérie in Montpellier. For critiques of these endeavors, see "Le Mémorial national de la France outre-mer: Un outil idéologique?" posted on www.indigenes-republique.org.

42. International conference on "Histoire et immigration: la question coloniale," Bibliothèque nationale de France, September 28–30, 2006.

43. Please refer to the collective resignation of eight historians from the scientific committee from the Cité nationale pour l'histoire de l'immigration on May 25, 2007, archived at www.ldh-toulon.net/spip.php?article2047.

CHAPTER SEVEN

Transient Citizens: The Othering and Indigenization of *Blacks* and *Beurs* within the French Republic

Didier Gondola

> Brazza[ville], Paris, des deux côtés, je suis bloqué
> Là-bas, ici, toujours le même qui va te croquer
> Le cul entre deux chaises, l'exil presse mon pas
> Vers quelle terre vont se diriger nos pas?
>
> —BISSO NA BISSO

Following the 2005 riots that wreaked havoc in several French *ban-lieues,* some *Black* and *Beur* civic organizations, including Indigènes de la République, have attributed the anger that fueled the riots to the persistence of colonial relations between France and its population of African descent, the so-called *Français issus de l'immigration* (first- and second-generation French) as opposed to *Français de souche* ("native" French). *Blacks* and *Beurs,* they contend, have earned French citizenship bereft of its psychological entitlement. Such an explanation was quickly dismissed by most French pundits and scholars as not only flawed but also dangerous, a cipher likely to drive a wedge into French society. Instead, these pundits have turned the table on the rioters by putting forth arguments that range from the breakdown of African families living in France, to polygamy, rap music, and more generally their unwillingness or perhaps inability to assimilate as more accurate explanations for their marginalization.

To put colonization on trial, as the Indigènes have attempted to do, is purely anachronistic according to French historian Michel Winock. Winock argues that in the 1950s, when Frantz Fanon wrote *The Wretched of the Earth* and Aimé Césaire *Discourse on Colonialism,* such discourse was necessary and useful to fight for Africa's emancipation.[1] Another French historian of colonization, Pascal Blanchard, asks quite rhetorically: "How could there be colonies in the metropolitan territory?" His off-the-cuff answer is unequivocal: "nonsensical."[2]

Although the main thrust of this paper deals with the pervasiveness of colonial paradigms in the way French society deals with its population of African descent, it is critical to disclaim the argument that confinement in the colonies is equivalent to incarceration in the *banlieues.* What I am arguing is that vestiges of old colonial ideas in French collective memory as well as new patterns of postcolonial exploitation in France's relations with African countries have contributed to the indigenization of *Beurs* and *Blacks* and their confinement in the French *banlieue.* Thus, the marginalization of Africans within French society is not merely a question of their epidermalization through blackness but the denigration of Africa and blackness in the French mediascape, in popular iconographies as well as in semantic representations.

Colonial Cronos

The myth of the Cannibal god that traverses African narratives of the colonial encounter and its postcolonial legacies was used by one of the very first African novelists, Mongo Beti, to characterize the colonial city and the colonial situation in general. To maximize colonial profit, the European presence in Africa required extensive economic, administrative, and military networks in which cities served as nodal points that facilitated the extraction of resources through labor and taxation. The colonial city, the epitome and locus of European promethean modernity, looms large in European as well as in African narratives of the colonial moment. European colonial propagandists relayed by the first European anthropologists and sociologists romanticized the colonial city and portrayed it as a tool of colonization, the showcase of European modernity, an ethnic melting pot and a cultural interface where Africans could morph from savages into civilized subjects.

Early European accounts even posited the colonial city as a foreign innovation, a one-dimensional construction owing little if any to African agency. As French geographer Jean Dresch put it, "*la ville africaine, création des blancs, se peuple de noirs*" (quoted in Gondola 1997: 35); an assumption echoed by George Hamdam, writing in the early 1960s: "Colonial capitals are entirely the *creation* of the new masters of the continent. An absolutely *novel* introduction in an entirely *virgin* land" (quoted in Gondola 1997: 36). Since African workers were viewed as strangers to the city, urban planning and policies tended to confine them and their families in spaces that lacked all urban amenities. In French Equatorial Africa, for example, well into the 1950s quarters where Africans lived within the perimeter of the colonial city were designated by the term *villages africains,* as opposed to *ville européenne* (European town), which grouped government offices, private-owned businesses, and European residential areas. Africans were kept at bay through an arsenal of prophylactic boundaries that included, among others, strict enforcement of the curfew and the presence of buffer zones between the European settlements and the African townships.

African accounts of the colonial city tended to lionize the obvious —cars, tall buildings, and street lights—and to lament the oppressive apparatus designed to regiment workers' lives and foster a labor discipline that became the linchpin of colonial capitalism. Mongo Beti's *Ville cruelle* (Cruel City), which he wrote in 1953 at age twenty-two, brings colonial oppression to the fore in its portrayal of the fictional city of Tanga as a colonial Cronos, a place of despair and the dissolution of ingrained social values and networks, a place where African migrants wrestled with the tentacles of colonial capitalism, whose ubiquity could be felt in all areas of African urban life. Lured by the promise of a new dispensation harnessed by the beacon of European modernity, young African migrants found themselves stranded between an illusive modernity and their "traditional" milieu. Saddled by compulsory taxation, men and women could only eke out a living by learning to dodge colonial prescriptions and engage in informal activities unless they accepted being co-opted within the colonial economic apparatus.

By invoking the colonial Cronos to define their exclusion and marginalization in the French *banlieues,* the Indigènes do not equate the squalor of the slums of Algiers or Dakar with the glooming atmosphere of the *cités* (ghettos) in Saint-Denis or Clichy-sous-Bois. What this parallel is intended to accomplish, however, is to historicize the oppression of blacks and Arabs and reopen the debate over colonization at a time when, as Elizabeth Ezra notes, "it is the atrocities of its colonial past that France represses, retaining only sanitized memories of the pomp and circumstance, the valor and the glory of France's *mission civilisatrice*" (Ezra 2000: xii).

Drawing from this highly contentious debate, this paper argues that the continuum between the French colonial past and her neocolonial meddling in her former African colonies, the continual demotion of blackness in the French mediascape, the pervasiveness of Afropessimistic discourses and policies, have all connived to exclude *Blacks* and *Beurs* from the benefits French citizens are entitled to.

A New France?

In the history of France, the period between the loss of Saint-Domingue (1803) and the defeat of Sedan (1870) witnessed the emergence of colonial discourses that allowed France to disavow her continual decline in Europe and in the New World. They presided over the creation of an overseas colonial archipelago, especially in Africa, that supplied the much-needed economic resources and imperial presence of which the independence of Haiti had deprived France. Examining these discourses in light of exacerbating racial tensions in France today can be particularly telling.

What seemed to have activated France's imperial drive, its indispensable impetus, was the myth that only colonial expansion could decisively set in motion ideas and interests that ultimately would fashion a new republican identity, what many then dubbed "a New France." While the nationalistic ideas and the desire to recapture France's standing among European nations that permeated the new brand of French imperialism were reaffirmed by the conquest of Algeria in 1830, relations between *métropole* and empire were set in place by the *mission civilisatrice;* it was the official ideology that France's mastery of overseas territory should serve to redeem "inferior peoples" and bestow upon them civic and moral virtues enshrined by the French Revolution. This idea, according to Conklin, that inferior races should be inculcated with "new needs and wants," through "the spread of French institutions and values deemed to be universally valid," gained currency with the conquest of Algeria (Conklin 1997: 18).

By the 1860s, the colonial lobby in France consisted of politicians, publicists, bankers, and industrialists who all adhered to the idea that the renewal of the *métropole* depended on imperial expansion, that a "New France" was in the making, and that this rebirth depended on the success of the *mission civilisatrice.* No one explained it better than Monsignor Lavigerie. In 1867, Lavigerie took on the daunting task of reorganizing the archdiocese of Algiers. In his farewell address to his constituency of Nancy, he declared, "I am leaving you so that I may contribute to this grand mission of Christian civilization which endeavors to bring forth a New France from the chaos and darkness of antiquated barbarism" (Biarnès 1987: 121).

More than any other territory of the French imperial domain, Africa loomed conspicuously in those propagandist narratives as the place of France's rejuvenation. It was precisely in these terms that the laissez-faire economist Leroy-Beaulieu proclaimed in 1874 that "France's future lies to a greater extent in Africa." A few years earlier, historian and political journalist Lucien Prévost-Paradol echoed an opinion shared by many in France that the conquest of Africa remained the only antidote against France's decline. In his popular compendium, *La France nouvelle,* published the same year he was inducted into the prestigious *Académie Française,* he wrote, "Africa should not be for us a trading post like India, or a training ground for our army, even less a testing ground for our philanthropists ; it is French soil and must be populated, possessed, and cultivated as soon as possible by the French if we want her in the future to weigh on our side in the arrangement of human affairs" (Biarnès 1987: 122).

Not only did Africa clearly emerge as a laboratory (*laboratoire*) that enabled the French to test out the universality of their revolutionary concepts, but it also buoyed France's languid economy and ultimately became her new frontier, a place where she could refashion herself. One can make the argument that *La plus grande France* (Greater France), as the French empire came to be known,[3] did inflate French patriotic sentiment until the demise of the Third Republic. "Greater France" also tended to supersede the notion that nationalism should be confined to metropolitan France alone and to bridle regionalist loyalties within France herself as French colonists of all walks of life responded to the colonial call of duty and poured from all areas of metropolitan France to the remote corners of empire. It is in that vein that Maréchal Hubert Lyautey, the main architect of the 1931 Colonial Exposition, lionized "colonial duty" as a "form of civic and patriotic duty." In his mind, "To love France [was] to love Greater France, that which is not closed in by borders but which shines its light into all parts of the world." One then could argue that since the Napoleonic wars of the early nineteenth century, no other political development had accomplished more for the idea of French nationhood than twentieth-century French imperial expansion and the rise of Greater France.

The Iconization of Blackness

There is, however, a seemingly glaring paradox in the construction of Greater France, a paradox that lies at the heart of France's reluctance to integrate her population of African descent as she has done for immigrants coming from Italy, Poland, Portugal, and Armenia. Hoisted as the cornerstone of "New France" and given a prominent place within Greater France, Africa became so heralded in the French imagination that François Mitterrand could quip that "[t]wenty-first century France will be African or will not be" (Mitterrand 1957: 237). At the same time, this vision of Greater France promoted archetypal ideas about Africans and the need for their redemption, namely their acceptance to be under the benevolent tutelage of French masters. As Sue Peabody perceptively observed, the image of blacks as dangerous creatures has a long pedigree in French history. Already in the eighteenth century, they were blamed for disrupting the public order, while fear of their sexuality, often perceived as a threat to French racial purity because it could result in an increasing population of *sang mêlé* (mixed blood), was the impetus for a series of racial immigration legislation that culminated with the *Police des Noirs* in 1777.[4] Although that image contrasted sharply "with the depiction of [black] slaves as victims who could be saved by the French champions of liberty" (Peabody 1996: 74), it remained entrenched in stereotypical representations of blacks and blackness in France. Thus, Mitterrand, like many of his contemporaries, could hardly conceal this ambivalent vision of a continent that he also pronounced as the "*cul-de-sac du monde*" (Mitterrand 1957: 169).

European modernity as a master narrative owes much to what Emmanuel Chukwudi Eze describes as "the explicit metaphysical negation and theoretical exclusion of Africa and Africans, archetypally frozen as 'savage' and 'primitive'" (Eze 1997: 13). This, however, is the darkest face of Janus, for as Fanon and Césaire have argued, it was not just the idea of European modernity that emerged from the encounter between Europe and Africa. To a larger extent, Europe's industrialization should also be attributed to Africa's incorporation into the rising world economic system of the sixteenth century, and it is indeed from that economic standpoint that Africa figures in French discourse as a fulcrum, an indispensable constituent of France's grandeur. Only when Africa is constructed as the recipient of French republican largesse and a land in need of culture do we encounter in French public discourse disparaging clichés that continue, by and large, to stigmatize Africans in France.

Of all the characteristics Africans possessed, their skin color seems to have elicited the most enduring tropes. Take, for example, the term *nègre*, which found its way from Iberia to France in the early sixteenth century. Immediately following its use to denote the color (black) and the status (slave) assigned to Africans (Peabody 1996: 61), this term was readily applied to the devil, known then as *Le Grand Nègre* (Hoffmann 1973: 17, 20). By then, it was firmly established in sacred as well as profane iconography that Satan could be only black, as its widespread portrayal in European medieval iconographies shows. Black, the color of damnation, became a convenient signifier that summoned evil tropes in a host of tangible as well as intangible signifieds. "Black like the walls of a jail cell, black like the soul of the accursed" consigned Castellan in 1842 (Ruscio 2002: 49). Black is associated with death, illness, mourning and despair. To describe sadness, for example, French poet Gérard de Nerval couched "the black sun of melancholy" (*le soleil noir de la mélancolie*). With the advent of the new industrial society in the West, there was no shortage of expressions that used black as (dis)qualifier, a litany that runs the gamut from "black market" to "black hole."

Whereas many derogatory expressions using "black" are no longer socially acceptable in many English-speaking countries, not only do they have a long history in the French language but their quotidian use is vindicated by the continual minorization of Africa and blackness in France. Two recent examples illustrate this. On December 22, 2001, the French daily *Le Monde* published a lead story remembering Léopold Sédar Senghor, who had passed away the day before at age ninety-five.

As fate would have it, Senghor's death had coincided with the launching of the euro, and *Le Monde*'s staff gleefully titled their eulogy "Léopold Sédar Senghor: l'Euronègre" without much ado ensuing. To add insult to injury, not a single high-profile French political official bothered to attend Senghor's national funeral in Dakar, prompting several commentators to lament that "*La France se moque désormais de l'Afrique*" (France no longer cares for Africa). Writer Erik Orsenna, a member of the Académie Française, struck a chord by expressing his shame that Senghor, a former African head of state, minister in de Gaulle's cabinet, member of the Académie Française since 1983, "*un ami indéfectible de la France en ce qu'elle a d'universel: sa langue, celle de la liberté*," and indefatigable apologist for *francophonie,* would be inflicted such an affront.[5]

The second example comes from the recent decision by Christiane Taubira (a French deputy from French Guyana) and Dieudonné Mbala Mbala, a French-Cameroonian stand-up comedian, and the poster boy for the African renaissance movement in France, to run for president in the 2007 elections. Their move was (dis)qualified by *Le Monde* as "*la tentation noire*" despite the fact that one recurring demand to come from young *Beurs* and *Blacks,* a demand that cannot be simply swept under the rug, has to do with their representation, or lack thereof, in the political arena and the mediascape.

No one has expressed France's negrophobia in a sharper vein than Johnny Hallyday, the French Elvis, a singer of Belgian extraction who has enjoyed in France a quasi-mythical status in spite of his foibles and wayward private life. His rendition of blackness in "*Noir c'est noir, il n'y a plus d'espoir*" ("Black is black, there is no more hope"), a song that did much to endear him to the French public, but also irretrievably fixed blackness in French popular culture as an undesirable quality, a forlorn condition.[6]

The Mysterious Rhizome

The French are known for one proverbial expression that has few equivalents in other languages: "*plus ça change, plus ça reste le même*" (The more things change, the more they stay the same). Rooted in the simplistic paradigm that France's international interests can be promoted only at the expense of Africa, this modus operandi has dictated France's postcolonial policies toward her former African colonies.

France is unique in the sense that of all the former European colonial nations, she is the only one that never really left the continent but continued to wield much influence through several political, economic, and cultural mechanisms that range from monetary policies, to military agreements, to *francophonie;*[7] in a word, a web of covert arrangements for which François-Xavier Verschave (1998) has coined the expression *Françafrique.*[8]

A question commonly asked by foreign commentators about *Françafrique* was bluntly formulated by Israeli journalist Tamar Golan, correspondent in Paris for the daily newspaper *Ma'ariv:* "How can France do everything that it does in Africa and get away with it?" (Golan 1981). To be sure, the criminalization of African governments has elicited much attention, from René Dumont's *L'Afrique noire est mal partie,* published in 1966,[9] to Jean-François Bayart's *La criminalisation de l'État en Afrique.*[10] However, French Africanists have shied away from exposing their own government's deleterious dealings in Africa, and, as a result, much of the literature devoted to this issue come from French independent journalists and activists.[11] There can be no doubt that French African policy remains a key element of Élysée's so-called *domaine réservé,*[12] a testimonial to the vital role Africa continues to play in French politics. However, since the 1960s it has been implemented solely in the interest of France and, more often than not, to the detriment of African nations (Martens 1983: 45).

The case of the Republic of Congo provides a unique window into French postcolonial interventionism on the threshold of the post–cold war era. In 1992, following a democratization process that culminated with the convening of a *Conférence Nationale Souveraine,* Congo started its topsy-turvy awakening from four decades of postcolonial dictatorship. President Sassou-Nguesso, who had been at the country's helm since staging a successful coup d'état in 1979, was defeated in the country's first democratic presidential elections by Pascal Lissouba. At stake was the control over Congo's vast oil deposits, which French company Elf had been exploiting since the late 1960s. By far the largest industrial company in France, Elf employed 85,500 people around the world in 1995. Most of its extractive activities and investments took place in Gabon, Congo, and Angola, three countries whose notorious overreliance on oil revenues has rendered their states both unstable and authoritarian. Elf had an operating budget of over $32 billion in 1995 and yielded annually an average of $1 billion in profits throughout the 1990s. These figures not only dwarf Congo's annual budget, around $300 million in 1995, but also provide a measure of the lopsided relations between transnational corporations and developing countries.

In Congo, Elf did not just act as a state within a state, as many multinational companies operate in developing countries, but more like a colonial power, buying off Congo's kleptocratic elite to ensure its loyalty. Elf also controlled both the state and the economy by mortgaging Congo's future oil revenues in exchange for oil-backed expensive loans. According to Global Witness, "Elf's system had two key elements. The first was that losses for the state were turned into private gains for the company, Elf officials, and the ruling elite of the country hosting its operations. The second was that the company created conditions of deliberate indebtedness though oil-backed lending, progressively securing its hold on the country's internal politics."[13]

In 2003, following a much publicized trial, known as "l'Affaire Elf," four of the main Elf executives, including former Elf chairman Loïk Le Floch-Prigent, were convicted on charges of siphoning off nearly half a billion dollars of the state-owned company to maintain a state-sanctioned corruption network that makes the Enron corruption scandal look like shoplifting in a convenience store. Through an intricate web of covert operatives, slush funds, and money-laundering schemes that spanned Europe, Africa, and Asia, Elf held Congo in its clutches in connivance with the country's elite.

After coming to power in 1992 Lissouba sought to tap into the opaque Elf network to strengthen his grip over an ethnically divided country where incipient democratic principles never supplanted antidemocratic habits inherited from the past. This was exacerbated by Elf's reluctance to relinquish its control over the country's economy. Matters came to a head in 1993 when Lissouba's request for an oil-backed loan to pay salary arrears of Congo's civil servants was turned down by Elf. He then decided to offset Elf's quasi-monopoly over Congo's offshore oil extraction by opening relations with U.S.-based oil company Occidental Petroleum (Oxy). The agreement called not only for immediate cash for oil, but also a durable partnership in which Oxy could potentially break Elf's monopoly in Congo. Although this agreement was later rescinded following intense pressure from Elf and the French government, Lissouba's "breach of loyalty" had sealed his fate, along with the future of Congo's newly gained democracy. During the remainder of his term in office, Elf would finance several covert operations to oust him until finally fanning the flames of an all-out civil war in 1997 by arming both Lissouba and French protégé Sassou Nguesso. On October 23, thanks to military logistics provided by Elf and the help of Angolan troops enlisted at the behest of Elf, Sassou Nguesso made his triumphant return into a ravaged city. More than three-quarters of Brazzaville's 900,000 residents fled the city, leaving all their possessions as spoils for looters and militias. Some sought refuge in the neighboring Democratic Republic of Congo, while others retreated into the forest.

There is an irony in Congo's four-month civil war. At no point did Elf stop pumping its 230,000 barrels of oil a day during a conflict that claimed the lives of more than fifteen thousand civilians according to the most conservative estimates,[14] destroyed the country's capital city, and drove thousands of residents from their homes. Elf's involvement in derailing Congo's democratization process as well as its active role in arming the belligerents prompted Multinational Monitor, a Washington-based watchdog organization, to include the French multinational in its "Ten Worst Corporations of 1997" list (Mokhiber and Weissman 1997). In France, a grassroots initiative known as "*Elf ne doit pas faire la loi en Afrique*" was led by two Green Party representatives, Noël Mamère and Marie-Hélène Aubert, and resulted in a parliamentary report denouncing Elf's unscrupulous practices in Africa.[15]

More importantly, France's predatory practices in Africa have created a double consciousness of marginalization among African youths living in the French *cités*.[16] Many feel confined between Scylla and Charybdis, between France's discriminatory arsenal meted out toward her citizens of African descent at home and her role as a "*pompier pyromane*"[17] in Africa. As in many other areas of the world, these disenchanted youths have expressed their double alienation through the discursive and corporeal strategies inherent to hip-hop culture, which in France has become a site of contestation and appropriation by *Black* and *Beur* youth (McCarren 2004). This double alienation contributes to the highly politicized hip-hop discourse that permeates youth culture in the *cités*. Take for example Bisso na Bisso, a group of rap musicians who hailed from Congo and grew up in Sarcelles, a destitute and segregated *banlieue* north of Paris. Bisso na Bisso, which in Lingala means "among us," took the French hip-hop scene by storm with their 1999 potpourri album *Racines* (Roots). The lyrics of some of the album's songs, especially *Après la guerre* (After the War) and *Le cul entre deux chaises* (The Ass between Two Chairs), leave no doubt about the impact that France's meddling in Africa has had on these youths, who feel torn as they witness the turmoil that ravages their parents' homeland. Ivorian artist Tiken Jah Fakoly is even more explicit in his critique of French involvement in the ongoing civil unrest in Côte d'Ivoire. His two albums, *Françafrique* (2002)[18] and *Coup de Gueule* (2004), overtly denounce the connivance between the French government and the African elite to maintain the status quo.

The Chickens Come Home to Roost

In Jean-François Richet's 1997 film *Ma 6-T va crack-er* (My "ghetto" is gonna crack), Arco, the main protagonist, and his coming-of-age buddies roam through their *cité* at night. Ironically named Beauval, the *cité* faces its twin, La Pierre Collinet, whose wide and tall towers shoot up eerily across the canal. The two *cités* sit on the outskirts of the old town of Meaux, famous for its twelfth-century gothic cathedral, the ecclesiastical see once occupied by French Bishop Jacques Bossuet, and Brie cheese. The three teenagers walk aimlessly until they reach a bus stop. As they sit inside the bus shelter, knowing well that it is too late to catch any bus, Arco bemoans their dereliction in a vein that strikes a responsive chord in his buddies:

> Seriously guys, what are we doing here?
> At a bus stop like three pieces of shit.
> Why the hell are we here?
> Nothing to do, nothing to say. Isn't that pathetic?
> Too many problems.
> We know where we want to go, but we'll never make it.

One of Arco's friends stands still besides him, his eyes looking down reflexively at the pavement as if the import of Arco's words compelled a deeper, well-thought reaction. He then replies:

> You know where to go? I don't know where I am going.
> They do what they want with us.
> We're just objects for this two-bit society.
> Three-penny society.
> You're a pawn. They do what they want with you.

As they carry on their conversation, a police car emerges from the dark, steers in front of them and comes slowly to a full stop. Arco warns his friends to keep a low profile: "What do they want?" he mutters with contempt and rage as if the police had intruded in his vital space to eavesdrop on his private conversation, to remind him of his worthlessness and nothingness. Then, just as slowly as it had appeared, the car moves away vanishing into the night.

Arco and his buddies, as many young people that live in the *cités* of the French *banlieues,* experience this ambiguous feeling of being trapped in one place and out of place at the same time, hoping to catch an elusive train called France; a train that never stops in the *cités,* a train where all the seats have been reserved for people that do not look like them; people who do not name their children Mamadou or Yasmina; who often believe that those who practice Ramadan and coax their daughters to wear the *hijab* (veil) have no place in France; people whose forebears were never colonized by the *République* or parked in human zoos in the City of Light; people who will never know how it feels to be labeled an "*immigré né en France*" (French-born immigrant). As Pierre Tévanian argues, the *immigré* has become a code phrase for race in political and popular parlance (Tévanian 2001: 21). According to this schema, there is little doubt that, let's say, a German or a white American who settles in France would ever suffer the indignity of being labeled an *immigré.* However, Arco and his friends, although they were born in France and feel alienated from Africa, have inherited the stigma of transience from their forebears in a process by which the label *immigré* no longer refers to a fluid social category but confines Africans to an indelible racial status.

If we grant that culture and race both remain the litmus test that would-be French citizens have to pass in order to be embraced by the *République,* we must nevertheless acknowledge that colonial vestiges as well as neocolonial policies, or what Maya Angelou terms "mutual history" and the guilt that it entails (see Gondola 2003), function as a palimpsest that creates social and psychological obstacles to the integration of *Beurs* and *Blacks.* France is hardly unique in that regard. Examining the interaction between race and class in postwar England, Paul Gilroy attributes anti-black racism to the "cultural legacy of empire," which "continues to saturate the consciousness of all Britons regardless of age, gender, income or circumstances" (Gilroy 1987: 27). Similarly, Allison Blakely's work on racial prejudice in the Netherlands proposes that associations in folklore, arts, literature, and religion between blackness and evil and between blacks and slavery have retained a lasting attraction that continues to shape popular attitudes toward blacks (Blakely 1993: 285). Once intended to act as hegemonic devices instrumental in establishing cultural boundaries and presiding over the othering of non-whites, stereotypical representations of blacks have migrated to a wide range of media and are now embedded within a myriad of popular cultures. These representations endure and remain potent in virtually all Western societies precisely because, as noted by Jan Nederveen Pieterse, they actively participate in the West's cultural hegemony and in the triumph of white supremacy (Nederveen Pieterse 1992: 15). They may be refashioned and readapted to suit a particular *zeitgeist,* but they are likely to persist as long as the process of Western hegemony continues to shape our global culture and whiteness continues to define access to power and privilege.

To return to the French context: racial tensions in this emerging multiethnic society should be singled out as they also stem from the refusal to accept the demographic changes that have taken place in France within the last forty years. While the proportion of immigrants in France has remained steady since the 1930s (around 7 percent of the total French population) its origins have witnessed several changes that advance in tandem. First, the increase in the influx of African immigrants has been such that for the first time since the 1990 census, African immigrants in France outnumbered their European immigrant counterparts 45.4 percent to 40.7 percent. Second, the overwhelming number of African immigrant youth,[19] which stands in stark contrast to the attritional birth deficit among most European groups, has become a defining feature of French demographics. This might explain their relative visibility as opposed to the invisibility that is associated with whiteness (Garner 2006: 259). When taken into account, these two phenomena point to new demographic patterns that have irreversibly altered France's ethnic makeup.

Greater Paris, especially, is no longer this racial monolith that has integrated scores of European working-class migrants who may have faced popular xenophobia at one time or another but who nonetheless managed to gain moral membership in the *République,* precisely because their integration meant more than just social equality. They have received by virtue of their whiteness not just the obvious economic and social privileges that come with whiteness but also what W. E. B. Du Bois aptly termed the "public and psychological wages of whiteness."

In fact, whiteness plays no part in the ways in which academics in France wrestle with notions that could gain clarity only when paired with this critical issue. Most of the recent works by noted French academics on slavery (Benot 2005), colonization (Blanchard, Bancel, and Lemaire 2005; Ferro 2003), immigration (Noiriel 1988; Schor 1996), and citizenship (Weil 2002) make no explicit engagement with the concept of whiteness. In none of these works are blackness and whiteness seen as correlated and mutually constitutive even though, as I have argued elsewhere, whiteness and Frenchness in twentieth-century France have been conflated as an exclusionary social category that enabled scores of European migrants to be assimilated at the expense of immigrants and French citizens of African descent (Gondola 2003: 212). Thus, this glaring omission mirrors the invisibility of whiteness in the French social landscape and, by contrast, magnifies the visibility of blackness and Arabness as inescapable conditions that account for the exclusion of *Blacks* and *Beurs*.[20]

This, of course, is not lost upon disenfranchised *Black* and *Beur* youths, who often attribute their exclusion to the ubiquity of racial categorizations in public discourse and media reports. During a group interview that I conducted with journalist Fatimata Wane in *cité* Pont-de-Créteil at Saint-Maur-des-Fossés,[21] a *banlieue* located on the eastern outskirts of Paris, young Djamel opined, "when a 'Rebeu' [*Beur*] or a 'Renoi' [*Noir* or *Black*] makes a mistake they [the French media] report about it but when he [the white French person] makes it they don't or, if they do, they say he is [merely] French." This rings particularly true for athletes, whose performances are scrutinized so much so that they have become a yardstick that measures their Frenchness. Tennis player Yannick Noah stands as a case in point. Born to a white French mother and a Cameroonian father, Yannick Noah could hardly escape the Janus-faced racial identity that his performances on the court seemed to have elicited from the media and the public. Pilloried as "*le Camerounais Noah a perdu*" after each one of his defeats on the court and lauded as "*le Français Yannick Noah a gagné*," following some his memorable victories, including his epic triumph over Swedish clay specialist Mats Wilander in the final of the 1983 French Tennis Open, Noah chaffed under this pendulum-like racial labeling. His exile to the United States at the peak of his game came as a blow to some in France who were wont to lionize him as a symbol of an incipient French multiculturalism. It was, however, as iconic victim of French versatile negrophilia that Noah took refuge in America's most cosmopolitan metropolis, New York City, to find solace from the burden of blackness and search for the ordinariness of being black. Ironically, Noah's American-born son Joakim, who led the Florida Gators to their first two consecutive NCAA basketball Championships in 2006 and 2007, faces no such racial prejudice from the American media and public, nor has his American citizenship been questioned (or vindicated) as a result of his performance on the basketball court.

Unlike high-profile athletes of Noah or Zidane's caliber, young *Blacks* and *Beurs* have little opportunity to have their Frenchness validated through sporting prowess.[22] Caught in the toil of ordinariness, many are marginalized for no other reason than that in France people of African descent cannot hope to enjoy full citizenship status unless their inescapable visibility is viewed in a positive light. While the average white French citizen is granted economic privilege by virtue of his or her whiteness and regardless of origin, place of residence, profession, and social status, ordinary *Blacks* and *Beurs* find themselves disqualified in spite of their French citizenship.[23] One of Djamel's buddies, Mohamed, puts it in a way that illuminates the intersection of race, class, and citizenship: "If you're successful as a soccer player or a stand-up comedian, you're integrated in their eyes. But if *we* want to integrate, we can't. In fact, it works in reverse. *They* integrate us." The same sentiment reverberates in their friend Raïm's blunt remark: "If somebody works for the city as a garbage man, he's not integrated. He is a foreigner. For them [the French], to be integrated is to have a good job and make a good living." *Blacks* and *Beurs* thus are put in a quandary that impedes both their integration and their social mobility in a society that sets higher expectations for them but refuses to level the playing field.[24] Tossed to and fro, between the African "cannibal state" (Mbembe 1993: 86) and the reincarnated colonial Cronos, they end up in the crease of cultures and are trapped in the interstitial recesses of the *République*.

Conclusion

Recent political rhetoric on immigration gives some sense of the slant and tropes that no doubt have shaped and incited French public opinion against the integration of *Blacks* and *Beurs*. Socialist prime minister Michel Rocard set the tone on March 19, 1990, declaring that France could no longer afford to "take in all the wretched of the world." On June 19, 1991, Jacques Chirac, then prime minister, launched his infamous tirade that came to be encapsulated in collective memory in two metaphors: "overdose" and "*les odeurs.*" Citing the commonest immigration data that show no foreign population increase in France since World War II, Chirac went on to denounce the growing number of "*musulmans*" and "*Noirs*" who, he claimed, pose far more problems than "Spanish, Polish or Portuguese foreign workers." There is an "overdose," he berated, especially when French hardworking families have to endure the smell ("*les odeurs*") that emanates from crowded apartments occupied by polygamist immigrant families. His words were later echoed by former President Valéry Giscard d'Estaing who sanctimoniously lectured on immigration issues and warned the public that France no longer dealt with "immigration" but with "invasion." Finally, interior minister Nicolas Sarkozy took this discursive assault to its most dangerous watermark when, in October 2005, he railed against some nondescript *banlieue* residents, branding them as "scum," and vowed to clean up the *cités* with Kärcher, the same jet hose used to remove graffiti and bird droppings from walls. Such incendiary language, according to columnist Doug Ireland, is "as close as one can get to hollering ethnic cleansing without actually saying so."[25] Sarkozy later declared, unapologetically:

> On en a plus qu'assez d'avoir en permanence le sentiment de s'excuser d'être français. On ne peut pas changer ses lois, ses coutumes parce qu'elles ne plaisent pas à une infime minorité. Si certains n'aiment pas la France, qu'ils ne se gênent pas pour la quitter. (April 23, 2006)

> (We're fed up with feeling like we need to apologize for being French. We cannot change our laws and customs because a tiny minority doesn't like them. If certain people don't like France, they should feel free to take their leave.)

Indeed, "La France, tu l'aimes ou tu la quittes" (France, you either love her or leave her), a motto long confined to right-wing extremists, now finds acceptance in mainstream political current and brings to the fore France's universal, indivisible, and secular dogma. The republican ideal of equality, the abstraction that posits the *République* as a great secular equalizer that dissolves all ethnic, racial, and cultural minorities, flies in the face of century-old racial discrimination both in the (post) colonies and in the *métropole*. Although, the nonexistence of racial and cultural distinctions, in demographic census for instance, has long been touted as one of the most salient features of French exceptionalism, *Blacks* and *Beurs* continue to be primarily defined by race, ethnicity, and culture in baffling anecdotal ways. Nowhere was this more clearly apparent than during the riots of October–November 2005 and the blame game that attempted to explain them afterward. Explanations used tropes that ranged from rap music to Islam to polygamy[26] but could hardly conceal damaging racial subtexts, thus suggesting the idea that *Beurs*' and *Blacks*' marginalization is attributable to their *communautarisme,* that is, the affirmation of minority status at the expense of national identification.[27] Yet, these youths aspire to nothing but the republican ideal of liberty and equality along with everything that it implies in terms of equal opportunity and access to education, employment, and housing. Their *cités* might be clustered and cut off from local urban cultures, yet they are saturated by global cultural flows, forms, and fads that allow these youths to partake in the production and consumption of the cosmopolitan vernacular that, impervious to boundaries, crisscrosses the globe.

As long as French society reneges in fulfilling these aspirations, as long as it falls short in making good on the republican promise of equality, *Blacks* and *Beurs* will find themselves incarcerated within the pernicious binary paradigm of non-whites as a social *problem* and/or historical *victims* (see Gilroy 1987: 11). This is precisely why when summoned by the *intégristes de la République*[28] to love France or leave it, many *Blacks* and *Beurs* riposte with an equally spurious claim: "*J'baiserai la France jusqu'à c'qu'elle m'aime*" ("I'll fuck France until she loves me"),[29] a slogan that figured boldly on the T-shirts that some of the juveniles donned during the riots. Exactly what these words might mean is subject to interpretation, of course, but such lyrics have been too hastily pilloried as yet again an example of anti-French sentiments that have been brewing in the *cités*. These lyrics do not exemplify anti-white racism and should not be taken as prima facie evidence of *Blacks*' and *Beurs*' nihilistic proclivity, but rather should be taken at face value, as a desperate, unrequited yearning for the *République*'s embrace. "[C]'est une phrase d'amour," explains Socrate, the author of the lyrics. "Quand je cherche son amour, la France ne me le renvoie pas. C'est pour lui dire: je ne veux pas de la vie que tu as calculée pour moi. Je suis français et il faut que tu fasses avec moi."[30]

The argument that I now turn to may serve as a coda for this exploration of the condition of *Blacks* and *Beurs* in France. There can be no doubt that the swelling number of the African diaspora and the status of second-rate citizens that indexes most Africans in France is attributable, albeit only partly, to the minorization of Africa. However, Africa's renaissance (especially in "French-speaking" Africa) hinges to a large extent on the ability of "Black France" to decolonize the *République* and respond to Gikandi's call that the "task of decolonization must be taken to the metropolis itself; the imperial mythology has to be confronted on its home ground" (Gikandi 1996: 27). Then perhaps a dual sense of belonging, a double heritage—as commonly experienced by many African Americans—could position the African diaspora in France as a lobby group and power broker between Europe and Africa, instead of the very precarious position *"le cul entre deux chaises."*[31] Then, perhaps, shedding the stigma of transience, the African diaspora in France could shape, following Mitterrand's prediction, France's twenty-first century and refashion the fabric of Frenchness.

Notes

The epigraph is from "Le cul entre deux chaises" from the 1999 album *Racines.* Lyrics in English:

> Brazza[ville], Paris, I'm blocked on both sides
> Here or there, it's the same, the man's gonna dog you
> My ass between two chairs, exile pushing at me
> In which place are these feet gonna land?

1. Michel Winock, "Une République très coloniale," special issue, "La colonisation en procès," *L'Histoire* 302 (October 2005): 41.
2. "Non à la guerre des mémoires. Entretien avec l'historien Pascal Blanchard," *Le Nouvel Observateur* 2144 (December 8–14, 2005): 30.
3. Robert Aldrich, *Greater France: A History of Overseas Expansion* (London: Macmillan, 1996).
4. Issued by Louis XVI, the *Police des Noirs* was aimed at regulating the entry of blacks to the kingdom of France.
5. Erik Orsenna, "J'ai honte," *Le Monde,* January 5, 2002.
6. Rama Yade-Zimet, a French conservative politician born in Senegal and recently appointed undersecretary for foreign affairs and human rights, recalls in a similar vein how she encountered the demotion of blackness as a sixth grader in her first year at a French public school; see Yade-Zimet (2007: 9–10).

7. It was mainly out of fear of "losing" Rwanda to their erstwhile Anglo-Saxon nemesis that motivated the French intervention in Rwanda; see Asteris C. Huliaras, "The 'Anglosaxon Conspiracy': French Perceptions of the Great Lakes Crisis," *Journal of Modern African Studies* 36, no. 4 (1998): 593–610. According to several testimonies and accounts, which are now backed by recently declassified Élysée archives ("Rwanda: les archives racontent ce que savait l'Élysée," *Le Monde,* July 3, 2007), the French government pursued a belligerent policy in Rwanda while ignoring recurrent warning signs of an impending genocide; see François-Xavier Verschave, *Complicité de génocide? La politique de la France au Rwanda* (Paris: Éditions La Découverte, 1994); Pascal Krop, *Le génocide franco-africain: faut-il juger les Mitterrand?* (Paris: J.-C. Lattès, 1994); Vénuste Kayimahe, *France-Rwanda: les coulisses du génocide* (Paris: L'Esprit Frappeur, 2001); and Patrick de Saint-Exupéry, *L'inavouable: La France au Rwanda* (Paris: Les Arènes, 2004).

8. The term was originally forged by Ivorian president Félix Houphouët-Boigny in the 1960s to qualify the symbiotic relations between France and her former African colonies.

9. The original English translation of Dumont's work appeared the same year as *False Start in Africa* (London: Deutsch, 1966).

10. The English language version came out in 1999 under the title *The Criminalization of the State in Africa* (Bloomington: Indiana University Press).

11. In addition to Verschave's *Françafrique,* other important titles include Pierre Péan, *Affaires africaines* (Paris: Fayard, 1983); Stephen Smith and Antoine Glaser, *Ces Messieurs Afrique: Le Paris-village du continent noir* (Paris: Calmann-Lévy, 1992); Mongo Beti, *La France contre l'Afrique. Retour au Cameroun* (Paris: Éditions La Découverte, 1992); Jean-Paul Gourévitch, *L'Afrique, le fric, la France: L'aide, la dette, l'immigration, l'avenir: vérités et mensonges* (Paris: Le Pré aux Clercs, 1997); Pascal Krop, *Silence, on tue: Crimes et mensonges à l'Élysée* (Paris: Flammarion [J'ai lu], 2001).

12. President Giscard d'Estaing once asserted this presidential prerogative, declaring on public television, "Je m'occupe de politique africaine, c'est-à-dire des intérêts de la France en Afrique" (quoted in Martens 1983: 45).

13. "Time for Transparency: Coming Clean on Oil, Mining and Gas Revenues," a report by Global Witness, March 2004.

14. "Mais que fait la France au Congo-Brazzaville? FrançAfrique ou droits de l'homme: il faut choisir," *Témoignage Chrétien,* February 18, 1999, p. 16.

15. Rapport d'Information, "Commission des Affaires Étrangères sur le rôle des compagnies pétrolières dans la politique internationale et son impact social et environnemental," no. 1859, October 13, 1999.

16. According to Isabelle Coutant's field research in the Parisian *banlieue,* many young people of African descent attribute Africa's problems to France's colonial exploitation and neocolonial meddling in African affairs (Coutant 2005: 184).

17. This refers to a practice in which the arsonist is actually a firefighter who sets an area on fire in the hopes that s/he will be called upon to put the same fire out.

18. On his personal website, www.tikenjah.net (accessed on January 15, 2008), Fakoly cites François-Xavier Verschave, the author of *La Françafrique,* as someone who had an intellectual influence on his musical work.

19. This is compounded by the high rate of returnees among the African immigrant population in France, who once they reach the retirement age tend to return to their homelands even though many have acquired French citizenship. For example, between 1984 and 1998, 20,147 African residents in France (and only 11,994 Europeans) have obtained monetary incentives (*aides à la reinsertion*) from the

French government to return to their original countries; see Office des Migrations Internationales, *Omnistats: Annuaire des migrations 98* (Paris: 1998): 151.

20. Racial equality, according to Patrick Lozès (2007: 13), president of the largest black organization in France, can be attained only if blacks in France obtain the right to "national invisibility," or what Rama Yade-Zimet (2007: 82) evokes as "le droit à l'indifférence."

21. Fatimata Wane and Didier Gondola, *Transient Citizens* (*Les citoyens de l'avion*), DVD documentary, 2006.

22. The soccer field remains about the only locus where France celebrates and embraces diversity, provided that *Les Bleus,* now ironically outnumbered by *Blacks,* win. This was especially true during the 2006 World Cup in Germany. The French team's slow start during the first round elicited a slew of criticisms from listeners on French radio, who lambasted a team with which, they claimed, they could hardly identify. Once they passed the first hurdle and went on to defeat Brazil and Spain, the *Bleus* suddenly were back in the public's good graces, their blackness fading from the public's radar screen with each one of their successive triumphs.

23. On November 22, 2007, Claude Bébéar, former CEO and chairman of Axa Group, handed Prime Minister Jean-Pierre Raffarin a report, "Des entreprises aux couleurs de la France," that deplored the discrimination "visible minorities" had to face and recommended the use of "anonymous cv" for all job applicants.

24. Nicolas Sarkozy's 2003 campaign in favor of "*discrimination positive*" (the French equivalent of affirmative action) was met with distrust and strong opposition from the French public and discredited by President Chirac, Prime Minister de Villepin, and most other main political figures. His decision to appoint a "Muslim prefect" was dismissed by Socialist leader François Hollande as a liberal, Anglo-Saxon ploy that could only undermine French ideals of equality and secular unity (Keslassy 2004).

25. Quoted in Jonathan Freedland, "France is clinging to an ideal that's been pickled into dogma," *The Guardian,* November 9, 2005.

26. Two French political figures, undersecretary of labor Gérard Larcher and National Assembly leader Bernard Accoyer, mentioned polygamy as one of causes of the French urban violence, while Hélène Carrère d'Encausse, an eminent member of the Académie Française, singled out polygamy as a prime suspect.

27. For a convincing critique of this claim, see Laurent Lévy, *Le spectre du communautarisme* (Paris: Éditions Amsterdam, 2005).

28. See Gèze (2006) for a cogent political mapping of this neoconservative group.

29. From "Hardcore 93," the lead song of an album called *C'est toujours pour ceux qui savent,* released in February 2005 by a rap duo of *Black* youths from Aubervilliers, Socrate and Makenzie. Tandem, the name of the duo, the most vocal representative of "le rap hardcore," have become the lightning rod for the state censorship. Their controversial line has been picked up by other rappers, including Monsieur R (real name Richard Maleka), who was prosecuted at the behest of Conservative member of Parliament Daniel Mach for inciting the riots.

30. "Raprophétie," *Libération,* November 3, 2005.

31. Hip-hop artists Bisso na Bisso (*Racines*), Disiz la peste (*Les histoires extraordinaires d'un jeune de banlieue*), La Rumeur (*Blessé dans mon ego*), and Diam's (*Dans ma bulle*), to mention just a few, weave this expression in their lyrics in one way or the other to encapsulate their feeling of alienation. For a sample of how rap artists elucidate their own lyrics and articulate the failure of the French social model, see "Raprophétie," insert in the French daily newspaper *Libération,* November 3, 2005.

CHAPTER EIGHT

The Law of February 23, 2005: The Uses Made of the Revival of France's "Colonial Grandeur"

Nicolas Bancel
Translated by Jane Marie Todd

I n the polemics following its passage, the law of February 23, 2005, has been understood as a legislative "accident," scandalous no doubt, but one, after all, that involved only a few opportunists on the "republican Right" seeking to pick up the votes of *rapatriés*.[1] The "incident," moreover, is said to have ended with the withdrawal—belated to be sure—of the most controversial provision of the bill (provision 4), which asserted the nation's duty to acknowledge the "positive [work] of colonization," required school textbooks to integrate that "positive" dimension, and oriented academic research in that direction. The stipulations of that provision, harking back to the terrible circulars of Vichy urging teachers to promote the National Revolution (let us note in passing that Vichy did not even dare promulgate a law), were a direct attack on democratic debates about the past, since they proposed a normative interpretation of the colonial period (judged "positive" overall). But they were also an attack on the constitution of academic knowledge: research programs would have been financed provided they dealt with the "positive aspects" of the colonial period, at the expense, of course, of all others and of any historical research that attempted to distance itself from such ideological stakes. In addition, the provision mounted an assault on the transmission of scholarly knowledge, obliging disciplines to take into account the accomplishments of the "civilizing mission."

It is clear why the legislation raised a real outcry among secondary-school teachers and professional historians. The historians, in fact, were practically unanimous in condemning it, a stance that created a fictive unity of circumstance that masked their profound disagreements on the subject of colonial history. It is true that the specifications of the law—centralist, reactionary—lent themselves to such a unanimous reaction. That is why the law, in its very excess, could be apprehended as a virtually incomprehensible legal monstrosity. More detailed analyses after the fact, however, have sought to understand the genealogy of the law (Bertrand 2006b; Manceron and Liauzu 2006).

Romain Bertrand looks for the explanation in the role of "outsider" deputies who, out of pure political opportunism, sought to occupy a more central position in public debate and to promote themselves within the political apparatus of the UMP.[2] Gilles Manceron and Claude Liauzu demonstrate the support from private associations and political groups that the drafters of the legislation enjoyed. It will become clear that the first explanation is hardly convincing, while the second, though more plausible, in my view bypasses an analysis of the larger context, characterized by the implementation of a concerted policy of memory within the state apparatus. It also overlooks the currency within the political body of statements ("discursive units," Michel Foucault would say) about the "grandeur" of colonization and, by extension, of France itself. I therefore advance the hypothesis that the law of February 23, 2005, was made possible by the rehabilitation of "colonial grandeur" through "realms of memory" projects and, alongside them, legislative proposals that predated the law of 2005. That rehabilitation process cannot be attributed solely to a faction of the "republican Right," and the lobbying efforts of certain associations of rapatriés are also not the only ones at fault. On the contrary, what is at stake in the law of February 23, 2005, is of national dimensions, by virtue of the actors—major political figures—who intervened in the construction of the discourses reviving imperial glorification, and by the very nature of the statements formulated at the time, which undertook a "reconquest" of national pride by turning to the history of the empire. We will see, finally, at a more localized level, that the field of the social sciences was affected by these polemics: the "sacred union" was followed by a polarization within institutional historiography regarding the acceptable interpretations of the colonial period.

The Genealogy of a Process

We must first return to the genealogy of the law, made possible by a set of related circumstances in the first years of the decade: the mobilization by certain associations of *rapatriés,* who had been militating for more than thirty years for an acknowledgment of their history, but also for a more "positive" view of the French presence overseas (especially in Algeria); the desire on the part of some lawmakers, on the Right and on the Left, to appropriate the *"rapatrié* vote" by moving in the direction of that "acknowledgment" through a certain number of local but also national actions; and finally, the "crisis of memory" set off by the polemics around General Paul Aussaresses's book, the testimony of a senior officer who assumed responsibility for the system of torture implemented by the French army in Algeria.[3] Let us try to untangle these different threads.

The public debate on France's colonial past is cyclical and narrowly focused. It concerns, in the first place, the history of Algeria, more specifically, the Algerian war, and even more precisely, the use of torture by the French army during that conflict. Since it is not the aim of this article to clarify in detail the reasons for that focus, let us move on to the essential: Algeria was a settler colony, theoretically a "jewel" of the French empire; the Algerian war mobilized conscripts, polarized the political debate between 1955 and 1962 (especially around torture), mobilized all the media throughout the period, led to the repatriation of 800,000 *pieds noirs* and tens of thousands of *harkis,*[4] and finally, had a lasting traumatic effect on the general public because the end of the conflict marked the collapse of imperial power.[5] The "French Algeria" question has thus resurfaced periodically: first, during debates, beginning in 1955, on the use of torture by the French army; then upon the 1997 publication of General Jacques Massu's *La vraie bataille d'Alger* (The Real Battle of Algiers), which relaunched the polemics around the same issue a generation later; and finally, in 2000, upon publication of General Aussaresses's *Services spéciaux (The Battle of the Casbah),* which recorded and took responsibility for a true institutionalized system of torture in Algiers. We know the importance that the question of torture assumed during the Algerian war. During the stir caused by that question the second time, the debates again became virulent, but reflections on it did not culminate in a broader inquiry into the colonial period itself.

The latest debate is not yet over: it is now at its crisis point, causing a remarkable polarization both in the social sciences and at the level of society, as various associations face off on the "colonial question," understood as a question of acknowledgment. There is thus a "generational effect" in debates on the colonial question, as if each generation was burdened with the inassimilable question of institutionalized torture by a democratic nation. Twice, these debates did not have real consequences for a general understanding of the colonial period: they did not advance beyond the question of torture. And twice, the polemics ended with a kind of status quo ante: the first time because the end of the Algerian war marked the fall of the empire and set in motion a period of forgetting (Stora 1991; Branche 2006); the second time because the debate ended without having allowed a reflection on colonization. That is not the case this time. On the contrary, the debates have radiated outward, well beyond the question of torture itself: to an assessment of the colonial past as a whole, extending to the history of slavery (which was in gestation for at least fifteen years, particularly in the overseas departments) (Vergès 2006); and to new inquiries into the connections between the colonial and postcolonial periods (the incursion into metropolitan France of the postcolonial question, that is, the effects in France of colonization after colonization, effects that were already broadly debated in the 1970s in all matters relating to the formerly colonized countries).[6] The cumulative effect of the burning questions raised by the colonial past of the Third, Fourth, and Fifth Republics, of the mobilization of the old *rapatriés, harkis,* and "descendants of colonization," of the polarization in the social sciences, and of the legislating of history has created a true maelstrom. It seems that everything was played out in the year 2000.

A Pivotal Juncture

The year 2000 could be called a "pivotal juncture," one of those years when events all shifted simultaneously, creating a sudden change in the configuration. First, as we have seen, there was the resurgence of the question of torture. Alongside Aussaresses's book came a wave of testimony about torture in Algeria, with, in particular, Louisette Ighilariz's statement on June 20, 2000, printed in the newspaper *Le Monde*, the 2002 broadcast of the documentary *L'ennemi intime* (Close Enemy) by Patrick Rotman, and the publication in 2001 of books by Raphaëlle Branche and Sylvie Thénault. Torture in Algeria became a major theme, far beyond the world of historians of the colonial period, making the front page of many mainstream weeklies and monthlies.

That undertow of memories of the Algerian war produced intense annoyance among certain *rapatrié* associations, which on their Web sites violently attacked historians considered "critical" of the period (that was the case for Benjamin Stora especially). It also led to the publication of *Le livre blanc de l'armée française en Algérie* (White Paper on the French Army in Algeria) (De Jaeghere et al. 2001), which denied the systematic use of torture (the army, supposedly, did nothing but preserve "human rights") and called into question Branche's thesis, Stora's studies, and, by extension, the academic world as a whole. The book stipulated, moreover, that since school textbooks are written "for hire," they ought to be revised at the opportune moment, in order to reestablish "the truth." A polarization of positions, already apparent during previous controversies, occurred with respect to the interpretation of the "Algerian war" phenomenon and of torture (or its denial). But several new elements were to play the role of catalyst, unleashing polemics of much greater magnitude.

First, the colonial period was invoked in very laudatory terms in a December 1996 speech by Jacques Chirac. Speaking of "the civilizing work of France," he declared: "Pacification, development of the territories, the spread of education, the establishment of modern medical practices, and the creation of administrative and legal institutions are all marks of that indisputable work to which the French presence contributed, not only in northern Africa but also on every continent." At the highest level, advances in what was politically "sayable" within the "republican Right" came about through a return, little noticed at the time, to the favorite themes of colonial propaganda, which until then had been confined to a few circles on the far right.[7]

At the same time, different memorial projects began to be elaborated, all of them clearly aimed at revalorizing the colonial past. Beginning in the earliest years of the decade, the plan for a "Museum of France in

Algeria," to be located in Montpellier, was developed under the leadership of Georges Frêche. Daniel Lefeuvre, a historian at the Université de Paris VIII and a member of the Conseil scientifique (science board), was charged with giving scientific legitimation to that operation. Frêche's "profile" is fairly characteristic: for more than twenty years he has engaged in a clientelist policy toward certain *rapatrié* associations, and his career is studded with remarks on "colonial grandeur."[8] As for Lefeuvre, he made his reputation through his work on colonial Algeria (Lefeuvre 1997) and through a recent pamphlet against a hypothetical group of "penitents" (Lefeuvre 2006) (yours truly was honored to be included, if only on the margins). In the pamphlet he argued, among other things, that Algeria was a money pit for the nation, and hence that colonial France was actually "generous."[9] He also returned to the massacres of the conquest, which he relativized with the help of strange anachronisms (the conquest of Algeria was no worse than certain episodes of World War I).

It was therefore on the alliance between these two key figures that the plan for the museum rested, a Plan Frêche was defined as follows in November 2005: "It entails creating a museum on France in Algeria and not a museum on the Algerian war or on colonial Algeria. It will pay tribute to the work accomplished, alongside the Arabs—inseparable from that history—by the French in Algeria." The museum's objective is thus to shed light on the benefits of the "civilizing mission," quite simply scotomizing the complexity of colonization in Algeria, and in particular its violent acts and crimes. Lefeuvre, under pressure, would ultimately resign as president of the museum. It seems for the moment, given the stir caused by Frêche, his ousting from the Parti Socialiste (PS), and the criticisms raised by the proposal, that the museum is at a standstill. Another museum of the same type is in the planning stages in Montredon-Labessonnié (in Tarn), with the participation of the academic Jean-Charles Jauffret. The museum is to be dedicated to the "events" of the decolonization of Morocco and Tunisia and to the Algerian war, from the standpoint, a priori, of military history. Finally, a Memorial to the Overseas Departments and Territories of France has also been in the planning stages in Marseilles since 2000, its science board headed by Jean-Pierre Rioux and Jean-Jacques Jordi. It is difficult to analyze the main lines of that last project's "realms of memory," these being quite unclear. It appears, however, that this memorial (which adopts colonial terminology: "la France d'outremer") will be dedicated in great part to the advance of the "civilizing mission" in northern Africa and other colonial locations. The plan for this memorial, like that for the museum in Montpellier, seems for the moment to be at an impasse, despite the millions of euros invested. That temporization may correspond to the intensity of current debates about the colonial past.

These three sites seem to correspond to a desire to "valorize" the French colonial presence, particularly in Algeria. It is clear that all three projects were developed in close collaboration with certain *rapatrié* associations, clientelist constituencies privileged in the south and southwest of France, which intervened directly in their scientific elaboration.[10]

The juncture of 2000–2004 was thus marked by a "conservative reaction" to the debates on torture in Algeria, deployed within the framework of certain *rapatrié* associations, which attracted interest among local elected representatives on the Right (especially) but also on the Left and took concrete form in the proliferation of memorial projects valorizing the colonial period. This cluster of factors came together in an extraordinarily rapid and concrete manner during those four years. The law of February 23, 2005, cannot be understood apart from it.

The Law of February 23, 2005

In some sense, the new "politics of memory" sketched out at the time culminated in the promulgation of the law of February 23, 2005. Hence that law was not an exceptional event. It was the outcome of a legislative and political trajectory that began in 2002 with the preparation of a piece of legislation, the Douste-Blazy-Léonetti bill, which was part of the "conservative reaction" (a particular sign of a period of more general regression, as we shall see).

Since the mid-1990s, Jacques Chirac, a veteran of Algeria, had validated the rapprochement between his party, the Rassemblement pour la République,[11] or RPR (and later the UMP), and the most active and nostalgic *rapatrié* associations. He attested to that rapprochement on the ideological level beginning in 1996, as we have seen. In 2002, he unveiled a national memorial to the Algerian war and to the battles of Morocco and Tunisia that occurred between 1952 and 1962. At the unveiling, between two expressions of regret about the cruelties of war, he returned to the old refrain of France's "civilizing work." Also in 2002, he approved the creation of an interministerial commission of *rapatriés* to work with the prime minister (Jean-Pierre Raffarin at the time). In addition, on

December 20 a decree was published creating a high council of *rapatriés* charged with presenting proposals, both social and memorial, on their behalf. The machine was in place that would allow the mobilization of deputies, most from districts in the south and southwest of France, where most *rapatrié* communities are located, around a plan to revalorize the memory of the *rapatriés* and—no doubt even more important and by extension—the imperial nation's "civilizing mission."

On February 24, 2004, the prime minister assigned Michel Diefenbacher, a UMP deputy known for his ultraconservative positions, the mission of "completing the efforts of material and moral acknowledgement of the *rapatriés* by the nation." On March 5, 2003, Philippe Douste-Blazy and Jean Léonetti had introduced a legislative bill comprising a single provision: "The positive work of all our fellow citizens who lived in Algeria during the period of the French presence is publicly acknowledged." The opening statement was particularly clear, since it adopted the main themes of Chirac's earlier speeches on the colonial question, explaining in particular that "the Republic . . . brought to the land of Algeria its scientific, technical, and administrative expertise, its culture and its language." The bill was not considered, but it confirmed the political and ideological configuration that had been gradually set in place since the president of the Republic's speech in 1996. It was against the background of that reactivation of "colonial grandeur" as resource for political discourse that Diefenbacher's report would be elaborated.

The deputy's method was simple: he questioned a hundred people, all of them belonging to *rapatrié* associations. A single (nonprofessional) historian was represented in the person of General Maurice Faivre, author of the preface to *Le livre blanc de l'armée française en Algérie,* which, as we have seen, dismissed out of hand accusations of torture by the French army in Algeria. General Faivre was also a member of the Haut conseil à l'intégration (high council on integration). The profile of the "historian" who was heard was thus very particular: there was no risk that he would contradict what the deputy wanted to hear about colonial Algeria and the "work" of the French of Algeria. In fact, the Diefenbacher report quite simply forgot about the Algerians and the academic world as a whole, which, however, is not lacking in specialists on that question, both in Algeria and in France.

As might have been expected, the Diefenbacher report was a monument of colonial lyricism: "France had asked its most fearless sons to ensure its influence beyond the seas: with courage, enthusiasm, tenacity,

[and] they did so. The land was farmed, illnesses battled, a true development policy promoted." No, we are not imagining things: this really was 2005, this really was a parliamentary report on colonial Algeria. The text as a whole was in the same vein, but with a particular insistence on the need to reestablish "the truth": "[The descendants of the French of Algeria] are waiting for their fellow citizens of France to assess the legacy of which they are the depositories and to preserve it with all the care it deserves. They are waiting for the state to reestablish the truth." It is clear that, through that report, a new threshold was crossed: in detailing all the merits of the "civilizing mission," its author intended to make that page of history a reference point for the identity of the republican Right, which could henceforth take France's colonial acts as an example of the "French genius." But the text goes even further: on one hand, and within an entirely colonial perspective, it ignores the "natives"; on the other, it suggests, since the "truth" must be reestablished, that someone has probably made off with it, or perhaps falsified it. Who other than the historians could be suspected of such villainy? Hence their absence from the hearings, and the prospect, already developing, of supporting the "truth" of the *rapatriés* against "that" (since historians were perceived, in a particularly stupid manner, as a homogeneous bloc) of the historians. According to that logic, then, France ought to move toward the articulation of a state discourse on colonization. This was confirmed by the content of the report, which suggested that the minister of national education should have a right to inspect textbooks, that the state should encourage academic research on "the actions conducted overseas" (one can guess from what point of view), and that the "associative world" (in other words, the associations connected with the plan) should participate in this research alongside historians and teachers. The result would be normative oversight of historical discourses, their restriction by the state and by *rapatriés* associations (a ratification, by the way, of the epistemological inversion of testimony, which here becomes an order of truth).

The government, not wasting any time, immediately created an interministerial commission of *rapatriés* comprising the Haut Comité des rapatriés, certain *rapatrié* associations, and the national education board, with the avowed objective of modifying the content of textbooks.[12]

The Diefenbacher report also contained several proposals that obviously set the stage for the law of February 23, 2005. Proposal 23, for example, would have provided a lump-sum allocation to restore the benefits of wage earners in the private sector who were exiled after the events of 1961–62 (in other words, the activists in the OAS).[13] It is found again, practically verbatim, in provision 13 of the law of February 23, 2005.[14]

Everything was now in place for the drafting of a formal law. On March 10, 2004, Michelle Alliot-Marie (UMP leader and minister of defense at the time) introduced a legislative bill "providing acknowledgment by the nation and national funds on behalf of French *rapatriés*." The opening statement adopted the edifying creed, now the norm, of colonial glorification, under cover of a tribute to the *rapatriés*: "Thanks to their courage, their spirit of enterprise, and their sacrifices, those countries were able to develop socially and economically; they thus contributed greatly to the influence of France in the world. To acknowledge the positive work of our compatriots in these territories is a duty of the French state: it will be, in particular, the mission of the Memorial of the Overseas Departments and Territories of France." Let us note in passing that the opening statement allows a connection to be made between the promulgation of the law and the memorial in Marseilles, tracing a true state politics of memory. The articulation of discourses on colonization would thus be controlled in the social sciences field (a research program on the "civilizing mission"), in the transmission of knowledge (supervised production of textbooks), and in their diffusion to the general public (a museum policy that embraced the bellwether Marseilles project, but that was also very much in line with colonially correct local initiatives). It is thus clear that at this stage, the crystallization of a new political and discursive configuration was coming about. The discourse revalorizing the work of the French overseas began as local initiatives (projects for colonial "realms of memory" but also steles dedicated at the local level to the memory of soldiers in the OAS) that were relayed by legislators, probably seeking to please a portion of the *rapatriés* to capture their votes.[15] But it gradually shifted to a revalorization of the nation through colonial history. Therefore, it is potentially one of the themes of "national pride," avidly sought by politicians at the national level. In that respect it has become a state discourse.

Consideration of the Bill

Consideration of the bill took place in June 2004. In charge was Christian Kert, UMP deputy from Bouches-du-Rhône, known for his conservative positions.[16] The individuals consulted in elaborating the bill shored up Diefenbacher's work: all were members of *pied noir* associations. As Thénault points out, associations disagreeing with the approach taken in the legislation, as well as *harki* associations, which broke away from that "acknowledgment" movement, were excluded (Thénault in Manceron and Liauzu 2006).

Apart from the attention, by now routine, paid to the "colonial grandeur" of France, the details of which I shall spare the reader, the principal objectives of the law were clear: colonial history had to be revised, both in the realm of scholarship and in the composition of textbooks. Thus, during the debate in the National Assembly on June 11, 2004, Kert expressed his "concern that textbooks take into account that human adventure and inscribe it in our country's history." Cécile Gallez, UMP deputy from Nord, went even further: "Hence it is necessary that the textbooks grant the history of France's overseas departments and territories its full place, not truncated and disfigured, but complete and impartial." Lionel Lucca, UMP deputy from Alpes-Maritimes and a secondary-school teacher of history and geography, later added that France "never enslaved the people it guided. . . . It is high time to assert our pride in the work accomplished. The time of bad conscience and cheap repentance is over." Meanwhile, the opposition demonstrated indifference, if not support, such as that of François Liberti, PCF deputy from Hérault,[17] acting on behalf of the communist group. The socialists did not vote for the bill, but not because the atmosphere of revisionism and normative history revolted them in any way; rather, they believed the bill *did not go far enough* in compensating the *rapatriés*. An amendment was passed creating an "endowment for the memory of the Algerian war and the battles of Morocco and Tunisia" within the Memorial to the Overseas Departments and Territories of France in Marseilles, a disturbing manifestation of the ideas expressed in the Diefenbacher report (centralization of the resources for academic programs dealing with colonial policy, with, of course, the participation of the *rapatrié* associations). That amendment came to complement, at the level of academic research, the work of the interministerial commission already set in place to revise textbooks.

During the vote in the Senate, the first clear reaction from the opposition came from Guy Fischer, Communist senator, who protested the "revisionism" of the law and the compensation of former OAS activists. Nevertheless, the law passed in the Senate without a hitch. Having been

returned to the National Assembly for a second vote, the bill was pas-
sionately supported by those deputies who had backed it on the first
vote, as well as by Kléber Mesquida, PS deputy from Hérault, and Rudi
Salles, UMP deputy from Alpes-Maritimes. Diefenbacher closed the
debate, asserting, "Never have lawmakers taken such a clear position on
the meaning to be given to the history of colonization and on the positive role played by the French presence."

We realize, therefore, that though the main supporters of the law
belonged to the rightist majority, others were located on the Left. The
traditional analysis of the political split is therefore inoperative here,
since, in any case, the law encountered practically no opposition during the various votes in the Assembly and the Senate. The mobilization
of deputies elected in regions where strong *rapatrié* communities are
concentrated is the most apparent, but an analysis would also need to
be done of certain deputies' connections with colonial history. In any
case, the passage of the law of February 23, 2005, came as the crowning
moment in a process that had begun ten years earlier, the relegitimation
of the "colonial epic" in political discourses.

The Law's Effects in Associations of "Visible Minorities"

The debate on the law of February 2005 had been preceded by numerous polemics regarding colonial history, particularly the Algerian war.
Several associations aspiring to represent "black" West Indian or African
minorities, most of them from the former empire, came into being in
that context. That was the case, for example, of Africagora, an association
of blacks seeking the acknowledgment of racial discrimination—in hiring and on the job—and the establishment of antidiscrimination policies; of the Comité marche du 23 mai 1998 (Committee for the March of
May 23, 1998), headed by Serge Romana, which had comparable objectives; and, in 2005, of the Conseil Représentatif des Associations Noires
(Representative Council of Black Associations), or CRAN, also created
to promote a "multicultural France" within a larger emerging movement
addressing the "black question" in France (Faes and Smith 2006). Les
Indigènes de la République (Native Peoples of the Republic), a more
radical movement basing itself on a postcolonial analysis of French
society, was also created in early 2005, at the initiative of militants who
defined themselves as "coming from the colonies, former or current, and
from postcolonial immigration." In its appeal, it asserted a kind of con-

tinuity between the colonial and postcolonial periods.[18] The signatories wanted to attract attention to the persistence of discrimination, which according to them is colonial in origin. The law of February 23, 2005, was thus being promulgated even as the movement of "visible minorities" in France was getting under way. The effects of that promulgation were obviously catastrophic: first, because one of the persistent demands of these associations was the acknowledgment of the history of slavery and colonization, which in their view is indispensable for understanding the history of the construction of modern French multicultural society; and second, because these associations were protesting (with greater or lesser virulence) against a republican and national discourse judged to be too conservative, which prevented the French from taking into account discrimination (that is, the concrete effects of racism, permanently scotomized by a discourse on the "France of the ideas of 1789," "French exceptionalism," the "French genius," and so on) or cultural differences (since every minority is supposedly capable of blending into the nation, thanks to the leveling effect of the "integration model *à la française*"). In the overseas departments and territories, particularly Martinique and Guadeloupe, reactions were extremely sharp for the same reasons. In particular, several demonstrations protested the law, and virulent declarations were made by intellectuals from the overseas departments, such as Édouard Glissant and Aimé Césaire. These emergent minorities, then, perceived the law of February 2005 as a real denial of their historical suffering but also as a brutal reminder of their marginality within the nation. It provoked a radicalization of positions that is now polarizing debates about colonial and postcolonial history in civil society.

Epilogue

Provision 4 of the law of February 23, 2005, was struck, after lengthy polemics, by Jacques Chirac, while the other provisions retained force of law. The debate on the colonial past is far from closed, and the process of reviving the main statements about France's "civilizing mission" in its colonial empire will have produced several effects. In the first place, the past (and its interpretation) has become a site of contention for all social groups claiming filiation to one or another of the episodes currently being debated (primarily colonization and slavery), whether these groups identify themselves as *rapatrié* communities or as the "descendants of slavery" and/or "colonization." The polarization of discourses is now beyond doubt and has also affected the social sciences. Hence books have appeared whose aim is to lament "critical aberrations" about the colonial past, which, according to their authors, have weakened useful points of reference for national cohesion. That was the objective, for example, of Rioux's 2006 well-documented and interesting book *La France perd la mémoire* (France Is Losing Its Memory), in which the author inquires into the uses made of the past by these social groups and laments that these uses destabilize the representations of French history.[19] In so doing, he neglects the complex relationship that the production of historical knowledge maintains with the construction of a national narrative with its own memory. That is truly the central issue raised for historians: they must allow themselves to undertake the study of certain difficult questions, foremost among them those raised by the postcolonial perspective, which is still largely taboo in the social sciences, without being stymied by the idea that this research might constitute a "self-fulfilling prophecy" (this is not very far from "magical thinking").

Historical work on the colonial, and especially the postcolonial, question is still largely perceived in academic circles as representing a risk for "national cohesion" tending to weaken the Republic. Yet it seems necessary to approach these matters from a strictly scientific point of view, without censoring oneself on the pretext that the resulting research may have negative sociopolitical effects. An epistemological revolution remains to be undertaken in that area. In addition, we find a few historians who wish to "set things straight" in the matter of colonization, either because their perspective is clearly conservative or because the current innovations contradict mental frameworks still largely dominated by Marxism. Lefeuvre belongs to the first category, but other historians (Bernard Lugan, for example) also engage in a large-scale revision of colonial history. In the second category are several historians who obviously do not understand current historiographical advances, since they reduce all questions to a post-Marxist analysis of class factions and the expansion of capitalism.[20] Hence the constant astonishment of a good number of colleagues abroad, who note the blocking of research in France on subjects that have been treated for more than two decades in the social science literature written in English.

The other notable effect of the debate on the colonial past and the law of February 2005 is that statements referring directly to the "glory days" of Greater France are back in style. This is obviously a regressive movement. It does not just affect small groups within the current majority, as some authors have claimed; it recomposes in its entirety the discourse on the nation. In this respect, it is likely to be continually reactivated, since the "critical return" to the past is far from realized and, for the time being, studies inspired by postcolonial studies are practically nonexistent. The discourse glorifying the empire has in reality become one of the possible resources for reinvigorating those devoted to "French exceptionalism," the "national genius," and the "grandeur of the nation," at the very moment when, for reasons it would take too long to detail here, these statements are being profoundly destabilized by France's integration into Europe, the blurring of boundaries, and the worries linked to "globalization." We still lack the necessary distance to fully appreciate the magnitude of these anxieties, but they probably provide fertile ground in our efforts to understand the deep ideological motivations behind the passage of the law of February 23, 2005.

Notes

1. *Rapatriés:* former colonists who have returned to metropolitan France. See, for example, the articles collected on the Web site of the Ligue des droits de l'homme (Human Rights League), Toulon branch, http://www.ldh-toulon.net.

2. The UMP (Union pour un Mouvement Populaire), created after the presidential and legislative elections of November 2002, sought to unite the "republican Right" as a whole. That operation, whose aim was to turn French politics into an American-style two-party system, failed in part because of the resistance of François Bayrou, who, despite many defections by elected representatives from his party (the UDF, Union de la Démocratie Française) to the UMP, succeeded in keeping his group alive. Since Nicolas Sarkozy was elected to head the UMP in November 2004, the party's discourse has shifted to the right, borrowing, in fact, a good number of its themes from the conservative Right in the United States.

3. In his book *Services spéciaux: Algérie, 1955–1957* (2000), Paul Aussaresses admitted and even justified the use of torture by the French army during the Algerian war, particularly during the "battle of Algiers." His statements unleashed a very sharp polemic, and in fact, Aussaresses was brought to court by the Ligue des droits de l'homme for "justification of war crimes."

4. *Pieds noirs:* French citizens born in Algeria; *harkis:* native Algerians who fought for the French cause during the Algerian war.

5. See Gervereau, Rioux, and Stora 1992; Harbi 1980, 1986; Pervillé 2002; and Sirinelli and Rioux 1988.

6. Catherine Coquery-Vidrovitch, "Le passé colonial entre histoire et mémoire," paper delivered to the forum of March 4, 2006, organized by the Comité de vigilance face aux usages publics de l'histoire, or CVUH (Vigilance Committee on the Public

Uses of History), and entitled "Sur les usages publics de l'histoire. Polémiques, com-
mémorations, enjeux de mémoire, transmission et enseignement," http://www.ldh-
toulon.net.

7. That is why, to borrow Romain Bertrand's terminology in *Mémoires d'Empire,*
it is anachronistic to say that the "politically sayable" in this regard emerged during
the elaboration of the law of February 23, 2005, as Bertrand claims (he cites Chirac's
remarks but does not take them into account). That "sayable" was very present much
earlier, and not only on the Right: remarks reiterated by Georges Frêche, mayor of
Montpellier, had long referred to that "glorious past." In addition, Bertrand totally
ignores the long maturation process of the law, which was preceded by a bill elaborated in 2003 but not considered at the time. That bill was introduced by Philippe
Douste-Blazy (not exactly an unknown) and Jean Léonetti, and its aim was to
acknowledge *the positive work of all our citizens who lived in Algeria during the period
of the French presence.* It was co-signed by 107 other deputies. Finally, Bertrand does
not take into account the different realms of memory that had been taking shape
since the early years of this decade, involving many political leaders from the highest
echelons (Jean-Claude Gaudin, for example), who very clearly declared the validity
of the discourse of colonial glorification. Is this a mere blunder on Bertrand's part or
a way of distorting the chronology in order to shore up his argument that the law of
February 2005 was an attempt by a few "outsider" deputies to impose a new discourse
about the colonial past so as to make inroads within the UMP leadership? In any case,
the "mechanical" aspect of that argument does not hold up to analysis: it would mean
that these deputies could have seized on any "transgressive" discourse at all (in fact,
the discourse of imperial glorification was no longer transgressive at the time). That
is to forget that words have a meaning, a history, and that their articulation by politicians depends on social groups capable of hearing them.

8. Let us point out that in 2007, after Frêche's declarations about the *harkis*—he
called them "subhuman"—the Parti Socialiste was compelled to make the decision,
long deferred, to oust him from its ranks.

9. Forgetting, in passing, that the aim of colonial domination was not to fill the
state's coffers but to enrich certain groups of speculators, and especially, to display
France's global power, whatever the cost to the "natives."

10. We will undoubtedly never know the real margin for maneuvering that was
available to certain honest historians (whose analyses we do not agree with, however),
such as Jordi and Rioux, since it seems that, in designing the project, they had to
negotiate closely with representatives of the associations and the government.

11. Union for the Republic.

12. Sylvie Thénauld (in Manceron and Liauzu 2006) points out that the history
textbook published by Éditions Nathan in 2005 devotes a chapter to the "positive and
negative effects of colonization": four paragraphs deal with the "positive effects," a
single paragraph with the "negative effects." It remains unclear whether it was a coin-
cidence, or an anticipation of reforms, that seemed ineluctable at the time.

13. OAS: Organisation de l'armée secrète (Secret Army Organization). That sedi-
tious group, headed by Raoul Salan in 1961, of senior officers and a few *pieds noirs,*
recruited members from the European population of French Algerian extremists and
professional soldiers. The OAS obstinately rejected the prospect of Algerian independence and used violent actions (attacks and assassinations) in Algeria and metropolitan France. In 1962, several attempted uprisings by the European population were
organized by the OAS, but they finally ended in failure and harsh repression.

14. Thénault notes (in Manceron and Liauzu 2006) that the application decree for that provision appeared very quickly, having been executed on May 26, 2005.

15. Here again, Bertrand is not very convincing when he argues that the *pieds noirs'* vote did not have any real influence on the passage of the law of February 23, 2005. In support of his thesis, he suggests that "several studies" demonstrate the insignificance of that vote. Apart from the fact that he cites only a single study (by Emmanuelle Contat), that observation demonstrates almost nothing. In the first place, one would require a much more convincing body of local political monographs attesting the insignificance of that vote. Second, one would have to be able to show that the recognized activism of the *pieds noirs* associations had no effect on the votes of the other representatives. And lastly, the "reality" of that vote is not everything: what matters far more is the way lawmakers viewed its significance (even if their view was false). We are compelled to note that the majority of the initiatives directed at the "acknowledgment" of the "positive work" of the French of Algeria have come from representatives of regions where the *pieds noirs* communities are the strongest. We find the same factor at work among the chief champions of the law (on the Right but also on the Left) during the debates in the National Assembly.

16. The deputy regularly attends ceremonies held by *rapatrié* associations. As an example, we offer this excerpt from the speech by René Andres at the ceremony dedicated to the Memorial to the French of Algeria and to the *Rapatriés* from the Overseas Departments and Territories at the Saint-Pierre cemetery in Aix-en-Provence, organized by the Association du mémorial national des Français d'Algérie et rapatriés d'outremer on October 22, 2005: "In classrooms where all the children of Algeria were to be found without distinction, the history of France was valued: the same history for all, Spanish, Italian, Maltese, Germans, and Arabs included, even for those whose ancestors were not Gauls. . . . And yet it seems that pseudointellectuals are now discovering that there are several histories of France in Algeria. . . . These third-rate historians, accustomed to looking for the horizon line above the clouds, fabricate lies and disinformation, which the newspapers—always the same ones—transform into truth. . . . Ladies and Gentlemen of the legislature, French citizens, beware, anti-France is being reborn. To combat it we must restore respect for the moral values of good citizenship and of our nation's Judeo-Christian culture, which would return to the French family its harmonious development and would serve as an example for the multidenominational and multiethnic societies whose growing emergence we are observing." See the Web site of the Ligue des droits de l'homme de Toulon: http://www.ldh-toulon.net/spip.php?article1102.

17. Parti communiste français, the French Communist Party.

18. That appeal is available in extenso at www.toutesegaux.net; see also *Le Monde,* February 22, 2005.

19. Less informed and more polemical works also attest to that annoyance. See Taguieff 2005, and, in the same vein, Slama 2005, Gallo 2006, and Paoli 2006.

20. There is undoubtedly an extensive analysis to be done on that second group, with respect to the generations to which the researchers belong and their maintenance against all odds of intellectual positions acquired at high cost within the institution. That undertaking, however, is beyond the scope of this article.

PART 3

Visions and Tensions of Frenchness

A Conservative Revolution within Secularism: The Ideological Premises and Social Effects of the March 15, 2004, "Anti-Headscarf" Law

Pierre Tévanian
Translated by Naomi Baldinger

F or almost two years, the campaign against "the headscarf at school" provoked political and media hysteria comparable to the Dreyfus Affair.[1] Launched by the right-wing government in April 2003, and quickly endorsed by a large portion of the Left, even the extreme Left, this campaign resulted in the law of March 15, 2004, which prohibited "wearing conspicuous symbols of religious affiliation." Although the so-called Islamic headscarf was worn at the time by only one to two thousand students, and although its presence has become increasingly accepted in the educational environment, numerous alarmist and aggressive speeches on prime-time television turned veiled students into agents of "Islamic fundamentalism" (*intégrisme islamique*), "anti-intellectualism" (*obscurantisme*), or even "green fascism."[2] These speeches established equivalence, usually implied but sometimes assumed, between the simple right to wear the headscarf and the obligation to wear it, as it is imposed in countries such as Iran. The headscarf was stigmatized as an attack on the principle of secularism, but also as the ultimate symbol of "the oppression of women," and even as an instrument of that oppression. Veiled teenagers were often accused of making other women

look like "sluts," implying that they were complicit with the chauvinism and rape committed by their "brothers." Thus, the public debate
quickly left the sphere of public education, evading attendant questions
of social stigma, humiliation, and marginalization in the school system
to become a vague, disembodied debate about the headscarf and Islamic
fundamentalism. We will return to the social stigma of the headscarf,
the adolescents who wear it, and their so-called brothers, who are suspected of forcing girls to wear the headscarf unless they manifest their
secular allegiances by denouncing it. But before we return to this idea
of stigmatization, let us first analyze the content of the March 15, 2004
law, and its implications for secular discourse, freedom of expression,
and the right to education.

The law, which was poorly received by the children of postcolonial immigrants when it was proposed to the National Assembly, was
often presented by its proponents (and sometimes by its detractors) as
an expression of the eternal "French essence."[3] For some, it gave new
life to the glorious *exception française:* a difficult concept for foreigners to grasp, yet considered a worthy lesson for the rest of the world.[4]
For others, however, it encapsulates all the arrogance and intolerance
of French society. In reality, the situation is more complex: although
the law enjoyed a large consensus among political elites and the mainstream French media, a large portion of civil society opposed its putative
exclusionism. At the beginning of the campaign, 45 percent of French
citizens were opposed to a ban on the headscarf at school (49 percent
supported it.) Better yet, only 22 percent supported the expulsion of a
student who refused to remove her headscarf (Tévanian 2005). Beyond
this, the anti-headscarf law has nothing to do with the essence of secular
French culture. It actually breaks with legislation justified in the name of
the secular. Paradoxically, the rhetoric of a "return to roots" has actually
been used to promote a new law, leading to a radical transformation of
French secularism. By imposing "neutrality" not only on the agents of
the public educational system, but on its users as well, the law transforms the founding laws of French secular politics (those of 1880, 1882,
1886, and 1905).[5] From 2003 to 2004, there has been a conservative revolution within the context of French secular politics, meaning that a "new
order" was supported by conservative or reactionary rhetoric idealizing
the past. By banning the headscarf at school, proponents of this rhetoric celebrate a supposed reaffirmation of forgotten principles, claiming

to have rediscovered the pertinence and relevance of Jules Ferry, Jean Jaurès, Léon Gambetta, and other monumental figures of the so-called Golden Age of the Third Republic, now "threatened" once again by the specter of religious values. I intend to show that deep within its objective and ideological presuppositions, the anti-headscarf law breaks with so-called progressive principles and is actually part of a profoundly reactionary ideology that can be summarized as: (a) the transition from a rational to a religious conception of the secular; (b) the transition from libertarian to "securitarian" secularism;[6] (c) the transition from democratic to totalitarian logic; and (d) the transition from egalitarian to "identitarian" secularism.[7]

From Rational to Religious Secularism

The improbable slogan *laïcité sacrée,* or sacred secularism, was featured on stickers and put up during a demonstration commemorating the centennial of the 1905 law. It demonstrates the transformation of secularism into a sacred symbol in public debates.[8] An organizing social principle, subject to democratic debate and perpetual critique and revision, has become a timeless value, open neither to criticism nor to amendment, whose mere utterance can supposedly exorcise all social problems. Thus, the alterity implied by the opposition between secular and religious values has become a *mimetic rivalry* exemplified by the phrase, "When you go to a mosque, you must remove your shoes. *Likewise,* when a student goes to class, she must remove her headscarf." This is a form of syllogistic reasoning repeated throughout the headscarf controversy, adopted in the lurching right-wing political pandering of Nicolas Sarkozy, the former minister of interior, elected as president in 2007, as well as those on the Left and the extreme Left. The word "likewise" (*de même*) is problematic because it positions the school as a site of worship and locates secular values within the terms of religious dogma. This form of dogma establishes an equivalence between secular and religious thinking that directly contradicts twentieth-century secular reason, which established another set of rules, in which sartorial interdictions were not a point of principle. The example of wearing the headscarf in a public school and wearing shoes in the mosque cannot be conflated for the simple reason that the classroom is not a mosque; the classroom is a *secular* rather than a *religious* space. As a secular space, the school establishes rules founded on pedagogical principles, allowing all that contributes and enhances the work of teachers and students. It forbids only that which functions as an obstacle to its pedagogical imperatives. A secular space is also a *non-dogmatic* space, open to discussion about the meaning of objects, phenomena, symbols, and articles of clothing. Only religious rituals assign unitary meanings to an article of clothing or a gesture, which may be considered acceptable or not to church dogma. By declaring that a headscarf is a sign that necessarily demonstrates contempt for secular values, the state turns the secular school day into a religious ritual in which its officials become clergy who monitor the actions, gestures, and attire of its congregation.[9]

This emerging "religious secularism" has its new theologians. Media-savvy philosopher Henri Péna-Ruiz has developed an abstract and apologetic rhetoric to present secularism, recalling metaphysics or catechism rather than law, political science, or sociology. The equally visible media intellectuals Régis Debray, Max Gallo, and Alain Finkielkraut, acknowledge and defend the religious dimension that the March 15, 2004 law imposes on public education. These figures, belonging to the spectrum of the French Socialist Left, claim that the loss of "transcendence" is the greatest threat to the social fabric, hoping that the second coming of the secular school will reestablish it as a "sacred space."[10] However, the public school system as it was conceived and implemented following the laws of 1880–86 and 1905 is neither transcendent nor sacred. It requires a secular attitude of its teachers and curriculum, assigning precious little significance to religious symbols worn by students.[11] It abstains from using religious precepts to interpret the significance of these symbols. The primary concern of such a school is to accommodate all students, whereas the law of March 15, 2004, presents the veiled student with an impossible dilemma: to remove her headscarf or to leave school permanently. After one year of enforcement, there have been hundreds of such cases resulting in the expulsion of veiled students.[12]

True secularism is radically different from today's religious secularism. Secularism as defined by the 1905 law and the legislation of the 1880s is a means rather than an end. In other words, it is not a dogma or an eternal value, but rather a means for a variety of opinions and beliefs to coexist while maximizing liberty and equality. However, current French discourse ignores these goals and treats secularism as an end in itself. Secularism today is frighteningly similar to religious doctrine.

From Libertarian Secularism to Securitarian Secularism

Secularism, as defined by the laws of the 1880s, is *libertarian* in the sense that the "neutrality" imposed on the enterprise of public education through its physical plant, personnel, and curricula is articulated in terms of liberty and equality. Its ultimate goal is to guarantee *maximum* individual liberty to all *equally*, ensuring that the liberty of the majority does not stifle that of the minority. In the French context, the term *libertarian* refers to the *equal liberty* of all, whereas the term *liberal* can be reserved for a more abstract valuation of individual liberty, blind to power hierarchies that increase the liberty of some and decrease that of others. The principle of *equal liberty for all* is at the heart of neutral public education. Although absolute neutrality is impossible for individual teachers, relative neutrality can be achieved by limiting the expression of personal convictions. Neutral education allows students to develop and think independently. Indeed, the teacher's opinions must be suppressed and neutralized so that their influence does not stifle the student's developing conscience. Likewise, scholastic curricula must not contain official ideology or religion. On the contrary, they must encourage the student to make spiritual, moral, aesthetic, and political choices based on the diversity and difference of human culture in its entirety.[13]

Freedom of conscience is the foundation of both neutral public education and students' freedom of expression. Very few limits are imposed on this freedom; slander, defamation, and (since 1972) incitement to racial hatred are prohibited, and certain pedagogical limits (such as the obligation to discuss the subject at hand and to wait one's turn to speak) are imposed. Because a free conscience requires that students form and discuss their own opinions, the founders of the secular school system imposed no other limits. Indeed, the laws of 1880–86 remain silent on the subject of the students' neutrality, permitting them to express their religious and political convictions.[14] Freedom is a pillar of French thought, structured around free speech, which includes the right to express absurdities or prejudices, which must be articulated before they can be fought.

The 2004 law marks a radical transformation of the concept of "libertarian secularism." By forcing neutrality on students, it questions the very foundations of secular education. Even if the law concerns only students' attire, it implies that Muslim students in particular must be discreet, reserved, and ultimately silent. The debate that preceded and provoked the adoption of this law was punctuated by incessant appeals to practice religion only in the private sphere, relegating religion to the home. Thus, the state implies not only that certain forms of expression are forbidden to Muslim students, but also that as students, they have no right to express their point of view on the subject. The 2004 law goes so far as to stifle any possibility for further debate. Furthermore, the state inflicts extraordinary violence by expelling girls who refuse to remove their headscarves. The state relegates these students to the status of sub-humans who are unfit for liberty, and incapable of benefiting from the lessons of emancipation provided by the school.

Securitarian secularism replaces libertarian secularism as "law and order" take the place of liberty and equality in the pantheon of French values. The new law's supporters argue that visible religious symbols must disappear from institutions caught in a "war of religion" in order to restore peace. Thus, if the law of 2004 has any historical precedent, it is neither the law of 1880 nor that of 1905, but that of 1936, in which Jean Zay's Ministry of Education temporarily prohibited students' political expression in reaction to violent confrontations between extreme right-wing leagues and militant communists within high schools. However, this law suspended public liberties only because public order was at risk in an exceptional circumstance. It did not tamper with the foundations of French secularism. Crucially, some proponents of the 2004 law invoked the 1936 law rather than the mythical "founding texts of secularism," making the deceptive claim that Jewish-Muslim relations in 2004 were causing disturbances similar to those of 1936.[15]

From Democratic to Totalitarian Logic (The "Neutrality of Public Space")

The slogan, "Republic versus democracy," first asserted by the essayist Régis Debray in 1989, following his first public involvement with the headscarf controversy, must be further examined. Nothing less than democratic logic has been called into question by the "republican secularism" of the past few years, especially in light of the current discourse employed by proponents of the anti-headscarf law on the necessity for "neutrality in public space." The idea of neutral public space can be understood in several different ways: if we disregard the thorny question of what is and is not public, there remain two radically different, even antithetical, ways to define this "space" and its "neutrality" (Lévy 2005). According to the first definition, "neutrality" means that everyone has the same *right to expression,* applied with neither privileges nor discrimination, and monitored by the authorities. Stated more directly, "neutrality" lies in the fact that no majority or dominant social force may monopolize speech or the use of public space, and that nothing prevents minorities from expressing themselves. Accordingly, the public *space* must be neutral, not the public itself. One might even say that the public space must be neutral precisely so that the public *does not have to be.* A woman may then wear her headscarf without calling into question the neutrality of public space. On the contrary, the neutrality of public space guarantees a woman's right to choose whether or not to wear a headscarf. Government policies or social conventions that require conformity to a single norm—such as going without a headscarf—threaten the neutrality of public space.

The other definition, prominent throughout the debate over the headscarf, imposes neutrality on the *public* itself. In this case, the Muslim woman who stands out by wearing a headscarf is essentially attacking the neutrality of public space. This conception of "neutral public space," while internally coherent, implies nothing less than a *total suppression of free speech.* When individuals are obliged to "remain neutral," public space becomes *totalitarian* space. Although this totalitarian logic is delusional, or at least unacceptable to anyone who values democracy, it has spread far beyond extremist circles, where it properly belongs. Its expression within mainstream media and politics has undoubtedly inspired the many acts of incivility and violence committed with impunity against veiled women in universities, banks, municipal buildings, police stations, and public transportation.

Because it is common knowledge that only veiled women, and not members of the general public, are expected to be "neutral," no one contests the conflation of the neutrality of public space with the neutrality of the public, and no one expresses concern over the advancing totalitarian tide infiltrating French thought and politics. Since the beginning of the headscarf controversy, the right to public expression of opinion has never actually been called into question, and everyone involved in the debate understands that only the public *space*, rather than the public itself, must be neutral, except for the practicing Muslim public. Exclusionism is totalitarian only with respect to the minority; the majority's democratic rights are left untouched. In other words, the majority may enjoy neutral public space without being neutral itself, whereas the minority must become neutral, that is, invisible and silent, as soon as it enters the public space.[16] Democracy and totalitarianism are no longer two types of regimes or societies diametrically opposed to each other; they now coexist within one model of society that is totalitarian for Muslims and democratic for the rest.

From Egalitarian Secularism to Identitarian Secularism
(The Question of Racism)

As curious as it may sound to a political scientist, this form of exclusionary politics is not at all exceptional to those who have studied or endured racism, sexism, or homophobia. When systematically applied, these forms of discrimination deny one segment of society the democratic rights accorded to the other. For example, many homosexuals are familiar with the underlying message for Muslims: "you may do what you like in the 'private sphere' but in public, be 'neutral' and inconspicuous." In both cases, the same false "respect" and "generosity" mask discrimination, invisibility, and submission to a totalitarian order from which the majority is spared. No one asks heterosexuals to hide their heterosexuality, nor does one ask Catholics, Protestants, Jews, Buddhists, atheists, communists, socialists, neoliberals, or centrists to "remain neutral" or to keep their opinions at home.[17]

The unequal treatment and double standards imposed by the new law have led many French citizens to term it *racist*. Having said that, I am not accusing everyone who approves of the law to be driven by hatred of Arabs or Muslims. On the other hand, the misconstrued notion of the neutrality of public and scholastic space that has served as the basis of the anti-headscarf campaign begs the question of racism. If racism can be defined as a system of thought and discriminatory practice founded on "race," "origin," "ethnicity," or "culture," then the anti-headscarf law is indisputably racist, because it establishes a glaring inequality. By banning the headscarf in the classroom, it directs violence against Sikhs and veiled Muslims, but casts a blind eye toward Christians who wear a cross under their sweaters. Such discrimination is not the result of chance; the law was created with this result in mind.[18] Indisputably, most arguments in favor of the law concern only the headscarf, even if they supposedly ban "all religious symbols." (This contradiction is most apparent in the anti-headscarf petition launched in May 2003 by the Union des familles laïques [Union of Secular Families (UFAL)] and in another petition published in December 2003 by *Elle* magazine.)[19] On December 17, 2003, Jacques Chirac asked Parliament to create legislation specifically targeting the headscarf. In spite of the good intentions of the progressive, even antiracist, activists who supported the law in the name of feminism or secularism, the 2004 law is an example of racist exclusionism.[20] Only racism can explain the collective hysteria and numerous contradictions characterizing the debate. When intelligent people suddenly become foolish, when kind, mild-mannered people suddenly become mean, when feminists call other women "sluts" (for participating in a feminist demonstration while veiled),[21] when defenders of liberty become antiauthoritarian anarchists (by allowing the state to regulate students' attire and turn "inappropriate dress" into a matter of discipline), no term is more appropriate than "collective phobia." How can we explain the indifference that met the expulsion of hundreds of mostly working-class students in a society so concerned with children and their education without taking into account deep-seated Islamo-phobia?

Although the debate has yet to be fully theorized, we can certainly say that it was riddled with racist arguments that reduce Islam to a series of amalgams: *voile-viol-excision-islamisme-intégrisme-terrorisme-fascisme-nazisme-antisémitisme* (headscarf-rape-excision-Islamic fundamentalism-terrorism-fascism-Nazism-anti-Semitism) (Tévanian 2005). Two examples are particularly worthy of further examination. The remarks of the Socialist Senator Jean-Luc Mélenchon and the philosopher Henri Péna-Ruiz are emblematic of the remarkable racist and exclusionary politics exposed within the heart of the French Left.

During the December 12, 2005, episode of the TV program *Mots croisés* (Crossword Puzzle), Mélenchon praised the March 15, 2004 law as the logical result of secular French values. In conciliatory tones, he gave an abstract description of secularism as a "universal" principle that permits "everyone to live together" while respecting individual convictions. Two guests (Christine Boutin and Amar Lasfar) pointed out the contradiction inherent in assigning a single, derogatory meaning to the headscarf without taking into account the opinions of the girls who wear it.[22] They also remarked that the anti-headscarf campaign effectively stigmatized an entire segment of the French population on the basis of prejudice and phobia, and that the law's effect was to expel many students who wished to remain enrolled in the secular school system. These objections seemed to incessantly annoy the senator; instead of engaging his opponents in a debate about these issues, he quickly ended the discussion with the exhortation, "Listen! We, the French, have our way of life: not to wear headscarfs in school!" The senator's reaction is characteristic of the inability of French political elites to accept dialogue, that is, the exchange of arguments between *equals,* especially when the subject of debate or the opponent has anything to do with immigration, the Arab world, or Islam. This instance is deeply emblematic of the contradictions within the sacred republican discourse of the French ruling classes. Despite a veneer of generosity, this discourse quickly becomes violent invective, stigmatizing immigrants and their children who demand that universal, libertarian, and egalitarian principles materialize into lived social conditions. When confronted with reality, the French political system passes with surprising ease from abstract universalism to narrow-minded and aggressive supremacism whenever the "French way of life" is challenged, particularly as a founding principle in the arbitration of student conduct.

Péna-Ruiz, one of the most passionate supporters of the 2004 law, advocated the passage from secular egalitarianism (founded on the principle of equality) to a secular form of exclusionary identity politics. During a 2004 public debate at the Montreuil City Hall, Péna-Ruiz declared, "As a teacher, I prefer not to know whether my students are Jews, Christians, Muslims, atheists, or anything else, because I must treat them all as equals." These sentiments were often repeated by other supporters of the anti-headscarf law. Interestingly, Péna-Ruiz does not denigrate egalitarianism, unlike other reactionary and "identitarian" pundits such as Alain de Benoist, the theorist of the New Right, or the neoconservative polemicist Alain Finkielkraut (see Rancière 2005). On the contrary, he reveres it as an ultimate goal. Inversely, Péna-Ruiz does not defend the exclusionism implied by forbidding the headscarf; rather, he denies that implication. The essence of his position is the opposition between the majesty of "Universalism" and the shadows of "particularism," "communitarianism," or even "exclusionary" identity formations. In contrast to the polemics of the extreme Right, neoconservative, or right-wing republicans, this speech is clearly not oriented toward the celebration of identity politics. Péna-Ruiz's position typifies left-wing republicanism, which disguises a majoritarian particularism as the "Universal," and identity politics as egalitarian discourse. Péna-Ruiz confuses *equality* with *identity*, thus demonstrating a total misunderstanding of egalitarian logic and its implications for the question of cultural difference.[23] How does the recognition of difference (for example, knowing whether someone is Jewish, Muslim, religious, nonreligious) prevent equal treatment? "Different" is the opposite of "identical" rather than "equal," and "equal" is the opposite of "unequal" rather than "different." By confusing the question of "equality/inequality" with that of "identity/difference," Péna-Ruiz makes identity a condition of equality. He believes that difference necessarily translates into inequality. This is the domain of racist thought. As a secondary school teacher, I can verify that the headscarf does not prevent me from treating my students equally. My pupils have, anyway (with or without a headscarf), thousands of manners of showing me who they are. And this identitarian affirmation is not in itself a problem. On the contrary, knowing one's pupils is a pedagogic necessity. What is dangerous is not identitary expression, but imposition of an exclusive identitarian norm. Recognizing difference based on religious identity never prevents me from treating my students as equals. If you are unable to treat two people equally because of religious difference, the problem is not with what a student wears on her head, but rather what is within yours, and this is a defining characteristic of racism.

An Affair of Consequence

Consistent media coverage of the headscarf controversy has only reinforced the climate of anti-Muslim racism in France that developed in the wake of September 11, 2001. Whether the debate focuses on "economic insecurity," "exclusionism," "secularism," "fundamentalism," "the condition of women in the slums," or "the new Judeophobia," *the Arab Muslim boy* functions as the stereotyped scapegoat.[24] On one hand the battle of the headscarf is the French equivalent of the American clash of civilizations, while also referring to a specifically French tradition predating the 9/11 attacks. It is the latest episode in the conflicted relationship between the cultural and religious majority and postcolonial immigrants and their children. From this point of view, the 2003–2004 campaign was reminiscent of the 1958 "battle of the headscarf," in which women in Algiers were forcibly unveiled to prove the "emancipating genius" of colonial France (Shepard in Nordmann 2004; Fanon 2001).

Placed within its proper political, economic, and social context, the headscarf controversy continues the social war conducted by the Right and the "social-liberal" Left against the working class. Like the national obsession with illegal immigration from 1993 to 1998 and the economic insecurity of 2001 and 2002, the headscarf controversy was actually a new occasion to deflect questions of unemployment, insecurity, and discrimination by imposing an ethnic and cultural rather than a socio-economic or political explanation of the situation. As Saïd Bouamama emphasized,

> [O]ne modality of social combat questions the border that sepa-
> rates opposing camps. Neo-liberalism certainly has an interest in
> downplaying social equality, which is why cultural, ethnic, religious,
> and national identity has played such an important role in the
> debate. The right to free education is one of the social inheritances
> questioned by neoliberalism. The process of challenging the neo-
> liberal social vision has only begun, and the government is already
> being questioned by educators. Given this fact, it is not surprising
> that the school has become the battlefield for the combat against
> the the new enemy: the "headscarf" and the "communitarianism" it
> supposedly represents. The term "secular" is mobilized to mask the
> reality of social disparities, to reunite what neoliberalism divides,
> and to divide what it unites. (Bouamama in Nordmann 2004)

One of the most marked effects of "the year of the headscarf" has truly been to reunite what neoliberalism divides. In fact, when the Raffarin government (which belongs to the right-wing Union for a Popular Movement [UMP])[25] attacked social gains (notably retirement and unemployment benefits) and public education, who would have guessed that Arlette Laguiller, spokeswoman for Lutte Ouvrière (the Trotskyite Workers' Struggle Party) would support the government's position along with the Socialist Malek Boutih and Raffarin's fellow UMP member in charge of prison construction, Nicole Guedj? Nevertheless, on March 8, 2004, during Women's Day, under the auspices of Ni putes ni soumises (Neither Prostitutes Nor Bullied),[26] a "sacred union" of the neoliberal Right, the social-democratic Left, and the working-class extreme Left came together in the battle of the headscarf. On the basis of common hostility to the headscarf and belief in the political virtues of disciplinary measures, the "secular" Left formed an alliance with the clerical Right, pro-Palestinian activists with stalwart supporters of Israel, feminists with misogynists, and, following a long strike, teachers joined with the minister who served as their erstwhile antagonist.

The breakup of old alliances is apparent in the ranks of many political, labor, and other organizations. Although there were a few dissenting voices within the right wing,[27] only the Left was truly divided by the debate over the headscarf. Ironically, although the right-wing government launched the "affair" for its own profit, only the Left was active in the pro- and anti-headscarf campaigns. Socialist senators and members of the National Assembly were the first to announce their intention to file a proposition banning the headscarf at school. National policymakers for Lutte Ouvrière and the Communist Revolutionary League fed the media machine at the beginning of the 2003 school year by starting the "Affair of Aubervilliers."[28] However, the members of Parliament most vehemently opposed to the law also came from the Left. Indeed, polls indicated a split between two approximately equal "camps" among leftists.[29]

Despite media claims to the contrary, the headscarf controversy is not a subject of political debate across the board, nor does it blur the division between Right and Left. In reality, the Left's own identity and unity were blurred. On the Right, politicians and voters alike were unanimously anti-headscarf and prohibitionist. This division within the Left limited any sizable mobilization against the government's initiatives in 2003 and 2004, with little hope for change. The Left is divided by several fundamental questions. Do bans and prohibitions contribute to or inhibit education? Can a woman be "emancipated" against her will? Can the Other be "enlightened" by "our" morals? Does the end of secularism justify the means of forcibly unveiling women? Most importantly, how can French leftists from the cultural majority relate to working-class, immigrant, and Muslim populations? Although the problem of the headscarf at school is a political and media construct, it inadvertently invoked these relevant questions. The headscarf controversy *veiled* real problems like the dismantling of public services and the welfare state, along with structural unemployment and economic instability. But it *unveiled* the postcolonial racism that has taken root in France. Although its existence is often denied, this racism is found among all social classes and political stripes, including self-described "progressive" or "revolutionary" movements.[30]

This *unveiling of the Left* has many consequences. By not opposing the media campaign against "veiled" students, and by sometimes actively participating in it, the leaders of leftist organizations—in particular the Socialist Party, Workers' Struggle, and the Communist Revolutionary League—showed the great social distance separating them from certain populations, their inability to understand these populations, their penchant for authoritarianism, their intermittent intolerance, and even their racism. These leaders have permanently alienated a large part of their potential base. Twenty years after it essentially ignored the *beur* movement of the 1980s, the mainstream French Left has catastrophically missed another opportunity.[31] Significantly, the twentieth anniversary of the December 1983 March for Equality, which was the first time postcolonial French citizens from immigrant backgrounds demanded entry into the national discussion, was commemorated only by a presidential speech banning the headscarf. This repressive measure, aimed principally at the marchers' children, veils the issue of social equality with a false "problem of cultural differences." The law of the headscarf is thus a Freudian symptom: it is a pathological manifestation of the return of the repressed, evoking a past that never goes away. It is also significant that the headscarf's visibility is at the heart of the "problem"; when veiled women and adolescents affirm themselves as equals by appearing in schools, universities, and businesses, the headscarf becomes unbearable. Headscarves worn by mothers at home never provoked such furor.[32]

Conclusion: "Collective Humiliation"

In conclusion, we must not lose sight of the most direct victims of the great debate. Among them are the forty-five teenagers who were confronted by disciplinary councils and expelled from school. In addition, three Sikh boys were expelled in Bobigny for wearing turbans, and sixty or so veiled students "chose," according to the euphemistic terms of the minister of national education, to resign from school in order to attend private schools or take correspondence classes. There are also those, impossible to count, who "expelled themselves," by not returning to school in September 2004, to avoid the ordeal of being summoned before a disciplinary council. We can, however, guess their number to be at least two hundred, if not more.[33] We also must not ignore the torment endured by those girls who removed their headscarves to stay in school. We must ask whether the republican values of secularism, liberty, equality, and fraternity, were served as these girls were forced to surrender to a litany of threats, insults, and humiliations.[34]

Finally, the media debate of the past few years and its concrete consequences have wounded tens of thousands of people: the hundreds of students expelled or compelled to remove their headscarves, their families, and the entire population of postcolonial immigrants and their descendents, who are reminded of the forcible unveilings of colonial days. This wound has been nursed in silence and invisibility. French politicians can rejoice that until now, it has not been particularly visible. School superintendents can congratulate themselves on the "educational character" of the disciplinary councils,[35] and the mainstream media can continue to perpetuate the belief that everything is for the best in the name of secularism. Nonetheless, the French state, its politicians, and its media will eventually have to reckon with the suffering of those who endured aggression, discrimination, and expulsion as a result of the anti-headscarf hysteria[36] and the March 15, 2004 law.

Notes

[The term "secularism," or *le discours laïque,* as used in the chapter title, refers to the bulwark of the French Republic and maintains ideals of national identity associated with secular humanism. —trans.]

1. See E. Terray, "Une hystérie politique," and H. Bouteldja, C. Grupper, L. Levy, and P. Tévanian, "Une nouvelle affaire Dreyfus," in Nordmann 2004.

2. The number of headscarf-related disputes, according to the French Ministry of Education, fell from 300 in 1994 to 150 in 2003. Of these incidents, 146 were quickly resolved through compromise. See Tévanian 2005.

3. Several corroborating enquiries show that more than two thirds (between 66 percent and 69 percent) of immigrant children and/or Muslim youths (18–25 years old) opposed the March 15, 2004, law. This hostility was even more marked among girls than boys. See Tévanian 2005.

4. [The term *l'exception française* originally conveyed the belief that the demand for human rights and social welfare was unique in its insight and place in French national culture. Yet the term has since given way to contentious notions of cultural purity, resistance to the perceived effacement of French culture, and criticism of supposedly "foreign" intrusions within that culture. —trans.]

5. The Jules Ferry laws of 1880 and 1882 established free, mandatory, and secular education. The law of 1886 required that teachers in public schools not be members of the clergy, and the law of 1905 legally separated church and state, stating that "the Republic neither recognizes, salaries, nor subsidizes any religion."

6. ["Securitarian" is a neologism that refers to the idea of the security state. The question of "security" is particularly oriented to the issue of criminality. —trans.]

7. ["Identitarian" is a translation of the notion "*laïcité identitaire*," and refers to a narrow form of identity politics that borders on a reaction formation that denies the right of the "other" on the basis of an essential difference. —trans.]

8. This slogan echoes Jacques Chirac's ironic declaration that "we must not meddle with the pillars of the temple" when asked whether the 1905 law separating church and state had been called into question.

9. The "mosque" argument is problematic for two reasons. First, it neglects the important difference between secular and religious space. It also equivocates the relative violence experienced by the tourist who removes his shoes with the far greater violence experienced by a veiled teenage girl who uncovers her head to enter the classroom. This argument compares the tourist's voluntary visit to a mosque with a girl's right to education, which is especially shocking because lack of education in French society means an assured drop in social status, especially for working-class girls, who make up the majority of veiled students.

10. See Finkielkraut 2003b, as well as Dominique Liebman's analysis, "Finkielkraut se dévoile!" at www.lmsi.net.

11. Indifference to students' attire has not always been the rule. It developed during the twentieth century when students were harassed, threatened, and even sent home because of their attire. However, such harassment has no legal basis, nor is it related to "secularism." Rather, it was based on arbitrary criteria: girls were expelled for wearing pants, and boys were expelled for long hair. Although such authoritarianism was supposedly put to rest by the student movements of May 1968 and the 1970s, the current debate suggests that it is alive and well.

12. For statistics on expulsions and students' perspective on the new law, see [the] Une école pour tou-te-s [collective], "Eléments d'un futur livre noir," at www.oumma.com.

13. Of course, this principle is more fictional than real. Until the 1960s, history lessons oriented toward nationalist, Franco-centrist, and colonialist ideology. Even today, curricula are full of official mythology that downplays the role of women and the working class (Citron 1987).

14. It is an elementary principle of law: the silence of the law is an implicit authorization.

15. On the exaggerated and socially constructed nature of the current debate, see in particular F. Kaoues, "Quand les médias attisent la haine," at www.oumma.com. See also "Quand la loi du marché s'impose à l'école. De la ségrégation sociale à la calomnie médiatique," at www.acrimed.org.

16. Veiled women, "visible" Muslims, practicing Muslims, "supposed Muslims," or just plain Muslims.

17. This is also not the case for students wearing Ché Guevara T-shirts, Palestinian scarves, political buttons or pins, or red ribbons symbolizing the fight against AIDS.

18. The law's goal was to expel veiled students. Sikhs are the "collateral victims" of a law that was not originally directed at them.

19. In addition, the delegates at a September 2003 UFAL meeting decided that for "tactical reasons" the organization must petition for a ban on *all* religious symbols: "neither headscarf, cross, nor kippah."

20. On the contradictions inherent in so-called feminist arguments against

the veil, see *Nouvelles Questions Féministes* 2006, Guénif-Soulimas and Macé 2004. See also the contributions by Christine Delphy, [the] *Femmes Publiques* [collective], Caroline Damiens, Houria Bouteldja, and Monique Crinon at www.lmsi.com. Although it is certainly paradoxical that antiracist activists would support an objectively racist law, it does not mean that these activists are racist themselves. Rather, it reminds us that no one is free of prejudice, especially in a society fraught with structural racism.

21. See Djamila Béchoua's testimony, "Et toi, pourquoi tu le portes pas, le foulard?" at www.lmsi.net.

22. Christine Boutin is a member of Parliament from the right-wing UMP. Amir Lasfar is rector and imam of the Lille Mosque, as well as principal of Averroès, a private Muslim school.

23. As the philosopher Michèle Le Doueff remarked, even a child can understand that regardless of the difference between feathers [*la plume*] and lead [*le plomb,*] a kilogram of feathers weighs as much as a kilogram of lead (Le Doueff 1999).

24. On the theme of "the new Judeophobia," see Anon. 2003. On the media treatment of the "condition of women in the slums," see Mucchielli 2005, and Guénif-Soulimas and Macé 2004. On the theme of "communitarianism," see Sylvie Tissot, "Le repli communautaire: un concept policier," at www.lmsi.net.

25. The UMP is France's mainstream conservative party, headed by former president Jacques Chirac. Jean-Pierre Raffarin served as prime minister from May 6, 2002, to May 31, 2005. Raffarin, one of France's most unpopular prime ministers since 1958, was an early supporter of the anti-headscarf law. In 2004, he established a committee to begin drafting the law.

26. This movement was founded by members of the Socialist Party to fight the oppression of young women from working-class neighborhoods. Although it lacks a real social base in these neighborhoods, it is a political darling on both ends of the spectrum. The movement is often attacked by immigrants, who have accused it of "ethnicizing" the issue of sexism, and contributing to the stigmatization of "Arab boys" and veiled Muslim girls.

27. On the Right, opposition to the law was restricted to lip service. No right-wing personality demonstrated against the law between December 2003 and March 2004. Members of the UDF (center-right) merely abstained from voting on the law instead of opposing it. The rare dissenting voices on the Right fell into three categories: neoliberals like Guy Sorman and Alain Madelin along with centrists like Jean-Christophe Lagarde, who called the law an attack on freedom of conscience and the Muslim community. Clerics like Christine Boutin deplored an attack on all religions, and finally, the extreme-right-wing leader Jean-Marie Le Pen called the law a "smokescreen" designed to divert opinion from "the problem of immigration."

28. At the beginning of the 2003 school year, teachers at Aubervilliers High School led a campaign that ended in the very publicized expulsion of two veiled students, Alma and Lila Lévy. See the complete account of the "affair" by Laurent Lévy on www.editionsamsterdam.com.

29. Prohibitionist activists fall into six categories: (a) the Socialist Party and its satellites (essentially SOS-Racisme and Ni putes ni soumises); (b) the "national-republican" movement, united by UFAL (Union of Secular Families); (c) a small contingent of anticlerical North African immigrants; (d) several movements on the extreme Left (the Worker's Party and Lutte Ouvrière); (e) a few feminist groups (Prochoice, the Women's Rights League, and SOS-Sexisme); (f) members of "divided"

organizations on the Left, such as ATTAC ("anti-neoliberal" Left), the Communist Party and the Trotskyite Revolutionary Communist League, and unionized teachers from the SGEN-CFDT (General National Educational Syndicate) and the FSU (Unified Federal Syndicate). The anti-prohibitionist camp, united since December 2003 around the collective Une école pour tou-te-s/Contre les lois d'exclusion (School for All/Against the Laws of Expulsion), brought together individuals from the entire range of leftist groups: environmentalists, communists (predominantly the Communist Revolutionary Youth and members of the LCR, or Revolutionary Communist League,) labor unionists (predominantly CGT, or General Confederation of Labor, and SUD) and many others (CEDETIM, the Léo Lagrange Federation, the Movement against Racism and for the Friendship of Peoples,) immigrants and their descendents (Association of Maghrebi Workers in France, Federation of Tunisian Citizens of the Two Banks, the Movement of Immigration and Suburbs), and feminists (Public Women, Pluralist Women, Les sciences potiches se rebellent, the Blédardes, Feminist Collective for Equality). The Collective Une école pour tou-te-s provoked much controversy because it contained two organizations associated with the Muslim intellectual Tariq Ramadan, the Muslim Collective of France and Muslim Participation and Spirituality.

30. On this point, see Masclet 2002; Bouamama 2004; Tévanian, "De la laïcité égalitaire à la laïcité sécuritaire: le milieu scolaire à l'épreuve du foulard islamique," in Bonelli and Sainati 2004, also posted at www.lmsi.net.

31. [The term *beur* was coined by French working-class youth of Arab descent to designate themselves. —trans.]

32. See P. Tévanian, "Le corps d'exception et ses métamorphoses," at www.lmsi.net.

33. For statistics concerning the law's effect on students, see [the] Une école pour tout-te-s [collective], "Eléments d'un future livre noir," at www.oumma.com.

34. "Liberty, Equality, Fraternity" is the national motto inscribed on the front of public buildings and at the top of all official documents.

35. The inspector of schools defended the disciplinary councils' "educational" character after expelling a fourteen-year-old junior-high-school student in Mâcon (Reuters, October 22, 2004).

36. For example: a veiled woman turned away from a voting booth, veiled mothers forbidden from accompanying school outings, veiled women denied participation in the "great debate over school," a mayor refusing to officiate in a marriage ceremony involving a veiled woman, along with many desecrations of Muslim ceremonies and attacks on religious places. See Collectif contre l'islamophobie in France: *Rapport d'étape du CCIF sur l'islamophobie en France,* 2003–2004, at www.oumma.com.

CHAPTER 10

Zidane: Portrait of the Artist as Political Avatar

Nacira Guénif-Souilamas
Translated by Naomi Baldinger

Zidane: idol, ex-soccer player, object of desire, commodity, political icon, emblem, enigma. Hard to believe that he's a being of flesh and blood (and nerves, some might add.) The star was born Zineddine Yazid Zidane on June 23, 1972, in Marseilles, to Algerian immigrant parents living in the Castellane housing projects. Although *Zineddine* is the most faithful transcription of the Arabic *Zin-ed-din,* the child's name was gallicized to become Zinédine. In Arabic, *Zin-ed-din* means "the beauty of indebtedness," which refers to the Muslim's debt to Allah. *Yazid* means "he who prospers, superior." The hero's family name, Zidane (which means "addition" or "increase") is associated with a village tribe in Petite Kabylie, east of Algiers. The star's ancestral ties with this tribe were ignored for many years, although today it attracts considerable attention. Above all, Zidane's image is an intersection of multiple identities that change depending on the viewer's perspective. A variety of conflicting discourses add layers to this network of often stereotyped identities, turning a man into a super-man. This text strives to understand the making of a hero. How did Zinédine Zidane become Zizou, a political avatar who represents the conflicts and tensions of postcolonial France?

The Making of a Hero

Zidane is in vogue. His legendary feet have trampled the greatest soccer stadiums of the world. He is the darling of the popular media: here he is on horseback, in an infomerical dedicated to fighting degenerative illness in children. Here, as well, his exploits on the field draw attention not merely as a soccer star, but as a twenty-first-century hero.[1] Here he is again, in the newspapers and daily television programs, and again, on an Algerian airport tarmac in December 2006, as television cameras document his "return." The prodigal son's televised "return" is like a cult film, in which he plays the romantic hero. Zidane appears in serious postcolonial editorials and glossy magazine spreads. He also finds himself at the center of an extreme-right, ultra-patriotic discourse that considers any immigrant one too many, especially those on the victorious soccer team. To an electorate divided along color lines, Zidane is more important than all of his teammates combined. He is exceptional, exemplary, unique, and he must stay that way.[2] He is perpetually Exhibit A, and always seems to embody exactly what is expected of him. If Lilian Thuram, the black soccer player from the French Antilles, estranged himself from the Right and much of the Left because of his incendiary comments on the "Sarko-ization" drawing on the "Le Pen-ization" of French politics since the 1980s,[3] both Right and Left still attempt to monopolize Zidane. But how long can it go on? He can be interpreted as a poster boy for the classic rags-to-riches tale, or he can be coopted as a representative of nationalism, be it French or Algerian. Zidane is infinitely exploitable to politicians, a fact partially due to his silence on the subject of politics. His only public political statement came during the 2002 presidential elections. When faced with a choice between merely a right-wing and an extreme-right-wing candidate, he said, "There is no choice." The portrait of the artist as a political avatar is a distorting yet revealing funhouse mirror of hearts and minds in postcolonial France. As France mourns its past and searches for its future, it creates Zidane the hero. Although the team that hired him expected nothing more than a sleeper champion, he has become a valuable political commodity. Sports commentators marvel that a player who has scored so few goals in so many qualifying matches could become such an idol.

Zidane's involuntary politicization reveals a certain glory that exceeds the magic of his skill.

This glory stems from his ability to represent France in all its contradictions. An entire nation's hopes are invested in Zidane, who is now the world's most famous Frenchman, to the astonishment of many. He is burdened with innumerable virtues and flaws by dint of his fame. Yet his reticence to speak publicly suggests that he does not want to be fully domesticated, and that he wants to maintain elements of the ethnicity that he has carefully constructed. This ethnicity, plastered all over public places and TV screens, fascinates even as it repels those who see the Other, the intimate enemy. Zidane complicates the notion of celebrity and troubles the distinction between identity and alterity. Some see in him the possibility (or the risk) of a new multiculturalism, in which French youth can retain their multiple identities and allegiances. His stardom complicates exclusive notions of citizenship and nationality. Like many French citizens, Zidane is bi-national, proving that it is possible to be both "here" and "there."

Indeed, he is ubiquitous both "here" and "there," both within France and outside its borders. His currency as an image is due not solely to his magical appearance on thousands of television screens, but also to his political relevance. His figure is made to obey the dictates of his followers, both athletic and political. The thousands of distorted images of a satanized Zidane and a self-righteous Materazzi, or vice versa, diffused throughout the Internet by facetious bloggers the day after the champion's infamous head-butt, showed Zidane's uncontainable rage. He resists all appeals to conform to the nation-state's norms, leading many to refuse to read him as anything but a sports figure. This amputates his otherness and naturalizes him after the fact as French. Thus, he represents the exclusivity of the nation-state and the contradictions that it imposes on some and not on others. He both embodies and resists the contradiction that dictates that some wear their multinationalism proudly, happily juggling their multiple passports, while others must hide their multiple identities like the shameful inheritance of a colonial past. Were he not a star, he would certainly be consigned to the second category—which includes a recent immigration law mandating DNA testing as a means of testing citizenship while reinforcing the politics of fear and innuendo.[4] The politics and rhetoric of the security state discourage newcomers from attempting to set foot in France, especially those who have endured a difficult journey from the African continent. These would-be citizens, as Sarkozy has described them in his July 2007 Dakar speech, are none other than eternal figures of the peasant imprisoned in their past and unable to take part in history and modernity.

Everyone has an opinion on Zidane, and everyone attempts to monopolize him for particular purposes. He belongs to everyone and thus cannot maintain sovereignty over his own persona. As a champion, his identity has slowly been stolen from him, and replaced with maudlin tales of exile, destitution, and immigration designed to please prime-time audiences. The hero's political fame brings his dispossession into sharp relief, revealing the inner workings of his glory. Although it is well hidden and difficult to decipher, behind the hero's fame lies a hidden knot of multiple identities. It is this knot that I will attempt to untangle in deconstructing the hero's body as the exception.[5]

Spoken Words, Silenced Words

Given the French taste for euphemism, the lexicon describing Zidane functions on multiple levels. Like a diver emerging from the depths surrounded by a halo of mystery, careful to ascend step by step to the surface in order not to destroy his respiratory system, anyone who describes the champion must proceed with caution. In France, taking the plunge into the discourse of ethnicity is like a dangerous foray into hostile territory. Ethnicity, especially when coupled with suspicious physical traits, is countered with discourse that functions as an antidote or a barrier. Thus, the discourse of ethnicity is one of levels and selections, avoiding any shocking words or slippery statements. At least, cultural gatekeepers would like to think so.

Seized by the Republic

The word *Republic* is the lexical key to Zidane's deconstruction, because it automatically resonates with all French citizens. From the limited perspective of sports, it may seem strange to introduce the Republic onto the soccer field. What could it possibly be doing there? In fact, the Republic seized the champion following the unexpected victory that he engineered. It claims his two out of three total goals scored during the 1998 World Cup, and it claims his ethnicity as a triumphal expression of the harmonious alchemy of *les bleus:*[6] *black, blanc, beur* rather than simply black, Arab, and white players.[7] The much vaunted multiculturalism of the French team troublingly resembles that of the blighted suburbs from which its players come and not the segregated neighborhoods of the elites. For this reason, it is subject to numerous intellectual and semantic distortions and reinterpretations. The guardians of the Republic watch over and cherish the champion. At the same time, they are hardly accustomed to his status as the Frenchman par excellence, which became unquestionable the day after the World Cup, when his image adorned the Arc de Triomphe.

The media's coverage of Zidane as a postcolonial "president," so to speak, was peppered with bitter notes as the champion's face adorned the monument to Napoleonic glory, marking it with the stigmas of a contested history that its beautiful bas reliefs cannot obscure. Can the memory of unsavory defeats be erased in one night celebrating a soccer champion with unexpected ethnic traits? Granted, the defeats in question were athletic rather than overtly political. But the hero of the day, the son of a former colonial "native," allows the Republic to forget its inglorious decolonization. Through a play of images, a champion born to immigrants achieves the highest rank in the monarchical republic. Yet Zidane's new regalia cannot quite mask his paradoxical mission, to engineer an ethnic and cultural reconciliation that has yet to materialize ten years later. The image of Zidane's face on the Arc de Triomphe, a dazzling inspiration due to nothing more than a sportswear company's marketing scheme, left no trace of the symbolic displacement it implied now that the image has been removed. After all, the unknown soldier turning over the flame does not share Zidane's origin as its ephemeral "president." As soon as the intoxication of victory wears off, the image is taken down, and classically "French" identity regains prominence at the expense of a renewal of ordinary racism. This moment is especially significant in terms of the concurrence of memories that saturates public space. In the absence of political discourse, the inflated importance of the memorial clashes with the stigmatization of ethnicity, particularly among the youth. After one blazing evening, the projected image is extinguished, leaving denial in its place. It is prudently relegated to the chapter of great events that must remain an exception. The evening's enchantment of the monument's rendezvous with the new France was followed by a disappointing morning. Like the France-Algeria match of 2001, which began with whistles against the opening anthem of La Marseillaise and ended with "territorial invasion," the event had great importance for young transnational denizens of the *banlieues* in search of excitement and change. The same youth give themselves periodically to other riots, in which fire comes gradually to occupy a central place. Once the intoxicating odor of glory evaporates, young French citizens of color see their country under a dark day, feebly lit by the flames of burning cars and perfumed with the odor of burnt rubber. "President Zizou" is exposed as an optical illusion, an ephemeral image in a fantasy tale of heroes, no more substantial than the mirage of his image on the Arc de Triomphe.

Yet almost overnight, Zidane became a symbol of the Republic and its power. Of course, some could argue that Zidane does not exercise this power. Despite his status as a cultural symbol, he keeps his distance from the discourse of French high culture, because he knows that he is a plebian hero rather than an elite one. But it would be false to state that his popular power is less than other figures' political or literary power; his decisive goals are incommensurable to any political decree. His appeal is the vulgar power of merit that is sometimes conferred within the Republic. Zidane created a precedent: the champion turned de facto politician, medals turned into badges of power. All this and he isn't even white!

But Zidane is white, you might say. Yes, but not white *enough;* he is at best Arab, "of North African origin." He is stained by a shadow, a shade, a dash, of his ethnicity. He recalls certain whispered words: Algerian, immigrant, Arab, Berber, Muslim, *indigène.*[8] Implicit within his stardom is a sense of the impostor, and a feigned meritorious legitimacy. He is undoubtedly successful, more so than all champions past and present, including his teammates. But up to a certain point: up to the point where he eclipses all the other champions of the moment, including his teammates, all past champions, and maybe even those to come. His exceptional fame is sometimes perceived as the impudence of one who ignores the dogmas of nation and Republic. Zinédine Zidane, son of Algerian immigrants who were formerly *indigènes,* displays this impudence in his excessive success in becoming the greatest champion in France. At the same time, the French are excited that a Frenchman is constantly and expensively courted by soccer clubs the world over. Gone, the stains of immigration, Berber folklore, Algerian refuse, Muslim rags, shadowy Arab-ness. Ethnicity is hidden beneath the discourse of glory, banished because of its impropriety and unseemliness. Ethnicity has no place within the discourse of the "egalitarian" and meritocratic Republic, which can sanction only a conventional rags-to-riches tale with no mention of ethnic identity. The Republic's crushingly proper process of domestication exerts its force on the champion,[9] who knows all too well that he cannot escape it. He is in no position to decline the offer of ethnic purification so kindly proffered by the Republic.

His naturalization is merely symbolic, because the Evian Accords decreed him French by birth, like all descendents of former Algerian *indigènes* born in France after 1963. In light of this fact, he knows he must make invisible and inaudible all traces of ethnicity, whether inherited or invented. The obscene words that describe this intimate and compulsory experience must not be heard, because they contradict and threaten the cherished universalism of the Republic. At the very least, the Republic must remain central to the identities of its increasingly multicolored progeny. Thus Zidane, emblem of the Republic's cultural goodwill, says the bare minimum about himself. In place of his private life, he must substitute his legendary shyness, his unparalleled modesty, and his deep respect for his parents, who are "everything" to him. These undoubtedly genuine qualities judiciously hide cultural penchants, ethnic attachments, and other markers of his origins that must never appear in broad daylight.

Recaptured by Islam

As champion of France, Zidane cannot be both the ideal citizen and a Muslim "subversive"; this would make him a sort of Trojan horse within the Republic. Like Monsieur Jourdain, who did not understand the aristocracy's rules of grammar, endorsing too visible identities exposes him to questionable minoritarian and ethnically displaced protuberances. By disguising his unsettling ethnic identity, he condemns himself to silence even as he benefits from the nation's adulation. A few days after the lost 2006 World Cup match and his liberating head-butt, he explained his behavior during a television interview. To the journalist interrogating him, he affirmed that he would do it all again: "I would leave it like that, because it was decided *up there.*" He referred to a superior force and a higher power against which he cannot prevail. By tracing an imaginary vertical line that connects him directly to Allah, the demigod committed a blunder that left him voiceless and estranged him from the discourse of the mainstream media.[10] Yet, the blunder was quickly justified by the idea that silence becomes Zidane and that his gestures speak for him, like the hero of an ancient legend. The hero's disgraceful affirmation of his religion baffled his dumbfounded interviewer, who was astonished to see Zidane the social climber rejecting the flawless pedigree the Republic had to offer him. Neither the Republic, eldest daughter of Reason rather than the Church, nor the blonde journalist expected such an affront from the hero. A true virtuoso must master his reason and not allow himself naïve, irrational translations of Muslim sayings whose well-known "fatalism" has fallen out of favor during this War on Terror. The head-butt transformed the great champion into a simple-minded believer, shocking the nation, which had to console itself with Pope Benedict XVI's pronouncements on the intrinsically irrational nature of Islam at Ratisbonne.[11]

Zidane's "coming-out" as a Muslim "proved" his irrationality and violence to those who were not already convinced by his famous head-butt in Berlin. This "gesture" demonstrated his unrestrained drive to violence, that had theretofore been pardoned in him, but would be no longer once he crossed the radioactive line of religion. Up to that point, he had succeeded so well in hiding his origins: he married the daughter of Spanish immigrants, gave his children Christian first names, and confined his shameful heritage to the realm of folklore. He hid his heritage behind a veneer of "civilization," enabling his assimilation. Yet his reference to religion seemed to imply Islamic extremism, rife with machismo and sexism, during this time of repackaged religious war.[12] Zidane's double transgression led to dismay, questioning, and regret for those who thought that his "dark side" had been conquered once and for all. Refusing to content himself with a simple declaration of faith, the champion concluded his explanation with a reminder that an Italian politician had declared that "Italy beat a team of Blacks, Muslims, and communists. For anyone who wants to combat racism, it's shocking to hear that. It's insulting, it's painful."

In the soccer stadium, like in everyday life, the hero is undoubtedly exposed to racial slurs that he deplores, and wishes to combat. But his reaction to them takes on religious overtones that expose the dilemma of ethnicity when he is compared to his religious alter ego of sorts, Franck

Ribéry.[13] Ribéry, who is of French origin, wears on his face the marks of a troubled adolescence,[14] and prays to Allah before each match. He created his own blend of Islam following his marriage to a daughter of Algerian immigrants, who brought him to Algeria following the loss of the World Cup. Ribéry's visit to the country that now belongs to him and his wife did not inspire the same controversy as Zidane's Algerian voyage. However, there is only a short leap from Zidane's inherited Islam to Ribéry's invented Islam. The routes of the two men from Marseilles toward Algeria are superimposed upon one another. As memory and emerging markets converge, the journeys of the two men from Marseilles toward Algeria converge, as the mixed-marriage couple paves the way for the demigod.

The Eternal Arab

The hero risks a fall as great as his rise; the threat of disgrace haunts the knight of the Legion of Honor.[15] These two poles, which appear diametrically opposed, can be described in the vocabulary of stigmatization and stereotyping, making use of the ultimate weapon, the word *Arab.* The word resounds in the historical discourse of French sovereignty as the bitter enemy of the Republic. Since the time of the Moorish Saracens, the Arab has alternately inspired fascination and fear within a historical discourse that recounts European attempts to open commercial and political routes to an undecipherable, stylized Orient.[16] France, which entered the slave trade and the colonial enterprise later than its Spanish, Portuguese, and British neighbors and its Arab opponent, has particularly strong feelings about the "foreignness" that lies beyond the Mediterranean. The Arab's supposed "opaqueness" is a key feature of the discourse that surrounds the intimate and lasting commerce between France and the Orient, which is represented by Levantines, Turks, and later by the North Africans who were to soon become the *indigènes* of the Empire. Alain Grosrichard describes the relationship as a "contrary intimacy," that takes place in the half-light of an Orient that is at once awe-inspiring, ambiguous, and corrupt (Grosrichard 1979). The West shivers with fright and desire, imagining that its fate, too, will be decided behind the Turkish sultan's Sublime Door. The figure of the Arab, which Edward Said subtly deconstructs, has oscillated between inspiring attraction and repulsion since the time of the Crusades (Said 1978, 1993).

The relationship between France and its Arabs remains equally ambivalent today, barely altered by the twists and turns of postcolonialism and the global fight against terrorism. The encounter between East and West occurs anew in France as it undergoes modernity's spectacular rites of passage. The Revolution and its ensuing Terror forged the concept of French Citizen. A century of colonialism came and went, and now gathers dust. The Republic will take any drastic action to suppress anything that deviates from its morally righteous universalism in its quest for a unified and uni-dimensional political space that does not support exceptions, unless dictated by insurgency. The Arab (and to an extent, the black) has replaced the proletariat as the scapegoat for all social ills.[17] The dangers of racial inferiority and social menace are represented by postcolonial figures who, freed of the confines of colonial exoticism, have come to inhabit a space of alterity at the very center of the Republic (Guénif-Souilamas 2006b). The figure of the Arab, drawing on the historical depth and semantic richness of the colonial imaginary, finds new dimension and resonance in the blighted suburbs. In the new, unpredictable France, the Other is once again constrained to play the villain. The Arab Other is, according to this role, perversely violent. He refuses to civilize himself or assimilate, as evidenced by his persistent violence against women. On the other hand, blacks are cast as collectively unable to understand the very concept of civilization, as their supposedly profligate polygamy demonstrates (Guénif-Souilamas 2006b). Zidane is the archetypal Arab. His body is the site of a performance of ambivalence and multiplicity. He reflects the many silhouettes of young French people struggling for a place in the social and cultural landscape. At the same time, since his head-butt and subsequent World Cup defeat, he has shared a reputation for incivility with the faceless Arabs and blacks of the peripheral suburbs. The champion, fallen from his pedestal, has become no better than the undignified, "indigenous" Arab, forever prisoner to his instincts. The absolution reluctantly given to the disguised Arab by Ségolène Royal doesn't ignore the adjacent worlds of the champion and of his former congeners when it comes to maintaining male honor and the submissive woman. On the contrary, it aims at indulging the hero in order to more effectively accuse insignificant figures. He is thus used to reinforce a climate of suspicion.

Even his well-publicized trip to Algeria demonstrates his return to dangerous "Arabness." The media's reaction to this voyage ranged from praise for Zidane's filial loyalty and humanitarian concern to ironic snips about his affinity for orphan causes. However, the trope of the prodigal son was the most frequently invoked. Zidane became a paper icon that anyone could manipulate or tear. On this unique journey, the Algeria of Zidane's ancestors had a very different meaning than the Bangladesh of impoverished yet dignified masses, which he had visited a few weeks earlier. Paradoxically, Zidane made his declaration of independence from the country of his birth, which began when he moved to his wife's native Spain, by returning to his parents' village. Zidane's voyage certainly does not display any sort of allegiance to the divided police state of Algeria. With his head-butt, he crossed the final frontier separating him from extraterritoriality and supranationality. He represents the unknown space of the singular, rather than universal, postnational, representing in his persona and his journey Arjun Appadurai's notion of the -*scape*, as that which escapes, incorporating elements of loss and the gaze (Appadurai 1996).

This voyage became possible because his professional engagements have lost some of their sacredness, like his loyalty to France and his too frequently invoked personal history. As he says hesitantly of the hyper-real world he escaped: "Until today, I was very ... watched, but now that I have the time, I can come back to real life, find my origins, the land of my parents. I want to experience it; I'll experience it little by little, that's what's left for me to experience." Through his discreet attitude, he attempts to evade this oppressive surveillance, instated because he is not only a soccer star, but the most famous Frenchman, thus crafting an image devoid of a publicly anticipated "racial" characterological will to excess.

Nevertheless, it would be inaccurate to see nothing but degradation and opprobrium in his "Arab" image. This image also represents an unspeakable and obscure desire oscillating between identification and possession. Like an island in a disputed sea, two states claim sovereignty over him. Yet he nourishes and cultivates the ambivalence at the heart of the unexpected image of the renowned Frenchman reduced to the status of an Arab "*indigène*" reinvented on his native soil. He is both same and other, average and exception, mediocre and sublime, who fascinates and yet repels.[18]

Behind the menacing face of the animal balking at domestication, we see that of the Arab boy (*garçon arabe*), eternal object of Orientalist

desire. This trope, rife with perverse colonialism, is reinvoked and reinterpreted for Zidane the demigod, the Adonis with an athlete's body.
Recent attempts to reestablish the hero on his Olympian pedestal go far
beyond attempts to defend his honor or admiration for his charitable
activities or his career. The authors of these panegyrics of praise, homosexual love, and Hellenic pederasty, just like their acid critics, are almost
exclusively men. Does this reflect praise for a universal hero, or contempt for a common kicker and dribbler? Either way, it demonstrates
the enduring desire of Western men for *garçons arabes,* who, like female
victims of rape, are held responsible for the perverse attraction they
inspire. Despite his status as virile hero, Zidane cannot escape colonial
narratives of colonial servitude, a narrative more violent than the more
conventional individuating forms of emasculation.[19]

Zidane-as-Adonis is also the object of platonic love. In an article
appearing in *Le Monde,*[20] a journalist swoons over Zidane's naked body,
portraying him as a mute star who speaks only with his body. If the body
of the champion truly speaks, his ethnic ancestry must be hidden under
suffocating laurels of praise. As such, Franck Baetens, a philosopher,
reads Zindane's body and the head-butt incident as a mythological sign
of the gods. Whether the love for Zidane is homosexual or platonic,
the idealized nude figure of the hero paradoxically disguises his unsavory traits (Baetens 2006). Like an eternal newborn, he is a blank slate
for the praise of his admirers, but he is also defenseless against them.
Yet within his mythologized and aestheticized body, the image of the
debased Arab rises to the surface with increasing frequency. His head-
butt lowered (or raised) him to the overdetermined status of the Arab in
France. Through this gesture, he returned to a world from which he had
carefully distanced himself, at least in appearance. By renewing these
slackened lines, he breaks out of the statuary mold created for him by
the media. His body may be suitable for the French Pantheon, but not
the flesh-and-blood man who struggles against the technologies of the
self prevalent in Foucauldian societies of surveillance.

Neither completely civilized or uncivilized, Zidane appears so
respectful and timid, yet cedes in an instant to his violent impulses.
Neither completely white nor black, as an Arab he is not white enough
to be fully accepted, nor black enough to be completely shunned. Zidane
is the emblem of the children of immigrants from the former colonies.
He, like all the others, is unpredictable, resisting all attempts at integra-

tion and assimilation. Displaying and "performing" the stigmas of a conspicuous ethnicity is the trademark of these stereotyped French men and women.[21] The simple presence of the "ethnic" label betrays their hopeless lack of integration and delimits their only niche of survival. As the actor, humorist, and producer Djamel Debbouze said, "for the press, I remain an Arab who succeeded." Debbouze, the second most famous Arab in France, renewed a connection with an obliterated past by producing and performing in the film *Indigènes,* which tells the story of colonized Maghrebi soldiers, often referred to as *Tirailleurs,* who were used to help liberate metropolitan France during the Second World War. For Debbouze, like Zidane, the conditions that permit his celebrity also lock him into a mimetic role. Can the infinite combinations of hybrid identities sprouting from the New France break out of the normative constraints of assimilationism to give rise to new forms of individuality and mutual acceptance? The quarrel over controlling Zidane's image exposes him as a pivotal figure in this game of mirrored identity.

The Algerian Underbelly of a "Kabyle" Image

Zidane's simultaneous censors and admirers take refuge in his Kabyle identity,[22] which until recently made up for the sinister Algeria/Arab dyad. If in spite of (or because of) the head-butt incident, Zidane is a great man in training, his Algerian and Arab identities are counterbalanced by his more palatable Kabyle and French identities. The first two identities are difficult to accept because they raise the specter of Zidane's binationality, which is actually codified into French and Algerian law. This binationality is true heresy for the neo-Hellenist "defenders of the Republic," although among others it is displayed as the mark of mutual recognition. Until recently, being Algerian was considered to be a crippling condition, either because of the leaden silence surrounding the legacy of the Algerian War or because of the supposed poverty, awkwardness, and primitivism associated with Algerian immigrants. If it was ideally better to be exclusively French, embracing the term "Kabyle" became thinkable only in wake of the recovery, even if it is just illusory, from the sound and fury of the protracted and contentious Algerian civil war.

The gulf between "Kabyle" and "Algerian," and their resonance, partially stems from Algeria's enduring, albeit stereotyped, presence in the French imagination. Two related developments are worth noting. On one hand, a new batch of (mostly female) recruits are rallying to Western modernity. Most of these come from stigmatized Muslim countries, such as the Algerian intellectuals (all considered Kabyles) who present the West as the bulwark against the fundamentalism that threatens their integrity and liberty, glossing over the West's complicity in doing little to denounce authoritarianism and repression in Algeria. In the gendered scene of a struggle between the West, as the arbiter of democracy and human rights, and the East, with its attendant totalitarianism and oppression, the blood-drenched warfare for women's rights and secular values is being fought in the trenches by sympathizers in Algeria (especially in Kabylie), Afghanistan, and Iran. Moreover, the martyrs in the struggle against male oppression have found a new battlefield: the ghettos *à la française.* This tumultuous entanglement of heterogeneous discourses comes as a slap in the marble-sculpted face of Zidane the French Berber, the only man who is spared in this epic struggle by reason of the androgynous exception that he incarnates, created by his too-virile head-butt.

The stereotype that hangs over immigrant men's heads is thus reinvented in the quarrel between fundamentalisms, be they religious or secular. The condescending gaze becomes a worried glare that haunts Algerian men and those unfortunate enough to resemble them. However, Algerian women have recently become trendy, even more so than the *beurettes,* those "daughters of North African immigrants" held up as models of French assimilation. Bloody images of the ancient colony extend to postcolonial France, recycling the tropes of sexist violence, and resulting in an unexpected and unequal alliance between Algerian and French women. The daughters of immigrants, taken under the wing of white women who "want the best for them," have become heroines in a just and unarmed war against Islamists both in France and abroad. The use of the ethnic marker "Kabyle" in this narrative says a great deal about the whitewashing of identity that women (and some men, like Zidane) must undergo in order to be accepted by these well-meaning, "open-minded" French advocates of liberty.

Imaginary and residual projections of the past crystallize in the political avatar of Zidane, the son of Kabyle immigrants from Marseilles. In 1998, as the horror and violence of the Algerian civil war began to die down, Zidane's face became ubiquitous all over France.[23] Minorities, in particular, viewed it as an affirmation and a badge of honor—Kabyles most of all, because more than other Algerians, they are viewed positively by the French for endorsing the fight against the Arab oppressor. During the colonial era, Kabyles were deliberately treated as higher on the ethnic hierarchy by the French when it became clear that the War of Independence was inevitable, perhaps in order to shore up the "civilizing mission." The colonizers hastily set up literacy campaigns and attempted to ameliorate sanitary conditions in rural, primarily Kabyle, zones near the governorship in Algiers. Although the effort was in vain, as colonial "modernization" broke down among the "natives," the colonizers desperately held on until the final days of the war. The story of the initiative and its failure resonate during these troubled times of riots and of despair nourished by inequality. Yesterday, like today, Kabyles, who are supposedly more docile and easily "civilized," are juxtaposed with Algerians, their supposed ideal Arab oppressors, who are perceived as shady and ferocious. This line of demarcation separates the immigrants who will conform to the injunction of invisibility and the recalcitrant ones that must be "straightened out."

This is why, when the silence about "Zizou's" origins lifts, the word "Kabyle" is reassuring, because it invokes a folkloric vision of "men who stand up straight." The word is rife with positive connotations absent from the "Algerian," which connotes insularity and unreliability, and especially the word "Arab," which slips into common parlance from the crooked and perverse Bedouin. Ever since the notorious head-butt incident, stereotypes of machismo and animal bestial violence have revived the long-entrenched distinction between "Kabyle" and "Algerian." Zidane crossed a fraught border by visiting the village of his parents and ancestors on his initial voyage to Algeria in December 2006. The head-butt scene played out in the context of a bloodbath that ensued when youthful demonstrators protesting for democratic rights in the Kabyle region were violently attacked by government forces. Zidane's journey, escorted and choreographed by the political powers that be, was an attempt to rediscover his own alternating identity as both Algerian and Kabyle, considered oppositional in the French context, but this contradictory duality became particularly emblematic in the time and place.

Can the prodigal son fuse the two sides of his identity, like two sides of a coin? Can he reconcile his "Algerian-ness" with its oppressed minority component? The opposition between Kabyle and Algerian is one symptom of a historical malaise that still exists between France and Algeria. It is also a symptom of the profusion of ethnic, cultural, and sexual characteristics attributed to Zidane by a sensationalist media. The marks of ethnicity that French assimilation almost succeeded in erasing from the hero's persona have invaded the scene, shocking sensitive spectators who are stunned to see their idol declare, "I'm proud to be Algerian." To put the icing on the cake, he added one last provocation: in front of the photographer's lens, he pays his respects to a *chibani* (literally, man with white hair) in his parents' village. This custom, that immigrants to France were obliged to suppress, was renewed in the prodigal son's affectionate gesture and the attentive gaze. His father looks proudly on as Zidane honors this man, whose connection to him is unknown.[24] The significance of Zidane's visit was vexing and disappointing to the French public, who were led to imagine him as a scorned seventeen-year-old sent back to complete military service as an immigrant son whose parents could not see the exceptionalism of a future world champion. Although the Algerian-Kabyle fusion of identities was played out in what was, until recently, enemy territory by a champion always conscious of his French nationality, the fact that a colonial hierarchy of ethnic difference is still in force remained unspoken. In fact, these ethnic hierarchies can now be more easily implicated and disavowed, overinvested or dislocated. They have returned to those with a psychic investment in them, in order to reinvent them through supplements and identifications that accentuate their meaning. In this time of postcolonial reorganization and infinite hybridization, Arabs and blacks no longer accept confinement to invisibility imposed by a previously shared myth and the fallacious doctrine of "color-blindness."

A Devouring Passion

The social uses of Zidane's political avatar make it clear that his supposed assimilation and propriety pose more problems than they resolve. His assimilation and his status as social object are fated to remain unsolved. The real man, independent of his avatar, proves indigestible to the French public. Its devouring passion for Zidane scorns the man of flesh and blood. For example, the frequently invoked image of his poor parents is far too simplistic. Not all immigrants are statistically poor, but the majority live modestly. Nevertheless, the media portrays Zidane's family as "poor" rather than "modest," because it fits in so well with the "rags-to-riches" story of the champion. The image of Zidane struggling to overcome the challenge of his immigrant and colonial origins magnifies his persona, obscuring the taint of his low extraction. The champion's role dictates that he *must* have poor parents so that he remains conscious of the indignity from which he rose. His parents are movie extras, disdainfully cast in the story of their son's life. They serve their son best by fading into the background, except during his trip to Algeria, when they were invited to pose next to their glorious offspring. But above all, signs of ethnic, cultural, and religious origin must not be seen, and must remain buried.

However, there is one ethnic scene that Zidane's "handlers" allow, that of food and ingestion. The champion and his family love to eat the cake his mother has always prepared. Here, his mother is called by her name—Malika—to lend evocative power to the scene. The interest shown in this simple, rustic meal that the mother prepares for her disdainful, jet-set son illustrates a well-documented tendency in France. The pleasures of multiculturalism in the *banlieues* are relegated to delight that the favorite son takes in his immigrant mother's cooking. Fears of ethnic "invasion" and the disappearance of jealously guarded traditions are temporarily set aside, and immigrant women receive a temporary reprieve from silence and invisibility. Eating is the quintessential act of a France proud of its *terroir* and cuisine, and in these times of hybrid globalization, Malika's cake is the most digestible sign of ethnicity. "When will we get the recipe for Malika's cake?" exclaimed the promoters of a new "pluriculinary" France, expressing an interest in the recipe of the champion's mother. These enthusiasts, of course, do not realize that Zizou's mother shares her recipe with the mothers of the ignored and demonized *banlieue* youth. Assimilation has taken on the unexpected contours of cooking, revealing its anthropophagic-political basis. The Republic is truly a devouring mother for all of its illegitimate children.[25]

Beyond Words: The Political Body as a Border

It is irrelevant whether the "real" Zidane is conscious or not of the identity wars he generates; their effects undoubtedly reach him. Zidane *is* political, because his persona represents so many conflicting identities. His image is politicized, whether he does anything about it or not. His every action takes place on a minefield of identity and memory. He is dangerously overdetermined, and he is expected to answer for this. One would think that his retirement from soccer would liberate him from his duties as a political symbol, as has been the case with other sports figures of his stature in years past, but he doesn't seem aware of it. Why does silence suit him so well? Several answers are possible. The argument that he is merely timid does not merit a closer look, because it is too easily inferred from his character. Prudence seems to be a better explanation, a trait that he has acquired from the immigrant milieu in which he was raised, developing the bitter conscience of an overexposure to the exterior gaze. Immigrants are constantly exposed to the inquisitive gaze of power, which seeks anomalies, defects, and irresoluble problems. Constantly aware of losing control of himself in the public eye, Zidane has thus developed a reflex for protecting himself and defending his family against attack. His story as the child of immigrants is in the making; he is careful not to tell it, and always remains mindful of what can be said and heard, that which can be perceived and anticipated. If he represents the theatrical expression of an interior narrative that cannot be spoken, then he is also a child of immigrants who knows not to cross certain perilous lines without a sense of vigilance. His interior narrative undoubtedly includes things that are not utterable, but he knows that he must tell his tale with vigilance.

Another explanation for Zidane's silence is his anger, which is expressed by the physical violence that has become one of his trademarks. His stinginess with words translates this other experience, which he shares with many children of immigrants. This is the experience of shame before the disdainful gaze that pierces minority children without truly seeing them.[26] This shame is ever-present behind the injunctions to assimilate and be "civilized." It is a subliminal message that produces powerful and durable effects. Zidane is certainly not immune to this banal, silent shame that is palpable among immigrants and the poor. Like so many others, he learned to hide his shame beneath a veneer of blind anger that threatens to erupt at any moment, displaying the shame he has tried so hard to forget. For him and many like him, anger is easier to bear than shame; the former is impulsive, while the second is mortifying. Zizou's many red cards symbolize the crimson of buried emotions that are all the more intense for his attempts to suppress them. For his shame, he substitutes violence and aggression that are perceived as savagery, whereas they are a mask for his vulnerability. Zidane is not mute, but he is reduced to silence. Thus Zidane, the "mute star" manipulated by the media, is actually an incarnation of the subaltern from whom Gayatri Spivak addresses the question, "Can the subaltern speak?" (Spivak 1988, 1999).

Beyond Borders: Plays of Words, Light, and Shadow

This analysis of Zidane's words and gestures is enriched by the improbable combinations that many other individuals and communities invent to express their multiple identities, multi-formed ethnicities, and complex affiliations. Zidane is both avatar and object of political morphing, pushed and pulled from all directions. Once his persona has exceeded the limits of his body, it is used to support all sorts of real and fictional projections of identity, but also for ideological, political, cultural, and social erasures. Everyone sees in him what he or she wishes. His likeness appears in video games, aesthetic retouching and deformations, thematic collages, and numerous other multidimensional representations. In Ukraine, Iceland, the United States, and countless other places, individuals customize his image to their own liking. He is shoved aside by his own ubiquitous image and the interminable symbols it produces. The virtual world of globalization produces a Zidane in continual flux, always reformed and reconfigured in order to be diffused, formatted, displayed, exaggerated, or erased. On the French side of the porous virtual border, a battle rages over local interpretations of Zizou, bearing on the future of France's postcolonial globality. Insularity is a thing of the past. The vast semantic and analytical mine of Zidane's fame remain to be discovered by the ethnographers of the virtual era.

While Zinédine, Yazid, Zidane, the being of flesh and blood, continues to lead the everyday life of a retired soccer star, commentators continue to analyze the numerous intrigues of his fame. The inexhaustible universe of his persona will surely outlive the man himself. He is charismatic, for sure, but also unique, lonely, rough-hewn, and poorly understood despite the multifarious discourse that surrounds him.[27] We have yet to understand the infinite ramifications of his social and political image. This text has attempted to forge the rudiments of a "Zidanology,"[28] which can, it is hoped, contribute to emerging narrative features of postcolonial worlds and their dissonant dissent,[29] whose effects have only begun to appear. The outline of Zidane's character can be traced as in a game of connect-the-dots. When the figure comes into view, the interconnected dots display the figure of a postcolonial landscape, creating new lines for the opening and closing of new spheres of action and representation of postcolonial French people. Through these new figures, a devastated political landscape can finally be separated from its double and the majority who reconfigure it.

Notes

1. In the film *Zidane, A Portrait of the 21st Century* (dir. Douglas Gordon and Philippe Parreno, 2006), Zidane's acumen on the soccer field is portrayed in a multi-focal and conceptual manner. This film was premiered at the Cannes Festival before its general release in May 2006.

2. On the idea of Zidane's exceptionality and exemplarity, see Abdelmalek Sayad's analysis of the Algerian émigré/immigrant (Sayad 1991, 1999).

3. In an interview following the infamous 2006 World Cup Final, Lilian Thuram, also member of the High Council for Integration and a former member of the Monaco soccer team, criticized then minister of the interior Nicolas Sarkozy for his response to the 2005 riots and Zidane's behavior during the match. See http://psg-manager.football.fr/2006/07/18/387-materazzi-c-est-une-maladie-estime-thuram.

4. See the editorial "Pseudoscientific Bigotry in France," at http://www.nytimes.com/2007/10/21/opinion/21sun2.html in the *New York Times*.

5. I will attempt here to take up again the enterprise of deconstruction in terms of the vocabulary that designates the descendents of North African immigrants in my earlier work, *Des Beurettes* (Guénif-Souilamas 2003: 31–51). On the sovereignty of the body and its defeat by exceptional bodies, see Hansen and Sepputat (2005); Barkat (2005). On the French exception, see the edited volume of the journal *Cosmopolitiques* (Chouquer and Guénif-Souilamas 2007).

6. "Les bleus" is the popular term for the French national soccer team.

7. The slogan "*black, blanc, beur,*" which employs colloquial terms for ethnic designations, was often repeated following the 1998 World Cup to vaunt the diversity of the French soccer team, and by extension, French society. Yet, as the *Washington Post* points out, while 17 out of 23 members of the winning team belonged to ethnic minorities, only 11 of 577 members of the French Parliament at that time were minorities. For elaboration on this issue, see http://www.washingtonpost.com/wp-dyn/content/article/2006/07/06/AR2006070601742.html.

8. The word *indigène* recalls the days of French colonialism. This was the term the French used to designate their colonial subjects; it contains negative connotations of backwardness and primitivism.

9. For more analysis of the French "civilizing" process, see Elias 1969a, 1969b. On its application to new subaltern groups, see Guénif-Souilamas 2006a.

10. Interview with Claire Chazal on the private channel TF1, July 12, 2006, which is available online at http://www.merci-zidane.com/interview_zidane_TF1_12juillet.asp. On the draconian conditions of visibility for Islam in France and its supposed corollary, communitarianism, see Nordmann 2004, Deltombe 2005, Tévanian 2005, Lévy 2005, Guénif- Souilamas 2006a.

11. This is a reference to a speech given by the pope, in September 2006, when he stated that Islam and democracy were incompatible.

12. Only one public figure, and not among the least, strayed from the general

reprobation the day after the head-butt: Ségolène Royal, the Socialist presidential candidate, who was then involved in the primary campaign. She stated, "I understand what Zidane did, because he wanted to defend the honor of women in his family; anyone else would have done the same." The vocabulary she used ("defend," "honor") was far from the feminist critique she normally performs. It is word for word the rhetoric she denounces that is used to describe the intolerant inhabitants of the suburbs. The reversibility of these arguments did not seem to astonish anyone. Although they had the same origin as the champion, she did not stop herself from stigmatizing, by borrowing citations to support her, the thundering declarations of the feminist movement NPNS (Ni putes ni soumises, which translates to "neither whores nor bullied"), which for its part had prudently kept silent in the "case" of Zidane. This misinterpretation or selective feminism was undoubtedly due to the paralysis that often struck politicians when facing the 2005 riots, controversial youth employment law which put the whole country on strike during Spring 2006, and the head-butt incident.

13. Ribéry currently plays for FC Bayern München. He converted to Islam after marrying a French-Algerian woman. He was Zidane's teammate during the 2006 World Cup.

14. Ribéry is known as "Scarface" because of a long scar on his cheek that is the result of a car accident.

15. Zidane was decorated as a knight in the French Legion of Honor in 1998.

16. On the political currency of the Arab, see Anidjar 2003.

17. For analysis of this emerging French debate, see Chevalier 1978; Blanchard, Bancel, and Lemaire 2005; Fassin and Fassin 2006; Castel 2007.

18. On the feminizing aspect of racist views of the othered body, see Guénif-Souilamas in Rigoni 2007.

19. See Rauch 2004, Guénif-Souilamas and Macé 2004, and Thomas Blom Hansen, "In Search of God's Hands: On Masculinity and Religion," keynote address at the International conference Gender and Religion in Global Perspectives, University of Copenhagen, October 26–28, 2006.

20. Laurent Greilsamer, "Et voilà pourquoi les stars sont muettes," *Le Monde*, December, 19, 2006. In its December 22 edition, the newspaper announced the appearance of the first books dealing with Zidane by inscribing him in the Western discourse of "melancholy," or by focusing on his moment of weakness. A recent exhibition at the Bibliothèque Nationale de France is titled "Héros, d'Achille à Zidane." It is aimed at displaying the exceptional and universal ties between Achilles, Heraclitus, Roland, Lancelot, Jeanne d'Arc, Condé, Napoléon, Jean Moulin, De Gaulle, Lucie Aubrac, Che Guevara, Jimi Hendrix, Superman, and Zidane. This mythologization enterprise can be read through George L. Mosse's lenses of "respectability and abnormal sexuality" (1985) and "creation of modern masculinity" (1996).

21. See Judith Butler's *Bodies That Matter* (Butler 1993: 32), where she writes, "the significance of something is to know how and why it matters, where 'to matter' means at once 'to materialize' and 'to mean.'"

22. The Kabyles are a Berber people whose traditional homeland is the highlands of Kabylie in northeastern Algeria. They are perceived in France as not "Arab," unlike the rest of Algerians. On the invention of the "Kabyle myth" by French colonizers see Lorcin (1995 and 2005).

23. Zidane received the Golden Ball for Most Valuable Player in the 1998 World Cup after scoring two decisive goals against Brazil.

24. On the ambiguity of masculine rituals in the Mediterranean and postcolonial France, see Guénif-Souilamas and Macé 2004. The photograph in question can be seen on numerous Web sites, including www.zidane.com.over-blog.com/.

25. Abdelmalek Sayad first attracted my attention to the "digestive" metaphor for assimilation, although he cautioned me as to its usage. He himself employed it best in "Les enfants illegitimes," appearing in Sayad 2006.

26. On shame and self-hatred, see Guénif-Souilamas 2003: 330–35.

27. On the figure of "one," see Appadurai 2006: 49–66.

28. I would like to thank Nikola Tietze, sociologist at the Institut für Sozialforschung in Hamburg, for having inspired this neologism that several colleagues and I are trying to make current. See her article entitled, "Zinedine Zidane oder das Spiel mit den Zugehörigkeiten, Zinedine Zidane or Games of Belonging" (Tietze 2006). Her article is accessible in German with an English summary at http://www.eurozine.com/articles/2006-08-28-tietze-de.html.

29. I draw here on Paul Ricœur's (1991) proposition to understand the real by the stories and temporalities that compose it.

CHAPTER ELEVEN

The State of French Cultural Exceptionalism: The 2005 Uprisings and the Politics of Visibility

Peter J. Bloom

In the 2004 Luc Besson–produced thriller *District B13* [*Banlieue 13*] (dir. Pierre Morel), a black American gangsta-rap cultural aesthetic promotes a specifically French vision of natural man against the authority of the corrupt state that has transformed exurban *banlieue* culture into a walled-off ghetto of the future. Though deriving its kinetic flow from a martial arts–style aesthetics of movement, it predicts that French *banlieue* culture recedes into a lost hetereotopia of the postcolony and is thus transported into a time capsule that merges communist apartment housing blocks with an American-style ghetto gestural vernacular. The self-proclaimed success of postcolonial France buoyed by universalism, in opposition to American ghettoization, is finally transformed into a dystopian vision of exclusionism. Although the film does not self-consciously attempt political allegory, it draws on the spectacle of current events and the popularity of *fin de millénaire* hip-hop aesthetics in France (Bazin 1995). The futuristic action genre setting nearly suggests, in a tongue-in-cheek manner, that the Asian, Maghrebi, sub-Saharan, and ethnic white French underclass will not merely be walled off from safe urban centers, but will be monitored at checkpoints. It predicts that by the year 2010 Americanization, or the global Taylorization of the prison-industrial complex, becomes the operative method for the management of the French *banlieue* crisis. It is, however, a partnership between the local avenger with street-smarts, Leïto (David Belle), and Damien (Cyril Raffielli), the politically naïve but highly trained secret agent, that ensures justice will eventually be served in a Western-style structure of revenge and the triumph of democratic virtues on the exurban frontier.

Parkour, a series of gymnastic techniques, marketed as a youth sub-culture phenomena, is featured in the film, and David Belle, the protagonist, is its best-known representative. Reference to *parkour,* which has been developing for more than ten years, became established in the international media as a discrete set of bodily movements after being featured in *Casino Royale* (2006), with James Bond (Daniel Craig) pursuing Mollaka, an African terrorist bomb maker, in the opening "Madagascar Construction" sequence. Played by Sebastien Foucan, the co-founder of *parkour,* Mollaka is shown running, jumping, and finally scaling a partially built structure in a death-defying chase sequence.[1] *Parkour* first appeared in Nike and Adidas sneaker commercials, French television documentary segments, and the popular 2002 advertising spot used to launch BBC One's new brand identity in Rush Hour.[2] The technique itself is most often presented with the backdrop of decaying or partially built structures that function as a perilous urban obstacle course, allowing practitioners to display a remarkable array of stunts. As a supplement to martial arts, *parkour* adapts military training exercises featuring running, jumping, climbing, and lifting. In fact, David Belle cites Georges Hébert (1875–1957), the early-twentieth-century theorist of modern French military training, as the founding father behind the *parkour* movement.

Parkour is most often framed by a narrative of pursuit in a partially built setting located on the exiled urban or global periphery. It is the setting—part obstacle course, part exurban living compound—that justifies adapted military gymnastic techniques of evasion. These movements represent defiance of the laws of gravity that are further exaggerated by the concrete edifices themselves. Without weapons or implements, *parkour* is the pursuit of visibility, and a means of escape from being cornered.

In situ: Containment and Exclusionism in the Built Environment

It is within this narrative of containment, being cornered by the forces of order for imputed wrongdoing, that Zyed Benna and Bouna Traoré, the *beur* and black youths from Clichy-sous-Bois, became trapped and finally electrocuted while trying to escape from an electrical substation on October 27, 2005. The refrain of police pursuit reinforces a failure of social integration and a geography of exclusionism. The intermittent violence, social protests, and appearance in the media has become part of a cyclical phenomenon in which the underlying causes of social precariousness has become increasingly difficult to confront. In this case, however, the sequence of events created a theatricality of confrontation indicating that the scale of the problem has metastasized, spreading throughout low-income *banlieue* communities. All totaled, nine thousand automobiles were set alight, along with the destruction of 230 public edifices and 75 private buildings. As mise-en-scène and historical context, the new found visibility of the *banlieue* crisis came to represent a forgotten human geographic body-double, which was broadcast live as the arrhythmia of political neglect.

The construction of massive exurban housing structures in France, which came to be known as the *grands ensembles,* can be dated to the mid-1930s (Rotival 1935: 57). The first and perhaps archetypal example of the *grands ensembles* was the *cité* of La Muette, located in a suburb of Drancy, just outside of Paris.[3] Completed in 1934, and designed by the architects Eugène Beaudouin and Marcel Lods, it was initially planned along the lines of a garden city, or *cité-jardin,* but as Robert Weddle explains, when the plans for the project were published in 1932, it became clear that it was to be a more formal and rigorous architectural model, employing strips or *barres* and towers linked axially by large open spaces (Weddle 2001: 168). It was inspired by industrial methods of prefabrication, dry assembly, and the rationalized organization of the worksite heralded by Taylorization. Of the 1,234 apartments projected at the site, only 1,033 were completed, and many remained unoccupied. At first, troops from the *gardes mobiles* were lodged there, and a portion of the structure was initially turned into a prison for suspected spies (Archer 1964: 70). Once the occupation began with the armistice on June 22, 1940, it was used for prisoners of war by the Germans, and with the large round-ups of Jews beginning in August 1941, it was transformed into the largest deportation camp in France. Consisting of five fourteen-story towers, and a horseshoe shaped array of three- and four-story structures, it was considered a marvel of the era for its innovative design, construction techniques, and use of aerated concrete, known as *béton cellulaire.* It was the horseshoe-shaped building at the center of the complex that later became the staging ground for sixty-eight convoys of deportees from January 1942 to August 1944.[4] Of the 75, 000 Jews who were deported from France, 61,000 passed through La Muette, and by the end of the war only 7,500 survived (A. Wieviorka 1994: 139).

The symbolic demolition of La Muette in 1976, just as most of the *grands ensembles* had been completed, illustrates how the metaphor of the transit camp haunts the *grands ensembles* and certain of the subsidized housing structures, known as HLMs (*habitations à loyer modéré*). As the centerpiece of the *cités* and located in the *banlieues,* the *grands ensembles* came to function as a model of containment and a solution to the postwar housing crisis. Not only is the vanishing point of the transit camps, as synonymous with the deportation of the Jews, a source of shame in the annals of French collaboration, but its memory is revived whenever a Jewish cemetery or site of worship is desecrated. These attacks are as much an attack against the French state as they are against the Jewish community, because they revive the specter of state violence against a minority population and are motivated in the first place to counteract the perpetrators' own condition of invisibility. The metaphor of the camp in the postwar imagination, as transit camp, concentration camp, garden community, gated community, or leisure setting, has been a crucial site for social control and a means by which to redefine citizenship and the reduction of the individual to what Giorgio Agamben has called "bare life." As a discontinuous space for interaction in which heterogeneous differences are subject to "new regimes of justification," which refers to the reinvention of the camp as existing on the margins of urban centers, the figure of the camp brings into focus the overlapping positioning of inside and outside, while blurring the boundaries between power and resistance (Diken and Laustesen 2006: 98). The camp functions as a metaphor for a space of non-commitment and non-equivalence in which the "common good" is transformed into a logic of networks, ownership, and differential access. It is from this perspective that we can come to understand how the rationalization of exurban lodging as a lived phobic landscape of the *grands ensembles* exists in relation to those trapped inside and in search of a visible means of public expression.

État d'urgence

During the events of October and November 2005, the projected negativity of the crowd was encapsulated in a series of derisive remarks

by French public figures and politicians, aimed at reducing the perpetrators to contemptible rabble.[5] Occurring five months before the
first round of French presidential elections, the events punctured the
fiction of universal rights for all while motivating a securitarian reaction, leading to the declaration of a state of emergency on November
8, 2005, twelve days after the disturbances began. Seven days after the
October 28th incident, attacks began in other regions, including Ile-
de-France, Dijon, Rouen, and Bouches-du-Rhone, and intensified in
the days to follow. Consisting of a curfew, censorship, house-to-house
searches without judicial oversight, checkpoints, and the deployment of
additional police, the state of emergency was declared by the Chirac government as a response to a perceived threat of insurgency from within.
Unlike a state of siege, which implies the imposition of martial law, the
state of emergency was first applied in Algeria at the beginning of the
War of Independence and was written into French law in 1955, after
which it was sporadically applied in metropolitan France until 1963.
The statute was revived nearly twenty years later, from 1985 to 1986, to
quell unrest in New Caledonia, a site that has been an important extension of French military power in the South Pacific. The return of the
modified 1955 statute in 2005 triggered a return to forgotten but familiar
patterns of administrative ultimatums that pair political repression with
the exercise of colonial authority.

As Sylvie Thibault suggests, the *état d'urgence* can be understood
in relation to the formula of *hors-la-loi,* used against those who contest the French republican order and are thus placed outside its protection (Thibaut 2007: 77). First established by decree in 1793 against
the Vendean counter-revolutionaries to the Republic, the *état d'urgence*
implied by its deployment in 2005 that the nature of the uprisings was
a form of terrorism against the French state. It was on this basis, and
against legal objections, that the mandated twelve-day *état d'urgence*
period was extended to three months.

In an ex post facto logic that activates political constituencies in the
name of a looming crisis, the call to order contributed to a useful set of
political fictions. Just as the state of exception functions at the threshold
of indifference, it is also an attempt to impose the rule of law against
the reigning specter of anomie (Agamben 2005). The state of emergency
is a subset of a state of exception in that it grants authority to take
immediate action. Further, a declaration of a state of emergency is more

clearly associated with releasing funds and resources necessary to combat natural disasters. It is precisely this type of synecdoche that assigns the uprising to the context of a state of nature, transforming the rioters themselves into a weather pattern, without will or agency to change their direction or potential for destruction. The display of negativity against state institutions, and the spectacular burning of automobiles, indicated that the rioters themselves saw no exit from their social condition of invisibility other than the spontaneous possibility of spectacle.

Describing the perpetrators as hoodlums, within the lexicon of *casseurs, sauvageons,* and *racaille,* turned them into violators of the public trust in a humiliating standoff with politicians as the purported guardians of public safety.[6] Positioned on the periphery of major cities throughout the country in the concrete expanse of postwar housing developments, the perpetrators came to represent not organized resistance, but rather a spontaneous reaction. Unlike the positioning of organized resistance *in situ,* beyond the boundaries of metropolitan France, as in the insalubrious hive-like casbah depicted in *The Battle of Algiers* [*La Battaglia d'Algeri*] (dir. Gillo Pontecorvo, 1967), the French identity of the perpetrators became obscured. While the human geography of anti-colonial liberation movements clearly assigned positions within the terms of hegemony and resistance, the relocation of resistance from within the Hexagon, among a second and third generation of postcolonial citizens, has redefined the terms of being inside and outside.

The Invisible Politics of Visibility

Advertising culture has been an important instrument for the relocation of symptoms and causes, seamlessly relocating the outside as inside that can be resolved through processes of identification and commodification. This paper started with a discussion of the 2004 film *District B13* as a procession of semiotic tokens in its deft reassignment of inside and outside, using the nondescript mise-en-scène of the impoverished *cité* as an obstacle course of the future.[7] This framework also suggests that certain of the low-income HLMs and *grands ensembles* have negated the crucial position of *territoire* in the formation of French national consciousness. The film itself uses an extended array of concrete and partially built expanses as an ideal site for a gymnastics of high-speed pursuit in hostile deterritorialized settings. Initially promoted as *Yamakasi,* it became widely known through Besson's 2001 martial arts film of the same title and specifically referred to a regime of uninterrupted movements in which a multiethnic group of seven Robin Hood–like avengers climb towering HLMs, among other built structures, with ease and Zen-like calm.[8]

Dubbed *parkour* by David Belle and Hubert Koundé, who was the African member of the trio of protagonists in Matthieu Kassovitz's *La Haine* [*Hate*] (1995),[9] it refers to the *parcours du combattant,* or military training for French soldiers. The name *parkour* also suggests a militant but nonviolent response to the *banlieue* context. Unlike *beur* as the back slang of *Arabe*, *parkour* is more analogous to "tagging" in the lexicon of graffiti art, in that it assigns individual identity as part of a collective, which is why practitioners of *parkour* are most often referred to as *traceurs,* whose actual trace can be seen only as an audiovisual recording and admired for its gymnastic grace. As a graffiti-like gesture that "infiltrates" the gigantism of the *grands ensembles*,[10] it presents these phobic spaces of dislocation as a towering gymnasium primed for an exiled *precariat.* That is, as Loïc Wacquant describes, a proletarian underclass in "the pincer of social and spatial marginalization" (Wacquant 2007: 72).

The *parkour* phenomenon helps us see how the politics of visibility relies on an aesthetics of representation in which bodily movements of evasion are transformed into a popular spectacle. Just as the news positions spectacular events, or the increasingly incredulous and humiliating assertions of politicians, in order to activate a response and dominate a discourse, political activists have also understood the power of merely generating a response, when the choice is to remain socially and politically invisible. In the case of *parkour,* it is the politics of exclusionism and social precarity that stages it as a popular commodity form. It functions as an extension of French hip-hop culture because it transforms the conditions and a vernacular of precarity into a form of entertainment. The evolution of hip-hop culture as a response to the effects of deindustrialization and low-income housing in New York, Philadelphia, Los Angeles, and Detroit, which Tricia Rose (1994) has so eloquently described, has also been adopted as a global emblem of displacement and a will toward visibility as a style that pairs violence and belonging with self-improvement and success.

Techniques of self-defense against the claustrophobic housing blocks as contiguous with a politics of exclusion represent a rhetorical response to geographic containment within contemporary France by reconsidering the history of physical education in relation to the racialized spectacle of combat; that is, an important shift can be discerned from an anthropometrics of difference to the rearticulation of national identity within an international media apparatus (Bloom 2008). The international media apparatus redistributes the significance of racial, ethnic, and class-based difference. It is within this context that *parkour* gestures toward remapping the urban/suburban/exurban sprawl as part of a continuous utopian flow of movement.

Reinventions of Natural Man and African American Aesthetics

The popularization of *parkour* also recodes racial otherness through movements across geographic boundaries while referencing an imputed black American aesthetics of violence. An overarching entropic media framework appropriates the aesthetics of African American social protest by foregrounding style as a means of encapsulating political and social rights. The valorization of the criminalized black American underclass also subtracts rights from the social equation in favor of reasserting male codes of honor and, from the French perspective, the reinvention of natural man.

My insistence on the theme of the reinvention of natural man in *District B13* refers to the implied presence of African American cultural aesthetics that functions as a social allegory in contemporary French films depicting French *banlieue* culture. This functions within a binary logic in which postcolonial French subjectivity cannot be made equivalent to black America because colonialism was not equivalent to the American plantation system of slavery. More crucially, however, a French-inspired critique of an Anglo-Protestant settler culture of moral uplift insists on a form of brutal human subjugation and penchant for the extermination of native cultures that, in turn, validates the survival of African American cultural aesthetics as genuinely authentic and, consequently, primed for a uniquely French form of artistic reappropriation. In this way, natural man can be inferred from the African American cultural idioms encoding the original French archetype of the pure, uncorrupted eighteenth-century vision of the "noble savage." By proxy, and through intermarriage, black Americans became the inheritors of this uncorrupted European heritage.

Though racially marked as descendants of the West African slave trade, they remained proto-European through an American Indian genealogical legacy as opposed to Anglo-Saxon European white settler culture. In other words, they are the last surviving genealogical vestiges of uncorrupted early Europeans, transformed from early conceptions of the noble savage and remade as natural man.

Furthermore, I would like to point to a shift in the representation of the *beur* and black community in France as increasingly detached from the possibility for social mediation, and increasingly inserted into an aesthetics of violence as media spectacle. This is part of a postcolonial logic of respatialization that has repressed the paradigm of colonial difference as the effect of immigration politics and consequently results in the disintegration of social cohesion. The proximity of a racialized underclass on the frontier of French urban centers has metastasized into a fear of the non-French-speaking French subject. Instead, the non-French French subject has appropriated a transnational African American ethnic idiom.

L'Esquive *and the Effect of Triple Exclusionism*

Abdellatif Kechiche's 2003 French film *L'Esquive* refers to the gesture of evasion, and the physicality of dodging a blow. Released in the United States as *Games of Love and Chance* in 2005 after the title of Marivaux's eighteenth-century play that serves as its centerpiece, the film focuses on the courtship between two adolescents in the northern Parisian conglomeration known as Franc-Moisin, located in the suburb of Seine-Saint-Denis. It features a play of language in *banlieue* culture as part of a subaltern aesthetic. In a theatrical style reminiscent of Peter Sellars's adaptation of *Hamlet* to the linguistic staccato of Los Angeles gang speech patterning, Kechiche's film focuses on the evasive tactics of the spoken word revealing the submerged contours of class consciousness and the game of courtship. Sprinkled with Arabic and various forms of verlan, the subtitled English version uses a black American vocabulary to render the dialogue in a contextual space of confrontation, and expressive close-ups.

An important element in the narrative structure of the film is not merely the opposition between the world of courtyards outside of the dormitory-like apartment structures that serve as the all-important site of encounters between the lycée-age (secondary school) adolescents, but the codes of ending a relationship and initiating one. The film begins with the protagonist, Krimou (Osman Elkharraz), distancing himself from his girlfriend, Magali (Aurélie Ganito), followed by her attempt to intimidate Krimou's new love interest, Lydia (Sara Forestier), who embodies the role of Lisette, the maidservant in Marivaux's *Games of Love and Chance*. Krimou remains mostly inarticulate and speaks only in hushed tones throughout the film, but falls in love with Lydia and attempts to play the role of the Harlequin in the school production of the play so he can interact more directly with her and enter into the parable of courtly love.

While rehearsing in the undefined space between the school and the anonymous apartment blocs, Krimou attempts to kiss Lydia in order to assert his sexual interest for her, which she then contemplates and plays out in the mise-en-scène of the *cité*, which scrambles the stakes of chance and courtship in the spirit of Marivaux's game-like narrative puzzle. It is Lydia's sense of deferment that brings into relief their respective roles in the community, particularly that of Krimou, whose ardor for Lydia turns him into a passive agent who is unable to speak for himself. Krimou's position in the narrative can be usefully understood in relation to Nacira Guénif-Souilamas and Eric Macé's notion of the triple exclusion of the *garçon arabe*. By "triple exclusion" they are referring to the end of a sense of colonial certainty as associated with the "good" Arab worker, soldier, or head-of-household in France. Secondly, they are referring to the sense of insecurity that young Arab men experience, such that they are cut off from making a difference in their own community and cultural context. And finally, Arab boys are at the center of a reaction formation, both from within and without. They may be considered troublemakers from within because of a code of male honor and a deflection of what might be considered "effeminate" behavior such as the ritual of courtly love and from without with the defamatory language in the popular discourse and a structure of policing that singles them out.

In *Games of Love and Chance*, Krimou's acquaintance Fathi (Hafet ben-Ahmed) exhibits many elements in this structure of triple exclusion through his attempt to serve as the patriarch-in-waiting elder-brother figure. At Magalie's urging, Fathi attempts to force Lydia to decide whether she wants to be with Krimou or not through a form of intimidation that leads, in turn, to a more serious form of police humiliation. In the penultimate sequence prior to Krimou's withdrawal from the prospect of a relationship with Lydia, they are subject to a police patrol and apprehended. It is in this scene that the use of police force becomes the overwhelming language of power, positioning them as subjects whose very presence and association is considered not merely suspect, but outside legal norms, in their clustered visibility on the street and in Fathi's stolen car.

It is within this state of overdetermined delinquency that Krimou's position in *Games of Love and Chance* is reduced to the position of the mute subject, who cannot be heard, and returns only as a distant outsider glimpsing through the glass doors to see the play that he was unable to participate in because he could not muster the linguistic and emotional wherewithal to express himself in a new language. It is a language that is not limited to words spoken precisely, but the gestures, a manner of intent, and space in which citizenship becomes nominated. Kechiche's adaptation of Marivaux presents the codes of class difference through the language of courtly love, which cannot be overcome by dressing the part of the master. In the guise of a master-servant opposition as a displacement of the Hegelian master-slave dialectic, this film demonstrates a nearly static sense of social mobility in the French housing projects, abandoned by the state as postcolonial archipelagos of exclusionary politics. The contemplative nature of *Games of Love and Chance* means that it functions as a social problem film, anchored by an awareness of the obstacles to achieving meaningful citizenship rights. Its mode of articulation is explanatory, and functions as an extension of a political project given voice through cinema.

The Housing Question and Cinema in a Postwar Context

It is within the reign of visibility that housing questions in the *banlieue* were first presented in French documentary films during the postwar period. Eli Lotar's 1946 documentary *Aubervilliers* was the first to portray the lived conditions of postwar squalor that paralleled the condition of the colonial city. With a spoken narration by Jacques Prévert, one of the best-known screenwriters associated with Poetic Realism filmmaking during the interwar period, it depicts the situation of slum children and their insalubrious living conditions in a northeastern suburb of Paris. Annie Fourcaut suggests that *banlieue* cinema begins with such well-known films as Julien Duvivier's *La Belle équipe* (1936),

Jean Renoir's *Le Crime de Monsieur Lange* (1936), and Marcel Carné's *Le Jour se lève* (1939), which are at once inflected by the politics of the Popular Front, the aesthetics of *film noir,* and the existential depiction of the *banlieue* setting (Fourcaut 1999). *Aubervilliers,* however, is perhaps equally rooted in a French documentary tradition of *cinéma direct* and avant-garde experimentation; Lotar, born into a Jewish Romanian cultural context that served as a defining source for European modernism,[11] worked as cameraman for Buñuel's Spanish ethnographic surrealist film *Las Hurdes: Tierra sin pan* [Land without Bread] (1933),[12] and Henri Storck's 1937 documentary film about worker slums in *Les Maisons de la misère* [Houses of Misery], which was made as an industrial film for the Belgium Fair Housing Association (Société nationale des habitations à bon marché). As part of the international legacy of politically engaged documentaries focused on worker's rights, a small group of films that begins with *Aubervilliers* depict the French *banlieue* in relation to fair housing and immigrant rights.[13]

Although the housing stock was in short supply and poor condition prior to the beginning of World War II, Allied strategic bombing of industrial cities and urban centers beginning in 1940 contributed to a severe housing crisis by the end of the war. With more than 150,000 residential buildings damaged or destroyed on the outskirts of Paris alone, 120,000 provisional dwellings were provided, which took the form of wooden huts, improvised arrangements, and temporary housing shipped from abroad (Bastie 1964; Fourcaut, Bellanger, and Flonneau 2007: 282). With rising demand for housing in urban areas, predominantly in cities with more than 50,000 people, housing became a national priority in the second *Plan national* (Voldman 1997). By 1949, a new target of 20,000 dwellings a month was set by Eugène Claudius-Petit, minister of reconstruction and urbanization. The plan envisioned housing as essential to the modernization and rationalization of the French economy and emphasized reconstruction as an immediate need, rather than establishing longer-term plans for renovation (Bullock 2007).

The question of whether the style and function of new architectural planning for housing development schemes was to be organized around economic priorities or a new social vision of planned communities remained an ongoing debate until the mid-1950s. Just as a number of innovative designs were considered and constructed, the need to simply create housing as quickly and efficiently as possible became a decisive factor once the forces of production were reconfigured under the state housing authority. The economic priorities of housing construction as *équipement national* that served as an emerging model of economic growth was a functional response to calls for hygienic and moderately comfortable housing, particularly given the visible signs of impoverishment represented by the *bidonvilles* and the ubiquitous transit camps. These conditions were a constant reminder of the policies under the occupation that reduced all outsiders to beings without humanity; in other words, the *bidonvilles* and the transit camps remained a living example of how the colonial condition was imposed upon Europeans, which was considered an ultimate form of humiliation. It is perhaps for this reason that Abbé Pierre's inspired call to action on behalf of those without shelter (*sans abri*) during a February 1, 1954, address on Radio-Luxemboug found a wide range of support, as the state of homelessness was the instantiation of *homo sacer* and "the scandal of the human as such" (Dillon 1999: 114).

Although his call for new housing for the *sans abri* was honored as part of an already established social benefits equation and a set of housing entitlements, it did little to change the emerging emphasis of quantity over quality. The *grands ensembles* constructed in the years to follow on the outskirts of major cities in France were built to accommodate families, and were located in close proximity to future centers of employment that included transit to major urban centers, but compartmentalized and contained within a model of an emerging postindustrial work flow of anchored unionized workers and intermittent floods of temporary ones.

The scale of demographic transformations within France during reconstruction was monumental. As late as 1954, 41 percent of the French population was rural, and twenty years later three quarters of this rural population moved toward urban centers, becoming members of the metropolitan work force along with an influx of foreign workers from Southern Europe and the colonies that were soon to become administratively independent of France. From 1945 to 1980, nearly ten million housing units were constructed in France, replacing destroyed housing units but also depopulating the countryside and creating a new demographics of French society, in which the effects of displacement and dislocation came to be negotiated in these rebuilt and expanded communities (Lion and Maclouf 1982: 13).

The Fonds d'Action Sociale and the Invention of Beur *Cinema*

The extensive internal migration and related shifts contributed to an expanded postwar social security system in which a system of benefits created the foundation for inclusion among French citizens, and various degrees of inclusion and exclusion among foreign-born and postcolonial workers. France has always been a country of immigration, but the legal status of the colonial worker created a differential hierarchy within the French social benefit equation. Algerian workers who came to France in the aftermath of the war who were from the three French departmental regions within Algeria had a special status. Known as French Algerian Muslims (Français musulmans d'Algérie [FMA]), they were from the three French administrative departments within Algeria considered French territory. Their status as French Algerian Muslims meant that they were denied access to the same family benefit allowances extended to French workers. Instead, reduced family benefits were offered to them on the basis of legislation dating from 1949, stipulating that full family benefits could be expanded only to families with children residing within the Hexagon. As Antoine Math has explained, the difference between full family benefits for French workers and the partial amount extended to French Algerian Muslims was used to create a fund to improve Algerian worker housing in metropolitan France beginning in 1952. Known as the Social and Sanitary Action Fund [Fonds d'action sanitaire et sociale [FASS]), it was created to improve the living conditions of North African workers living in France. On the basis of this funding in association with the family allowance administration, 2.85 billion francs was budgeted and used to create more than six thousand beds in over forty-two housing complexes (Math 1998: 38).

The FASS was the predecessor of the Social Action Fund (Fonds d'action sociale [FAS]), which was founded in 1958 under de Gaulle. Although some political rights were extended to French Algerian Muslims under this mandate, they still received only limited allowances within the social benefits equation. This regime of differential allowances was justified on the basis that the cost of maintaining a family in France was much higher than in the French colonies. However, this policy ignored arguments for compensation based on the long-term separation from one's family, nor did it take into account the need to visit or reunite families. This bureaucratic regime was conceived within a colonial mandate. Furthermore, the difference of income between

French family allowances and the limited one offered to foreign workers was used to finance the activities of the FAS until this administrative regime was replaced in 1964 by a fixed contribution determined by presidential decree (Revol 1968: 9).

The history of the FAS remains important today because of its role as an instrument of social benefits that embodies colonial ideology. That is, the bureaucratic regime of holding back benefits in order to finance a housing authority set up in their name justified withholding benefits on the basis that the cost of building infrastructure was something the immigrants themselves should pay for from their own salary, as opposed to the industries, or the state, who were their employers and under obligation to provide adequate conditions. With the founding of SONACOTRAL in 1956, which was charged with building housing for Algerian workers, the FAS became the continuation of this project in a different guise.[14]

As Violaine Carrère explains, the FAS established a system of social rights and services for Algerian workers and their families living in France as a continuation of colonial policy that then evolved into the broader mandate of social insertion (Carrère 2007: 3). As the work of the FAS continued through the 1970s and 1980s, a significant portion of their budget was devoted to nearly five thousand associations working in the realm of immigration that included training, literacy, education, social mediation, and cultural activities that finally fell under the purview of the state. As a state-sanctioned agency, the FAS became the arbiter of these associations related to immigrant rights and discrimination that, in turn, might be used by the state to guide policy.[15] The FAS also had an influential role in legitimizing *beur* cultural expression, serving as an intermediary for local film production beginning with immigrant cinema of the 1970s.

Cinema and the Politics of Social Insertion

Institutionally, the political project of *beur* cinema began with a series of short films and became associated with the cinema of immigration that began in the late 1970s. The 1981 film *Zone Immigrée* stands as a transitional film in this respect, made on Super 8 by the Mohammed Collective based in Vitry-sur-Seine. As I have explained elsewhere, it was shown as part of the annual *Cinéma du réel* documentary film festival held at the Pompidou Center and addressed the procession of bureaucratic zones established as a means of social insertion and exclusion among the second generation (Bloom 1999). In fact, the transformation from immigrant cinema of the early 1980s to *beur* cinema later in the decade was primarily motivated by large public demonstrations such as the 1983 *Marche pour l'Égalité* and the 1984 *Convergences* rally, among other protest movements related to many of the same issues evoked during November 2005. *Beur* consciousness, which Boubeker and Battegay later described as *beur*-geois-ification, became identified with the release of Mehdi Charef's 1985 film, *Thé au harem d'Archimède* [Tea in the Harem], which established the position of the *beur* protagonist as *banlieusard* insider but an outsider to the norms of the French workplace. Significantly, the FAS was one of the organizations that attempted to bridge this gap, albeit functioning as an apology for it. That being said, the FAS did reinforce legislation written into law in 1981 allowing immigrants full rights to join and organize associative structures (Yahiel 1988: 109). These structures became the basis for a number of well-known antiracist organizations such as SOS-Racisme and France Plus.

A lineage of filmmaking aesthetics and style long associated with the political impetus behind Soviet-style agit-prop filmmaking that located political activism within the craft of filmmaking itself made its way into the "immigrant cinema" of the late 1970s and early 1980s. By the late 1980s, at the end of a cycle in which the urban peripheries were rebuilt, the *banlieue* became a site for the emergence of feature-length films alternately known as *beur* and *banlieue* films (Bosséno 1992). Whereas depictions of the living circumstances in the increasingly de-industrialized *banlieues* can be associated with the mise-en-scène depicted in French Poetic Realism on the one hand, hence the assignation *banlieue* films, the emphasis on *beur* identity, referring to the second and third generation of postcolonial North African French citizens born in France, and their emergent style within a French hip-hop aesthetic, is most often associated with *beur* cinema (Tarr 2005).

The Auteur and Constructions of French Cultural Exceptionalism

Although *beur* cinema directly refers to an Anglo-American critical vocabulary that nominates institutional access and redress, the new visibility of *beur* cultural identity by the early 1990s was couched in terms of the limits of a French republican discourse of assimilation in relation to American civil rights activism and identity politics. This opposition was partially resolved through the well-protected position of the auteur as filmmaker and social critic who embodies the features of the cultural exception.[16] As an exception to the rule, the auteur as an independent creative agent represents a perspective that contests dominant social meanings. The role of the auteur, typically associated with François Truffaut's celebrated 1954 essay "A Certain Tendency in French Cinema," opposed what was known as the "Tradition of Quality" to the cinéma d'auteurs (Truffaut 1959: 68). For Truffaut, and the circle of critics/filmmakers writing for the Cahiers du cinéma, auteurs were embodied by particular filmmakers who were able to express a particular worldview that privileged human potential against a corrupt society.

It is important to remember, however, that it was written in response to an article entitled "The Cinema of Quality,"[17] and directed against a state system of financing known as the Fonds de soutien, which automatically funded projects with popular appeal and bankable talent that did not take significant risks or attempt to showcase emerging talent. Starting in 1953, a new experimental regime of funding was established that rewarded quality short films. It was extended to feature films in 1955, and transformed into what became known as the avance sur recettes system, which uses a portion of box-office receipts for French film production funding; this system still remains in place today. The debate about quality that Truffaut challenged was, in fact, a new argument within the French film production system and became the basis for a new system of financing, but also had a significant impact on the nature of film production as a social good, not only intended as a form of consumption. It is from this perspective that a network known as the Groupe des trente (Group of Thirty), first established in 1953, came to redefine the autonomy of cinema and the terms of quality, which aligned its network with the public interest and public service (Gimelo-Mesplomb 2006: 141–50). It was on this basis that by the end of the 1950s the collective of filmmaker critics associated with the Cahiers started to receive financing for their films. The cinema-of-quality argument was crucial in reestablishing the Arts et essais tradition first organized in 1930, but transformed into an associative structure with access to production funding and distribution outlets starting in 1955.[18]

The argument for quality, as a protected category of cultural funding, became institutionalized and represented a means by which

professionals in the field were able to develop their own artistic autonomy and promote the development of the art form itself. Crucially,
however, debates about quality as synonymous with aesthetic values
were later embodied as a form of cultural exceptionalism, which became
a significant argument when Jack Lang began to serve as minister of culture in 1981. Cultural exceptionalism positioned the concept of discrimination as both the positive act of being intellectually discriminating and
a response to discriminatory global market forces dominated by the
Hollywood culture industry. Furthermore, it was used to accentuate a
distinctive vision of Frenchness and the projective patina of enlightened
cultural policies with international ambitions.

French cinema is part of an extended political bureaucracy that
assigns meaning and cultural value as a decisive source of film production funding and distribution. Within this context, *beur* cinema became
linked to new sources of public financing that empowered the FAS to
serve as an intermediary for small-scale productions through the French
National Film Center. Closely paralleling francophone African filmmaking structures under the rubric of the now defunct Agency of Cultural
and Technical Cooperation (ACCT), the shift toward emboldening
postcolonial media producers, such as Yamina Benguigui, as political
personalities transforms the significance of politically engaged cinema
related to the question of immigration, in the sense that the exceptional
personality becomes norm, but can no longer adequately represent a
normalized political problem. In fact, Rachid Bouchareb, the director of
the 2005 film *Indigènes* that opened to popular acclaim, began directing
films within this very limited scale of production, starting with such films
as *Baton Rouge* (1985), *Cheb* (1991), and *Vivre au Paradis* (1998), among
others. This scale of production served as a political zone of mediation,
neutralizing rather than activating public discussion, given that most of
these films never made it beyond the circuit of theaters in the Quartier
latin in Paris or the international French cultural affairs circuit of offices
that loan films to universities, museums, and festivals to promote the
diversity of French culture. In fact, none of the films produced within
this mode of production were widely screened or seen. As the Senegalese
filmmaker Djibril Diop Mambéty wryly observed some years before he
died, so many of our films are taking place in a carefully orchestrated
bubble that does not matter to the world outside.

Conclusion: The Return of Mise-en-scène

Just as arguments in favor of cultural diversity have benefited from governmental support, they have primarily been used as a vehicle for French exceptionalism rhetorically constructed in opposition to the discriminatory market forces associated with U.S. cultural imperialism—which has always been an all too easy target. Continual references to American discriminatory global economic practices and the caricature of identity politics in the United States have positioned the impoverishment of certain *banlieues* and their association with postcolonial identity within France as merely a case of the unassimilated, who are, by definition, uneducated. The symbolic role of the auteur as filmmaker and embodiment of the cultural exception thus becomes a means by which to incorporate minority representation on the basis of an aesthetic argument. Once again, it is through an argument about a discriminatory global climate of competition that the discriminating role of the auteur becomes recognizable as a symbol of inclusionism, but might actually function as an apology for a more decisive context enabling exclusionary minority politics. Discrimination as an analogy to market forces and cultural diversity has been used to stage an international political strategy on the basis of intrinsic national cultural values. The 2001 UNESCO Universal Declaration on Cultural Diversity proclaims that cultural diversity is synonymous with biological diversity, which is linked to freedom of expression. This rendering of discrimination suppresses the role of racial exclusionism that is further covered over by the nation-state as its vanishing point.

The reinvention of a republican model of universalism has been challenged from a number of fronts. Probably the best known has been associated with the Indigènes de la République, founded in January 2005, and the establishment of the Conseil Représentatif des Associations Noires in November 2005 in the aftermath of the November 2005 uprisings. They have focused on how the state has deployed colonial strategies by which to manage the postcolonial underclass as part of a project of colonial memory and redress. The emphasis on postcolonial subjects, racialized and excluded on the basis of their race as a synecdoche for a diffusionist view of formerly colonized cultures, has been a recurrent feature in recent commentary about 2005 uprisings.

Finally, film and media representations that have addressed the *banlieue* crisis began with debates around the naming of *beur* cinema as a film movement, and its relationship to a political movement. Just as the political movement has shifted in recent years, it is perhaps the less than intentional mise-en-scène revealed through depictions of the *banlieue* crisis that has revived the possibility for a deeper renegotiation of the social equation. It was on the basis of mise-en-scène that the *politique des auteurs* became a powerful argument for a new type of international cinema entering the register of the universalized cultural exception. Instead, the emerging terms of exceptionalism cannot be anchored merely by the *auteur,* but rather by the mise-en-scène and the emergence of these shadowy figures as agents of their own representation.

Notes

1. In fact the "Madagascar Construction" sequence was shot at the abandoned Coral Harbor Royal Bahamas Defense Training Base. Information about this particular sequence can be found in the production notes. See "Casino Royale: Production Notes," *Seattle Post-Intelligencer,* n.d., http://seattlepi.nwsource.com/movietimes/moviepn.asp?movieID=39756.

2. The popular 2002 BBC One advertising spot entitled "Rush Hour" was used to launch BBC One's new brand identity. In the spot, Belle spires by foot across the London cityscape as cars are snarled in traffic. He runs and jumps from one building to the next, risking life and limb to arrive just in time to sit on the couch and watch the news. See the Web site, http://parkour.net/modules/videos/singlefile.php?cid=3&lid=28. Most recently, *parkour* was the subject of a 2007 feature article in *The New Yorker Magazine.* See Alec Wilkinson, "No Obstacles," *The New Yorker,* April 16, 2007.

3. The other two best-known early examples of the *grands ensembles* include the Maisons-Alfort and Plessis-Robinson, also located just outside of Paris.

4. Comité national du mémorial du camp de Drancy, *Drancy: Le camp d'internement pour la déportation des Juifs* (Société Drancéene d'Histoire et d'Archéologie et le Service Culturel Municipal, n.d.). As cited by Weddle 2001: 168.

5. A week after Nicolas Sarkozy's too well known brandishment of *racaille* for the protesting youth, the well-known French academic and public intellectual Hélène Carrère d'Encausse was the first to refer to the polygamous marital practices of Muslim immigrants from West Africa as the root of the problem, while she was on an official visit to Moscow; she made the comment, which was seconded by the French minister of employment, Gérard Larcher, when queried by Moscow news.

6. For an analysis of the term *racaille* and its use, see Abdallah 2006: 54–62, and Jobard 2006: 59–80.

7. For a discussion of semiotic tokens see Eco 1976: 50, 183–84.

8. "Yamakasi-l'art du déplacement," *Les Périphériques vous parlent* 12 (Summer 1999): 12–16.

9. "Parkour History: Completed Timeline," http://parkour.net/modules/newbb/viewtopic.php?viewmode=flat&topic_id=4990&forum=1.

10. "Saute qui peut," http://parkour.net/modules/articles/.

11. For more on the history of Dadaism see Sandqvist 2006: 278–88.

12. For more on ethnographic surrealism and Buñuel's *Land without Bread*, see Lastra 1999: 52.

13. See for example, *Enfants des courants d'air* (dir. Edouard Luntz, 1959, 29'); *Etranges étrangers* (dir. Marcel Trillat et Frédéric Variot, 1970, 60'); *Les immigrés en France, le logement* (dir. Robert Bozzi, 1970, 56'); *Est-ce ainsi que les hommes vivent?* (dir. Claude Dityvon, 1975, 11'); *Du bidonville aux HLM* (dir. Mehdi Lallaoui, 1993, 51').

14. SONACOTRAL (Société nationale de construction de logements pour les travailleurs algériens et leurs familles) was established in 1956 as a means of providing housing for Algerian workers in France, and in 2007 was renamed Adoma, which now manages 450 buildings throughout France with 70,454 occupants.

15. In 2001, the FAS was disbanded and renamed FASILD (Fonds d'action et de soutien pour l'intégration et la lutte contre les discriminations) with its mandate shifting to discrimination and away from worker's rights and housing issues. In March 2006, in the months following the 2005 uprisings, the FASILD was renamed L'ANCSÉ (L'Agence nationale pour la cohésion sociale et l'égalité des chances), again emphasizing discrimination and moving toward further integration with urban renewal in its association with ANRU (l'Agence nationale pour la rénovation urbaine). See their website for further information: http://www.lacse.fr/.

16. Thanks to Jonathan Buchsbaum for his careful reading of an earlier version of this discussion and disagreements with the way in which I have represented the arguments about the auteur and cultural exceptionalism in France.

17. This article was written by Jean-Pierre Barrot, see Barrot 1953: 26–37.

18. Michaël Bourgatte, "L'exploitation Cinématographique dite d'Art et Essai," from the conference Mutations des industries de la culture, de l'information et de la communication, September 2006 at: http://www.observatoire-omic.org/colloque-icic/pdf/Bourgatte%201_5.pdf.

CHAPTER TWELVE

Let the Music Play: The African Diaspora, Popular Culture, and National Identity in Contemporary France

Charles Tshimanga

In the wake of the riots that caused widespread upheaval in France between October 27 and November 17, 2005, mainstream politicians, social critics, and journalists argued that rap lyrics fueled rebellion in the French suburbs, or *banlieues*.[1] Policymakers such as Nicolas Sarkozy, then interior minister and conservative candidate in the 2007 presidential elections, along with scholars including Alain Finkielkraut,[2] André Glucksmann,[3] and Hélène Carrère d'Encausse,[4] suggested that because the young rioters were mostly Muslims of African or Maghrebi descent, their "cultural differences" would make integration into French society impossible. Moreover, these representatives of "authentic France" and the mainstream media interpreted the riots as an expression of the rioters' hatred for France and the Western world. They accused the young *Blacks* and *Beurs* living in the suburbs of playing the victim without asking whether they themselves were responsible for these young people's exclusion from the system (Soullez 1999: 22). However, this theory is implausible because it is founded on the interlocking binary paradigms of "Westernized" vs. "non-Westernized," and "high" vs. "low" culture. It rejects multiculturalism, constructing a homogenous concept of French identity and culture. This approach underlines contemporary France's difficulty accepting its own diversity.

Rappers responded to these aspersions by arguing that their music was neither violent nor discriminatory by nature, nor was it the root cause of the violence of 2005. They explained that violence certainly existed prior to the emergence of rap music, and defined themselves as "street journalists" who merely described the unrest in the *banlieues*.[5] As rappers Joey Starr and Kool Shen put it, the provocative metaphors and mocking tone of their songs are an attempt to force mainstream politicians and media figures into a public debate about the plight of ethnic minorities.[6] Although official state discourse portrays *banlieue* youth as violent delinquents, African French rappers lend legitimacy to the *banlieue* revolt. They argue that the riots were a response to the legislative and economic policies that unfairly impact ethnic minorities in France. Moreover, an attentive reading of rap lyrics exposes the strong political discourse that fueled the riots, which African French rappers have pointedly expressed for decades. Through the medium of popular music, they interrogate the hypocrisy of a country that preaches humanist values while engaging in racial discrimination. In addition, rappers expose a different point of view on France's colonial past, which has little to do with the colonial and imperial version of history taught in French schools.[7] They are extremely critical of Africa's postcolonial evolution, marked by dictatorships and failed governments. Rappers such as Fabe consider it their duty to produce "an alternative discourse" that will represent *banlieue* youth and awaken their political consciousness.[8] These are the terms of the debate that has divided France for the past thirty years, in which both sides draw support from France's rich cultural traditions.

My goal in this paper is to develop a preliminary analysis of the emergence of this musical genre in France and its discourse on French identity. My reflections result from the primary research I conducted in Paris in July and August 2007. Likewise, my interviews with rappers in Paris and its suburbs increased my familiarity with the popular culture of French youth of African and Maghrebi descent. Thus, my paper will focus on the cultural critique constituted and embodied by the French rappers over the intersection of French national identity with the political rights of French citizens of African and Maghrebi origin. Rap music in France underlines the multiple challenges that the African diaspora has faced in its attempts to integrate into French society. Although many members of this community theoretically enjoy the privileges of French citizenship by virtue of their French birth, they are nonetheless considered "immigrants" even into the second and third generations, and accused of being inassimilable to French society. My analysis of rap lyrics centers on the pertinence (or lack thereof) of rap music in addressing the discriminatory treatment of second- and third-generation descendents of the African diaspora in France. I also intend to explore rap's role in addressing the construction of cultural identity in contemporary France, implying a critical reexamination of the ideals of the French Republic and its attendant motto of "Liberty, Equality, and Fraternity." Thus, this essay explores how, through popular music,[9] members of the African diaspora in France are challenging the notion of "Frenchness" implicit in the dominant discourse.

French Rap: Challenging the Politics of Cultural Difference

French rap and hip-hop, heavily influenced by their American precursors, emerged within the French musical scene in the early 1980s (Prévos 1996). Recent studies on this relatively new musical phenomenon have mostly focused on the history, styles, and subcultures of French rap.[10] Others, such as Jean-Marie Jacono (2002), address Marseilles' identity through a study of the group IAM. Paul Silverstein (2002) examines the economic aspect of rap music, exposing the ambivalence of musicians who criticize French capitalism even as they depend on it to sell records. Boucher analyzes whether rap has the potential to become a social movement in the suburbs, and Marti explains that rap "expresses the malaise of a disoriented population" and that African French rappers "keep their distance from a country in which they could not or would not find a place" (Marti 2005: 9, 11). In other words, Marti believes that African French citizens belong to a separate culture that cannot integrate into mainstream French culture. Each of these works, many of which suggest a paradigm of assimilation, provides a piece of the puzzle. To give as complete a portrait as possible of French rap today, I will provide its basic history as well as its historical and political context. As Tricia Rose (1994) and Robin Kelley ([1994] 1996) suggest in their studies of U.S.-based rap, historical context gives "a more multilayered interpretation of cultural forms that takes account of context and aesthetics, politics and pleasure," while avoiding simplistic explanations (Kelley 1996: 186). In France, rap is best situated in the colonial context and the post–World War II period.

History, Themes, and Evolution of Rap in Post-Industrial France

Rap music originated in the United Sates and arrived in France after the jazz of the 1910s and 1930s, the folk music of the 1960s, and the disco of the 1970s (Prévos 1996: 713; 2002). Sydney and Dee Nasty, Parisian DJs in the late 1970s and early 1980s, were the first to play hip-hop in French nightclubs.[11] Following their lead, DJs on the free radio, such as Radio 7 and Radio Nova (which were created following the 1981 election of the Socialist president François Mitterrand), brought rap into mainstream French consciousness.[12] In 1984, Sydney hosted the first hip-hop television program on TF1. During these early years, the repetition of certain English lyrics as well as rappers' adoption of American names signified strong American influence.[13] However, some rappers adopted French or African names later on.[14] Lionel D, Jhongyo, and Destroy Man were the first to rap in French.

Since its inception in the 1980s, rap has attracted emblematic as well as controversial figures, such as Joey Starr and Kool Shen, youths from Seine Saint-Denis, one of the most hazardous suburbs of northern Paris. Passi, another key figure in French rap, grew up in Sarcelles, a blighted suburb northwest of Paris. Rap came into its own as a musical genre during the critical period of the 1973 and 1979 oil crises, which ended thirty years of economic growth and plunged France into a serious depression. As a result, massive restructuring of the industrial sector led to widespread unemployment, primarily among unskilled workers in the *banlieues*. As Daniel Bell (1973) explains, the emergence of post-industrial societies has been marked by a decrease in blue-collar jobs and the ensuing decline of the unions. In France, this phenomenon has naturalized the revival of populist discourse of the extreme-right and conservative parties for so many French citizens. Thus, the themes of rap and hip-hop reexamine the origin of the first urban riots, which occurred in 1979 at Vaulx-en-Velin and in 1981 in the Minguettes housing projects in the Lyon suburb of Venissieux, as well as the undocumented immigrants' movement of 1996–97.[15] French rap also interrogates the popularity of Jean-Marie Le Pen, leader of the xenophobic, extreme-right National Front, which blames ethnic minorities for a host of problems in France.

In the 1990s exceptional CD sales and awards legitimated rap's presence within the French musical scene. In 1995, MC Solaar, a rapper of

Chadian origin, received the Best Male Singer of the Year award, and IAM was awarded Best Musical Group at the tenth annual Victoires de la Musique (Musical Victories) awards.[16] The next year, 1996, Alliance Ethnik was named Best Musical Group during the same awards. Menelik, a Cameroonian rapper, was named "Discovery of the Year." In 1997, Passi's first solo album, "Les Tentations," went gold three weeks after its release, a record in the world of French rap music.[17] These successes signaled rap's acceptance within a musical landscape dominated by classical French songs by talented singers such as Charles Aznavour, Georges Brassens, Patrick Bruel, Johnny Hallyday, Patricia Kaas, Mireille Matthieu, Renaud, Michel Sardou, and Charles Trenet. Major record labels were attracted by the success of rap music, and began to see it as a lucrative investment (Bocquet and Pierre-Adolphe 1997; Mucchielli 2003).

The majority of French rappers have roots in the former French Empire.[18] Their music grew out of the economically depressed French suburbs where they were raised. For example, KDD is from the Le Mirail neighborhood of Toulouse, while IAM, Fonky Family, Faf la Rage, and Le 3ᵉ Oeil hail from the northern suburbs of Marseille (Mucchielli 2003: 332). Artists from the Parisian *banlieues* include Ministère AMER, Suprême NTM (from Seine Saint-Denis), Arsenick, Passi and Bisso na Bisso, the brothers Lino and Calbo (from Val d'Oise), Les Sages Poètes de la Rue, the Beninese brothers Zoxea and Melopheelo, Lim and Dany Dan (from Hauts-de-Seine), Youssoupha and Monsieur R (from Seine-et-Marne), Kamnouze, Jango Jack and Ol Kainry of the group Factor X, and Diam's, who hails from Essonne. These neighborhoods are composed predominantly of subsidized housing projects (the infamous HLMs, or moderate-rent dwellings). Although some poor French whites live in the *banlieues,* they are populated mostly by African foreign workers and their descendents. The *banlieue* has come to symbolize a host of social problems, including poverty, inequality, discrimination, violence, delinquency, drugs, and social disintegration (Prévos 1998). French rap songs deal with such social turmoil as well as themes of African diasporic identity, postcolonial Africa, and the artists' personal experiences as marginalized citizens in France.

Some French rappers are university-educated, like MC Solaar, the first "mainstream" French rapper. After graduating high school in 1988, MC Solaar studied English, Spanish, and Russian at the Jussieu campus of the University of Paris. Passi, who graduated high school in 1998, studied agronomy for two years while making music as well. Ekoué, a member of the group La Rumeur, has a master's degree in political science, and his colleague Hamé, from the same group, has completed the first sequence in the cinema and media sociology Ph.D. program at the Sorbonne. Abd al Malik has an undergraduate degree in philosophy. Rocé, who writes rap songs with Djohar, has an undergraduate degree in French and Anglo-American law, and has begun his Ph.D. in philosophy.[19] These "children of hip-hop and Derrida," to use Elsa Vigoureux's phrase, draw on the work of Gilles Deleuze, Jacques Derrida, Pierre Bourdieu, Edward Said, Spinoza, Victor Hugo, Frantz Fanon, and Nina Simone, in their songs.[20] Even as rappers seek financial success, they are most of all trying to convey a message, and deconstruct ethnic stereotypes. La Rumeur's songs "Le poison d'Avril" (April Poison), "Le Franc-tireur" (The Straight Shooter), "Le Bavard" (The Talker), and "Le Paria" (The Pariah) refer specifically to African history, colonialism, the Algerian War, and neocolonialism. Hamé, member of La Rumeur, explains that their own work refers to France's industrial transformation and its social costs for those living in the suburbs.[21]

Major Styles of French Rap

French rap has spawned many offshoots over the last thirty years. Although French rap can be divided into "purist" or "hardcore" rap and commercial rap, classification is never easy, as many artists change their style with time.[22] Others combine political lyrics with commercial style. Some rap music has become, in the words of Jacques Denis (2006), a "product" that has been "commodified." Commercial rap often loses its political dimension as it adapts to demands of radio stations and record labels. One example of such an artist is MC Solaar, who was the first French rap star to sell over a million albums worldwide due to his poetic lyrics. However, even MC Solaar is not devoid of political consciousness. In 1991 he starred in a Costa-Gavras short film entitled *For Kim Song-Man*, which was an appeal for the liberation of the South Korean political prisoner Kim Song-Man. The rapper Diam's, aka Mélanie Georgiades, became a commercial phenomenon after selling 740,000 copies of her album, *Dans ma bulle* (In My Bubble) as well as 430,000 singles. According to *Le Figaro*, Diam's, whose albums earned €2.7 million (or $3.8 million in 2007 U.S. dollars), was the third-top-grossing French artist of 2006. Moreover, she was named French Artist of the Year at the 2006 MTV European Music Awards and won three mentions at the 2006 NRJ Music Awards. In July 2006, Universal ULM hired her as the artistic director of its new label, Motown France. Despite her commercialization allied with her success, Diam's music remains politically engaged, as in songs like "Ma France à moi" (My France) and "Marine," which I will discuss in the second part of this essay.

Another current in rap is called "hardcore" or "purist." Groups such as NTM (made up of Joey Starr and Kool Shen) and Ministère AMER (which included Passi) made hardcore music in the early 1990s. Today, many of these artists, like Passi and Joey Starr, have become more mainstream. When they were hardcore artists, NTM and Ministère AMER were among the first to challenge the government for the conditions in the *banlieues*. In the 1991 song "Le monde de demain" ("Tomorrow's World"), Kool Shen of NTM invites current political leaders to visit the *banlieues* to experience firsthand the conditions that ethnic minorities face in the rhyme.

> What luck, what luck to live in France! Too bad so many people are incompetent / No one cares, scourges develop—that's normal / In my 'hood, violence is becoming too common / So, take a trip to the suburbs / Look your youth in the eyes, you who command from on high / My call is serious so don't treat it as a game / Because the youth is changing, that's what bothers you.

In response to the continuing apathy of political leaders and the mainstream media, Joey Starr, also a member of NTM, brutally asked the following question in the song "Qu'est-ce qu'on attend?" (What Are We Waiting For?):

> How long is this going to last? / It's already been years since all of this should have exploded / Too bad that unity hasn't been on our side / But you know that it's going to end badly, all of it / You have asked for a war of the worlds, here it is / But what, but what are we waiting for to light the fire? / But what are we waiting for before we stop following the rules of the game?

These lyrics appeal to government leaders, imploring them to improve the situation in the *banlieues,* now referred to by the bureaucratic acronym ZUS, or *Zones Urbaines Sensibles* (Fragile Urban Zones). Following the 1973 and 1979 oil shocks, the beginning of the 1980s saw the dramatic restructuring of the iron, steel, carbon, and potassium industrial sectors as well as the textile and shipping industries. The economic crisis led to widespread unemployment that primarily affected unskilled workers from the suburbs. According to Kool Shen and Joey Starr, the unemployment rate in the *banlieues* rose, drug trafficking intensified, and the gap between whites, blacks, and Maghrebis widened.[23] Moreover, respected teachers refused to teach in suburban schools, and the misconduct of young, inexperienced policemen was striking. This situation, Kool Shen maintains, necessitates urgent governmental measures, as verified by official government statistics (Jacquesson 2006).

The political turmoil that followed the oil shocks enabled the rise of Jean-Marie Le Pen, who won his first electoral victories in the early 1980s on a political platform that blamed ethnic minorities for France's difficulties. According to Le Pen, "massive, unregulated immigration took away more than a million jobs from Frenchmen."[24] Le Pen has also declared that "foreigners" threaten the very fabric of French identity (Singer 1991). In order to preserve the purity of this identity, Le Pen has suggested revoking French nationality for all persons of non-European origin who were naturalized after 1970. Some figures from the left have joined conservative politicians in support of Le Pen's National Front ideology, suggesting a dangerous philosophical shift within French politics. Over the past thirty years, a series of particularly repressive laws have been adopted, such as those implemented by successive ministers of interior, including Pasqua (1986 and 1993–94), Debré (1997), Sarkozy (2003 and 2006), and Hortefeux (2007), that directly target ethnic minorities. The Pasqua laws barred automatic access to French citizenship for children born in France of foreign parents, and established new police protocols discriminating against minorities. Police officers now have the legal right to request to see anyone's identity card. Once again, this law has most often been used as a justification to profile ethnic minorities.[25] It was in an attempt to evade a police identity checks on October 27, 2005, that a youth of Tunisian and another of Mauritanian origin accidentally electrocuted themselves at Clichy-sous-Bois, sparking the 2005 riots.

Joey Starr and Kool Shen have been accused of inciting suburban youth to violence. Eric Raoult, minister of cities and integration in the mid-1990s, accused them of engaging in a facile critique of the government without investing any of their CD sales in improving the situation in the suburbs (Caramel 1996). The minister's critique recalls the violent stereotypes that some critics employ to discredit rap music, and shows how the words of ethnic minorities are often turned against them in order to discredit them (Lapeyronnie and Mucchielli 2005).

In a 2007 interview that I conducted with the rappers Passi and Hamé, I asked them about the minister's comments. From their perspective, the taxes they pay as musicians and citizens fulfill their duty to the national community. These taxes should serve to improve the lives of all citizens, including those in the *banlieues,* which is the government's responsibility. They also explained that they have initiated and participated in numerous humanitarian projects. Another subtext of the minister's comments is that the French government has launched numerous social, educational, preventative, and repressive measures to respond to the suburbs' problems since the 1981 Minguettes riots and the 1983 "Marche des Beurs" (Serafini, Tourancheau and Vital-Durand 2005). The housing projects were refurbished in order to give their inhabitants a better standard of living, and many especially difficult suburbs were declared "priority educational zones" (ZEP) in an attempt to improve the level of education for suburban youth. In areas where 20–40 percent of the population is unemployed, social measures were enacted to help families survive the first oil shock in 1973. Preventative social measures were extremely varied. During summer vacations, the minister of culture often financed cultural activities such as dance, music, and theater for suburban youth (Thibodat 1996; Prévos 1998). Some suburban municipalities organized and sometimes financed summer camps for poor children. Also, suburban police forces sometimes organized sporting activities, which allowed them to gather information on delinquency while establishing better relationships with the inhabitants of the *banlieues.*

Sarkozy suspended this program upon being named interior minister in 2002. According to him, the job of the police is to arrest criminals rather than to play soccer with kids from the *banlieues.* Following the 2005 riots, the government recognized "weaknesses and flaws" in its fight against discrimination, and presented a legal program intended to establish an "equal playing field."[26] According to Les mots sont importants (Words Are Important) collective, most of the measures contained in the law for the "level playing field" increase repression and social control, and thus do not constitute an appropriate response to the 2005 riots.[27] The government's policies have since attempted to respond to the crises of underprivileged areas, but seem unable to grapple with the multinational nature of these communities or French national identity. If they would only recognize that fact, a more creative and pragmatic politics might emerge.

On the other hand, rap's language of machismo and reference to violence could undermine the message it seeks to convey. These clichéd characteristics could discredit rappers and trap them in a vicious circle. Critics who reduce rap to these clichés reject all discussion of the subjects it addresses. This is the case of the group Nique ta Mère (Fuck Your Mother). In a well argued article, Marie-Victoire Louis (1996) attacked the group's name, which she sees as a reflection of male violence against women. She asserts that the name "Fuck Your Mother" constitutes a hostile, insulting act toward women. A group representing French mothers sued NTM and its record company for using sexist, offensive language (Guyot 1997; Prévos 1998). Such machismo and misogyny is also present in American gangsta rap (Kelley [1994] 1996: 187), but in the French case it is part of a longstanding French musical tradition that predates rap.

"Purist" or Hardcore Rap: A Politically Charged Music

The "street rap" of Tandem, Casey, Alibi Montana, Rhoff, Salif, Medine, Al Peco, Monsieur R, 113, Booba, and 2Bal, as well as the underground, subversive rap of La Rumeur, represent the hardcore/purist current in French rap. Like American gangsta rap, hardcore interrogates French society in harsh, unflinching language. Extremely political, it deals with difficult, disturbing, even taboo subjects, such as colonialism, drugs, police brutality, and the bleak conditions in the *banlieues*. Street rappers, who claim to be the voice of suburban youth, sing about the hardships faced by young immigrants. As rappers Makensy and Socrate put it, "the words cannot be gentle. In our lyrics and videos, we show things that France does not want to see. . . . As long as we are not integrated (into French society), we will continue to say what we want, however we want to."[28] These rappers' lyrics and videos can undoubtedly be shocking. In his song entitled "FranSSe," the rapper Monsieur R calls France a "chick" and suggests "treat[ing] her like a whore."[29] In the music video version of "FranSSe," France takes the form of lascivious white naked women. Moreover, Monsieur R's replacement of the letter C with "SS" refers to the Schutzstaffel, Hitler's "Praetorian Guard" largely responsible for the vast majority of war crimes perpetrated during the war. La Rumeur's underground subversive rap has a singular approach, attempting to resist cooptation and commodification by the mainstream media, by keeping its distance from mainstream radio and television. The group promotes its own CDs and concerts, and posts its news on underground websites. Moreover, La Rumeur rejects the title "French rap," preferring the term "immigrant children's rap." In the current historical context in France, where they are "immigrants" despite their French birth, the group has taken the risk of an essentialist cultural identification. Stuart Hall (1992) provides a means by which to understand La Rumeur's approach, in which the term "immigrant children's rap" in place of "French rap" is actually a response to the binary paradigm that defines whiteness in relation to what is not white.[30] The children and grandchildren of immigrants are redefining a previously operative white/non-white divide as part of an emerging demographic shift within France.

La Rumeur is extremely critical of commercial rap and accuses it of "whoring out" the spirit of hardcore rap to satisfy the demands of the market. The group's members are convinced that rap must remain "pure," ever critical of French society. In the April 29, 2002, edition of *La Rumeur Magazine,* a member of the group, Mohamed Bourokba (aka Hamé) criticized the police because of the misconduct that culminated with the death of young people in the suburbs. Hamé added that "the reality in our suburbs is economic abandonment, psychological fragility, discrimination in employment and housing, routine instances of police humiliation . . . unfair imprisonment, with no horizon. . . . Our life is a fast train to prison or death." Nicolas Sarkozy, then interior minister, pressed charges against the rapper in July 2002 for what he perceived as slander of the national police. Hamé was tried first by the Correctional Tribunal and then by the Paris Court of Appeals, and both times found innocent, but his last acquittal was annulled on June 10, 2007, by the Court of Appeals, and he will be tried a third time for these charges.[31] Street rap and underground rap are the most radical and harsh current within French rap, as well as a favorite of suburban youth, who recognize their daily lives in its lyrics.

Hardcore rap does not hesitate to address several other issues that ethnic minorities in France have been grappling with for decades. In the song "The Third Estate Is Dead," Socrate, of the group Tandem, offers his opinions about discriminatory hiring practices. He condemns the system that has made it extremely difficult for members of the African diaspora to establish careers as professionals. Furthermore, Socrate explains in an interview that "we refuse to accept the notion that our ambitions have hit a glass ceiling. We want to be able to reach our dreams in the country that we love. In our quarters, when someone studies long and hard, his entire family sacrifices. So, when he is stopped in mid stride because he can't find work despite his degrees, it causes rage." According to Socrate, the lyrics "I will fuck France until she loves me" are an expression of love. "When I search for love, France refuses to return it. . . . I don't want the life that you have imposed on me. I am French, and you need to deal with it."[32] Socrate's comments exemplify rappers' response to raging debates over ethnic minorities that have finally reached the boiling point in France.

To prevent discrimination in hiring practices, Sarkozy himself has suggested the use of anonymous CVs that would keep employers from seeing the names of job applicants in order to ensure equal opportunity. But it was a form of window dressing, considering the defamatory ethnic stereotypes that have contributed to his ascendant media persona. He regularly refers to minorities in derogatory terms, and from 2002 to 2007 he proposed laws that targeted and further marginalized minorities. Like a firefighting arsonist, his proposal to omit the names of job applicants on CVs does not solve the problem of discrimination, because candidates must still appear in person during the interviewing process. In fact, the anonymous CV was first used by the National Employment Agency (ANPE) in Lormont, located in southwest France. This experiment demonstrated a huge flaw in the system: when businesses called potential candidates to schedule interviews, applicants had to give their names. Businesses prone to practices of discrimination during the hiring process were still able to refuse candidates based on ethnicity. Concerns over hiring practices and career advancement, as Socrate points out, once again go unanswered despite Sarkozy's grudging rhetorical acknowledgement of the problem.[33]

Police violence is one of the most popular themes for French rappers. Groups such as NTM, Assassin, Bams, and La Rumeur denounce the fact that acts of police brutality go unpunished. They emphasize that the police are state workers and question why they are never investigated for acts of violence against ethnic minorities. Through a combination of deliberate provocation and examination of police brutality, the song

"The Assassin State" by the group called "Assassin" forcefully shows that, since justice is never served when ethnic minorities are murdered by the police, rappers and disaffected youth for whom they speak are driven to embrace hatred. "The State assassinates, one example Malek Oussekine, / Bing, bang, the police are like a gang / Because the State assassinates, Makome was a victim of it / Bing, bang, the police are like a gang."[34] Later, the song adds, "You want us to respect your Police State [. . .] / But it's done, the people have awakened and are asking us for accounts / Judiciary power needs to take what we're saying seriously / Because the atmosphere's heavy when violence strikes." These lyrics deal with police brutality, while the other rap texts that I mention in this section demonstrate the growing politicization of French rap. As Chris Barker explains, "popular culture is constituted through the production of popular meaning located at the moment of consumption" (2005: 69). Thus, French rap is not simply an entertainment commodity because it creates counter-narratives that contradict dominant discourse, but suggests that popular culture is the site at which cultural hegemony is being challenged (Hall 1996a and 1996b).

French Identity: Set in Stone, or in Constant Flux?

Over the past few decades, France has been engaged in passionate debates over the construction and redefinition of French identity. Rappers such as Passi, Hamé, Ekoué, and Diam's have certainly contributed their own notions to this debate. This section will examine the post-1945 context of today's debates over race, identity, and French rap.

The New Right and Le Figaro Magazine: Hegemony in Motion

Between 1945 and 1960, the presence of immigrant populations did not create anything like the political tension on today's scale. In fact, following the defeat of the Vichy regime and the end of World War II, public expressions of anti-Semitism and racism were virtually unheard of. The French Right was greatly discredited and weakened by the conservative elite's collaboration with Maréchal Pétain during World War II (Dupin 2007). As Charles de Gaulle wrote in 1959, Maréchal Pétain and the French Right were guilty of collaboration with Nazi Germany, undermining the French resistance, and even deporting France's Jewish population along with foreign refugees. Thus, the French Right was particularly discreet in the years following the war. Nevertheless the same Charles de Gaulle considered the French "a Caucasian, European people with Greco-Roman culture and Christian religion" (Peyrefitte 1994: 51–52). This perspective, prevalent among other leaders as well, led him to limit the possibility of French citizenship for Mediterranean peoples (including Arabs), Asians, and blacks (Weil 2002: 221).

The 1960s and Algerian independence brought with them several extreme-right groups, including neo-Nazis, which were known for their shared xenophobia, racism, and bitterness over the loss of Algeria as a colony. Included in the ranks of these groups are Alain Madelin, Patrick Devedjian, Gérard Longuet, and Alain Robert from the "West," who today constitute a portion of the conservative wing of the French government. The New Right associated with the Group for the Research and Study of European Civilization (known as GRECE) is the most influential of these groups, particularly among historians. According to Nathalie Krikorian (1986), Anne-Marie Duranton-Crabol (1988), and Yvan Gastaut (2000), the New Right was established in January 1968 by a group of militant members of the extreme Right, who justified their racist discourse as a "right to difference" and argued for "the superiority of the white race." Since its inception, numerous repatriated French citizens from Algeria joined GRECE, especially in southern France. In 1969, just one year after the student riots of May 1968, GRECE began actively targeting the academy, especially the School of Political Sciences (Sciences politiques), and the School of Hautes études commerciales in Paris, the University of Lyon, and the University of Aix-Marseille. The organization created a number of study groups and committees, such as the "Cercle de l'Horloge" (Watch Circle), the CLOSOR, and the GENE,[35] which aimed for ideological control of the military as well as the academy. Conservative activists belonging to these groups attempted to resurrect and revivify right-wing, racist ideologies and to counteract the influences of Marxism and left-wing ideologies in France.

During the late 1970s, the New Right's theories inundated French public opinion in simplified versions due, to a large extent, to the active collaboration between Robert Hersant, a conservative politician acting as owner and CEO of Le Figaro, and Louis Pauwels, editor of Le Figaro Magazine, the weekly supplement created in 1977. Le Figaro Magazine, with a circulation in the hundreds of thousands, served as propaganda for the New Right in its effort to win over public opinion. The crux of the magazine's ideology was the defense of white French identity based upon an Indo-European heritage. It asserted that France, along with the rest of Europe, has experienced a demographic decline in the white race. According to the New Right, this demographic decline symbolizes the decadence of France and other Western nations and has resulted in a loss of racial identity. Thus, the New Right argues for increased birth rates among whites and opposes abortion. *Le Figaro Magazine* is a tool in the New Right's remarkable strategy for conquering public opinion. It opposes "cosmopolitanism," which it considers synonymous with the entry of non-European immigrants into France. It famously asks the question, "Will we still be French in another thirty years?"[36] Such New Right notions, as espoused by the extreme Right and other conservative parties, have led France to a major turning point in its history, where racism against blacks and Arabs is becoming increasingly overt and commonplace. Writing about this school of thought in 1980, one analyst accurately noted:

> Ten years have gone by. They have already succeeded. They have placed their men in Ministerial positions, within the ranks of the military, and amongst those at the University. They possess a publishing house and create their own reviews. They [the New Right] have a strong foothold, thanks to Louis Pauwels, in *Le Figaro Magazine*, that allows them to spread this profanity throughout large sectors of the population. Their books have been approved by the Academy. Some of their businesses are subsidized by the state. When any one of the highest movers and shakers in the Republic writes a book of general political interest, they [the New Right] provide the research. (Duranton-Crabol 1988: 187)

The New Right also draws on Ernest Renan's work on identity (1882)[37] as well as the ideas of Charles Maurras (1954). Its rallying cry to preserve "Indo-European" identity is undoubtedly central to the construction of right-wing cultural identity in the 1960s and 1970s, thanks to the support of *Le Figaro Magazine*. Other ideological groups and media outlets, such as Jean-Marie Le Pen's National Front, took over this role in the 1980s.[38]

According to Le Pen, who was one of the first politicians after World War II to capitalize on nationalism and identity politics, African, Maghrebi, and Turkish immigration is "the most serious problem threatening France." He added that non-European immigrants cannot assimilate because of their cultural differences and Muslim religion, going on to argue that they are a menace to France's historical continuity.[39] This has been a fruitful political strategy for Le Pen, allowing him and the National Front to achieve several important electoral victories since the 1980s.[40] Le Pen's success also stems from the oil crises, industrial upheavals, and urban riots of the late 1970s and early 1980s. Le Pen conveys the simplistic message to unemployed French workers that their jobs were "stolen" by ethnic minorities rather than lost to fluctuations in the job market. Conservative leaders, along with some notable left-wing figures, have rallied around the National Front. In France, this is known as the "Lepenization of the mind." In a notoriously publicized June 1991 statement, Jacques Chirac, then mayor of Paris, used the term "overdose" to refer to foreign populations in France. He also spoke of the "noise and odors" emanating from Africans living in the nineteenth arrondissement of Paris, a quarter perceived as highly populated by immigrants (Drozdiak 1991; Hall 1991: 18). Three months later, in September 1991, former president Valéry Giscard d'Estaing unhesitatingly stated that France was under "invasion" by foreign populations (De la Gorce 1991: 30; Singer 1991: 814).

Certain notable academics contributed to the New Right's ideological offensive. The demographer and economist Alfred Sauvy developed the theme of "foreign invasion" in his works on demography in France. Between 1946 and 1987, it became an increasingly obsessive theme in his work. As he writes,

> Europe and France affected by depopulation will be too weak to play an effective role in peace ... because history is strewn with violence, wars, population migrations, territorial conquests, invasions. Is it necessary to evoke the occupation of Spain by the Arabs who pushed northward as far as Poitiers in 732? An enfeebled Europe will not be sufficiently able to resist countries from the south that will be motivated by aggressive leaders. And, most importantly, an aging Europe will not be able to oppose cultural resistance by aggressive foreign cultures bent on snuffing out ours. This tragic scenario will be a disaster. (Sauvy 1984; Sauvy and Dumont 1984: 153–55)

For Sauvy, French and European cultures stand in stark opposition to the other cultures of the world. There can be no beneficial exchange between "civilized" cultures and their barbaric, "aggressive," and "unciv-ilized" counterparts, particularly those of Arab origin.

More recent studies on French colonial history, immigration, and identity by the well-known scholars Max Gallo (2006), Gérard Noiriel (1988), and Africanists such as Daniel Lefeuvre (2006) bear certain ideo-logical similarities to the New Right and political conservatives. These authors develop a paradigm of integration in which ethnic minorities would abandon all distinctive cultural or linguistic traits and embrace a monolithic Franco-European culture. They accuse minorities who com-plain of racism or advocate American-style affirmative action of shatter-ing the foundations of the Republic through ethnic particularism. The rappers Passi, Hamé, and Casey note the inherent contradiction within this theory, namely that members of the African diaspora were born in France and studied there.[41] How can one "assimilate" to the culture of one's own country? As Said Bouamama (1993), Ahmed Boubeker (2003), and Nacira Guénif-Souillamas (2004; 2006) have consistently argued, it is imperative that the paradigm of assimilation be deconstructed, and as I will demonstrate, it is defamatory rhetoric, in the name of the French republic, that is used to discriminate against minorities.

In the late 1990s, a significant number of left-wing intellectuals known as "neo-reactionaries" or "intellectual militants," began to espouse aspects of conservative and extreme-right-wing ideologies. Alain Finkielkraut, André Glucksmann, Pierre-André Taguieff, Alexandre Adler, and Jean-Claude Milner are such intellectuals, as Daniel Lindenberg (2002) and Maurice T. Maschino (2002) point out along with reports published in *Libération* and *Le Nouvel Observateur*. These intellectuals privilege the use of so-called straightforward language (*langage décomplexé*) when speaking about ethnic minorities. In other words, they claim to speak openly about current issues directly, without the taint of "political cor-rectness." They scorn civil rights organizations and left-wing groups who criticize essentialist critiques of ethnic minorities. Laurent Joffrin, along with several French journalists writing for *Le Nouvel Observateur*, defines the "neo-reactionaries" as representatives of a "New Right" informed by the political agenda of Nicolas Sarkozy and his call for "frank dialogue."

Neo-reactionaries support the overly simplistic theory that ever since September 11, 2001, the West and its values of civilization have been under attack by Islamic movements acting not only in Iraq and Afghanistan, but in metropolitan centers such as New York, London, and Madrid. Ethnic minorities who arrived in a "massive" wave of immigration are foot soldiers in this war of civilization. They argue that left-wing parties, such as the Socialist Party in France, along with the moderate right, do little to thwart the new dangers threatening Western countries (Joffrin 2005; 2007a; 2007b). Moreover, according to Jacques Rancière (2005), "neo-reactionaries" attack "democratic individualism" and "egalitarianism," claiming that any philosophy that advocates universal human rights creates problems that drive humanity toward suicide. It is difficult to extrapolate an all-out war on Western civilization from the 2005 riots. The neo-reactionary thesis lacks any substantiating evidence.

According to a confidential report from the French domestic intelligence organization, known as the Renseignements Généraux (RG), during the three weeks of riots, France moved from a state of "urban guerrilla" warfare following incidents linked to the deaths of two youths from Clichy-sous-Bois on October 27th, to an "urban insurrection" and finally a "movement of popular revolt." The report specifies that the "social condition of exclusion from French society" was at the root of the urban violence from October to November 2005. It explains that "youth in volatile districts feel penalized by poverty, the color of their skin, and their names." They are disadvantaged by their "absence of interaction with French society." The report describes enormous levels of social disenchantment among the young and "a complete loss of confidence in the Republic." It indicates that ethnicity was not the principal motivation for violent riots. Likewise, the riots were neither organized nor manipulated by any Islamic groups. To the contrary, the report claims that responsible Muslims "had every interest in a return to calm so that any implication of Islamic extremism was avoided." This investigation contradicts the theses of Nicolas Sarkozy and the neo-reactionaries, who claim that the riots were orchestrated by Islamist groups. Instead, the RG's official report underscores two main causes for the riots: the deaths of two youths on October 27, 2005, and unceasing discrimination toward ethnic minorities in contemporary France.

Neo-reactionaries invented the concept of "anti-white racism" to demonstrate that hatred of Western civilization and the white race is at the heart of the riots. Because the young rioters were all linked to the African diaspora in one way or another, and because the vast majority was Muslim, neo-reactionaries claim that these events constitute a declaration of war between civilizations that can be controlled only by forcefully preventing further threats. Daniel Lindenberg (2002) rejects this viewpoint and argues that the neo-reactionaries offer a drastically oversimplified analysis of far more complex issues. In a statement that eerily prefigures the riots of fall 2005, Maurice Maschino (2002) warned that when "people are muzzled and democracy is in jeopardy, insurrection is the most sacred of duties." Such ideas evoke Charles Tilly's assertion that we should not treat "violence," "protest," or "disorder" as a phenomenon distinct from high politics or as a mere reaction to stress. He argues that popular collective action is not an epiphenomenon. Instead, "it connects directly and solidly with the great political questions. Through actions that authorities categorize as 'disorder,' ordinary people fight injustice, challenge exploitation, and claim their own place in the structure of power" (Tilly 1986: 403–404).

Antonio Gramsci's concept of hegemony addresses how a subtle process of domination is set in motion, where mainstream cultural institutions create a nearly consensual system of compliance. *Le Figaro Magazine,* along with other newspapers, television stations, and radio programs, are outlets that the New Right uses to promote their values into the very heart of French society. Through such media institutions, the New Right and other conservative movements have been able to assume a "position of leadership." The central thesis that the New Right sells to the public as "common sense" is that an immutable French identity has existed since the dawn of time. The rise of racism in France since the end of the 1970s demonstrates the New Right's success. However, this hegemony cannot be taken for granted and is under constant challenge from new ideas and theories. As a result, the New Right and the conservatives must continually renegotiate their position (Barker 2005: 80–82). The recent alliance of formerly left-wing neo-reactionaries with the New Right is an example of this renegotiation. This alliance marks an important stage in the New Right's strategy to maintain political leadership. The neo-reactionaries' former alliance with the Left provides a moral veneer for the New Right's racist ideas. In 1997, several rappers teamed up to produce the song "Eleven Minutes 30 against Racist Laws," in which they call the French people to task for the rise of racism and the National Front in France.[42] They sing:

> More excuses / People know very well who they're voting for / 52
> percent of those sons of bitches from Vitrolles / One time for all,

that's clear / Ditto for these smooth tongued venomous ministers / Voting for laws that seduce this kind of electorate.

African French Rappers: Deconstructing the Master Narrative

Nationalist fears are at the base of the National Front's electoral victories, placing Le Pen and his party at the center of French political life since the early 1980s. Conservative politicians attempt to employ the National Front's electoral and political cachet to increase their own electoral base. Nicolas Sarkozy's presidential victory stems partially from his recycling of National Front themes. As the conservative presidential candidate, Sarkozy stigmatized ethnic minorities as the source of problems in the *banlieues* from March to May of 2007. In a Le Pen–accented discourse, Sarkozy declared that "there is a clear link from the unregulated immigration policies of the past thirty or forty years to the social unrest in the suburbs" (Auffray and Tassel 2007). Moreover, although France is officially a secular nation, Sarkozy called Christianity a "determining" part of French identity and claimed that Europe's "Christian roots" were incontestable. He added that "Christianity bequeathed an immense heritage of cultural, moral, intellectual, and spiritual values" to France.[43] Sarkozy's strategy and statements are strikingly similar to the discourse in Thatcherite Britain of the 1980s that figures such as Paul Gilroy and Stuart Hall, initially associated with the Center for Contemporary Cultural Studies, analyzed in their work of this period. An important dimension of their analysis was the construction of a new type of cultural racism advocated by British conservatives during the 1970s, which stigmatized blacks by portraying them as inherently criminal. Sarkozy's rise to power is similar to that of the Tories under Margaret Thatcher. Like Thatcher's party did in Great Britain, Sarkozy places the blame for the nation's woes on ethnic minorities. However, minorities in Britain seem to be better integrated and accepted than in France.

Once elected president, Sarkozy created the new Ministry of National Identity in May 2007, headed by Brice Hortefeux.[44] According to Hortefeux, the preservation of French identity "is a response to both globalization and identity politics. There is nothing wrong with linking immigration, assimilation, and identity. To hide our identity from those who wish to settle in France is to deny the values that forged our history."[45] In response to Hortefeux's comments, academics in France, the United States, and the rest of the world called on the French government to rename the ministry, pointing out that the association of immigration with a threat to national identity has its precedent in the Vichy regime.[46] They add that accusing African and Maghrebi immigrants of disrespecting the values of the Republic treats them as a threat to French identity (Coroller 2007a, 2007b, and 2007c; Joffrin 2007a and 2007b). The French government refused to change the ministry's name, arguing that Nicolas Sarkozy has a political mandate to create such an institution.

This political decision and the immigration legislation since the 1980s, as Manthia Diawara (2003) has so aptly argued, are really identity regulations aimed specifically at blacks and Maghrebis. As a whole, these new laws lay the foundation for what Étienne Balibar calls a "European apartheid," that is, the construction of "internal borders within European countries" constructed on the basis of racial identity (Balibar 2004). In a world that has become increasingly globalized and multicultural, Balibar invites Europeans to invent a new concept of citizenship that respects the rights of ethnic minorities. In response to discriminatory laws which affect their lives in the *banlieues,* the rappers of "Eleven Minutes 30 against Racist Laws" demand the repeal of laws that target ethnic minorities. At the beginning of the song, Jean François Richet and Madj explain,

> Deffere Laws, Joxe Laws, Pasqua or Debre Laws, one sole logic / The pursuit of the immigrant. And don't forget all the decrees and pamphlets / We will never excuse the barbarity of their inhuman laws / A racist state can only create racist laws / So, enough with anti-racist folklore and the child-like euphoria of holidays / Immediately rectify the situation for those undocumented immigrants and their families / Repeal all the racist laws governing immigrant stays in France / We demand the emancipation of all the exploited in this country / Whether they be French or immigrants.

Produced as a critique and response to the Debré Laws on immigration proposed by a conservative government, it also attacked the Defferre and Joxe Laws, ratified by previous socialist governments.[47] Rappers blame the socialist government for being particularly hesitant to apply a left-wing philosophy to the issue of immigration legislation. They also criticize it for failing to abolish immigration laws passed by conservatives. In the words of La Rumeur rapper Hamé, rap and hip-hop artists believe that they have a responsibility to speak out as citizens. They cannot "just sit around watching, sniveling and whining." They must "promote the idea of an alternative, emergency politics."

In the song "Marine," released in 2006, Diam's directly addresses Marine, Jean-Marie Le Pen's daughter and the leader of the National Front, in the following terms: "But Marine / You perpetuated the same bullshit as he did / Thinking that whites can't mix with others." In another song, entitled "Ma France à moi" (My France), she directly addresses Nicolas Sarkozy, accusing him of demagoguery:

> It's not my France this traditional France / That makes us ashamed and wants us gone / My France doesn't live lies / With heart and rage, in the light, not the shadows. [...] / It lives on American time, KFC, MTV Base, Foot Locker, Mac Do, and 50 Cent / It's kids playing basketball in their spare time / Dreaming they're Tony Parker on the Spurs' court / [...] My France is mixed, yeah, it's a rainbow/ It bothers you, I know, because it doesn't want you as a model.

Diam's song reads as an unequivocal response to current debates about the concept of "French identity." She rejects an exclusivist notion of French identity espoused by the National Front, conservative parties, and certain French academics. Her songs demonstrate the response of diaspora cultures that unceasingly question and destabilize the essentialist model, which defines French identity in contrast to ethnic minorities, who represent the Other. Diam's, along with other rappers, describe a pluralist France and call for the recognition of "cultural and racial diversity." She challenges the idea of a singular cultural identity as supported by the New Right, the National Front, and the conservatives, evoking the notion of *civic* identity integral to the spirit of the French and American revolutions. According to these two movements, "citizens make up the Nation." They have rights and responsibilities (such as the right to vote and the responsibility to pay taxes). This supports Stuart Hall and Amin Maalouf's assertion that no identity is set in stone; rather, identities are continually rebuilt and reshaped.

Diam's songs are highly inventive and offer many perspectives on the debate between rappers and the New Right, the National Front, and political conservatives. She incorporates the tropes of globalization by invoking the United States, as a symbol of multiculturalism, and Tony Parker, the black French-American basketball star. She also mentions the restaurants KFC and McDonald's, along with MTV, Foot Locker, and the American rapper 50 Cent. These personalities and brands demonstrate the continuing processes of globalization and mass migration that bring various minority groups into the discursive center. According to Diam's, France is a "rainbow" nation thanks to immigration from the Third World. In Stuart Hall's words, Europe, including France, is "already hybridized [and] multicultural" (1991). Diam's critical perspective tears down the wall between the dominant (French) Self and the marginalized (minority) Other, deconstructing the myth of a homogeneous, white France that has remained unchanged for centuries, which conservatives brandish for political and economic gain.

Amin Maalouf synthesizes these two concepts of identity, cultural and civic, and states that an idea's status as dominant does not justify this dominance. Just because French identity has historically been portrayed as monolithic does not make it so. Maalouf suggests that a country welcoming new migrants is neither a blank slate nor a uniform entity, but is undergoing a fascinating phase of flux. Certainly, "history must be respected," but at the same time, since the future of a country cannot simply rely on veneration of the past, Maalouf argues that new immigrants and natives must write, together, the history of their new homeland "with profound changes," as "was the case in all the great eras of the past" (Maalouf 1998: 40).

François Mitterrand once espoused the concept of civic identity that rappers now defend. Mitterrand formerly stood apart as one of the few French politicians to incorporate minority rights into his concept of French civic identity. As such, he advocated an extension of the right to vote in local elections to legal immigrants. He argued that any tax-paying individual deserves a certain level of input into the community. By including this proposition in his 1981 and 1988 campaign platforms, Mitterrand pushed the notion of "civic identity" further than it had ever gone before. In 1999, the right to vote in local elections was finally granted to all EU citizens living in France, but this right was never extended to Africans living legally in the country. France's Parliament, where conservatives generally make up the majority, has never been willing to extend this right to legal African residents. According to these conservatives, Africans are citizens neither of France nor of Europe; therefore, they cannot benefit from the rights reserved for the French and members of the European Union. In the meantime, European and non-European legal immigrants now living in countries such as Belgium, Denmark, Estonia, Finland, Hungary, Ireland, Lithuania, Luxembourg, Netherlands, Slovakia, Slovenia, and Sweden have been granted these rights. The debate over Mitterrand's proposition highlights the larger debate, which pits the Right's notion of a monolithic cultural identity against the Left's broader notion of civic identity.

Conclusion

Ongoing globalization continues to bring different cultures and ethnic minorities to the banks of the Seine. Their arrival in France (and in Europe in general) challenges the very concept of nation-state and its identity and the significance of transnational cultural values. The hegemonic struggle between rappers and their political foes among the New Right, the conservatives, and the neo-reactionaries must be viewed within this context. Likewise, we must also place this struggle within the context of industrial changes that followed the oil shocks of the 1970s. In this new and uncertain environment, marked by mass unemployment, the National Front and other conservative parties launched a political agenda characterized by exclusive cultural identities. Over the last thirty years the New Right and other conservatives have successfully advanced their notion of French identity among the majority of French citizens. They have obtained the substantial support of supposedly left-wing scholars who lend scientific validation to the right-wing paradigm of integration. This strategy allows the New Right and political conservatives undeniable political benefits. On one hand, it allows them to mask their failure to significantly address the problem of unemployment—ever since the oil crisis, France has had one of the highest unemployment rates in the EU. On the other hand, the Right has succeeded in marginalizing ethnic minorities as "dangerous foreigners."

Through rap, the African diaspora continually challenges the notion of "Frenchness" that is a mainstay of the dominant discourse. In response to Le Pen and Sarkozy's notion of a uniformly Christian France, unchanged for millennia, rappers present a concept of civic identity rooted in the French Revolution, the defining moment of the French modern nation. Rappers assert that ethnic minorities are "at home" in France, although they maintain multiple allegiances. Mainstream politicians portray the subject matter addressed by rappers as so controversial and distasteful that they must silence it at all costs.[48] Yet rappers counter their critics by arguing that they give voice to the ethnic minorities in the *banlieues* by expressing their quotidian experience, as well as the lived social, economic, and political challenges that go along with their "immigrant" and "foreign" status in a culturally conservative and increasingly racist French nation. A segment of the French Left (i.e.,

socialists and communists) denounce the official prosecution and censorship of rappers by arguing that such legislation limits freedom of
expression and silences the voices of those dwelling in the *banlieues*.[49]

The identities of ethnic minorities are multiple and hybrid, as befits
this age of globalization. Crucial works by authors like Stuart Hall ([1989]
1996), Paul Gilroy (1993), Amin Maalouf (1998), and Robin Kelley and
Tiffany Patterson (2000), have helped deconstruct the dichotomy of Self
and Other, suggesting concepts of "double consciousness" and "hybridity." They have suggested that identities are socially and historically constituted, reconstituted, and reproduced. Second- and third-generation
offspring of the African diaspora attend French schools, speak French
along with African languages, and eat *baguettes* along with traditional
African foods. In other words, they are neither exclusively French nor
exclusively African, but rather both. In fact, every identity is in the process of being rebuilt and reshaped. Amin Maalouf (1998) further argues
that identity "is built up and changes throughout a person's lifetime."
As such, it is a shifting composite of a great number of different, often
conflicting, allegiances and attachments, including allegiances to one's
family, neighborhood, village, and country, to one's religious, ethnic,
linguistic, and racial group, and to one's profession, favorite soccer team,
or political movement (Badin 2002: 341). The struggle between rappers
and the New Right exposes a passionate debate at the heart of contemporary France's difficulty in assuming its cultural diversity. Rap lyrics
also produce political meanings and show the influence of the diaspora
in redefining and recasting French identity and republicanism. Rappers
deconstruct the artificial borders between different elements of the contemporary French nation through their songs, and urge their fellow
citizens to write, together, the new, glorious history of their nation in
their everyday lives, as in the 1998 World Cup.

Notes

This study was made possible by the Junior Faculty Research Grant of the University
of Nevada, Reno.

This article first appeared in different forms, which were delivered respectively at the
colloquium Scripts of Frenchness at the University of California at Santa Barbara,
and at the 49th Annual Meeting of the African Studies Association in San Francisco
(2006). In San Francisco, this paper was presented on a panel that I chaired, entitled
"Why Is Paris Burning? The African Diaspora and Identity Issues in Contemporary
France." I would like to thank my colleagues who were kind enough to read and

comment on earlier versions of this article. I am particularly indebted to the following for their critical comments: Peter J. Bloom, Dennis Dworkin, Geoff Eley, Didier Gondola, Louis Marvick, Esra Mirze, and Bruce Moran. I am also grateful for the insightful feedback of the anonymous reviewers at Indiana University Press. I would like to thank Toufa Biramah, who taught me a great deal about French rap, and who introduced me to this musical universe. Without her precious help and availability I never would have accomplished my research on French rap. I would also like to thank Naomi Baldinger for editing this article. This paper is part of a book project, in which I plan to elaborate on other aspects of French rap.

1. Ted Swedenburg, "French Lawmakers Accuse Rappers of Inciting Riots," November 24, 2005. See http://swedenburg.blogspot.com/2005; "French MP Blames Riots on Rappers," November 24, 2006, http://newsvote.bbc.co.uk/mpapps/pagetools/print/news.bbc.co.uk/2/hi/europe/4467068.stm; "Le rap criminalisé," *Le Monde,* January 4, 2005.

2. Interview in the Israeli weekly *Haaretz,* November 18, 2005. See also *Le Monde,* November 24, 2005.

3. "Les feux de la haine," *Le Monde,* November 21, 2005.

4. See: "La polygamie jetée en polémique," *Libération,* November 16, 2005; Elaine Sciolino, "Citing of Polygamy as a Cause of French Riots Causes Uproar," in *New York Times,* November 17, 2005.

5. "La Rumeur devant ses juges": http://www.acontresens.com/contrepoints/societe/29.html; and "Joey Starr: se préoccuper des autres, c'est déjà faire de la politique," *Libération,* October 19, 2006.

6. Gilles Médioni et al., "L'affaire NTM en sept questions," *L'Express,* November 21, 1996; Laurence Caramel, "Nos chansons, c'est un constat, pas de la provocation," *Le Nouvel économiste,* November 29, 1996, 80–81.

7. For further discussion of the 2005 law, see Nicolas Bancel's article in this volume.

8. Fabe, aka Fabrice, is a French rapper born in 1971 in the tenth district of Paris. After receiving his bachelor's degree, he enrolled in the philosophy department at the University of Nanterre. He left the university and began to rap in the early 1990s. He released his first album, *Bafa surprend ses frères* (Bafa Surprises His Brothers), in 1994. After his 2001 release, *La rage de dire* (The Rage of Speaking), Fabe converted to Islam, halted his musical career, and moved to Quebec to study theology. Fabe is a politically engaged rapper, articulating what others only dare whisper. In 1997, he contributed to the fabled hit "Onze minutes 30 contre les lois racistes." Refer to: http://www.ramdam.com/art/f/fabe.htm. See also, "Rap et politique," January 20, 1999, http://www.davduf.net/.

9. I am also indebted to Joan Gross, David McMurray, and Ted Swedenberg (1996).

10. See Prévos 1996; Bocquet and Pierre-Adolphe 1997; Mucchielli 2003; Cachin 2006.

11. Syndey, aka Patrick Duteil, was born in the Antilles in 1960, and Dee Nasty, aka Daniel Bigeault, was born in Paris in 1962.

12. Before 1981, radio was controlled by the French state, whose bias partially controlled information. The only stations authorized to broadcast at the time were public stations like Europe 1, RMC, and RTL. Toward the end of the 1970s, many pirate community stations began broadcasting. The creators of these stations invoked the freedom of expression the state was inhibiting and broadcast on FM wavelength with

low-cost material from rooftops. After François Mitterrand's election as president in May 1981, the law of July 29, 1982, finally allowed free stations to broadcast and definitively destroyed the state's monopoly. Refer to: http://www.pointsdactu.org/article.php3?id_article=671.

13. These African American–inspired names included Dee Nasty, IAM, MC Solaar, Mafia K'1 Fry, Alibi Montana, Sniper, Kery James, La Fonky Family, Tandem, among others.

14. The most notable among them include Passi, Menelik, Youssoupha, Amara, La Fouine, La Boussole, La Rumeur, Bouchées Doubles, and Diam's.

15. These riots in southern France were the first confrontations between the police and African and Maghrebi youth. They also marked the first occasion of joyriding and car burning. The 1981 Minguettes riots were extensively covered by the media. Since then, there have been more riots in Minguettes (1983), in Vaulx-en-Velin (1990), and in many other suburbs.

16. MC Solaar, aka Claude M'barali, was born on March 5, 1969, in Dakar, Senegal, to Chadian parents. When he was six months old, he moved with his family to the Parisian suburb of Villeneuve-Saint-Georges.

17. Since then, Passi has won twenty other awards for these and other albums: *Ma 6-T va crack-er,* which went gold in March 1998, and *Laisse parler les gens* (platinum in September 2003).

18. Joey Starr, MC Solaar, Passi, Monsieur R, Disiz La Peste, Stommy Buggsy, Socrate, Menelik, Oxmo Puccino, Doc Gyneco, Booba, Ekoué, Hamé, Casey, Blacko, Tunisiano, Medine, Fabe, Salif, Abd Al Malik, Axiom First, and many others are all of African or West Indian origin.

19. The rapper Rocé is the son of a Russian Jewish father and an Algerian, black, and Muslim mother.

20. Elsa Vigoureux, "Enfants du hip-hop et de Derrida. Les intellos du rap," *Le Nouvel Observateur,* no. 2167 (May 18, 2006).

21. Also see "Hamé, de la Rumeur." Interview with Hamé and Benjamin Chevillard, October 2003, at http://www.indesens.org/.

22. Prévos suggests three majors tendencies that he terms "hardcore," "Zulu," and "pharaohism" (1996: 719).

23. According to the statistics of the Institut National des Statistiques et des Études Économiques, the unemployment rate among youth in Clichy-sous-Bois, where the 2005 rioting began, is around 30 percent. This is more than twice the national average.

24. See Front National, "300 mesures pour la renaissance de la France," at http://www.frontnational.com/doc_frater_emploi.php.

25. The Pasqua Law of 1993 is part of a major oppressive current, because it allows police officers great liberty to check identity cards "regardless of the behavior" of the individuals in question. See Jobard 2002.

26. "Projet de loi pour l'égalité des chances présenté par M. Jean-Louis Borloo, Ministre de l'emploi, de la cohésion sociale et du logement." Recorded at the Assemblée nationale on January 11, 2006; see http://www.assemblee-nationale.fr/12/projets/p12787.asp. This legal project, which "intends to create an equal playing field for all, is composed of five components: (1) education, employment, and economic development, (2) creation of equal chances and the fight against discrimination, (3) parental authority, (4) reinforcement of municipalities, (5) and the creation of a voluntary civil service." Refer to: http://www.assemblee-nationale.fr/12/projets/p12787.asp.

27. Collectif Les mots sont importants, "Chronique du racisme républicain. Les années Sarkozy," April 30, 2007; see http://lmsi.net/.

28. Stéphanie Binet, "Rap et la banlieue," www.labanlieuesexprime.org, April 21, 2006.

29. H. Schofield, "French Rappers' Prophecies Come True," November 16, 2005; see www.newsvote.bbc.co.uk/.

30. I am indebted to the remarkable analysis of Dennis Dworkin in his *Class Struggles* (2007: 68).

31. See Anne Gaelle Rico, "Pour l'avocat des rappeurs de La Rumeur, 'la liberté d'expression est en péril,'" lemonde.fr, July 11, 2007.

32. Stéphanie Binet, "Banlieues. Les rappeurs l'avaient bien dit," *Libération*, November 14, 2005.

33. Housing discrimination poses another serious problem. After the 2005 riots, Prime Minister Dominique De Villepin decided to legalize "testing" as a means of fighting all types of discrimination. "Testing" involves planting undercover minority participants at the entrances to nightclubs, restaurants, and campsites, as well as placing them as potential job candidates or as would-be renters, in order to document cases of discrimination that have been alleged. But, just as quickly, the National Union of Real Property Owners (UNPI), consisting of property owners, openly opposed it. The discriminatory attitude of the UNPI even went so far as to threaten to no longer list vacant rentals on the market if "testing" was applied. Moreover, the anonymous-CV proposition and the UNPI's attitude underline several questions about the application of laws discouraging discrimination in France. The anti-racist association SOS-Racisme has criticized the slowness and hesitancy of the French justice system in prosecuting and condemning discriminatory practices brought to light by plaintiffs. For further discussion of this issue see Laetitia Van Eeckhout, "Le premier ministre légalise le 'testing' contre les discriminations," *Le Monde,* December 2, 2005; "Testing: menace des propriétaires," December 2, 2005, Nouvelobs.com.

34. Malek Oussekine, Makomé, Abdelkader Bouziane, and other young members of the African diaspora died following acts of police brutality. The officers involved were never investigated or prosecuted for their actions.

35. CLOSOR (Reserve Officers' and Sub-Officers' Liaison Committee) was aimed at military milieus. GENE (Study Group for a New Education) sought contact with the Department of Education and published the review *Nouvelle Éducation* (Duranton-Crabol 1988: 47).

36. *Le Figaro Magazine,* October 26, 1985. See also Louis Pauwels, "Immigration: la controverse," *Le Figaro Magazine,* November 9, 1985: 109–19.

37. The New Right employs a partial reading of Renan's definition of the nation, focusing on the determining role of heritage in the making of cultural identity. They ignore the notion of the "daily plebiscite" that is the basis of Renan's philosophy of the nation (Eley and Suny 1996). See the insightful articles in the edited volume by Eley and Suny that shed light on the notion of nation and identity.

38. Eric Dupin indicates that other study groups were created beginning in the 1980s. The media, including the television stations TF1 and France 2, also participate in the diffusion of conservative attitudes toward cultural identity (Dupin 2007).

39. Jean-Marie Le Pen, "Immigration et souveraineté," January 27, 2002, http://www.frontnational.com/.

40. Since the early 1980s, Le Pen has run on a consistently racist platform and has been elected and reelected to Parliament by the French public. Nonetheless, the

majority of the population does not agree with the rhetoric and practices of political oppression and racial persecution advocated by the extreme-right and conservative parties.

41. Interview by author with Passi, Hamé, and Casey, July–August 2007.

42. Passi, Fabe, Stomy, Rockin' Squat, Akhenaton and Freeman, Mystic, Soldafada, Yazid, Rootsneg, Sleo, Kabal, and Aze were among these rappers.

43. See the interview with Sarkozy in the Catholic weekly *Famille chrétienne* from April 21, 2007; "Pour Sarkozy, le christianisme est 'déterminant,'" April 17, 2007, Nouvelobs.com, http://tempsreel.nouvelobs.com/speciales/elysee_2007/; "A quelques jours du scrutin, Nicolas Sarkozy se drape de christianisme," LeMonde.fr, April 17, 2007, www.lemonde.fr/web/article/.

44. Decree No. 2007-999 (May 31, 2007) mandated the new Ministry of Immigration, Assimilation, National Identity, and Co-development (*Journal officiel,* No. 125, June 1, 2007: 9964).

45. "Pourquoi un ministère de l'immigration?" *Le Figaro,* June 1, 2007.

46. See the petition published in the daily newspaper *Libération* on June 22, 2007.

47. The 1996 Debré law restricted the ability of foreigners to enter France. According to its critics, this new law is oppressive to immigrants. It extends the power of the police, allowing them to raid businesses for "black market" workers, among other infractions (refer to: http://socialisme.free.fr/c). Since 2003, new immigration legislation has been passed every year or two, which worries observers.

48. In 2005, member of Parliament (MP) François Grosdidier along with two hundred other Conservative MPs asked the minister of justice to actively prosecute rappers and rap groups such as Fabe, Salif, Monsieur R, 113, Ministère AMER, Bougnoul, Smala, and Lunatic for "inciting hatred against certain races and the Republic." In April 2006, the same politician (François Grosdidier) sponsored legislation aimed at rappers, condemning them for songs with lyrics deemed to be "discriminatory, violent, hate-filled" or "anti-white." Under this legislation, they may receive a year in prison and a fine of up to €45,000 (or $58,842 in 2007 U.S. dollars) (Jon Henley, "Grosdidier s'en prend au rap anti-blanc," 2005, http://forums.france2.fr/france2/toutlemondeenparle/Grosdidier-prend-anti-blanc-sujet-14820-1.htm).

49. Jérôme-Alexandre Nielsberg, "Rap: la réponse aux censeurs," *L'Humanité,* November 30, 2005.

APPENDIX 1

A Call to Action: "We Are the Natives of the Republic!" January 18, 2005

Translated by Florence Bernault

Discriminated against in their access to jobs, housing, health care, education, and leisure, those born in past and present colonies, and others originating from postcolonial immigration, are the first victims of social exclusion and increased social vulnerability. Independent of their actual origins, inhabitants from these *quartiers* find themselves indigenized and relegated to the margins of society. The *banlieues* are labeled as zones of disorder that the Republic sets out to conquer all over again. Identity checks based on profiling, and various provocations and persecutions, continue to multiply. Meanwhile, police brutality, sometimes extreme, has become acceptable in a two-track system of justice. In order to exonerate the Republic, our parents have been accused of abdicating their responsibilities, when we know of their immense sacrifice, struggle, and suffering. The old colonial tactics to control Islam are recycled with the establishment of the French Council for Muslims,

On January 19, 2005, "Le Mouvement des Indigènes de la République" launched the online petition originally entitled, "L'Appel 'Nous sommes les Indigènes de la République!'" After this petition was circulated, they formed as a permanent association. The petition called for a mass demonstration, held in Paris on May 8, 2005, and the creation of a Conference for Postcolonial Anti-Colonialism [Assises de l'anti-colonialisme postcolonial]. Florence Bernault's translation of this manifesto was edited by Peter J. Bloom and Charles Tshimanga. See Florence Bernault's contribution in this volume for further discussion of the Indigènes. —Eds.

under the authority of the Ministry of Interior. Discriminatory, sexist, and racist, the anti-headscarf law is a law of exception reeking of colonialism. It is as colonial in essence as the residential segregation of the *harkis* and their children. People of immigrant and colonial origin are also discriminated against as political subjects. Their few elected *beur* or black officials are merely the veneer of representative politics. The right to vote is refused to those who are not legally French. For those who are, but do not appear to be, they remain under constant suspicion. The tradition of citizenship based on being born in the country, or the right-of-soil (*jus soli*), is under attack. Deprived of rights and protection and living under the constant threat of arrest and deportation, tens of thousands of people are deprived of their legal rights. Freedom of circulation is denied; an increasing number of people from the Maghreb and Africa are forced to cross borders illegally, at risk of losing their lives.

Once a Colonial State . . . For more than four centuries, France participated in the slave trade and the deportation of people from sub-Saharan Africa. At the cost of terrible massacres, colonial rule put dozens of nations under its yoke, spoiling their riches, destroying their cultures, ruining their traditions, denying their history, and erasing their memory. The *tirailleurs* of Africa, canon fodder during the two World Wars, remain victims of a scandalous inequality as their pensions as war veterans are denied.

Still a Colonial State! In New Caledonia, Guadeloupe, Martinique, Guyana, Reunion, and Polynesia repression and the contempt of electoral rights still reign unscathed. The children of these colonies are, in France, relegated to the status of immigrants, of French citizens of lesser value, and deprived of equal rights. In some of the former colonies, France continues to assert a policy of domination. A disproportionate part of local riches is siphoned off by the ex-imperial nation and international capital. In the Ivory Coast, for example, the French army behaves as if in a conquered land.

The Treatment of People of Colonial Origin Continues Unabated as a Colonial Policy of Old. Not only is the principle of equality before the law routinely violated, but the law itself does not insist on equal treatment (one glaring example is the case of double jeopardy immigration legislation that penalizes those who enter France illegally with imprisonment, followed by deportation without the right of return for several years; another example is the way in which legislation against wearing

This poster called for the second demonstration of the "Indigènes," in Paris, on May 8, 2006. It reproduces a French national identity card that plays on the stigmatizing of French citizens of color. Instead of the usual demographic elements normally listed on French identity cards, this one reads: Name: Native of the Republic; Birth Date: May 7, 1802: reinstatement of the slavery by Napoleon Bonaparte; Birth Place: Metropolis, ex-colonies, Overseas Departments and Territories; Birth Marks: Black, Arab, Muslim, discriminated, stigmatized, media-vilified. The poster ends with the words: "liberty, equality, freedom for our elders, parents and children."

the headscarf by young women of Maghrebi and sub-Saharan origin becomes a means of denying them access to educational settings). The image of the "native" continues to haunt political, administrative, and judicial action. It revives and articulates with the structures of oppression, discrimination, and social exploitation. For instance, in the context of contemporary neoliberalism, immigrant workers are accused of being the agents of deregulation, an accusation that allows the silent extension of more precariousness and flexibility to the detriment of the working class as a whole.

The Colonial Gangrene Is Taking Over. The exacerbation of global conflicts, particularly in the Middle East, has gripped current debates in France. The interests of American imperialism and the Bush administration's neoconservatism joins with the legacy of French colonialism. An active stratum of intellectual, political, and media elites has turned away from the progressive struggles that they pride themselves on, repositioning themselves toward a Bush-inspired mode of thinking.

Dominating the media, these ideologues endlessly repeat the clash of the civilizations credo, translating it into a local idiom of the conflict between the Republic and communitarianism. As during the glorious days of colonialism, the Berbers were opposed to the Arabs, the Jews to the Arabo-Muslims and the blacks. Youth of immigrant origin are accused of being the vectors of an anti-Semitic revival. Under the amorphous term of fundamentalism, persons of African, Maghrebi, or Middle Eastern origin are now stereotyped as the Fifth Column of the New Barbarism that threatens the West and its values. Fraudulently camouflaged in the name of the secular, and in defense of the putative semantics of citizenship and feminism, this reactionary offensive has become an ingrained stereotype, reconfiguring the political arena, and ravaging French society. It has already succeeded in imposing its rhetoric among progressives, like gangrene. To dispel the colonial and racist imaginary as merely a fantasy of the extreme Right is a form of political and historical denial. Colonial ideology endures, traversing ideological currents that define the French political landscape.

Decolonizing of the Republic Remains on the Agenda! The Republic of Equality is a myth. The state and society must critically examine their colonial past and present. The time has come for France to question its role as the beacon of Enlightenment thought and universal egalitarian values, once associated with the French Revolution, and asserted in the name of a national culture. They are, in fact, indebted to the legacy of a "universal chauvinism" aiming to "civilize" the savages and their children. Radical measures must be taken so justice and equality may prevail in adjudicating racial discrimination at work, in the housing market, in the access to culture and citizenship. Institutions that confine people of colonial origin to subhuman status must be reformed.

Our parents and grandparents have been enslaved, colonized, and dehumanized, but they have not been destroyed. They have preserved their human dignity through heroic resistance that they organized to tear themselves away from the colonial yoke. We are their heirs as like those Frenchmen who resisted the Nazi barbarism, and the many who helped the oppressed, demonstrating, maintaining a sense of engagement and sacrifice. Thanks to them, the anti-colonial struggle is connected to the struggle for social equality, justice, and citizenship. Dien Bien Phu was their victory. Dien Bien Phu was not a defeat but the victory for liberty, equality, and fraternity!

For these reasons, we ally ourselves with those (from Africa to Palestine, from Iraq to Chechnya, from the Caribbean to Latin America ...) who fight for their own emancipation, against all forms of domination, be it colonial or neo-colonial.

WE, descendents of slaves and African deportees, daughters and sons of the colonized and the immigrants, militants involved in the battle against oppression and discrimination produced by the postcolonial Republic, call those engaged in these struggles to come together in the Conference for Anti-Colonialism. We ask you to contribute to the emergence of a movement that calls for the accountability of the political system and its agents, and beyond, to all of French society, as part of a common struggle of the oppressed and the exploited, for a truly egalitarian and universal social democracy.

On May 8, 1945, the paradox of the Republic was revealed: on the same day that France celebrated the Nazi capitulation, an unbelievable act of repression was perpetrated by France against the colonized of North Constantine in Algeria, resulting in thousands of deaths!

On May 8, 2005, the sixtieth anniversary of this massacre, let us continue the anti-colonial struggle with the first demonstration of the Natives of the Republic!

GLOSSARY

A number of French terms and acronyms that appear throughout the text are described below thanks to a joint effort between the editors and collaborators in the volume. In addition to drawing on our shared knowledge, when appropriate we cite specific authors who have contributed their specific knowledge to particular entries (*Au S.*), sources listed in our bibliography (*Bib.* [last name, date]), and specific contributions in the present volume addressing the term (*Vol.* [author and chapter number]).

[*The*] *Algerian War* [*of Independence*]: Typically refers to the period of 1954 to 1962, with the signing of the Evian Peace Accords, culminating in the declaration of Algerian Independence from France. (*Bib.:* Stora 2005; *Vol.:* Bernault 6).

Association Connaissance de l'histoire de l'Afrique contemporaine (ACHAC) [Research Association on Contemporary African History]: ACHAC is a consortium of scholars and researchers founded in 1989 whose work has addressed the representation and legacy of colonial and postcolonial iconography as well as the interrelated history of immigration. They have been at the forefront of staging debates in the French public sphere about these questions, and have worked with more than three hundred international authors and researchers on numerous conferences, film screenings, exhibitions, and publications. The collective has pursued a series of research agendas including Colonial Ideologies and Postcolonial Legacies, Immigration from the South to France, and Colonial Culture in France. They have also created French colonial collections that include the ACHAC Collection, held at the Getty Research Institute in Los Angeles. Pascal Blanchard has been a leading figure in this group, along with Nicolas Bancel, Gilles Boëtsch, Francis Delabarre, Éric Deroo, and Sandrine Lemaire, among others. (*Au S.:* Bancel, Blanchard, Bloom; *Bib.:* Bancel et al. 1997, 2002, 2003; Blanchard et al. 1993, 1998, 2005; *Vol.:* Bancel 8, Bernault 6).

Banlieue: Outlying areas of French cities that are characteristically impoverished and primarily populated by immigrant families, especially African foreign workers and their descendents. The *ban-lieue* has come to symbolize a host of social problems, including poverty, inequality, discrimination, violence, delinquency, drugs, and social disintegration. (*Au S.:* Bloom, Gondola, Lapeyronnie, Tshimanga; *Bib.:* Hargreaves 2002).

Beur: According to the *Le Petit Robert* dictionary, the term "beur" desig-nates a young Maghrebi born in France to Algerian, Moroccan, or Tunisian immigrant parents. The *Beurs,* most of whom are French citizens, are the second or third generation of Maghrebi immi-grants. This is, of course, a *verlan* term, or French slang, character-ized by the inversion of a word's letters or syllables—as in the trans-formation of "arabe" to "beur." Today the term, although coined by *banlieue* youth themselves, is gradually falling into disrepute. Other back-slang derivations, such as *rebeu[x]* and *rhors,* are also asso-ciated with the term. (*Au S.:* Bloom, Boubeker, Tshimanga; *Bib.:* Bouamama 1994; Boubeker 1999, 2003; *Vol.:* Bloom 11, Boubeker 4, Gondola 7, Guénif-Souilamas 10, Tshimanga 12).

Bidonville: It refers to communities that were to be replaced by the HLMs, or housing projects located in the *banlieues.* As Ahmed Boubeker explains, *bidonville* literally means the borderline between the dis-posal of refuse and the assumption of responsibility for immigrant worker housing by slumlords. (*Au S.:* Boubeker, Tshimanga; *Bib.:* Boubeker 1999, 2003; *Vol.:* Bloom 11, Boubeker 4).

Black: Currently used by young people of African descent in France to identify themselves. It symbolizes not only a rejection of such terms as *Noir* or *Africain* (which continue to label "older" Africans in France) but also a fascination with the Black American cul-tural experience. (*Au S.:* Gondola, Tshimanga; *Vol.:* Gondola 7, Tshimanga 12).

Cité: Typically refers to housing estates (British), or housing projects (American), but has a broader meaning that refers to an industrial township. (*Au S.:* eds.; *Vol.:* Bloom 11, Gondola 7).

Code de l'Indigénat: A set of laws creating an inferior legal status for natives in the French colonies from 1944–1947. First instituted in Algeria, it was applied across the French Colonies from 1887–1889. (*Au S.:* eds.; *Vol.:* Cooper 5).

Communitarianism: Refers to the idea that ethnic communities preserve their cultures without fully integrating within the *creuset français* (the French "melting pot"). Unlike in the United States, communitarianism has a negative connotation in France because of its purported opposition to republicanism, universalism, and secularism. (*Au S.:* Tshimanga; *Bib.:* Noiriel 1988; *Vol.:* Bernault 6, Tévanian 9).

Conseil Représentatif des Associations Noires (CRAN): A lobbying group established in November 2005 under the leadership of Patrick Lozès, Louis-Georges Tin, and Pap Ndiaye to promote the rights of black French men and women. CRAN's ideas stand firmly on the side of universalism, and the defense of the French Republic and its model of integration. The purpose of the group is to reinforce the visibility, representation, and power of black citizens in France. (*Au S.:* Bernault, Tshimanga; *Vol.:* Bernault 6, Gondola 7).

Créolité: A literary movement associated with Martinican writers, including Patrick Chamoiseau, Jean Bernabé, and Raphaël Confiant. Edouard Glissant is frequently associated with this movement, although he did not contribute to their well-known 1989 text, *Éloge de la créolité,* which carved out a new literary sphere in relationship to *Négritude. Créolité* is a neologism that refers to the cultural and linguistic heterogeneity of the Antilles, or the French Caribbean. (*Au S.:* Bernault, eds.; *Vol.:* Bernault 6).

Dien Bien Phu: A French garrison located to the west of Hanoï in Vietnam, near the Chinese and Lao DR border, first established in November 1953 by General Navarre under orders from the French Military High Command. Ten thousand eight hundred soldiers under French command were dispatched to fortify this strategic position, including 4,300 Legionnaires as well as colonial troops from the African continent, in order to assert control over numerous provinces in the Tonkin delta. On March 13, 1954, Viet Minh forces, under the command of General Giap, encircled this position with 35,000 soldiers, and 75,000 reinforcements. After a fifty-seven day siege of the garrison, Colonel Casties, the French commander, capitulated. This was the bloodiest of battles since World War II, 25,000 Vietnamese were killed, as were 2,300 men from the French forces. The defeat of French forces at Dien Bien Phu had a profound impact on French public opinion, and precipitated Vietnamese independence from France under the Geneva Accords, signed on May 7, 1954, partitioning the country between North and South along the 17th parallel. (*Au S.:* Bancel, Bloom, Tshimanga; *Bib.:* Martin 1988: 134–35; *Vol.:* Indigènes Manifesto [Appendix: A Call to Action: "We are the Natives of the Republic!"])

[*L'*]*Exception française:* This term originally conveyed the belief that the demand for human rights and social welfare was unique in its insight and place in French national culture. Yet the term has since given way to contentious notions of cultural purity, resistance to the perceived effacement of French culture, and criticism of supposedly "foreign" intrusions within that culture. (*Au S.:* Bloom, Mbembe; *Vol.:* Bloom 11; Mbembe 2).

Fonds d'Action Social [FAS] (Social Action Fund): The *Fonds d'Action Social* was founded in 1958 under Charles de Gaulle as an instrument of social benefits for North African workers in France. It is the administrative descendant of the Fonds d'Action sanitaire et sociale (FASS), founded in 1952 as a fund to improve living conditions for North African workers living in France. (*Au S.:* Bloom; *Bib.:* Revol 1968, Math 1988, Yahiel 1988; *Vol.:* Bloom 11).

[*Le*] *foulard islamique* (the Islamic Headscarf): The Islamic Headscarf [controversy] is a metonym for Islamic Fundamentalism and, at the outer limits, Islamofascism. Political movements against the headscarf assert their solidarity with the rights of women. This position is most often voiced by policymakers in the French media. The Islamic headscarf, as a social issue, has been a powerful weapon used to champion a republican notion of universal citizenship rights in opposition to the purported will toward ethnic minority difference. As Pierre Tévanian argues in this volume, the Islamic Headscarf controversy is an exclusionary rhetoric that stereotypes a Black and *Beur* underclass as part of a strategy of social containment. (*Au S.:* Bloom, Tévanian; *Bib.:* Guénif-Souilamas et al. 2004, Tévanian 2005; *Vol.:* Tévanian 9).

[*La*] *Fracture coloniale:* Refers to an amalgam of social processes originating in the colonial period that continue to inform cultural and social norms in contemporary France. The resonance of these features is often masked and analogous to blind spots, creating the condition for "la fracture coloniale" as a working-through that recovers the split between a *banlieue* culture of colonial containment and the universal rights of French citizens. Reconciling the fracture of deterriorialization that has been grounded in the legacy of colonial racism is also a means of intervening into a fiction of French national identity, and perhaps the possibility for reconciliation. (*Au S.:* Bancel, Bloom; *Bib.:* Blanchard et al. 2005; *Vol.:* Bancel 8, Bernault 6).

Françafrique: A term at first used by Ivorian president Félix Houphouët-Boigny in the 1960s to qualify the symbiotic relations between France and former African colonies. It was later appropriated by François-Xavier Verschave to refer to covert military arrangements and abuse of power on the African continent supported by the French government in the name of cooperation in African countries formerly colonized by France. It is also the dark side of *la francophonie*. (*Au S.:* Bloom, Gondola; *Bib.:* Golan 1981, Verschave 1998; *Vol.:* Gondola 7).

Français de souche: Literally, French citizens who have multigenerational roots in France as opposed to the newly naturalized French or people born in France to foreign parents. The term, *souche*, refers to the idea of stock, or blood, that is part of a myth of a racial purity as the basis for French national identity. (*Au S.:* Bloom, Gondola; *Vol.:* Gondola 7).

Français issus de l'immigration: First and second generations of the population to attain French citizenship. It is a phraseology that refers to the memory of immigration and points to perceptible social difference. (*Au S.:* Gondola; *Vol.:* Gondola 7).

Français musulmans d'Algérie [FMA] (French Algerian Muslims): Those from the three French administrative departments within Algeria considered French territory before the end of the Algerian War of Independence that recognized Algerian Muslims as a distinct category of citizen so that social programs could be directed to them. (*Au S.:* Bloom, Cooper; *Bib.:* Shepard 2006; *Vol.:* Bloom 11, Cooper 5).

Grands ensembles: Large housing developments built outside of French cities as part of a post–World War II slum clearance mandate to accommodate families. These developments are most often linked to the larger cities, such as Paris, with an extensive rail system such as the RER, or other forms of public transportation with limited access to the urban centers. (*Au S.:* Bloom, Tshimanga; *Bib.:* Hargreaves 1997; *Vol.:* Bloom 11, Gondola 7, Tshimanga 12).

Habitations à Loyer Modéré [HLM]: Subsidized housing structures usually associated with the *grands ensembles,* but the term is typically used as a generic term to refer to low-income housing developments. It may also refer to institutionally subsidized housing located in the *cités* predominantly populated by immigrants and low-income French nationals. These *banlieue* neighborhoods are composed predominantly of subsidized housing projects. (*Au S.:* Tshimanga; *Bib.:* Hargreaves 1997; *Vol.:* Bloom 11, Gondola 7, Tshimanga 12).

Harkis: Algerians who fought on the side of the French during the Algerian war of independence, and were repatriated to France at the end of the war to avoid the ire of the new nationalist government. (*Au S.:* Bancel; *Bib.:* Stora 2005; *Vol.:* Bancel 8).

Identitarian: This term refers to a narrow form of identity politics that borders on a "reaction formation" that denies the right of the "other" on the basis of an essential difference. This term is a translation of the concept *laïcité identitaire,* employed in Pierre Tévanian's contribution to this volume. (*Au S.:* Bloom, Tévanian; *Bib.:* Tévanian 2005; *Vol.:* Bernault 6, Tévanian 9).

[*Les*] *Indigènes de la République* (the Natives of the Republic): A coalition of activists of immigrant origin organized by Houria Bouteldja in late 2004 and early 2005. It soon attracted followers across a constellation of smaller militant groups. The *Indigènes* argue that France bears the signs of its colonial past, and nurtures the policies of a postcolonial state. The term *indigène* is a French colonial term used euphemistically by the movement to underscore how connotations of backwardness and primitivism are directed toward them, as the remaining putative but unspoken colonial subjects. (*Au S.:* Bernault, Gondola; *Vol.:* Bernault 6).

Kabyle, Kabilya: The Kabyles are a Berber people whose traditional homeland is the highlands of Kabylia in northeastern Algeria. Perceived in France as primed for French cultural assimilation during the colonial era, they were considered to be living in the Middle Ages. Not necessarily Muslim, the Kabyles were considered different, and their difference as early Christians, in some versions, or Jews in others, also justified the myth of a Holy French Empire that replaced the Holy Roman Empire. Kabyles were also among the most important contingents of immigrant foreign laborers in the post–World War II period. (*Au S.:* Bloom, Guénif-Souilamas; *Bib.:* Bloom 2008; *Vol.:* Bloom 11, Guénif-Souilamas 10).

Le Penism: Refers to partisans of the extreme right, and the figure of Jean-Marie Le Pen, leader and co-founder of the National Front Party. Founded in 1974 by Le Pen, with Jean Bompard (a former member of the short-lived far-right paramilitary French nationalist underground military movement in Algeria, known as the OAS), and Roland Gaucher (known to be a Vichy collaborator), *Le Penism* has come to mean a racist, anti-immigrant political platform that also points to the contradictory policies of the French political establishment. It has also become the recurrent theme in the French hip-hop idiom, as Tshimanga explains. (*Au S.:* Bloom, Tshimanga; *Vol.:* Bernault 6, Tshimanga 12).

[*Les*] *Minguettes/The Minguettes Generation:* refers to one of the largest housing projects built during the 1960s and became a euphemism for the *banlieue* problem; *Les Minguettes* is located in a suburb of Lyons and consists of nine thousand housing units. The 100,000-strong demonstration as part of the 1983 March for Equality in Paris featured what became known as the Minguettes Generation, or youths who grew up in projects such as *Les Minguettes,* and who came of age as politically minded activists who demanded full citizenship rights beyond that of immigrants. (*Au S.:* Boubeker; *Vol.:* Boubeker 4, Introduction).

Négritude: A literary and political movement developed in the 1930s by a group that included the future Senegalese president Léopold Sédar Senghor, Martinican poet Aimé Césaire, and the Guianan Léon Damas. The *Négritude* writers found solidarity in a common black identity as a rejection of French colonial racism. They believed that the shared black heritage of the African diaspora was the best means of fighting against French political and intellectual hegemony and domination. (*Au S.:* eds.; *Vol.:* Mbembe 3, Introduction).

Parkour: A series of urban gymnastic techniques, associated with extreme sports culture, first associated with David Belle and Sebastien Foucan in France as of 1997 through the *Yamakasi* movement, and featured in commercials for Nike, Adidas, and BBC One. It has since became the subject of documentary films, and incorporated into a number of action feature films, including *Yamakasi* (dirs. Ariel Zeitoun and Julien Seri, written by Luc Besson, 2001), *Banlieue 13* (dir. Pierre Morel, prod. Luc Besson, 2004), and *Casino Royale* (dir. Martin Campbell, 2006). Since it first appeared, it has become an international movement, with splinter groups, including *traceurs.* Georges Hébert, the twentieth-century theorist of French military training, is often cited as inspiration for the techniques developed as *parkour.* (*Au S.:* Bloom; *Vol.:* Bloom 11).

Pieds noirs: European immigrant settlers, including Sephardic Jews, established in colonial Algeria from 1830 to 1962. A majority came from poor farming communities in France, Italy, and Malta, seeking a better life in North Africa. Some of the early and most successful settlers were from the Alsace-Lorraine region, who resettled in Algeria after its annexation during the 1870–71 Franco-Prussian War, including Lyautey. After Algeria declared independence, over a million *pieds noirs* settled in France, and now represent an important, but heterogeneous, lobby in French politics. (*Au S.:* Bernault; *Vol.:* Bernault 6).

Precariat: A term coined by Loïc Wacquant to describe a proletarian underclass in an international amalgam of exurban situations. (*Au S.:* Bloom; *Bib.:* Wacquant 2007; *Vol.:* Bloom 11).

Quatre Communes (Four Communes of Senegal): St. Louis, Rufisque, Dakar, and Gorée Island were the four municipalities located in present day Senegal, that later became known as the Four Communes. They were initially settled under the *ancien régime.* Other parts of Africa colonized by France were largely established under the Third Republic, or after 1870. A well-established bourgeoisie developed in the Four Communes because each of these municipalities was successively granted the same rights of a locally elected administration as well as civil rights equivalent to municipalities in France, as of 1871 (in St. Louis and Gorée), 1880 (in Rufisque), and 1887 (in Dakar). (*Au. S.:* Bloom; *Bib.:* Conklin 1997; Bloom 2008, *Vol.:* Cooper 5).

Racaille: A term associated with Nicolas Sarkozy's outburst against North African *banlieue* youth in November 2005. The term refers to scum, hooligans, dirt. The related term *cailleras* is back slang for *racaille,* and used by *banlieue* youth to refer to themselves. Other terms such as *casseurs* and *sauvageons* are also associated with this term. (*Au. S.:* Boubeker; *Bib.:* Mucchielli et al. 2005; *Vol.:* Bloom 11, Boubeker 4, Gondola 7, Introduction).

RER (*Réseau Express Regional*): The RER is a network of trains serving the Île de France Region, particularly the Parisian *banlieue* (suburbs) that have become a symptom of immigrant and working-class containment. The RER has also served as the basis for various literary works, including François Maspero's 1990 book, *Les passagers du Roissy-Express,* translated as *Roissy-Express: A Journey through the Paris Suburbs* (trans. Paul Jones, London: Verso, 1994). (*Au. S.:* Bloom; *Vol.:* Tshimanga 12).

Sans papiers: Undocumented immigrants. Several organizations have routinely staged demonstrations to demand that undocumented immigrants with no criminal record and their children born in France be granted legal status. (*Au. S.:* eds.; *Vol.:* Bernault 6, Tshimanga 12).

Sans-parts: Jacques Rancière's term for those who do not share in the benefits of society and thus have no stake in it. (*Au. S:* Mbembe; *Bib.:* Rancière 1995; *Vol.:* Mbembe 3).

SOS-Racisme: Initially set up as a close associate to the French Socialist Party during François Mitterrand's tenure as president. Founded in October 1984, it became an important associative structure for antiracist campaigns related to practices of racial discrimination against immigrants. Harlem Désir was the first president of the association from 1984–1992. (*Au. S.:* eds.; *Vol.:* Bernault 6; Gondola 7).

Zupiens: Derived from the abbreviation ZUP (*zone à urbaniser en priorité,* which may be translated as priority development zones), the term refers to citizens from such zones. (*Au. S.:* Tshimanga; *Vol.:* Tshimanga 12).

BIBLIOGRAPHY

Abdallah, Mongiss. 2006. "La France: Love it or Leave it." *Index on Censorship* 35, no. 3 (August): 54–62.

Agamben, Giorgio. 1998. *Homo Sacer: Sovereign Power and Bare Life.* Trans. Daniel Heller-Roazen. Stanford, Calif.: Stanford University Press.

———. 2005. *State of Exception.* Trans. Kevin Attell. Chicago: University of Chicago Press.

Aldrich, Robert. 2005. *Vestiges of the Colonial Empire in France: Monuments, Museums and Colonial Memories.* New York: Palgrave Macmillan.

Amselle, Jean-Loup. 1996. *Vers un multiculturalisme français. L'empire de la coûtume.* Paris: Flammarion.

———. 2008. *L'Occident décroché: Enquête sur les postcolonialismes.* Paris: Stock.

Anidjar, Gil. 2003. *The Jew, the Arab: A History of the Enemy.* Stanford, Calif.: Stanford University Press.

Anon. 2003. *Antisémitisme: l'intolérable chantage.* Paris: Éditions La découverte.

Appadurai, Arjun. 1996. *Modernity at Large: Cultural Dimensions of Globalization.* Durham, N.C.: Duke University Press.

———. 2006. *Fear of Small Numbers.* Durham, N.C.: Duke University Press, Public Planet Books.

Archer, Georges. 1964. *De Terentiacum à Drancy. Histoire d'une commune de la Seine.* Montpellier: Déhan.

Archer-Shaw, Petrine. 2004. *Negrophilia: Avant-Garde Paris and Black Culture in the 1920s.* New York: Thames and Hudson.

Arendt, Hannah. 1963. *Eichmann in Jerusalem: A Report on the Banality of Evil.* Rev. and enlarged ed. New York: Viking.

Ariès, Philippe. 1999. *Essais de mémoire.* Paris: Seuil.

Askolovitch, Claude. 2005. "Colonisation, d'une vérité l'autre." *Le Nouvel Observateur,* December 8, 2005.

Auffray, Alain, and Tassel, Fabrice. 2007. "Sur l'immigration, un candidat immaîtrisable." *Libération,* April 3, 2007.

Augé, Marc. 1998. *Les formes de l'oubli.* Paris: Payot.

Aussaresses, Paul. 2000. *Services spéciaux. Algérie, 1955–1957.* Paris: Perrin.

Awenengo, Séverine, Pascale Barthelemy, and Charles Tshimanga, eds. 2004. *Écrire l'histoire de l'Afrique autrement?* Paris: L'Harmattan.

Badie, Bertrand. 1997. "Quelles citoyennetés à l'heure de la mondialisation?" *Hommes et migrations* 1206: 5–13.

Badin, Sandra J. 2002. "Book Notes." *Harvard Human Rights Journal* 15 (Spring 2002): 341–42.

Baecque, Antoine de. 1991. *Les Cahiers du cinéma: Histoire d'une revue.* Vol. 1: *À l'assaut du cinéma, 1951–1959.* Paris: Éditions Cahiers du Cinéma.

———. 2003. *La Cinéphilie: Invention d'un regard, histoire d'une culture, 1944–1968.* Paris: Fayard.

Baetens, Frank. 2006. "Le coup de tête de Zidane. Pour une lecture mythologique." *Esprit* 329 (November): 127–47.

Balandier, Georges. 1955. *Sociologie actuelle de l'Afrique noire.* Paris: Presses universitaires de France.

Baldwin, James. 1955. *Notes of a Native Son.* Boston: Beacon.

Balibar, Étienne. 2004. *We, the People of Europe? Reflections on Transnational Citizenship.* Princeton, N.J.: Princeton University Press.

———. 2006. "Uprisings in the banlieues." *Lignes* 21 (November): 50–101.

Bancel, Nicolas, and Pascal Blanchard. 1998. *De l'indigène à l'immigré.* Paris: Gallimard.

Bancel, Nicolas, Pascal Blanchard, and Delabarre Francis, eds. 1997. *Images d'Empire, 1930–1960.* Paris: La Martinière.

Bancel, Nicolas, Pascal Blanchard, and Françoise Vergès, eds. 2003. *La République coloniale: Essai sur une utopia.* Paris: Albin Michel.

Bancel, Nicolas, et al., eds. 2002. *Zoos humains: Au temps des exhibitions humaines.* Paris: La Découverte.

Barbeau, Arthur, and Florette Henri. 1974. *The Unknown Soldiers: Black American Troops in World War I.* Philadelphia: Temple University Press.

Barbier, Christophe, and Eric Mandonnet. 2005. "Colonisation, le mal de la repentance." *L'Express,* December 15, 2005.

Barkat, Sidi Mohamed. 2005. *Le corps d'exception.* Paris: Éditions Amsterdam.

Barker, Chris. [2000] 2005. *Cultural Studies: Theory and Practice.* 2nd ed. London: Sage Publications, 2005.

Barrot, Jean-Pierre. 1953. "Une Tradition de Qualité." In *Sept Ans de Cinéma Français,* ed. H. Agel, et al., 26–37. Paris: Les Éditions du Cerf.

Bastié, Jean. 1964. *La Croissance de la Banlieue Parisienne.* Paris: Presses Universitaires de France.

Battegay, Alain, and Ahmed Boubeker. 1993. *Les images publiques de l'immigration.* Paris: L'Harmattan.

Baudouï, Rémi. 1992. "La cité de la Muette à Drancy (1933–1945)." In *Banlieue rouge, 1920–1960,* ed. Annie Fourcaut, 207–20. *Série Mémoires* 18. Paris: Éditions Autrement.

Bayart, Jean-François. 2007. "La novlangue d'un archipel universitaire." In *La situation* coloniale. *Les postcolonial studies dans le débat français,* ed. Marie Claude Smouts, 268–72. Paris: Presses de Sciences Po.

Bayart, Jean-François, and Romain Bertrand. 2006. "De quel legs colonial parle-t-on? *Esprit* (December 2006): 134–60.

Bazin, Hugues. 1995. *La culture hip hop.* Paris: Desclée de Brouwer.

Beau, Nicolas, and Ahmed Boubeker. 1986. *Chroniques métissées: L'histoire de France des jeunes Arabes.* Paris: Alain Moreau.

Beaud, Stéphane. 2002. *80% au bac . . . et après? Les enfants de la démocratisation scolaire.* Paris: La Découverte.

Beaud, Stéphane, and Younes Amrani. 2004. *"Pays de Malheur!" Un jeune des cités écrit à un sociologue.* Paris: La Découverte.

Beaud, Stéphane, and Michel Pialoux. 2003. *Violences urbaines, violence sociale: Genèse des nouvelles classes dangereuses.* Paris: Fayard.

Bédarida, François, ed. 1995. *L'histoire et le métier d'historien en France, 1945–1995.* Paris: Éditions de la Maison des sciences de l'homme.

Belaïd, Chakri, et al. 2006. *Banlieue, lendemains de révolte.* Paris: La Dispute.

Bell, Daniel. 1973. *The Coming of Post-Industrial Society: A Venture in Social Forecasting.* New York: Basic Books.

Benbassa, Esther. 2004. *La République face à ses minorities.* Paris: Mille et Une Nuits.

Benot, Yves. 2005. *Les lumières, l'esclavage, la colonisation.* Ed. and presented by Roland Desné and Marcel Dorigny. Paris: La Découverte.

Bensaïd, Daniel, Samuel Johsua, and Roseline Vachetta. 2005. "Quand la raison s'affole." *Libération,* March 21, 2005.

Beriss, David. 2004. *Black Skins, French Voices: Caribbean Ethnicity and Activism in Urban France.* Boulder, Colo.: Westview.

Berl, Emmanuel. 1957. *La France irréelle.* Paris: Grasset.

Bernault, Florence. 1996. *Démocraties ambigües en Afrique centrale, Congo-Brazzaville, Gabon, 1940–1965.* Paris: Karthala.

———. 2001. "L'Afrique et la modernité des sciences sociales." *Vingtième siècle* 70: 127–38.

Bertrand, Romain. 2006a. "La mise en cause(s) du fait colonial. Retour sur une controverse publique." *Politique africaine* 102: 28–49.

———. 2006b. *Mémoires d'empire. La controverse autour du "fait colonial."* Clamecy, France: Éditions du Croquant.

———. 2007. "Faire parler les subalternes ou le mythe du dévoilement." In *La situation postcoloniale: Les postcolonial studies dans le débat français,* ed. Marie Claude Smouts, 276–84. Paris: Presses de Sciences Po.

Biarnès, Pierre. 1987. *Les Français en Afrique noire de Richelieu à Mitterrand.* Paris: Armand Colin.

Binet, Stéphanie. 2005. "Banlieues. Les rappeurs l'avaient bien dit." *Libération,* November 14, 2005.

———. 2006a. "Rap et la banlieue." Available at http://www.labanlieuesexprime.org/, April 21, 2006.

———. 2006b. "Prendre conscience qu'on peut s'unir." *Libération,* December 23, 2006.

———. 2006c. "Radio hip hop à hit-parade civique." *Libération,* December 23, 2006.

Binet, Stéphanie, and Fabrice Tassel. 2006. "Joey Starr: Jeunes et policiers, on leur a promis plein de choses et rien n'a été fait." *Libération,* October 20, 2006.

Blakely, Allison. 1993. *Blacks in the Dutch World: The Evolution of Racial Imagery in a Modern Society.* Bloomington: Indiana University Press.

Blanchard, Pascal, and Armelle Chatelier. 1993. *Images et colonies.* Paris: La Découverte.

Blanchard, Pascal, and Nicolas Bancel, eds. 2006. *Culture post-coloniale, 1961–2006.* Paris: Éditions Autrement.

Blanchard, Pascal, Nicolas Bancel, and Sandrine Lemaire, eds. 2005. *La fracture coloniale: La société française au prisme de l'héritage colonial.* Paris: La Découverte.

Blanchard, Pascal, and Sandrine Lemaire, eds. 2004. *Culture impériale: Les colonies au cœur de la République, 1931–1961.* Paris: Éditions Autrement.

Blauner, Robert. 1969. "Internal Colonialism and Ghetto Revolt." *Social Problems* 16, no. 4 (Spring).

Blévis, Laure. 2004. "Sociologie d'un droit colonial: Citoyenneté et nationalité en Algérie (1865–1947): une exception républicaine?" Doctoral thesis, Institut d'Études Politiques, Aix-en-Provence.

Bloch, Marc. 1946. *L'étrange défaite. Témoignage écrit en 1940.* Paris: Société des Éditions Franc-tireur.

———. 1949. *The Historian's Craft.* Trans. Peter Putnam. New York: Vintage Books, 1953.

Bloom, Peter J. 1999. "Beur Cinema and the Politics of Location: French Immigration Politics and the Naming of a Film Movement." *Social Identities* 5, no. 4 (December): 469–487.

———. 2008. *French Colonial Documentary: Mythologies of Humanitarianism.* Minneapolis: University of Minnesota Press.

Bocquet, José-Louis, and Philippe Pierre-Adolphe. 1997. *Rap ta France.* Paris: Flammarion.

Boilley, Pierre. 2005. "Loi du 23 février 2005, colonisation, indigènes, victimisation. Évocations binaires, représentations primaires." *Politique africaine* 98: 131–38.

Boilley, Pierre, and Ibrahima Thioub. 2004. "Pour une histoire de la complexité." In *Écrire l'histoire de l'Afrique autrement,* ed. S. Awenengo, P. Barthelemy, and Ch. Tshimanga, 23–45. Paris: L'Harmattan.

Boltanski, Luc, and Laurent Thévenot. 2006. *On Justification: Economies of Worth.* Trans. Catherine Porter. Princeton, N.J.: Princeton University Press.

Bonelli, Laurent, and Gilles Sainati, eds. 2004. *La machine à punir: Discours et pratiques sécuritaires.* Paris: L'Esprit Frappeur.

Bordes-Benayoun, Chantal, and Dominique Schnapper. 2006. *Diasporas et Nations.* Paris: Odile Jacob.

Bosséno, Christian-Marc. 1992. "Immigrant Cinema: National Cinema—The Case of *beur* Film." In *Popular European Cinema,* ed. Richard Dyer and Ginette Vincendeau, 47–57. London: Routledge.

———. 1992. "Les environs de Paris au fil du cinéma." In *Banlieue rouge, 1920–1960*, ed. Annie Fourcaut, 242–51. *Série Mémoires* 18. Paris: Éditions Autrement.

Bouamama, Saïd. 1992. "De l'assimilation à l'intégration: genèse d'une mystification." In Bouamama, Cordeiro, and Roux 1992, 171–96.

———. 1993. *De la galère à la citoyenneté. Les jeunes, la cité, la société.* Paris: Desclée de Brouwer.

———. 1994a. *Contribution à la mémoire des banlieues: Avec les contributions de Hadjila Sa-Saoud & Moktar Djerdoubi.* Paris: Éditions du Volga.

———. 1994b. *Dix ans de marche des Beurs. Chronique d'un mouvement avorté.* Paris: Desclée de Brouwer.

———. 2004. *L'affaire du foulard islamique: La production d'un racisme respectable.* Roubaix: Éditions Le Geai Bleu.

———. 2005. "Indigènes de la République. Une contribution au débat." June 13, 2005. Available at http://www.oumma.com.

———. 2006. "De la visibilité à la suspicion: la fabrique républicaine d'une politisation." In *La République mise à nue par son immigration*, ed. Nacira Guénif-Souilamas, 196–216. Paris: La Fabrique Éditions.

Bouamama, Saïd, Albano Cordeiro, and Michel Roux, eds. 1992. *La citoyenneté dans tous ses états. De l'immigration à la nouvelle citoyenneté.* Paris: L'Harmattan.

Bouamama, Saïd, and Pierre Tévanian. 2005. "Peut-on parler d'un racisme post-colonial?" In *Culture post-coloniale, 1961–2006*, ed. Pascal Banchard and Nicolas Bancel, 243–54. Paris: Éditions Autrement.

Boubeker, Ahmed. 1999. *Familles de l'intégration. Les ritournelles de l'ethnicité en pays jacobins.* Paris: Stock.

———. 2001. "Des mondes de l'ethnicité. La communauté d'expérience des héritiers de l'immigration maghrébine en France." Ph.D. diss., Paris: EHESS.

———. 2003. *Les mondes de l'ethnicité. La communauté d'expérience des héritiers de l'immigration maghrébine.* Paris: Balland.

———. 2005. "'Le creuset français' ou la légende noire de l'intégration." In Blanchard et al. 2005, 183–90.

Boucher, Manuel. 1998. *Rap, expression des lascars: Significations et enjeux du rap dans la société française.* Paris: L'Harmattan.

Bourdieu, Pierre. 1986. "L'illusion biographique." *Actes de la Recherche en Sciences Sociales* 62/63: 69–72. (Translated as "The Biographical Illusion." In *Working Papers and Proceedings of the Center for Psychosocial Studies*, No. 14. Chicago: Center for Psychosocial Studies.)

———. 1994. *Raisons pratiques. Sur la théorie de l'action.* Paris: Seuil.

Bowen, John R. 2007. *Why the French Don't Like Headscarves: Islam, the State and Public Space.* Princeton, N.J.: Princeton University Press.

Branche, Raphaëlle. 2001. *La torture et l'armée pendant la guerre d'Algérie 1954–1962.* Paris: Gallimard.

———. 2006. *La guerre d'Algérie: Une mémoire apaisée?* Paris: Seuil, coll. "Points histoire."

Braudel, Fernand. 1986. *L'identité de la France: espace et histoire.* Paris: Arthaud-Flammarion.

Brubaker, Rogers. 1992. *Citizenship and Nationhood in France and Germany.* Cambridge, Mass.: Harvard University Press.

———. 1998. *Citizenship and Nationhood in France and Germany.* Cambridge, Mass.: Harvard University Press.

Buchsbaum, Jonathan. 2006. "'The *Exception Culturelle* Is Dead.' Long Live Cultural Diversity: French Cinema and the New Resistance." *Framework* 47, no. 1 (Spring): 5–21.

Bui Trong, Lucienne. See under Trong.

Bullock, Nicholas. 2007. "Developing Prototypes for France's Mass Housing Programme, 1949–53." *Planning Perspectives* 22 (January): 5–28.

Burguière, André. 2006. *L'École des Annales. Une histoire intellectuelle.* Paris: Odile Jacob.

Butler, Judith. 1993. *Bodies That Matter: On the Discursive Limits of "Sex."* New York: Routledge.

Butler, Kim. 2001. "Defining Diaspora, Refining a Discourse." *Diaspora* 10, no. 2: 189–219.

Cachin, Olivier. 2006. *Les 100 albums essentiels du rap.* Paris: Éditions Scali.

Caramel, Laurence. 1996. "Nos chansons, c'est un constat, pas de la provocation." *Le Nouvel économiste* (29 November): 80–81.

Carrère, Violaine. 2007. "Quelles politiques pour quelle intégration?" *Plein droit* 72, no. 2 (March), available at http://www.gisti.org/spip.php?article885.

Castel, Robert. 2007. *La discrimination négative. Citoyens ou indigènes?* Paris: La République des idées/Seuil.

Castells, Manuel. 1983. *The City and the Grassroots.* London: Arnold.

Castoriadis, Cornélius. 1975. *L'institution imaginaire de la société.* Paris: Seuil.

Cavell, Stanley. 1987. *Disowning Knowledge in Six Plays of Shakespeare.* New York: Cambridge University Press.

Centre for Contemporary Cultural Studies. 1978. *Policing the Crisis: Mugging, the State, and Law and Order.* London: Macmillan.

———. 1982. *The Empire Strikes Back: Race and Racism in 70s Britain.* London: Hutchinson.

Chartier, Roger. 1998. *Au bord de la falaise: L'histoire entre certitudes et inquiétude.* Paris: Albin Michel.

Chevalier, Louis. 1978. *Classes laborieuses, classes dangereuses.* Paris: Librairie Générale Française.

Chouquer, Gérard, and Nacira Guénif-Souilamas, eds. 2007. Special issue, "Une exception si française," *Cosmopolitiques* 16 (November).

Chrétien, Jean-Pierre. 2005. "Le passé colonial: le devoir d'histoire." *Politique africaine* 98, (June): 141–48.

Chrétien, Jean-Pierre, Catherine Coquery-Vidrovitch, and Jean Copans. 2006. "Autour d'un livre: La Fracture coloniale." *Politique africaine* 102 (June): 189–208.

"Cité dans le texte." 2005. Selected interviews in 2005–2006, with inhabitants of the housing project La Grande Borne, Grigny (Essonne). Available at http://www .liberation.fr.

Citron, Suzanne. 1987. *Le Mythe national: l'histoire de France en question.* Paris: Éditions Ouvrières.

———. 2006. "L'impossible révision de l'histoire de France." In Bancel and Blanchard 2006, 42–52.

Clark, Kenneth. 1965. *Dark Ghetto.* New York: Harper and Row.

Cléris, Céline. 2005. "La politique cinématographique de Jack Lang de 1981 à 1986." Thesis, University of Rennes. Available at http://www.rennes.iep.fr/IMG/pdf/ cleris-2.pdf.

Cobb, Richard. 1970. *The Police and the People: French Popular Protest 1789–1820.* New York: Oxford University Press.

Collectif. 2003. *Antisémitisme: l'intolérable chantage.* Paris: La découverte.

Collins, Randall. 1990. "Stratification, Emotional Energy, and the Transient Emotions." In *Research Agendas in the Sociology of Emotions,* ed. Theodore D. Kemper, 27–57. Albany, N.Y.: SUNY Press.

———. 2004. *Interaction Ritual Chains.* Princeton, N.J.: Princeton University Press.

Conklin, Alice L. 1997. *A Mission to Civilize: The Republican Idea of Empire in France and West Africa, 1895–1930.* Stanford, Calif.: Stanford University Press.

Conklin, Alice, and Julia Clancy-Smith. 2004. "Introduction: Writing Colonial Histories." *French Historical Studies* 27, no. 3: 497–505.

Cooper, Frederick. 1996. *Decolonization and African Society: The Labor Question in French and British Africa.* Cambridge: Cambridge University Press.

———. 2002. "Decolonizing Situations: The Rise, Fall and Rise of Colonial Studies, 1951–2001." *French Politics, Culture and Society* 20, no. 2 (Summer): 47–76.

———. 2005. *Colonialism in Question: Theory, Knowledge, History.* Berkeley and Los Angeles: University of California Press.

Cooper, Frederick, and Randall Packard, eds. 1997. *International Development and the Social Sciences: Essays in the History and Politics of Knowledge.* Berkeley and Los Angeles: University of California Press.

Cooper, Frederick, and Ann Laura Stoler, eds. 1997. *Tensions of Empire: Colonial Cultures in a Bourgeois World.* Berkeley and Los Angeles: University of California Press.

Coquery-Vidrovitch, Catherine. 1999. "Plaidoyer pour l'histoire du monde dans l'université française." *Vingtième siècle* 61: 111–25.

———. 2001. "Nationalité et citoyenneté en Afrique Occidentale Française: Originaires et Citoyens Dans le Sénégal Colonial." *Journal of African History* 42, no. 2: 285–305.

Corbin, Alain. 2001. *Historien du sensible. Entretiens avec Gilles Heuré.* Paris: La Découverte.

Coroller, Catherine. 2007a. "L'État ne peut définir l'identité nationale, qui n'est ni unique ni figée." *Libération,* June 22, 2007.

———. 2007b. "La vision de la nation est ethnicisée." *Libération,* June 29, 2007.

———. 2007c. "C'est toujours la droite qui a évoqué le sujet." *Libération,* July 16, 2007.

Coutant, Isabelle. 2005. *Délit de jeunesse: la justice face aux quartiers.* Paris: Éditions la Découverte.

Creton, Laurent. 2004. *Histoire économique du cinéma français: Production et financement 1940–1959.* Paris: CNRS Éditions.

Crubellier, Maurice. 1991. *La mémoire des Français: Recherches d'histoire culturelle.* Paris: Henri Veyrier.

Davidson, Alastair. 1999. "Open Republic, Multiculturalism and Citizenship: The French Debate." *Theory and Event* 3, no. 2: 49–71.

De Gaulle, Charles. 2000. *Charles de Gaulle: Mémoires.* Paris: Gallimard-Bibliothèque de la Pléiade.

De Jaeghere, Michel, et al. 2001. *Le livre blanc de l'armée française en Algérie.* Paris: Contretemps.

De la Gorce, Paul Marie. 1991. "Chirac joue du tam-tam." In *Jeune-Afrique,* July 3–9, 30–31.

Debray, Régis. 2005. "Malaise dans la civilisation, suite." *Le Monde,* November 26.

Decottignies, Roger, and Marc de Biéville. 1963. *Les nationalités africaines.* Paris: Pedone.

Décret No. 2007–999 du 31 mai 2007 relatif aux attributions du ministre de l'immigration, de l'intégration, de l'identité nationale et du co-développement. Available at http://www.legifrance.gouv.fr.

Décret No. 2005–1386 du 8 Novembre 2005 portant application de la loi n° 55-385 du 3 avril 1955. Available at http://www.assemblee-nationale.fr/12/projets/p12673.asp.

Deleuze, Gilles. 1986. *Foucault.* Trans. Seán Hand. Minneapolis: University of Minnesota Press.

———. 1997. *Pourparlers.* Paris: Minuit.

Deleuze, Gilles, and Félix Guattari. 1980. *Mille plateaux.* Paris: Minuit.

Delphy, Christine, and Nacira Guénif-Souilamas. 2006. "Une exigence d'égalité." Available at http://www.indigenes-republique.org.

Deltombe, Thomas. 2005. *L'islam imaginaire.* Paris: La Découverte.

Denis, Jacques. 2006. "Songs of Protest." *Le Monde diplomatique,* July 23.

Diawara, Manthia. 2003. *We Won't Budge: A Malaria Memoir.* New York: Basic Civitas Books.

Diken, Bülent, and Carsten Bagge Laustesen. 2006. *The Culture of Exception: Sociology Facing the Camp.* London: Routledge.

Dillon, Michael. 1999. "The Scandal of the Refugee: Some Reflections on the 'Inter' of International Relations and Continental Thought." In *Moral Spaces,* ed. D. Campbell and M. J. Shapiro, 92–124. Minneapolis: University of Minnesota Press.

Dimier, Véronique. 2004. "For a Republic 'Diverse and Indivisible': France's Experiences from the Colonial Past." *Contemporary European History* 13: 45–66.

Diouf, Mamadou. 1998. "The French Colonial Policy of Assimilation and the Civility of the Originaires of the Four Communes (Senegal): A Nineteenth Century Globalization Project." *Development and Change* 29: 671–96.

Dirks, Nicolas B. 1996. Foreword in Bernard S. Cohn, *Colonialism and Its Forms of Knowledge: The British in India.* Princeton, N.J.: Princeton University Press.

Downs, Laura Lee, and Stéphane Gerson, eds. 2007. *Why France? American Historians Reflect on an Enduring Fascination.* Ithaca, N.Y.: Cornell University Press.

Drozdiak, William. 1991. "French at Odds over Immigrants." *Washington Post* (July 12), A-24.

Du Bois, W. E. B. 1946. *The World and Africa.* New York: International Publishers, 1965.

Dubet, François, and Didier Lapeyronnie. 1992. *Quartiers d'exil.* Paris: Seuil.

Dubet, François, et al. 1989. *Pobladores, luttes sociales et démocratie au Chili.* Paris: L'Harmattan.

Dubois, Laurent. 2004a. *A Colony of Citizens: Revolution and Slave Emancipation in the French Caribbean, 1787–1804.* Chapel Hill: University of North Carolina Press.

———. 2004b. *Avengers of the New World: The Story of the Haitian Revolution.* Cambridge, Mass.: Harvard University Press.

Duby, Georges, and Guy Lardreau. 1992. *Dialogues.* Paris: Flammarion.

Duchesne, Sophie. 1997. *Citoyenneté à la française.* Paris: Presses de Sciences-Po.

Duclert, Vincent, and Christophe Prochasson, eds. 2002. *Dictionnaire critique de la République.* Paris: Flammarion.

Dulucq, Sophie, and Colette Zytnicki. 2005. *Décoloniser l'histoire? De l'histoire coloniale aux histoires nationales en Amérique latine et en Afrique, XIXe–XXe siècles.* Saint-Denis, France: Société française d'histoire d'outre-mer.

Dulucq, Sophie, et al. 2006. "L'Écriture de l'histoire de la colonisation en France depuis 1960." *Afrique & Histoire* 6, no. 2: 235–76.

Dupin, Eric. 2007. *A droite toute.* Paris: Éditions Fayard.

Durand, Alain Philippe, ed. 2002. *Black, Blanc, Beur: Rap Music and Hip-Hop Culture in the Francophone World.* Oxford: Scarecrow Press.

Duranton-Cabrol, Anne-Marie. 1988. *Visages de la Nouvelle Droite: Le GRECE et son histoire.* Paris: Presses de la Fondation nationale des sciences politiques.

Dworkin, Dennis. 2007. *Class Struggles.* London: Pearson.

Eco, Umberto. 1976. *A Theory of Semiotics.* Bloomington: Indiana University Press.

Einaudi, Jean-Luc. 1991. *La bataille de Paris: 17 octobre 1961.* Paris: Seuil.

Eley, Geoff, and Ronald Grigor Suny, eds. 1996. *Becoming National.* New York: Oxford University Press.

Elias, Norbert. 1969a. *La civilisation des mœurs.* Paris: Agora Presse Pocket, 2003.

———. 1969b. *La dynamique de l'Occident.* Paris: Agora Presse Pocket, 2003.

Ellison, Ralph. 1952. *The Invisible Man.* New York: Random House.

Eze, Emmanuel Chukwudi, ed. 1997. *Postcolonial African Philosophy: A Critical Reader.* Cambridge: Blackwell.

Ezra, Elizabeth. 2000. *The Colonial Unconscious: Race and Culture in Interwar France.* Ithaca, N.Y.: Cornell University Press.

Faes, Géraldine, and Stephen Smith. 2006. *Noir et Français!* Paris: Panama.

Fanon, Frantz. 2001. "L'Algérie se dévoile." In *L'an V de la révolution algérienne*. Paris: La Découverte.

Farchy, Joëlle. 1999. *La fin de l'exception culturelle?* Paris: CNRS Éditions.

Farge, Arlette. 1997a. *Des lieux pour l'histoire*. Paris: Seuil.

———. 1997b. *Le goût de l'archive*. Paris: Seuil.

Fassin, Didier, and Eric Fassin, eds. 2006. *De la question sociale à la question raciale? Représenter la société française*. Paris: La Découverte.

Faure, Alain, et al., eds. 1991. *Les Premiers Banlieusards: Aux origines des banlieues de Paris (1860–1940)*. Paris: Éditions CREAPHIS.

Ferro, Marc, ed. 2003. *Le livre noir du colonialisme. XVIe–XXIe siècle: de l'extermination à la repentance*. Paris: Robert Laffont.

Finkielkraut, Alain. 1989. *La défaite de la pensée*. Paris: Gallimard.

———. 2003a. *Au nom de l'autre: Réflexions sur l'antisémitisme qui vient*. Paris: Gallimard.

———. 2003b. "Le foulard et l'espace sacré de l'école." *L'Arche* 544–45 (June–July). Available at http://www.nouveau-reac.org/docs/FA/AF_arche544.htm.

———. 2005. Interview in the Israeli weekly *Haaretz*, November 18, 2005. (See also *Le Monde*, November 24, 2005.)

Foltz, William. 1965. *From French West Africa to the Mali Federation*. New Haven, Conn.: Yale University Press.

Fouilloux, Etienne. 1990. "Hiver 1954." *Vingtième Siècle. Revue d'histoire* 27 (July–September): 107–108.

Fourcaut, Annie. 1999. "Aux origines du film de banlieue: Les banlieuesards au cinéma (1930–1980)." *Sociétés et Représentations* 8 (December): 113–27.

Fourcaut, Annie, Emmanuel Bellanger, and Mathieu Flonneau. 2007. *Paris/Banlieues: Conflits et solidarités: historiographie, anthologie, chronologie*. Paris: Éditions CREAPHIS.

Gallo, Max. 2006. *Fier d'être Français*. Paris: Librairie Arthème Fayard.

Gamson, William. 1990. *The Strategy of Social Protest*. Belmont, Calif.: Wadsworth.

Gamson, William, Bruce Fyreman, and Steven Rytina. 1982. *Encounters with Unjust Authority*. Homewood, Ill.: Dorsey Press.

Gans, Herbert. 1962. *The Urban Villagers: Group and Class in the Life of Italian-Americans*. New York: Free Press.

Garner, Steve. 2006. "The Uses of Whiteness: What Sociologists Working on Europe Can Draw from US Research on Whiteness." *Sociology* 40, no. 2 (April): 257–75.

Gastaut, Yvan. 2000. *L'immigration et l'opinion en France*. Paris: Seuil.

Geisser, Vincent. 2000. "Discours républicain et rhétorique de la spécificité française." *Hommes et migrations* 1223: 33–40.

———. 2006. "L'intégration républicaine: réflexion sur une problématique postcoloniale." In Blanchard and Bancel 2006, 145–64.

Genova, James. 2004. "Constructing Identity in Post-War France: Citizenship, Nationality, and the Lamine Guèye Law, 1946–1953." *International History Review* 26: 55–79.

Gervereau, Laurent, Jean-Pierre Rioux, and Benjamin Stora, eds. 1992. *La France en guerre d'Algérie (novembre 1954–juillet 1962)*. Nanterre, France: Édition Bibliothèque de documentation internationale contemporaine.

Gèze, François. 2006. "Les 'intégristes de la République' et les émeutes de novembre." *Mouvements* 44 (March–April): 88–100.

Gikandi, Simon. 1996. *Maps of Englishness: Writing Identity in the Culture of Colonialism*. New York: Columbia University Press.

Gilroy, Paul. 1987. *There Ain't No Black in the Union Jack*. London: Routledge.

———. 1993. *The Black Atlantic: Modernity and Double Consciousness*. Cambridge, Mass.: Harvard University Press.

———. 2000. *Against Race: Imagining Political Culture beyond the Color Line*. Cambridge, Mass.: Belknap Press of Harvard University.

———. 2004. *Postcolonial Melancholia*. New York: Columbia University Press.

Gimello-Mesplomb, Frederic. 2006. "The Economy of 1950s Popular French Cinema." *Studies in French Cinema Journal* 6, no. 2: 141–50.

Girard, Bernard. 2006. *Banlieues: insurrection ou ras-le-bol?* Le Kremlin Bicêtre, France: Les points sur les i éditions.

Giudicelli, Anne. 2006. *Caillera . . . Cette France qui a peur*. Paris: Jean-Claude Gawsewitch Éditeur.

Golan, Tamar. 1981. "A Certain Mystery: How Can France Do Everything That It Does in Africa—and Get Away with It?" *African Affairs* 80, no. 318 (January): 3–11.

Gondola, Ch. Didier. 1997. *Villes miroirs: migrations et identités urbaines à Brazzaville et Kinshasa, 1930–1970*. Paris: L'Harmattan.

———. 2003. "But I Ain't African, I'm American! Black American Exiles and the Construction of Racial Identities in Twentieth-Century France." In *Blackening Europe: The African American Presence*, ed. Heike Raphael-Hernandez, 201–15. New York: Routledge.

———. 2007. *Africanisme: La crise d'une illusion*. Paris: L'Harmattan.

Gournay, Bernard. 2002. *Exception Culturelle et Mondialisation*. Paris: Presses de Sciences PO.

Green, Nancy L. 2002. *Repenser les migrations*. Paris: Presses Universitaires de France.

Greilsamer, Laurent. 2006. "Et voilà pourquoi les stars sont muettes." *Le Monde*, December 19.

Grémion, Catherine. 1996. "L'accès au logement social." In *L'exclusion: L'état des savoirs*, ed. Serge Paugam, 519–29. Paris: La découverte.

Grosrichard, Alain. 1979. *Structure du sérail*. Paris: Editions du Seuil.

Gross, Joan, David McMurray, and Ted Swedenberg. 1996. "Arab Noise and Ramadan Nights: Raï, Rap, and Franco-Maghrebi Identities." In *Displacement, Diaspora, and Geographies of Identity*, ed. Smadar Lavie and Ted Swedenberg, 119–55. Durham, N.C.: Duke University Press.

Guénif-Souilamas, Nacira. 2003. *Des Beurettes*. Paris: Hachette Pluriel.

———. 2005. "La réduction à son corps de l'indigène de la République." In Blanchard, Bancel, and Lemaire, 199–208.

————. 2006a. "The Other French Exception: Virtuous Racism and the War of the Sexes in Postcolonial France." *French Politics, Culture and Society* 24, no. 3 (Winter): 23–41.

————, ed. 2006b. *La république mise à nu par son immigration.* Paris: La Fabrique.

————. 2007. "L'iconographie républicaine des Marianne 'multicolores.' Une arme de destruction massive au service de l'universalisme abstrait." In *Qui a peur de la télévision en couleurs?* ed. Isabelle Rigoni, 85–107. Montreuil: Éditions Aux Lieux d'être.

Guénif-Souilamas, Nacira, and Eric Macé, eds. 2004. *Les féministes et le garçon arabe.* Paris: Éditions de L'Aube.

Guèye, Lamine. 1966. *Itinéraire africain.* Paris: Présence Africaine.

Guyot, Jean-Pierre. 1997. "Mères de famille en guerre contre NTM." *Le Figaro,* February 13, 1997: 12.

Hajjat, Abdellali. 2005. *Immigration post-coloniale et mémoire.* Paris: L'Harmattan.

Halbwachs, Maurice. 1925. *Les cadres sociaux de la mémoire.* Paris: Félix Alcan.

————. 1968. *La mémoire collective.* 2nd ed. Paris: Presses Universitaire de France.

Hall, Catherine. 2002. *Civilising Subjects: Colony and Metropole in the English Imagination, 1830–1867.* Chicago: University of Chicago Press.

Hall, Stuart. 1988. *The Hard Road to Renewal: Thatcherism and the Crisis of the Left.* London: Verso.

————. 1990. "Cultural Identity and Diaspora." In *Identity, Community, Culture, Difference.* London: Lawrence and Wishart.

————. 1991. "Europe's Other Self." In *Marxism Today* 35, no. 8: 18–19.

————. 1992. "Cultural Studies and Its Theoretical Legacies." In *Cultural Studies,* ed. Lawrence Grossberg et al., 277–86. London: Routledge.

————. [1989] 1996. "New Ethnicities" In *Stuart Hall: Critical Dialogues in Cultural Studies,* ed. David Morley and Kuan-Hsing Chen, 441–49. London: Routledge.

————. 1996a. "The Question of Cultural Identity." In *Modernity and Introduction to Modern Societies,* ed. Stuart Hall, 596–634. Oxford: Blackwell.

————. 1996b. "What Is This 'Black' in Black Popular Culture?" In *Stuart Hall: Critical Dialogues in Cultural Studies,* ed. David Morley and Kuan-Hsing Chen, 465–75. London: Routledge.

Hannerz, Ulf. 1969. *Soulside: Inquiries into the Ghetto Culture and Community.* New York: Columbia University Press.

Hansen, Thomas Blom, and Finn Stepputat, eds. 2005. *Sovereign Bodies: Citizens, Migrants, and States in the Postcolonial World.* Princeton, N.J.: Princeton University Press.

Harbi, Mohammed. 1980. *Le FLN: Mirage et réalité.* Paris: Éditions JA.

————. 1986. *La guerre commence en Algérie. 1954.* Paris: Éditions Complexe.

Hargreaves, Alec G., ed. 2005. *Memory, Empire, and Postcolonialism: Legacies of French Colonialism.* Oxford: Lexington Books.

Hargreaves, Alec G., and Mark McKinney, eds. 1997. *Postcolonial Cultures in France.* London: Routledge.

Haut Conseil à l'intégration. 1993. *L'intégration à la française*. Paris: Union générale d'éditions.

Hirsch, Francine. 2005. *Empire of Nations: Ethnographic Knowledge and the Making of the Soviet Union*. Ithaca, N.Y.: Cornell University Press.

Hobsbawm, Eric. 1959. *Primitive Rebels: Studies in Archaic Forms of Social Movements in the Nineteenth and Twentieth Centuries*. Manchester: Manchester University Press.

Hobsbawm, Eric, and Terence Ranger. 1983. *The Invention of Tradition*. Cambridge: Cambridge University Press.

Hoffmann, Léon-François. 1973. *Le nègre romantique : personnage littéraire et obsession collective*. Paris: Payot.

Honneth, Axel, ed. 1992. *Philosophical Interventions in the Unfinished Project of Modernity*. Trans. William Rehg. Cambridge, Mass.: MIT Press.

———. 1995. *The Struggle for Recognition: The Moral Grammar of Social Conflicts*, trans. Joel Anderson. Cambridge, Mass.: Polity.

Houillon, Philippe. 2005. Rapport fait au nom de la commission des lois constitutionnelles, de la législation et de l'administration générale de la République sur le projet de loi (n° 2673) prorogeant l'application de la loi n° 55-385 du 3 avril, 15 novembre 2005. Available at http://www.assemblee-nationale.fr/12/rapports/r2675.asp#P246_26812.

Huntington, Samuel P. 1996. *The Clash of Civilizations and the Remaking of World Order*. New York: Simon and Schuster.

Iliffe, John. 1979. *A Modern History of Tanganyika*. Cambridge: Cambridge University Press.

Illich, Ivan. 2003. *Œuvres complètes*. Paris: Fayard.

Indigènes de la République. 2005. "Qui sommes-nous? Synthèse du premier débat en séance plénière de l'Agora des Indigènes." Available at http://www.indigenes-republique.org/article phpd3?id_article=2.

Ivekovic, Rada. 2006. "Le retour du politique oublié par les banlieues." *Lignes* 19 (February): 64–88.

Jacono, Jean-Marie. 2002. "Musical Dimensions and Ways of Expressing Identity in French Rap: The Groups from Marseilles." In Durand 2002, 22–32.

Jacquesson, Françoise. 2006. "Les zones urbaines sensibles franciliennes: des réalités diverses." *INSEE Ile-de-France à la page*, no. 271 (August 2006).

James, C. L. R. 1963. *The Black Jacobins*. New York: Vintage, 1938.

Janowitz, Morris. 1968. *Social Control of Escalated Riots*. Chicago: University of Chicago Center for Policy Studies.

Jazouli, Adil. 1985. *La formation de l'action collective des jeunes issus de l'immigration maghrébine en France*. Doctoral thesis directed by Alain Touraine, École des Hautes Études en Sciences Sociales.

Jobard, Fabien. 2002. "La loi de la peur." *Passant* 39 (March–April). Available at http://www.passant-ordinaire.com/revue/39-384.asp.

———. 2006. "Sociologie politique de la *racaille*." In *Émeutes urbaines et protestations*, ed. Hugues Lagrange and Marco Oberti, 59–80. Paris: Presses de la Fondation Nationale de Sciences Politiques.

Joffrin, Laurent. 2005. "Les 'néoréacs.'" *Nouvelobs.com*, December 1, 2005.

———. 2007a. "Mélange." *Libération*, June 22, 2007.

———. 2007b. " Phénomènes émergents." *Libération*, July 16, 2007.

Johnson, G. Wesley. 1971. *The Emergence of Black Politics in Senegal: The Struggle for Power in the Four Communes, 1890–1920.* Stanford, Calif.: Stanford University Press.

Jones, Gareth Stedman. 1971. *Outcast London: A Study in the Relationship between Classes in Victorian Society.* London: Penguin.

Jules-Rosette, Bennetta. 1998. *Black Paris: The African Writers' Landscape.* Urbana: University of Illinois Press.

Julliard, Jacques, and Michel Winock, eds. 2002. *Dictionnaire des intellectuels français: Les personnes. Les lieux. Les moments.* Paris: Seuil.

Keaton, Trica Danielle. 2006. *Muslim Girls and the Other France: Race, Identity Politics, and Social Exclusion.* Bloomington: Indiana University Press.

Kelley, Robin D. G. [1994] 1996. *Race Rebels: Culture, Politics, and the Black Working Class.* New York: Free Press, 1996.

Kelley, Robin D. G., and Tiffany Ruby Patterson. 2000. "Unfinished Migrations: Reflections on the African Diaspora and the Making of the Modern World." Special issue, "Africa's Diaspora," *African Studies Review* 43, no. 1 (April 2000): 11–45.

Keslassy, Éric. 2004. *De la discrimination positive.* Paris: Éditions Bréal.

Kleinberg, Aviad. 2005. *Histoire des Saints: Leur rôle dans la formation de l'Occident.* Paris: Gallimard.

Kohler, Catherine, and Suzanne Thav. 1990. *Les immigrés et leur famille au recensement de 1990.* Paris: Insee.

Kokoreff, Michel. 2004. *La force des quartiers.* Paris: Payot.

Krikorian, Nathalie. 1986. "Européanisme, nationalisme, libéralisme dans les éditoriaux de Louis Pauwels dans *Le Figaro Magazine (1977-1984)*." *Mots*, no. 12 (1986): 171–88.

Kundera, Milan. 2005. *L'ignorance.* Paris: Gallimard.

Lagrange, Hugues, and Marco Oberti. 2006. *Émeutes Urbaines et Protestations: Une singularité française.* Paris: Presses de Sciences PO.

Lapeyronnie, Didier. 1993. *L'individu et les minorités: La France et la Grande-Bretagne face à leurs minorities.* Paris: Presses Universitaires de France.

Lapeyronnie, Didier, and Laurent Mucchielli. 2005. "Piégés par la République." *Libération*, November 9, 2005.

Lastra, James F. 1999. "Why Is This Absurd Picture Here? Ethnology/ Equivocation/ Buñuel." *October* 89 (Summer): 51–68.

Laurence, Jonathan, and Justin Vaisse. 2006. *Integrating Islam: Political and Religious Challenges in Contemporary France.* Washington, D.C.: Brookings Institution Press.

Laurent, Pierre. 2005. "La banlieue, c'est la France." *L'Humanité,* November 5.

Le Cour Grandmaison, Olivier, ed. 2001. *Le 17 octobre 1961: Un crime d'État à Paris.* Paris: Éditions La Dispute.

Le Doueff, Michèle. 1999. *Le sexe du savoir.* Aubier.

Le Goaziou, Véronique, and Laurent Mucchielli. 2006. *Quand les banlieues brûlent . . . Retour sur les émeutes de novembre 2005.* Paris: La Découverte.

Le Goaziou, Véronique, and Charles Rojzman. 2001. *Idées reçues sur la banlieue.* Paris: Éditions Le cavalier bleu.

Le Goff, Jacques. 1988. *Histoire et mémoire.* Paris: Gallimard.

———. 1996. *Une vie pour l'histoire. Entretiens avec Marc Heurgon.* Paris: La Découverte.

———. 2006. *La nouvelle histoire.* 3rd ed. Paris: Éditions Complexe.

Le Pors, Anicet, ed. 1997. *Le nouvel âge de la citoyenneté: Avec les contributions de Laurent Fabius, Robert Hue and Philippe Séguin.* Paris: Les éditions de l'Atelier.

Le Pourhiet, Anne-Marie, ed. 1999. *Droit constitutionnel local: égalité et liberté locale dans la constitution.* Paris: Economica.

Lebovics, Herman. 1992. *True France: The Wars over Cultural Identity, 1900–1945.* Ithaca, N.Y.: Cornell University Press.

———. 2004. *Bringing the Empire Back Home: France in the Global Age.* Durham, N.C.: Duke University Press.

Lefeuvre, Daniel. 1997. *Chère Algérie. Comptes et mécomptes de la tutelle coloniale, 1930–1962.* Saint Denis, France: Société française d'histoire d'Outre-mer.

———. 2006. *Pour en finir avec la repentance coloniale.* Paris: Flammarion.

Leglise, Paul. 1977. *Histoire de la politique du cinéma français.* Vol. 2: *Le Cinéma entre deux Républiques (1940–1946).* Paris: Filméditions, Pierre L'Herminier Éditeur.

Leininger-Miller, Theresa. 2000. *New Negro Artists in Paris: African American Painters and Sculptors in the City of Light, 1922–1934.* New Brunswick, N.J.: Rutgers University Press.

Lemaignen, Robert, Léopold Sédar Senghor, and Prince Sisonath Youtévong. 1945. *La communauté impériale française.* Paris: Alsatia.

L'Estoile, Benoît de. 2000. "Science de l'homme et domination rationnelle. Savoir ethnologique et politique indigène en Afrique coloniale française." *Revue de synthèse* 4, nos. 3–4: 292–323.

Lévy, Laurent. 2005. *Le spectre du communautarisme.* Paris: Editions Amsterdam.

Lewis, James I. 1998. "The MRP and the Genesis of the French Union." *French History* 12 (1998): 276–314.

Liauzu, Claude, and Gilles Manceron, eds. 2005. *La colonisation, la loi et l'histoire.* Paris: Syllepse.

Liebman, Dominique. 2003. "Finkielkraut se dévoile!" November 2003. Available at http://www.lmsi.net.

Lindenberg, Daniel. 2002. *Le rappel à l'ordre. Enquête sur les nouveaux réactionnaires.* Paris: Éditions du Seuil et la République des Idées.

Lion, Antoine, and Pierre Maclouf. 1982. *L'Insécurité Sociale: Paupérisation et Solidarité.* Paris: Éditions ouvrières.

Londres, Albert. 1927. *Marseille porte du sud.* Paris: Éditions de France.

Lorcin, Patricia M. 1999. *Imperial Identities.* London/New York: I.B. Tauris/St. Martins Press.

———. 2005. *Kabyles, Arabes, Français: identités coloniales.* Limoges: PULIM.

Louis, Marie-Victoire. 1996. "NTM, injure sexiste." *Libération,* December 9, 1996.

Lozès, Patrick. 2007. *Nous les Noirs de France.* Paris: Éditions Danger Public.

Maalouf, Amin. 1998. *In the Name of Identity: Violence and the Need to Belong.* Trans. Barbara Bray. New York: Arcade Publishing, 2000.

MacNamara, Francis T. 1989. *France in Black Africa.* Washington, D.C.: National Defense University.

Mamdani, Mahmood. 1996. *Citizen and Subject: Contemporary Africa and the Legacy of Late Colonialism.* Princeton, N.J.: Princeton University Press.

Manceron, Gilles, and Claude Liauzu, eds. 2006. *La colonisation, la loi et l'histoire.* Paris: Syllepse.

Manchuelle, François. 1997. *Willing Migrants: Soninke Labor Diasporas, 1848–1960.* Athens: Ohio University Press.

Marcuse, Herbert. 1964. *One-Dimensional Man: Studies in the Ideology of Advanced Industrial Society.* Boston: Beacon.

Marlière, Eric. 2005. *Jeunes en cité: Diversité des trajectoires ou destin commun?* Paris: L'Harmattan.

Martens, Guy. 1983. "Les fondements historiques, économiques et politiques de la politique africaine de la France." *Genève-Afrique* 21, no. 2: 39–68.

Marti, Pierre-Antoine. 2005. *Rap 2 France. Les mots d'une rupture identitaire.* Paris: L'Harmattan.

Martin, Jean. 1988. *Lexique de la colonisation française.* Paris: Dalloz.

Marx, Gary T. 1967. *Protest and Prejudice: A Study of Belief in the Black Community.* New York: Harper and Row.

Marx, Karl. 1963. *The Eighteenth Brumaire of Louis Bonaparte.* New York: International Publishers.

———. 1964. *The Class Struggles in France.* New York: International Publishers.

Maschino, Maurice T. 2002. "Les nouveaux réactionnaires." *Le Monde diplomatique,* October.

Masclet, Olivier. 2002. *La gauche et les cités. Enquête sur un rendez-vous manqué.* Paris: La Dispute.

———. 2003. *La Gauche et les exclus, enquête sur un rendez-vous manqué.* Paris: La Dispute.

Massengo, Gualbert-Brice. 2004. *L'économie pétrolière du Congo.* Paris: L'Harmattan.

Massu, Jacques. 1997. *La vraie bataille d'Alger.* Monaco: Éditions du Rocher.

Math, Antoine. 1998. "Les allocations familiales et l'Algérie coloniale: À l'origine du FAS et de son financement par les régimes de prestations familiales." *Recherches et Prévisions* 53: 35–44.

Mauger, Gérard. 2006. *L'émeute de Novembre 2005: Une révolte proto-politique.* Bellecombe-en-Bauges, France: Éditions du Croquant.

Maurras, Charles. 1954. *Œuvres capitales. Essais politiques.* Paris: Flammarion.

Mbembe, Achille. 1993. "Écrire l'Afrique à partir d'une faille." *Politique africaine* 51 (October): 69–97.

———. 2000. *De la postcolonie. Essai sur l'imagination politique dans l'Afrique contemporaine.* Paris: Karthala.

———. 2005. "La République et sa Bête: À propos des émeutes dans les banlieues de France." *Africultures.* Published December 1, 2005. Available at http://www.afri cultures.com/index.asp?menu=affiche_article&no=4099.

McAdam, Doug. 1982. *The Political Process and the Development of Black Insurgency.* Chicago: University of Chicago Press.

McCarren, Felicia. 2004. "Monsieur Hip Hop." In *Blackening Europe: The African American Presence,* ed. Heike Raphael-Hernandez, 157–69. London: Routledge.

McGaffey, Janet, and Rémy Bazenguissa-Ganga. 2000. *Congo-Paris: Trans-National Traders on the Margin of the Law.* Bloomington: Indiana University Press.

Medioni, Gilles. e.a. 1996. "L'affaire NTM en sept questions." *L'Express,* November 21, 1996.

Merle, Isabelle, and Emmanuelle Sibeud. 2003. "Histoire en marge ou histoire en marge? La colonisation entre repentance et patrimonialisation." Conference paper presented at conference entitled "La politique du passé," University of Paris 8, September 2003. Available at http://www.histoire-sociale.univ-paris1.fr/Collo/ Merle.pdf.

Meynier, Gilbert. 2005. "Le piège des mémoires antagonists." *Le Monde,* May 12.

Ministère de l'Intérieur. 2002. *Rapport au Parlement. Les titres de séjour des étrangers en France en 2001.* Quatrième rapport établi en application de l'article 45 de la loi du 11 mai 1998, quatrième trimestre.

Mitterrand, François. 1957. *Présence française et abandon.* Paris: Plon.

Mohammed, Marwan, and Laurent Mucchielli. 2006. "La police dans les quartiers populaires: un vrai problème!" *Mouvements* 44 (March–April): 58–66.

Mokhiber, R., and R. Weissman. 1997. "Beat the Devil. The Ten Worst Corporations of 1997." *Multinational Monitor* 18, no. 12 (December).

Mollat, Michel, and Philippe Wolff. 1970. *Ongles Bleus, Jacques et Ciompi: Les révolutions populaires en Europe aux XIVe et XVe siècles.* Paris: Calmann-Lévy.

Montvalon, Jean-Baptiste de. 2005. "Nicolas Sarkozy s'engage dans la querelle des memoires." *Le Monde,* December 25.

Moore, Barrington, Jr. 1978. *Injustices: The Social Bases of Obedience and Revolt.* London: Macmillan.

Mosse, George L. 1985. *Nationalism and Sexuality: Respectability and Abnormal Sexuality in Modern Europe.* New York: H. Fertig.

———. 1996. *Image of Man: the Creation of Modern Masculinity.* New York: Oxford University Press.

Moulier-Boutang, Yan. 2006. *La Révolte des banlieues ou les habits nus de la République.* Paris: Éditions Amsterdam.

Mucchielli, Laurent. 2003. "Le rap de la jeunesse des quartiers relégués. Un univers de représentations structuré par des sentiments d'injustice et de victimation collectives." In *Emergences culturelles et jeunesse populaire. Turbulences ou médiations?* ed. Manuel Boucher and Alain Vulbeau. Paris: L'Harmattan.

———. 2005. *Le scandale des "tournantes": Dérives médiatiques, contre-enquête sociologique.* Paris: La découverte.

Mucchielli, Laurent, and Véronique Le Goaziou, eds. 2006. *Quand les banlieues brûlent . . . Retour sur les émeutes de novembre 2005.* Paris: La Découverte.

Muchembled, Robert. 1978. *Culture populaire et culture des élites dans la France moderne (XVe–XVIIIe siècle).* Paris: Flammarion.

———. 1998. *La société policée: Politique et politesse en France du XVIe au XXe siècle.* Paris: Le Seuil.

Murray, Christopher John, ed. 2004. *Encyclopedia of French Modern Thought.* New York: Fitzroy Dearborn.

Muthu, Sankar. 2003. *Enlightenment against Empire.* Princeton, N.J.: Princeton University Press.

Nederveen Pieterse, Jan. 1992. *White on Black: Images of Africa and Blacks in Western Popular Culture.* New Haven: Yale University Press.

Nettelbeck, Colin. 2007. "Narrative Mutations: French Cinema and Its Relations with Literature from Vichy towards the New Wave." *Journal of European Studies* 37, no. 2: 159–86.

Nicolas, Jean. 2002. *La rébellion française: Mouvements populaires et conscience sociale, 1661–1789.* Paris: Le Seuil.

Noël, Erick. 2006. *Être Noir en France au XVIIIe siècle.* Paris: Tallandier.

Noiriel, Gérard. 1988. *Le creuset français: Histoire de l'immigration, XIXe–XXe siècle.* Paris: Seuil.

———. 1996. *Sur la crise de l'histoire.* Paris: Belin.

———. 1998. *Qu'est-ce que l'histoire contemporaine?* Paris: Hachette.

———. 2001. *État, nation et immigration. Vers une histoire du Pouvoir.* Paris: Gallimard.

———. 2003. *Penser avec, penser contre. Itinéraire d'un historien.* Paris: Belin.

———. 2006a. "'Color Blindness' et constructions des identités dans l'espace public français." In *De la question sociale à la question raciale. Représenter la société française,* ed. Didier Fassin and Éric Fassin, 158–74. Paris: La Découverte.

———. 2006b. "Itinéraire d'un engagement dans l'histoire." *Mouvement* 45–46 (August): 209–19.

———. 2007. *Immigration, antisémitisme et racisme en France (XIXe–XXe siècle): Discours publics, humiliations privées.* Paris: Fayard.

Nora, Pierre, ed. 1983–93. *Les Lieux de mémoire,* 8 vol. Paris: Gallimard.

———, ed. 1987. *Essais d'ego-histoire.* Paris: Gallimard.

———, ed. 1997. *Les lieux de mémoire.* Paris: Gallimard.

———. 2005. "Plaidoyer pour les indigènes d'Austerlitz." *Le Monde,* December 13.

———. 2006a. "La France est malade de sa mémoire." *Le Nouvel Observateur*, February 18, 20–27.

———. 2006b. "Malaise dans l'identité historique." *Le Débat* 141 (September–October): 48–52.

Nordmann, Charlotte, ed. 2004. *Le Foulard islamique en questions*. Paris: Editions Amsterdam.

Noudelmann, François. 2006. *Hors de moi*. Paris: Éditions Léo Scheer.

Nouvelles Questions Féministes. 2006. "Sexisme et racisme," vol. 25, no. 1.

Oberschall, Anthony. 1973. *Social Conflict and Social Movement*. Englewood Cliffs, N.J.: Prentice-Hall.

Otayek, René. 2000. *Identité et démocratie dans un monde global*. Paris: Presses de la Fondation nationale des Sciences politiques.

Palmer, Colin. 1998. "Defining and Studying the Modern African Diaspora." *Perspectives: American Historical Association Newsletter* 36, no. 6 (1): 22–27.

Paoli, Paul-François. 2006. *Nous ne sommes pas coupables*. Paris: La Table ronde.

Paul, Kathleen. 1997. *Whitewashing Britain: Race and Citizenship in the Postwar Era*. Ithaca, N.Y.: Cornell University Press.

Peabody, Sue. 1996. *"There Are No Slaves in France": The Political Culture of Race and Slavery in the Ancien Régime*. New York: Oxford University Press.

Peabody, Sue, and Tyler Stovall, eds. 2003. *The Color of Liberty: Histories of Race in France*. Durham, N.C.: Duke University Press.

Pervillé, Guy. 2002. *Pour une histoire de la guerre d'Algérie (1954–1962)*. Paris: Picard.

Pétré-Grenouilleau, Olivier. 2004. *Les traites négrières: essai d'histoire globale*. Paris: Gallimard.

———. 2005. "Les identités traumatiques. Traites, esclavage, colonization." *Le Débat* 136 (September): 93–107.

Peyrefitte, Alain. 1994. *C'était de Gaulle*. Paris: Editions Fayard.

Piven, Frances F., and Richard A. Cloward. 1977. *Poor People's Movements: Why They Succeed, How They Fail*. New York: Vintage Books.

Prévos, André J. M. 1996. "The Evolution of French Rap Music and Hip Hop Culture in the 1980s and 1990s." *French Review* 69, no. 5 (April 1996): 713–25.

———. 1998. "Hip-Hop, Rap, and Repression in France and in the United States." *Popular Music and Society* 22, no. 2: 67–84.

———. 2002. "Two Decades of Rap in France: Emergence, Developments, Prospects." In Durand 2002, 1–21.

———. 2003. "'In It for the Money': Rap and Business Cultures in France." *Popular Music and Society* (December): 445–67.

Prost, Antoine. 1996. *Douze leçons sur l'histoire*. Paris: Seuil.

Rajsfus, Maurice. 1995. *La police de Vichy: Les forces de l'ordre françaises au service de la Gestapo 1940–1944*. Paris: Le Cherche Midi.

———. 1996. *Drancy: Un camp de concentration très ordinaire, 1941–1944*. Paris: Cherche Midi Éditeur.

Rancière, Jacques. 2005. *La haine de la démocratie.* Paris: Editions La Fabrique.

Ranger, Terence. 1993. "The Invention of Tradition Revisited." In *Legitimacy and the State inTwentieth-Century Africa: Essays in Honour of A.H.M. Kirk-Greene,* ed. Olufemi Vaughan and Terence Ranger, 62–111. Houndmills, Basingstoke, Hampshire: Macmillan.

Rauch, André. 2004. *L'identité masculine à l'ombre des femmes: de la Grande Guerre à la gay pride.* Paris: Hachette.

Redecker, Robert. 2006. "Le nihilisme et l'assourdissant silence des émeutes banlieusardes." In *La République brûle-t-elle? Essai sur les violences urbaines françaises,* ed. Raphaël Drai and Jean-François Mattéi. Paris: Édition Michalon.

Régent, Frédéric. 2005. *Esclavage, métissage, liberté.* Paris: Grasset.

Regourd, Serge. 2002. *Qui sais-je? L'exception culturelle.* Paris: Presses Universitaires de France.

Renan, Ernest. 1947–61. *Qu'est-ce qu'une nation?* Conférence prononcée à La Sorbonne le 11 mars 1882. In *Œuvres Complètes,* vol. 1, 887–906. Paris: Calmann-Lévy.

———. 1996. "What Is a Nation?" In *Becoming National: A Reader,* ed. Geoff Eley and Grigor Suny. New York: Oxford University Press, 41–55.

Revol, Joseph. 1968. "Le fonds d'action sociale pour les travailleurs migrants." *Revue française des affaires sociales* 1 (January–March): 1–45.

Rey-Goldzeiguer, Annie. 2001. *Aux origines de la guerre d'Algérie: 1940–1945. De Mers-el-Kébir aux massacres du Nord-Constantinois.* Paris: La Découverte.

Rico, Anne Gaelle. 2007. "Pour l'avocat des rappeurs de La Rumeur, 'la liberté d'expression est en péril.'" Available at lemonde.fr, July 11, 2007.

Ricœur, Paul. 1975. *La métaphore vive.* Paris: Seuil.

———. 1991. *Temps et récit.* Paris: Point-Seuil.

———. 2000. *La Mémoire, l'Histoire, l'Oubli.* Paris: Seuil.

Rigoni, Isabelle, ed. 2007. *Qui a peur de la télévision en couleurs?* Montreuil: Editions Aux Lieux d'être.

Rioux, Jean-Pierre. 2004. *Au bonheur la France.* Paris: Librairie académique Perrin.

———. 2006. *La France perd la mémoire: Comment un pays démissionne de son histoire.* Paris: Librairie académique Perrin.

Rivet, Daniel. 1992. "Le fait colonial et nous. Histoire d'un éloignement." *Vingtième siècle* (January–March): 127–45.

Robine, Jérémy. 2006. "Les 'Indigènes de la République': Nation et question postcoloniale." *Hérodote* 120: 118–48.

Rosanvallon, Pierre. 1998. *Le peuple introuvable.* Paris: Gallimard.

Rose, Tricia. 1994. *Black Noise: Rap Music and Black Culture in Contemporary America.* Hanover, N.H.: Wesleyan University Press.

Rossi, Peter H. 1970. *Ghetto Revolts.* New York: Transaction.

Rotival, Maurice. 1935. "Les grands ensembles." *L'Architecture d'aujourd'hui* 6 (June): 57.

Rousso, Henry. 1990. *Le syndrome de Vichy, de 1944 à nos jours.* 2nd ed. Paris: Seuil.

———. 1998. *La hantise du passé. Entretiens avec Philippe Petit.* Paris: Éditions Textuel.

————. 2001. *Vichy. L'évènement, la mémoire, l'histoire.* Paris: Gallimard.

Rudé, George. 1959. *The Crowd in the French Revolution.* Oxford: Clarendon Press.

Ruscio, Alain. 2002. *Le credo de l'homme blanc.* Paris: Éditions Complexe.

Saada, Emmanuelle. 2003. "Citoyens et sujets de l'Empire français: Les usages de droit en situation colonial." *Genèses* 53: 4–24.

————. 2006a. "Il faut distinguer travail historique et positions militants." *Le Monde,* January 21, viii. .

————. 2006b. "Un racisme de l'expansion. Les discriminations raciales au regard des situations colonials." In *De la Question sociale à la question raciale? Représenter la société française,* ed. Didier Fassin and Éric Fassin, 55–71. Paris: La Découverte.

————. 2007. *Les enfants de la colonie: Les métis de l'Empire français entre sujétion et citoyennete.* Paris: La Découverte.

Saada, Emmanuelle, et al. 2003. "Sujets d'Empire." Special issue, *Genèses* 53 (December).

Sabeg, Yazid, and Pierre Méhaignerie. 2004. *Les oubliés de l'égalité des chances.* Paris: Institut Montaigne.

Safran, William. 1991. "Diasporas in Modern Societies: Myths of Homeland and Return." *Diaspora* 1 (Spring): 83–84.

Said, Edward. 1978. *Orientalism.* New York: Vintage.

————. 1993. *Culture and Imperialism.* New York: Vintage.

Sala-Molins, Louis. 1987. *Le Code Noir ou le calvaire de Canaan.* Paris: Presses universitaires de France.

————. 2006. *Dark Side of the Light: Slavery and the French Enlightenment.* Trans. and with an introduction by John Conteh-Morgan. Minneapolis: University of Minnesota Press.

Sandqvist, Tom. 2006. *Dada East: The Romanians of Cabaret Voltaire.* Cambridge, Mass.: MIT Press.

Sarkozy, Nicolas. 2007. *Discours d'investiture.* Palais de l'Élysée. Paris, May 16, 2007. Available at http://www.latribune.fr/info/Le-discours-d-investiture-de-Nicolas-Sarkozy-.

Sauvy, Alfred. 1984. "La grande migration." *Le Monde,* January 7, 1984.

Sauvy, Alfred, and Gérard-Francois Dumont. 1984. *La montée des déséquilibres démographiques. Quel avenir pour une France vieillie dans un monde jeune?* Paris: Economica.

Sayad, Abdelmalek. 1991. *L'immigration ou les paradoxes de l'altérité.* Brussels: De Boeck-Waesmell.

————. 1994. "Qu'est-ce que l'intégration?" *Hommes et migrations* 1181: 8–14.

————. 1999. *La double absence.* Paris: Le Seuil. (Translated into English as *The Suffering of the Immigrant,* Cambridge: Polity Press, 2004.)

————. 2006. *L'immigration ou les paradoxes de l'altérité. 1. L'illusion du provisoire.* Paris: Raisons d'agir.

Schnapper, Dominique. 1991. *La France de l'intégration. Sociologie de la nation en 1990.* Paris: Bibliothèque des sciences humaines.

———. 1994. *La communauté des citoyens: Sur l'idée moderne de nation.* Paris: Gallimard.

———. 2000. "Comment reconnaître les droits culturels?" In *Comprendre les iden-tités culturelles,* ed. Sylvie Mesure and Will Kymlicka, 253–69. Paris: Presses Universitaires de France.

Schor, Ralph. 1996. *Histoire de l'immigration en France: de la fin du XIXe siècle à nos jours.* Paris: Armand Colin. Selected interviews in 2005–2006 with inhabitants of the housing project La Grande Borne, Grigny (Essonne). See the *Libération* web-site for further documentation, at http://www.liberation.fr.

Sebbar, Leïla. 2008. *The Seine Was Red: Paris, October 1961.* Trans. Mildred Mortimer. Bloomington: Indiana University Press.

Serafini, Tonio, Patricia Tourancheau, and Brigitte Vital-Durand. 2005. "Politique de la ville: trente ans de traitements d'urgence." *Libération,* November 8, 2005.

Sevran, Pascal. 2007. *Le privilège des jonquilles.* Paris: Garnier Flammarion.

Shepard, Todd. 2004. "La bataille du voile pendant la guerre d'Algérie." In *Le fou-lard islamique en questions,* ed. Charlotte Nordmann, 134–41. Paris: Editions Amsterdam.

———. 2006. *The Invention of Decolonization: The Algerian War and the Remaking of France.* Ithaca, N.Y.: Cornell University Press.

Sibeud, Emmanuelle. 2002. *Une science impériale pour l'Afrique? La construction des savoirs africanistes en France, 1878–1930.* Paris: EHESS.

Sibony, Daniel. 1997. *Le "racisme" ou la haine ordinaire.* Paris: Christian Bourgois Éditeur.

Sieffert, Denis. 2005. "Ce que disent les "Indigènes de la République." *Politis* (April 14): n.p.

Silverstein, Paul. 2002. "Why Are We Waiting to Start the Fire? French Gangsta Rap and the Critique of State Capitalism." In Durand 2002, 45–67.

———. 2004. *Algeria in France: Transpolitics, Race, and Nation.* Bloomington: Indiana University Press.

Singer, Daniel. 1991. "Le Pen's Pals-Blood and Soil." In *Nation* (December 23): 814–16.

Sirinelli, Jean-François. 2005. *Comprendre le XXe siècle français.* Paris: Fayard.

Sirinelli, Jean-François, and Jean-Pierre Rioux. 1988. *La guerre d'Algérie et les intellec-tuels français.* Paris: Institut du Temps Présent.

Slama, Alain Gérard. 2005. *Le siècle de Monsieur Pétain.* Paris: Perrin.

Smith, Andrea, ed. 2003. *Europe's Invisible Migrants.* Amsterdam: Amsterdam University Press.

Smouts, Marie-Claude, ed. 2007. *La situation postcoloniale. Les Postcolonial Studies dans le débat français.* Paris: Presse de Sciences Politiques.

Soullez, Christophe. 1999. *Les violences urbaines.* Toulouse: Editions Milan.

Spire, Alexis. 2003. "Semblables et pourtant différents. La citoyenneté paradoxale des 'français musulmans d'Algérie' en métropole." *Genèses* 53: 48–66.

———. 2005. *Étrangers à la Carte: L'administration de l'immigration en France (1945–1975).* Paris: Grasset.

Spivak, Gayatri Chakravorty. 1988. "Can the Subaltern Speak?" In *Marxism and the Interpretation of Culture*, ed. Cary Nelson and Lawrence Grossberg, 271–313. London: Macmillan.

———. 1999. *A Critique of Postcolonial Reason.* Cambridge, Mass.: Harvard University Press.

Stoler, Ann Laura. 2002. *Carnal Knowledge* and Imperial Power: Race and the Intimate in Colonial Rule. Berkeley and Los Angeles: University of California Press.

Stora, Benjamin. [1991] 2005. *La gangrène et l'oubli. La mémoire de la guerre d'Algérie.* Collection "Poche." Paris: La Découverte.

Stora, Benjamin, and Thierry Leclère. 2007. *La guerre des mémoires: La France face à son passé colonial.* Paris: L'Aube.

Stovall, Tyler. 1996. *Paris Noir: African Americans in the City of Light.* Boston: Mariner Books.

"Sujets d'Empire." 2003. Special issue, *Genèses: sciences sociales et histoire* 53: 4–92.

Taguieff, Pierre-André. 2005. *La République enlisée.* Paris: Éditions de Syrtes.

Tarr, Carrie. 2005. *Reframing Difference: Beur and Banlieue Filmmaking in France.* Manchester: Manchester University Press.

Tarrius, Alain. 2004. *La mondialisation par le bas. Les nouveaux nomades de l'économie souterraine.* Paris: Balland.

Tévanian, Pierre. 2001. *Le racisme républicain: Réflexions sur le modèle français de discrimination.* Paris: L'Esprit frappeur.

———. 2004. "De la laïcité égalitaire à la laïcité sécuritaire: le milieu scolaire à l'épreuve du foulard islamique." In Bonelli and Sainati 2004, 178–217.

———. 2005. *Le voile médiatique: Un faux débat: "l'affaire du foulard islamique."* Paris: Raisons d'Agir.

Thénault, Sylvie. 2001. *Une drôle de justice: Les magistrats dans la guerre d'Algérie.* Paris: La Découverte.

Thibaut, Sylvie. 2007. "L'état d'urgence (1955–2005). De l'Algérie coloniale à la France contemporaine: destin d'une loi." *Le Mouvement Sociale* 218 (January–March): 63–78.

Thibodat, Jean-Pierre. 1996. "Les bonnes intentions et les vraies limites de la politique culturelle dans les quartiers." *Libération,* April 20–21, 1996, 28–29.

Thomas, Dominic. 2006. *Black France: Colonialism, Immigration, and Transnationalism.* Bloomington: Indiana University Press.

Tietze, Nikola. 2006. "Zinedine Zidane oder das Spiel mit den Zugehörigkeiten, Zinedine Zidane or Games of Belonging." *Mittelweg* 36, 4/15 (August/September): 73–92.

Tilly, Charles. 1986. *The Contentious French: Four Centuries of Popular Struggle.* Cambridge, Mass.: Harvard University Press.

Tissot, Sylvie. 2004. "Le repli communautaire: un concept policier." Available at http://www.lmsi.net.

Touraine, Alain. 1988. *La parole et le sang, politique et société en Amérique latine.* Paris: Odile Jacob.

Tribalat, Michèle, ed. 1991. *Cent ans d'immigration, étrangers d'hier Français d'aujourd'hui—Apport démographique, dynamique économique et familiale de l'immigration.* Paris: Presses universitaires de France/INED.

———. 2004. "The French Melting Pot: An Obsolete Ideal or One to Be Reinvented." In *Reinventing France, State and Society in the Twenty-First Century,* ed. Susan Milner and Nick Parson, 127–42. London: Palgrave.

Trong, Lucienne Bui. 2003. *Les racines de la violence.* Paris: Audibert.

Trouillot, Michel-Rolph. 1995. *Silencing the Past: Power and the Production of History.* Boston: Beacon Press.

Truffaut, François. 1959. "Une certaine tendance du cinéma français." *Cahiers du Cinema* 100, no. 17 (October): 27–38.

Van Eeckhout, Laetitia. 2005. "Le premier ministre légalise le 'testing' contre les discriminations." *Le Monde,* December 2, 2005.

Vergès, Francoise. 2002. "Post-Scriptum." In *Relocating Postcolonialism,* ed. David Theo Goldberg and Ato Quayson. Oxford: Blackwell.

———. 2006. *La mémoire enchaînée. Questions sur l'esclavage.* Paris: Albin Michel.

Verschave, François-Xavier. 1998. *La Françafrique, le plus long scandale de la République.* Paris: Stock.

Veyne, Paul. 1971. *Comment on écrit l'histoire: essai d'épistémologie.* Paris: Seuil.

Viet, Vincent. 1999. "La Politique du logement des Immigrés, 1945–1990." *Vingtième Siècle* 64 (October–December): 91–101.

Voldman, Danièle. 1997. *La reconstruction des villes françaises de 1940 à 1954: Histoire d'une politique.* Paris: Éditions l'Harmattan.

Wacquant, Loïc. 2006. *Parias urbains. Ghetto, banlieues, état.* Paris: La Découverte.

———. 2007. "Territorial Stigmatization in the Age of Advanced Marginality." *Thesis Eleven* 91 (November): 66–77.

Weddle, Robert. 2001. "Housing and Technological Reform in Interwar France: The Case of the Cité de la Muette." *Journal of Architectural Education* 54, no. 3 (February): 167–75.

Weil, Patrick. 1991. *La France et ses étrangers. L'aventure d'une politique de l'immigration depuis 1938 à nos jours.* Paris: Gallimard, 2005.

———. 2002 [2005]. *Qu'est-ce qu'un Français? Histoire de la nationalité française depuis la Révolution.* Paris: Gallimard.

———. 2005. *La République et sa diversité. Immigration, intégration, discrimination.* Paris: Seuil.

Wieviorka, Annette. 1994. "Jewish Identity in the First Accounts by Extermination Camp Survivors From France." Special issue, "Discourses of Jewish Identity in Twentieth-Century France," *Yale French Studies* 85: 135–51.

Wieviorka, Michel. 1993. *La démocratie à l'épreuve. Nationalisme, populisme, ethnicité.* Paris: La Découverte.

———. 1999. *Violence en France.* Paris: Éditions du Seuil.

———. 2001. *La différence.* Paris: Balland.

Wihtol de Wenden, Catherine. 1988. *Les immigrés et la politique: Cent cinquante ans d'évolution.* Paris: Presses de la Fondation Nationale des Sciences Politiques.

———. 1997. "Que sont devenues les associations civiques issues de l'immigration?" *Hommes et Migrations* 1206: 53–66.

Wilder, Gary. 2003. "Colonial Ethnology and Political Rationality in French West Africa." *History and Anthropology* 14, no. 3: 219–52.

Winders, James. 2006. *Paris Africain: Rhythms of the African Diaspora.* New York: Palgrave Macmillan.

Wright, Richard. 1940. *Native Son.* New York: Harper and Brothers.

Yade-Zimet, Rama. 2007. *Noirs de France.* Paris: Calmann-Lévy.

Yahiel, Michel. 1988. "Le FAS: questions de principe." *Revue Européenne des Migrations Internationales* 4, no. 1–2: 107–14.

Zantop, Susanne. 1997. *Colonial Fantasies: Conquest, Family and Nation in Precolonial Germany, 1770–1870.* Durham, N.C.: Duke University Press.

Discography

Assassin. 1995. *L'Etat assassine.* Believe.

Bisso na Bisso. 1999. *Racines,* V2.

Diam's. 2006. *Dans ma bulle.* EMI Music France.

Monsieur R. 2005. *Politikment incorrect.* Diamond Entertainment/BMG.

NTM. 1991a. *Le monde de demain.* Sony Music Entertainment Inc.

———. 1991b. *Qu'es-ce qu'on attend?* Sony Music Entertainment Inc.

Stomy Bugsy, Menelik, Passi, et al. 1997. *Onze minutes 30 contre les lois racistes.* Crépuscule.

Filmography

Aubervilliers. 1946. Dir. Eli Lotar.

Banlieue 13 (District B13). 2004. Dir. Pierre Morel.

The Battle of Algiers (*La Battaglia d'Algeri*). 1967. Dir. Gillo Pontecorvo.

Du Bidonville aux HLM. 1993. Dir. Mehdi Lallaoui.

Casino Royale. 2006. Dir. Martin Campbell.

Enfants des courants d'air (Children Adrift). 1959. Dir. Edouard Luntz.

Est-ce ainsi que les hommes vivent? (Is This Where Men Live?) 1975. Dir. Claude Dityvon.

Étranges étrangers (Strange Foreigners). 1970. Dir. Marcel Trillat et Frédéric Variot.

France, le logement (France, Housing). 1970. Dir. Robert Bozzi.

La Belle équipe (They Were Five). 1936. Dir. Julien Duvivier.

Las Hurdes: Tierra sin pan (Land without Bread). 1933. Dir. Luis Buñuel.

Le Crime de Monsieur Lange (The Crime of Monsieur Lange). 1936. Dir. Jean Renoir.

Le Jour se lève (Daybreak). 1939. Dir. Marcel Carné.

Les Maisons de la misère (Houses of Misery). 1937. Dir. Henri Storck.

L'Esquive (Games of Love and Chance). 2003. Dir. Abdellatif Kechiche.

Ma 6-T va crack-er (My ghetto is gonna crack). 1997. Dir. Jean-François Richet.

Thé au harem d'Archimède (Tea in the Harem). 1985. Dir. Mehdi Charef.

Yamakasi. 2001. Dirs. Ariel Zeitoun and Julien Seri, written by Luc Besson.

Zidane, A Portrait of the 21st Century. 2006. Dirs. Douglas Gordon and Philippe Parreno.

Zone Immigrée (The Immigrant Zone). 1981. Prod. Mohammed Collective.

CONTRIBUTORS

Nicolas Bancel is Professor of History at the University of Lausanne (Switzerland) and the University of Strasbourg II (France). His most recent published work includes *Lyon, capitale des Outremers; La République coloniale;* and *La Fracture coloniale.* His current research focuses on postcolonial cultural processes, immigration, and sociocultural histories of colonization and decolonization. He is also one of the founding members of ACHAC Collective, with Pascal Blanchard among others.

Florence Bernault is a specialist of contemporary Central and Equatorial Africa and teaches African History at the University of Wisconsin–Madison. She has published *Démocraties ambigües en Afrique centrale: Congo-Brazzaville, Gabon, 1940–1965;* and edited *A History of Prison and Confinement in Africa.* Her current research project focuses on the history of witchcraft and cannibalism in colonial and postcolonial Central Africa.

Peter J. Bloom is Associate Professor of Film and Media Studies at University of California Santa Barbara. His ongoing research examines the relationship between colonial media, the history of ethnographic film, and pre-cinema. In addition to his monograph, *French Colonial Documentary: Mythologies of Humanitarianism,* he has published more than a dozen articles on francophone African cinema, colonial media, pre-cinema, and the history of French anthropology. He is currently co-director of the African Studies Multi-Campus Research Project in the University of California system.

Ahmed Boubeker is Professor of Sociology and Anthropology in France at the University of Metz. For the last 20 years, he has been conducting research in the fields of the *banlieues* and French immigration that attempts to construct a perspective of ethnicity from the standpoint of the heirs of Maghrebi immigration. He has published several works, including *Chroniques métissées; Familles de l'intégration; Les mondes de l'ethnicité;* and *Histoire politique des immigrations (post)coloniales: France, 1920–2008.*

Frederick Cooper is Professor of History at New York University. He is the author of a trilogy of books on labor and society in East Africa and more recently *Africa since 1940: The Past of the Present* and *Colonialism in Question: Theory, Knowledge, History.* He is currently completing a book co-authored with Jane Burbank on *Empire and the Politics of Difference in World History* and is working on the history of citizenship in France and French West Africa between 1945 and 1960.

Didier Gondola is Professor of History and Africana Studies at Indiana University–Purdue University, Indianapolis. His publications include numerous articles and chapters on popular cultures, gender, and post-colonial issues in central Africa and the African diaspora in France. His most recent book, *Africanisme: La crise d'une illusion,* explores the connections between African studies in France and French policies in Africa.

Nacira Guénif-Souilamas is Associate Professor at the University of Paris Nord and Research Fellow at Experice (Paris 13–Paris 8). She is author of *Des beurettes aux descendantes d'immigrants nord-africains.* She has co-authored with Éric Macé *Les féministes et le garçon arabe* and edited *La république mise à nu par son immigration.* In addition to publishing her work in numerous edited collections and journals in French and English, she is in the process of completing a book entitled *The Otherness from Within.*

Didier Lapeyronnie is Professor of Sociology at the University of Paris–La Sorbonne. His research focuses on questions of urban margin-ality (the *banlieues*), deviance, immigration, and racism. Most recently he has published *Ghetto urbain: Pauvreté, violence et ségrégation en France aujourd'hui; L'individu et les minorités: La France et la Grande-Bretagne face à leurs immigrés;* and *Les quartiers d'exil* (with François Dubet). His work consistently appears in journals and anthologies in French and German.

Achille Mbembe is Professor of History and Politics at the University of the Witwatersrand (Johannesburg-South Africa), and a senior researcher at the Witwatersrand Institute for Social and Economic Research (WISER). He has published numerous articles and books, including *Afriques indociles; La naissance du maquis dans le Sud-Cameroun;* and *On the Postcolony.* He is also co-editor with Jean-François Bayart and Comi Toulabor of *La politique par le bas en Afrique noire.*

Pierre Tévanian teaches Philosophy at the Lycée Eugène Delacroix, Drancy (Seine-Saint Denis, France). He is co-founder and co-facilitator with Sylvie Tissot of the Collective "Les mots sont importants" (www .lmsi.net). He has published *Le racisme républicain; Le ministère de la peur; Le voile médiatique;* and *La république du mépris.* He is co-author, with Sylvie Tissot, of *Dictionnaire de la lepénisation des esprits,* and, with Ismahane Chouder and Malika Latrèche, *Les filles voilées parlent.*

Charles Tshimanga teaches African History, Diaspora Studies, and Core Humanities at the University of Nevada, Reno. He is author of *Jeunesse, formation et société au Congo, 1890–1960.* He is also co-author with Benoit Verhaegen of *L'Abako et l'indépendance du Congo Belge,* and co-editor with Catherine Coquery-Vidrovitch and Odile Goerg of *Histoire et devenir de l'Afrique noire au XXème siècle,* and with Séverine Awenengo and Pascale Barthélemy of *Écrire l'histoire de l'Afrique autrement?* His current research focuses on the African diaspora in France, popular culture, and Afro-European children in the Belgian Congo.

INDEX

Abd al Malik (rapper), 253, 274n18
ACHAC. *See* Association Connaissance de l'histoire de l'Afrique contemporaine (ACHAC)
Adoma, 246n14
"l'Affaire Elf," 155
affirmative action, 7, 80, 166n24; French, 66; *promotion musulmane* and, 107; public condemnation of, 83. *See also discrimination positive*
Africa: anti-France sentiment in, 50; *banlieue* riots and, 49; culture, 9; France's exploitation of, 92; France's minorization of, 152–153, 164; governments of, criminalization of, 154; labor migration from, 108–109; policy, 49, 50; slave trade and, 49, 61
Africagora, 178
Africain, 284
African(s): cultural differences, 5; marginalization of, in *cités*, 156; migrants, 113, 148; neocolonialism and, 149; skin color, 152
African Americans: *banlieues* and, 16n1, 234; exiles, 8; ghettoization of, 16n1; *parkour* and, aesthetics, 234–237; police and, 30; vocabulary, 235. *See also* United States
African colonies, 49; citizenship and, 95; France and relations with, 13, 49; French union and leaders in, 104–105; nationality/nationalities of, 106–107; neocolonialism and, 149; postcolonial policies toward, 153–154; standard of living in, 103. *See also* colonialism

African descendents: citizenship status, 12–13, 94, 161, 270; integrating population of, 151
African diaspora, 248–276; in *banlieues,* 10; Frenchness and, 7; rap and, 271
African French, 5, 12–13, 108–113, 147; cultural integration and, 250; rappers, 267–270
African immigrants: returnees, rate of, 165n19; urban planning and, 148. *See also* immigrants (*immigrés*)
African Member States, 106
Al Peco (rapper), 257
Algeria: decolonization of, 111; *état d'urgence* in, 231; independence of, 114; massacre, 281; "Museum of France in Algeria," 171–172; OAS and, 182n13; *pieds noirs* exodus from, 112; torture used by French army in, 169–171, 181n3; Zidane's trip to, 213–215, 219–220
Algerian(s): citizen category of, 109–110; citizenship status of, 95; curfew targeting, 17n11; FAS and rights for, 241; *Français musulmans d'Algérie,* 107; French migration of, 112–113; labor migration, 112–113; massacres of, 143n10; migration of, 112–113; Muslim, 109–110; *promotion musulmane,* 112; religious law ruling, 95; rights of, 109, 241; stereotypes, 218; violence inflicted on, 96
Algerian *colons,* repatriation of, 61–62
Algerian identification documents, 112
Algerian War, 107, 283; Algerian supporters of France in, 111–112; April 3, 1955

law of, 5; history of, 178; memories, 171; national memorial to, 173; torture used in, 169–171, 181n3
Alibi Montana (rapper), 257, 274n13
aliens, 62; in France, law regarding, 62; race and, 56, 75; representations of, 52
Alliance Ethnik, 252
Altrun, Muhittin, 3
ancien régime, 290
Annales complex, 136–139
anti-Americanism, 8
anticolonialism, 104–105, 280
anti-French sentiment, 163
anti-headscarf legislation, 2004, 14; "Aubervilliers Affair," 199, 203n28; education, public and, 188–190; *exception française* and, 188; opposition, 201n3; racism and, 194–195; religious dimension in, 190; Right and, 203n27; in schools, 188–190, 202n11; secularism and, 187–204; UMP and, 203n25; victims of, 200–201
anti-Semitism, 61
anti-white racism, 16, 265–266
apartheid, 60
Appel, 126
April 3, 1955 law, 5; curfew, 17n11; reenactment of, 18n12
Arab boys (*garçon arabe*), 214, 236
Arabs, 213; France and its, 214; as scapegoats, 214; Zidane's image as, 214–215
Arendt, Hannah, 48, 75
Arsenick (rapper), 252
Assassin (rap group), 259–260
Assemblée Nationale Constituante, 98; second, 100
assimilation, 11; colonized people's, 99; to French culture, 98; French strategies of, 123–124; immigrant, 5–6; Indigènes de la République's issues with policies of, 129–130; policies, 124
Association Connaissance de l'histoire de l'Afrique contemporaine (ACHAC), 123, 283–284
athletes: diversity and French, 166, 166n22, 224n7; racial identity of, 160–161. *See also* French soccer team
Aubervilliers, 237–238; 2005 riots, 23
"Aubervilliers Affair," 199, 203n28

auteurs, 242–244; *politique des,* 246
avance sur recettes, 243

Bams (rap group), 259
Bancel, Nicolas, 13, 167–183
Banlieue 13. See District B13 (Banlieue 13)
banlieues, 284; Africa and riots in, 49; African Americans and, 16n1, 234; African diaspora in, 10; *bidonvilles* within, 284; cinema, 237–238; crisis in, root cause of, 55; discrimination and, 60; drug trafficking, 255; education within, 67; ethnicity, 252; *la Fracture coloniale* and, 287; French acknowledgment of, 21; ghettos, American compared with, 61; history of, 79; HLM and, 288; language, 86; *les Minguettes/the Minguettes Generation* and, 289; *non-droit* of, 5; North African, 291; pacification policy in, 50; Palestinization of, 53; police and, 29, 77; *racaille* and, 85–86, 291; race and, 56; raids, 51–52; rap music and, 271; rappers, 16, 252; renovation, 74, 76; RER serving, 291; riots, 3–4, 49; self-defence and, 233–234; social measures enacted in, 256; social mixing within, 80; threat, perceived of, 53; underlying issues, 21; uprising, politics and, 75–76; urban planning and, 79; voting rights in, 69; youth, 29, 31, 249. *See also specific banlieues*
Barker, Chris, 260, 266
bavure policière, 3, 17n4. *See also* police
Bayrou, François, 181n2
Belle, David, 228, 233, 246n2, 290
Benguigui, Yamina, 244
Benna, Zyed, 3, 228–229
Besson, Luc: *District B13,* 15, 227–228, 232; *Yamakasi,* 232–233
*beur-*geois-ification, 242
beurs, 74, 88n1, 284; cinema, 240–242, 246; citizenship, 146–147; cultural identity, 242–243; indigenization of, in France, 146–166; integration of, 158, 161–162; marginalization of, 163; othering of, in France, 146–166
Bhabha, Homi, 69

bidonvilles, 79, 239, 284; within *banlieues,* 284
Bilal Mosque, Clichy-sous-Bois, 35
Binet, Stéphanie, 275nn28,32
Bisso na Bisso (rap group), 156–157, 166n31, 252
black(s), 284; citizenship, 146–147; as derogatory expression, 152; image of, 151; indigenization of, in France, 146–166; integration of, 158, 161–162; marginalization of, 163; othering of, in France, 146–166; representation of, 151; term, 7
blackness: France's minorization of, 152–153; iconization of, 151–153; representation of, 151; symbolism, 152
Blanchard, Pascal, 10, 18n17, 144n30, 147, 164n2, 283–284
Booba (rapper), 257, 274n18
Bouamama, Said, 127, 133, 198, 264
Boubeker, Ahmed, 11, 70–88, 133, 242, 264, 284, 319
Bouchareb, Rachid, 141n1, 244
Bourokba, Mohamed, 258. *See* Hamé (rapper Mohamed Bourokba)
Boutelja, Houria, viii, 125–126, 205n20, 288
built environment, 228–234
Bush, George W., 279

cailleras, 88n1, 291
Calbo (rapper), 252
Carrère d'Encausse, Hélène, 166n26, 246n5, 248
Casey (rapper), viii, 16, 257, 264, 274n18
Cassen, Bernard, 5
casseurs, 291
Césaire, Aimé, 63, 145n22, 147, 152, 179, 289
Chevènement, Jean-Pierre, 88n1
Chirac, Jacques, 171; anti-headscarf legislation and, 195; immigrants and, 263; national memorials unveiled by, 173–174
cinema, 244; auteurs, 242–244; *banlieue,* 237–238; *beur,* 240–242, 246; funding, 243; housing question and, 237–242; quality, 243–244; social insertion politics and, 241–242

cités, 284; African youths in, marginalization of, 156; anti-French sentiment in, 163; hip-hop in, 156–157; HLM and, 288
citizens/citizenship, 12, 67, 89–183; African colonies and, 95; African descendent, 12–13, 94, 161, 270; Algerian, 95, 109–110; *beurs,* 146–147; black, 146–147; civil status and, 101; colonialism and, 96, 105; colonized peoples as, 99–100, 105; cultural differences and, 68; Declaration of the Rights of Man and of the Citizen, 93; distinction among different kinds of, 95–96, 99; DNA testing, 207–208; draft constitution provision of, 101; economic dimensions of, 102–103; ethnicity and, 56; *Français musulmans d'Algérie,* 107; French colonies and, 105; generalized, 99; immigration and, 48–49; *indigène,* 127; "integrated," 133; Malian, 111, 114; nationality and, 58–59, 106, 110; "non-integrated," 133; nonwhite, treatment of, 62–63; "qualities" of, 99; race and, 64–65; republican, 94–96; right-of-soil, 278; rights, 12–13, 94, 237; second-class, 52; Senegalese model of, 116; social dimensions of, 102–103; transient, 146–166; universal, 63–64; World War I and, 96; would-be, 208
citoyenneté dans le statut, 94; Senegal and, 96
civic identity, 270
civil rights movement, 8; riots, 27, 39
civil status: citizens without, 101; regulating admission to, 103–104
class, 59; "dangerous," 76–78. *See also* working class
Clichy-sous-Bois riots, 2005, 3–4, 21, 28; police action during, 35–37; silent march, 32–33. *See also* 2005 riots
Code de l'Indigénat, 52, 285; crimes detailed in, 52; state racism and, 52–53
Collomb, Gérard, 44n11
colonial debt, 125; *réparations/repentance* and, 136

"colonial grandeur," 167–183; attention paid to, 177; February 23, 2005 law and, 168
colonial imperialism, 61
colonial paradigm, 134, 136–137, 141
colonial period, 286–287
colonialism, 121, 278; academic study of, 123; African, 13, 49; African, postcolonial policies and, 153–154; African colonies and, 13, 49; aim of, 182n9; Cronos of, 147–149; debate regarding, 179; discrimination, racial and, 121, 123; history of, 8, 18n16, 122, 135, 140, 180; history of, revalorization of nation through, 176; history of, revising, 177; ideology and, 135; immigrants and paradigms of, 5; legacies, 141n2; Memorial to the Overseas Departments and territories of France, 172–173; memory and, 135; "Museum of France in Algeria," 171–172; polarization regarding, 170; racism and, 123; rap music and, 249; republicanism and, 92; revalorizing of, 171–173, 176, 280; Soviet, 144n25; studies of, 123, 134, 137; syndrome, 120–145; theorists, 136; World War II and, 96
colonization, 5, 89–183; debate over, 170; North African, French, 5; polarizing opinions regarding, 170; positive view of, 13–14, 50; positive work of, 167–168; stereotypes, 6
colonized peoples, 94–96; assimilation of, 99; citizenship status of, 99–100; formerly, treatment of, 278–279; Frenchness of, 110
Comité de vigilance face aux usages publics de l'histoire (CVUH), 133, 145n37
Comité march du 23 mai 1998 (Committee for the March of May 23, 1998), 178
Committee for the March of May 23, 1998. See Comité march du 23 mai 1998
Communism, 57
communitarianism, 59, 163, 285

Community citizenship, 111. See also citizens/citizenship
Conférence Nationale Souveraine, 154
Conseil Représentatif des Associations Noires (CRAN), 13, 121, 178, 245, 285; Conseil scientifique, 132; Indigènes de la République v., 129; minority rights promoted by, 128–129; organization of, 128; public support of, 130
containment, 89–183; in built environment, 228–234; exclusionism and, 228–234
Convergences rally, 242
Cooper, Fred, 12, 91–120, 144n24, 320
Coste-Floret, Paul, 100, 117n8
Côte d'Ivoire, 107; France's involvement in, 157, 278. See also Africa
La Courneuve, riots of 1988, 32
CRAN. See Conseil Représentatif des Associations Noires (CRAN)
créolité, 64, 285
le creuset français. See French melting pot (le creuset français)
criminality, poverty and, 66
criminalization, 65
critical race theory, 57. See also race
Cronos of colonialism, 147–149
cultural differences, 4; African/French, 5; assimilation and, 5–6; citizenship and, 68; immigrant, 262–263; integration and, 248, 250
cultural elitism, 57–58
cultural globalization, 68
cultural identity: beur, 242–243; heritage and, 275n37; hip-hop and, 16
culture: African, 9; hip-hop, 233; race and, 140–141. See also French culture
curfews, 5, 18n12; French Algerian-targeted, 17n11
CVUH. See Comité de vigilance face aux usages publics de l'histoire (CVUH)

Dammarie-lès-Lys, riots of 1997, 28, 32
"dangerous classes," 76–78
Dany Dan (rapper), 252
de Gaulle, Charles, 105–107, 109, 112, 119n36, 240, 260–261, 286
Debbouze, Djamel, 217

Debré, Michel, 105–106, 119n36, 255
Debré Laws, 268, 276n47
Declaration of the Rights of Man and of the Citizen, 93. See also citizens/citizenship
decolonization, 280; of Algeria, 111. See also colonization
deconstruction, 224n5
Defferre Laws, 268
democracy: European, 57; race and, 64–65
dependency theory, 122
Derrida, Jacques, 253, 274n20
Destroy Man (rapper), 251
détournement, 5
Devedjian, Patrick, 261
Dia, Mamadou, 106–107, 118n26
Diagne, Blaise, 96
Diam's (rapper Mélanie Georgiades), 16, 166n31, 253–254, 260, 269–270
diasporic issues, 5
Diefenbacher, Michel, 174, 178
Diefenbacher report, 174–176
Dien Bien Phu, 285–286
Diop Mambéty, Djibril, 244
discrimination, 245; colonialism and, 121, 123; ethnic, 83; February 23, 2005 law and, 179; in hiring practices, 259; housing, 275n33; housing and, 80; nation and, 81–83; racial, 60, 121–123; secularism and, 194–197; "testing" and, 275n33
discrimination positive, 7
disengagement, 112
Disiz la peste (music group), 166n31, 274n18
District B13 (Banlieue 13), 15, 227–228, 232
diversity: cultural, 245; ethnic, of French soccer team, 166, 166n22, 224n7
Djohar (rapper), 253
DNA testing, citizenship, 207–208
Douste-Blazy, Philippe, 174, 182n7
Douste-Blazy-Léonetti bill, 173
draft constitution, 100; citizenship provision of, 101; multiple civil regimes allowed under, 103
drug trafficking, 255

La Duchère: riots, 1997, 27–28; 2005 riots, 23–24

education: banlieue, 67; "ego-history" and, 138–139, 145n35; world history studies in, 138
education, public: anti-headscarf legislation, 188–190, 202n11; freedom of expression in, 191; religion and, 189–190; secular, 190–192
"ego-history," 138–139, 145n35
Ekoué (rapper), viii, 16, 253, 260, 274n18
Elf, 154–156
emotion: mobilizing, 32–37; solidarity and, 34
equal opportunity, 81, 83
equality, 162–163; identités, 197; libertarianism and, 191; racial, 166n20
L'Esquive (Games of Love and Chance), exclusionism, triple and, 235–237
État de siège, 142n7
état d'urgence, 142n7; in Algeria, 231; history of, 231; 2005 riots, 230–232
état-civil, 118n14
ethnic minorities, 11. See also minority populations
ethnicity/ethnicities, 85; banlieue, 252; differences in, 4; discrimination and, 83; in France, 87, 159; French citizens stigmatized by, 56; French soccer team's diverse, 166, 166n22, 224n7; multiple, 223; rappers and, 274n18; stereotypes, 259; Zidane's, 208, 210
"ethnobusiness" neighborhoods, 80
European Union, 65
Europeanization, 59
Evian Peace Accords, 111, 283; naturalization and, 211
evolutionism, 130–133
l'exception française, 286; headscarf laws and, 188
exceptionalism, 77–78, 84, 227–247
exclusion, 76–77
exclusionism, 194; in built environment, 228–234; containment and, 228–234; L'Esquive and effect of triple, 235–237; social, 6
extreme-right, 261. See also Right

exurban housing, 229. *See also* public housing

Fabe (rapper), 249, 273n8, 274n18, 276nn42,48
Factor X (rap group), 252
Faf la Rage (rapper), 252
Faivre, Maurice, 174
Fakoly, Tiken Jah, 157–165n18
Fanon, Frantz, 145n33, 147, 152, 253
FAS. *See Fonds d'Action Sociale* (FAS) (Social Action Fund)
FASS. *See* Fonds d'Action sanitaire et sociale (FASS)
February 23, 2005 law, 13, 167–183; "colonial grandeur" and, 168; consideration of, 176–178; controversy, 124–125; Diefenbacher report and, 175–176; discrimination and, 179; effects of, 178–179; maturation process, 182n7; passage of, 178; petitions, 139; *pieds noirs'* vote, 183n15; Provision 4, 179; *rapatriés* compensation and, 177; reaction to, 168; senate vote, 177–178
federalism: failure of, 117; imperial, 104
50 Cent (rapper), 269
Le Figaro/Le Figaro Magazine, 260–267; New Right theories and, 261–262
Finkielkraut, Alain, 6, 18n19, 190, 196, 248, 264
FMA. *See Français musulmans d'Algérie* (FMA)
Fofana, Youssef, 77–78
Fonds d'Action sanitaire et sociale (FASS), 240, 286
Fonds d'Action Sociale (FAS) (Social Action Fund), 240–241, 286; Algerian rights and, 241; history of, 241; renaming of, 247n15
Fonky Family (rap group), 252, 274n13
"foreign invasion," 263–264
Foucault, Michel, 168
le foulard islamique (the Islamic Headscarf), 133, 286; feminist arguments against, 202n20; hostility toward, 198–199; rights and, 204n36; social stigma, 188; wearing of, in schools, 188–189, 202n11. *See also* anti-headscarf legislation, 2004

Four Communes of Senegal. *See Quatre Communes* (Four Communes of Senegal)
Fourth Republic, 97–98
fracture sociale, 18n17
Françafrique, 154, 287
Français de souche, 146, 287
Français issus de l'immigration, 146, 287
Français musulmans d'Algérie (FMA), 12, 107, 109, 287. *See also* Algeria
France: Africa and, minorization of, 152–153, 164; Africa exploited by, 92; African migration to, 113; African policy, 49, 50; African sentiment towards, 50; African-descendents in, 147, 151; Africans in, 5, 108–113; Algerian migration to, 112–113; Algerian supporters of, in Algerian war, 111–112; aliens in, law regarding, 62; anti-Americanism, 8; anti-Semitism in, 61; Arabs in, 214; "authentic," 248; *banlieues* acknowledgement in, 21; *beurs* in, 146–166; blackness in, minorization of, 152–153; blacks in, 146–166; "civilizing work of," 171; colonial ideologies in, present, 126–127; Côte d'Ivoire and involvement of, 157, 278; denial, 58–59; ethnicity in, 87, 159; federal, 102–105; historians, 139–141; immigration, 48–51; imperial and national, 93–94; integration model in, 84; metropolitan, demographics, 8; minority groups, 9, 50; multicultural, 9; national and imperial, 93–94; "New," 150; North African presence of, 5; pluralist, 100–101, 269; racialization in, 55; racism in, 61–62; reconstruction, 239; riots and, 6; Rwanda and intervention of, 164n7; self-inflicted disaster in, 56–58; slave trade, African in, 49; slave trade in, 61; social model, 71; unitary, 102–105
France terre de liberté, 18n18
la francophonie, 287
la Fraature coloniale, 286–287
free circulation, 113, 115
freedom of expression, 193; headscarf controversy and, 193–194; in public education, 191. *See also* right(s)
"freedom of passage," 119n31

French colonies: citizenship status of, 105; Fourth Republic and, 97–98; subjects of, including/accepting, 108. *See also* colonialism; *specific colonies*

French Community, 105, 113–114; nationality in, 105–106

French culture, 68–69; African French and, 250; assimilation into, 98, 123–124; diversity, 245; Islam and, 10; race and, 48; secular, 188

French empire, 96–101; glorification of, 181; *métropole* and, 149–150

French identity, 6; concept of, 269; construction of, 260–270; forging new, 65–69; globalization and, 56; hip-hop and, 16; national, 111; recognition and, 84–87; redefinition of, 260–270; reinventing, 55–69. *See also* cultural identity; *identités;* national identity

"French Katrina," 5

French melting pot (*le creuset français*), 82, 124, 285; immigrants in, 82; outsiders in, 70–88

French Republic: postcolonial, 6; racism and, 47–54

French soccer team, 208–209; ethnic diversity of, 166, 166n22, 224n7. *See also* Zidane, Zinédine

French Socialist Party, 291

French Union, 118n14; African political leaders' power in, 104–105; Assembly of, 101

Frenchness, 7; African diaspora and, 7; of colonized peoples, 110; notion of, 10; tensions of, 185–276; visions of, 185–276

fundamentalism, 58

Gallo, Max, 190, 264

Games of Love and Chance. See L'Esquive (Games of Love and Chance)

garçon arabe, 236. *See also* Arab boys

Georgiades, Mélanie. *See* Diam's (rapper Mélanie Georgiades)

ghettos: *à la française*, 79; African American, 16n1; *banlieues* compared with American, 61; U.S., 53

Gilroy, Paul, 69, 158, 267, 272

Giscard d'Estaing, Valéry, 162, 165n12; immigrants and, 263

Glisant, Édouard, 63–64, 145n33, 179, 285

globalization, 7, 269; cultural, 68; French identity and, 56; national identity and, 271; race and, 59; racism and, 65

Glucksmann, André, 248, 264

de Gobineau, Joseph-Arthur, 84

Gramsci, Antonio, 266

grands ensembles, 229, 246n3, 287–288; postwar housing crisis and, 230

GRECE. *See* Group for the Research and Study of European Civilization (GRECE)

Group for the Research and Study of European Civilization (GRECE), 261

Groupe des trente (Group of Thirty), 243

"guest worker program," 72

Guèye, Lamine, 100–102

Habitations à Loyer Modéré (HLM), 230, 288

Hajjat, 18n17

Hall, Stuart, 69, 258, 260, 267, 269, 272

Hamé (rapper Mohamed Bourokba), viii, 16, 253, 256, 258, 260, 264, 268, 274nn18,21

harkis, 112, 181n4, 278, 288

Haut Comité des rapatriés, 175

headscarf affair, 14–15, 278–279; freedom of expression and, 193–194; media coverage, 197, 201

hegemony, 260–267

heritage, 275n37

hip-hop, 166n31; cultural identity and, 16; culture, 233; themes, 251; youth culture and, 156–157

HLM. *See Habitations à Loyer Modéré* (HLM)

Hollande, François, 166n24

homogenous citizenry, 116. *See also* citizens/citizenship

hors-la-loi, 231

Houphouët-Boigny, Félix, 104, 107, 165n8, 287

identitarian, 288

identités, 131; equality and, 197; multiple, 223; Le Pen and, 262–263; Zidane's, 205, 217–220. *See also specific identities*

identity checks, 255, 277
Île de France, 291
immigrants (*immigrés*), 158, 263; assimi-
    lation, 5–6; colonial paradigms and
    dealing with, 5; cultural differ-
    ences, 5–6; cultural differences and,
    262–263; French melting pot and, 82;
    Maghrebi, 88n1; public housing, 80,
    88n3; recognition, 85; republican/
    republicanism and adaptation of, 91;
    rights, 72; second generation, 88n1;
    social rights of, 72; threat of, 131;
    undocumented, 75; unemployment,
    73; urban planning and, 147; working
    class and, 72–73
immigration, 48–51; citizenship and,
    48–49; controlling, 52; Debré Laws
    and, 268, 276n47; French society and,
    87; history of, 140; as national iden-
    tity threat, 268; policy, 50–51; restric-
    tions, 115; *sans papiers*, 291. *See also
    Français issus de l'immigration*
immigrés. See immigrants (*immigrés*)
imperial federalism, 104
imperialism, 150; American, 279; colo-
    nial, 61; egalitarian, 97; legacy of, 123;
    postwar, 97
L'Indigène, 126, 143n12
indigènes, 125, 224n8, 288; citizenship
    and, 127
Indigènes de la République (the Natives
    of the Republic), 13, 121, 125–126,
    178, 245, 288; assimilation policies
    and, 129–130; CRAN v., 129; demon-
    stration, 126, 279; hostile reactions
    against, 130; integration policies and,
    129–130; in media, 127–128, 141n1;
    petition, 277
indigenization, of *beurs*/blacks in
    France, 146–166
Indo-European identity, 262
injustice: frame, 45n23; identity, 31;
    police hostility and sense of, 28–29;
    rioting and, 27–32; "us" and "them"
    feeling of, 31–32
integration, 64, 81; African descendent,
    151; of *beurs*, 158, 161–162; of blacks,
    158, 161–162; cultural differences and,
    248, 250; dissenting studies, 133–134;

French, model, 84; "grand model"
    of, 124; Indigènes de la République's
    issues with policies of, 129–130;
    paradigm of, 264; policy, 83; process,
    130–133
Islam, 9; French culture and, 10; Western
    civilization and, 264–265
Islamic extremism, 212
Islamic Fundamentalism, 286
the Islamic Headscarf. *See le foulard
    islamique* (the Islamic Headscarf)
Islamic law, 95
Islamofascism, 286

Jango Jack (rapper), 252
Jhongyo (rapper), 251
Joey Starr (rapper), 249, 251, 254, 273n5,
    274n18; violence incited by, 255–256
Joxe Laws, 268
Jules Ferry laws of 1880 and 1882, 201n5
Jules-Rosette, Bennetta, viii, 9
Julien, Isaac, 46n64, 69

Kabyle, Kabilya, 288–289
Kabyle identity, 217–220
Kabyles, 225n22, 288–289; treatment of,
    218–219
Kamnouze (rapper), 252
KDD (rap group), 252
Kechiche, Abdellatif, 235
Kelley, Robin, 250, 272
Kerner Commission, 30
Kim Song-Man (rapper), 253
Kool Shen (rapper), 249, 251, 254–256
Koundé, Hubert, 233

labor migration, 17n9; from Africa,
    108–109; Algerian, 112–113
laïcité identitaire, 288
laïcité sacrée, 189
language, 7
Lapeyronnie, Didier, 10–11, 21–46, 124,
    142, 256, 320
Lefeuvre, Daniel, 132, 145n41, 172, 180
Left, 199
left-wing intellectuals, 264
Lemaire, Sandrine, 18n17, 144n30, 284
libertarianism: equality and, 191; secular,
    191–192

Lino (rapper), 252
Lionel D (rapper), 251
Lotar, Eli, 237–238
L'Ouverture, Toussaint, 93
Lozès, Patrick, 128–129, 144n21, 166n20, 285
Lumpenproletariat, 72
Lyautey, Maréchal Hubert, 151, 290

Maalouf, Amin, 270
Madelin, Alain, 203n27, 261
Maghrebi immigrants, 88n1
Makensy (rapper), 257
Mali: collapse of, 113–114; Union Soudanaise and, 119n45
Mali Federation, 107
Malians, citizenship of, 111, 114
Mambéty, Djibril Diop, 244
Mamère, Noël, 156
mandarinat, 137
March 15, 2004 law. *See* anti-headscarf legislation, 2004
March for Equality (*Marche pour l'Égalité*), 74, 200, 242. *See also* equality
Marche pour l'Égalité. See March for Equality (*Marche pour l'Égalité*)
Marxism/neo-Marxism, 138
Matthieu, Mireille, 252
Mbembe, Achille, 11–12, 47–69, 286, 289, 291, 321
MC Solaar (rapper), 251–253
media, 67; *Le Figaro/Le Figaro Magazine,* 260–267; headscarf affair in, 197, 201; *L'Indigène,* 126, 143n12; Indigènes' in, 127–128, 141n1; postcolonial, 244; riots and, 36, 44n9; Zidane in, 206, 209
Medine (rapper), 257, 274n18
Mélenchon, Jean-Luc, 195
Melopheelo (rapper), 252
member states, independence of, 108
mémoire, 7
Memorial to the Overseas Departments and territories of France, 172–173, 176
Menelik (rapper), 252, 274nn14,18
métropole, empire and, 149–150
migrants: African, 113, 148; *rendre français,* 130; representations of, 52
military training, 228

"Minguettes generation," 74
les Minguettes/the Minguettes Generation, 289; *banlieues* and, 289; policy changes due to riots of, 38; riots, 1981, 3, 24, 73–74
Ministère AMER (rap group), 252, 254, 276n48
Ministry of National Identity, 267–268
minority populations: cultural/ethnic differences and, 4; equal opportunity, 83; France, 9, 50; identities, 272; rights of, CRAN and, 128–129; rise of, 131–132; visible, 178–179; war on terror and, 4
mise-en-scène, 245–246
mission civilisatrice, 6, 149–150, 179
Mitterrand, François, 73; civic identity and, 270
Monsieur R (rapper), 166n29, 252, 257–258, 274n18, 276n48
moral indignation, 43; rioting and, 27–32, 35–36
Morocco, battle of, national memorial to, 173
Mosaic law, 95
mosques, 189–190, 202n9
La Muette, 229–230
multiculturalism, 132; of French soccer team, 208; promotion of, 178–179. *See also* culture
multiethnicities, 159, 223. *See also* ethnicity/ethnicities
multinationalism, 207. *See also* nationalism
"Museum of France in Algeria," 171–172
Muslim(s): Algerian, 109–110; in France, 109; headscarf affair and, 14–15; headscarfs, wearing of, 133; racism directed towards, 197; Zidane as, 211–213

National Front Party, 251, 255, 262–263, 266–267, 271, 289; Sarkozy and, 267
national identity, 131, 248–276; French, 12; globalization and, 271; immigration as threat to, 268
National Revolution, 167
National Union of Real Property Owners (UNPI), 275n33

nationalism: French, 150–151; Le Pen and, 262–263

nationality, 105–108; African colonies and, 106–107; citizenship and, 58–59, 106, 110; double, 110; French, 255; French Community, 105–106; "superposed," 106

"native," image of, 279

the Natives of the Republic. *See* Indigènes de la République (the Natives of the Republic)

naturalization, 211

Ndiaye, Pap, 128, 285

nègre, 152

Négritude, 63–64, 285, 289

Negrophilia, 9

negrophobia, 153

neocolonialism, 149. *See also* colonialism

neoconservatism, 279

neutrality, 193

"New France," 150

New Right, 6, 260–267; *Le Figaro/Le Figaro Magazine* and, 261–262; racism and, 262; rappers and, 272; theories, 261. *See also* Right

nihilism, 43n2

1955 law. *See* April 3, 1955 law

Nique ta Mère (rap group), 257

Noah, Yannick, 160–161

noir, 7, 284. *See also* black(s); *pieds noirs; Police des Noirs*

Noiriel, Gérard, 11, 124, 132–133, 139, 145n37, 254

non-droit, 5

North Africa, 5, 291. *See also* Africa

OAS. *See* Organisation de l'armée secrète (OAS)

Occidental Petroleum (Oxy), 155–156

October 5, 1961, 17n11

oil shocks, 254–255

Ol Kainry (rapper), 252

113 (rapper), 257

Organisation de l'armée secrète (OAS), 182n13

originaires, 96

Oxy. *See* Occidental Petroleum (Oxy)

pacification policy, 50

Palestinization, 51–54

Papon, Maurice, 17n1, 18n14

parcours du combattant, 233

Paris Pogrom, 5

Paris 7 initiative, 122

parkour, 15–16, 228, 290; African American aesthetics and, 234–237; in films, 228; military training and, 228

Pasqua Law, 255, 274n25

Passi (rapper), viii, 16, 251–254, 256, 260, 264, 274nn14,17

Pauwels, Louis, 261–262, 275n36

Le Pen, Jean-Marie, 251; identity politics and, 262–263; nationalism and, 262–263; racism, 275n40; rise of, 255

Le Pen, Marine, 5, 269

penal repression, 65–66

Péna-Ruiz, Henri, 190, 195–197

Le Penism, 48–49, 62, 289

"Le Pen-ization," 206, 263

pieds noirs, 181n4, 290; exodus of, from Algeria, 112; February 23, 2005 law and, 183n15

Plan national, 238

pluralism, 100–101, 269

pluviôse, 12

police: African Americans and, 30; *banlieue* youth targeted by, 29; *banlieues* controled by, 77; Clichy-sous-Bois riots, 2005 and actions of, 35–37; death due to, 27–28; graffiti, antipolice, 29; harassment, 30; injustice and hostility towards, 28–29; perception, 30–31; race and, 60; racism, 51, 67; rioting and, 27–32; 2005 riots and, 28, 35–37; "us" and "them" feelings toward, 32; working class and, hostility between, 29–30

Police des Noirs, 151

police violence/brutality, 60, 277; rap music and themes of, 259–260

polygamy, 246n5

popular culture, 248–276

postcolonialism, 57, 278; Africa and, 153–154; history and, 180; Republic of Congo and, 154–155; theorists, 136. *See also* colonialism

poverty: criminality and, 66; rioting and, 41

precariat, 290

Prévost-Paradol, Lucien, 150

primordialism, 130–133

prise de parole, 43n2

promotion musulmane, 107, 109–110, 112, 166n24. *See also* Muslim(s)

provincialism, 78

public housing: cinema and, 237–242; discrimination and, 80; economic priorities and construction of, 239; immigrant, 80; immigrant percentage living in, 88n3; postwar, 237–242; refurbishing, 256; urban planning and development of, 238–239

public space, 192–194

Quatre Communes (Four Communes of Senegal), 94–95, 290. *See also* Senegal

racaille, 88n1, 291; *banlieues* and, 291; Sarkozy and, 5, 85–86, 162

race: of aliens, 56, 75; athletes and, 160–161; *banlieues* and, 56; categorizations, 160; citizenship and, 64–65; class and, 4; colonialism and, 121; culture and, 140–141; democracy and, 64–65; discrimination, 60, 121; equality, 166n20; Europeanization and, 59; French culture and, 48; globalization and, 59; "inferior," 149–150; looking beyond, 63–65; penal repression of, 65–66; police and, 60; racism between, 255; religion and, 53–54; riots and, 59; *sans-parts,* appearance of and, 60–63; segregation, 60; stereotypes, 6; war on terror and, 59

racial profiling, 277

racial vocabulary, 85

racialization, 11–12, 55, 65

racism: anti-headscarf legislation and, 194–195; anti-Muslim, 197; "anti-white," 16, 265–266; Code de l'Indigénat and, 52–53; colonialism and, 123; in France, 61–62; French Republic and, 47–54; globalization and, 65; New Right and, 262; Le Pen, 275n40; police, 51, 67; between races, 255; riots and, 11, 42; secularism and, 194–197; state, 52–53

radio, control of, 273–274n12

Raffarin, Jean-Pierre, 166n23, 203n25

Rancière, Jacques, 265, 291

rap music: African diaspora and, 271; *banlieues* and, 16, 271; censorship of, 166n29; colonialism and, 249; commercial, 253, 258; evolution, 251–253; hardcore, 253–254, 257–260; history, 251–253; language, 257; lyrics, 254–255; political message in, 253, 257; prosecution of, 276n48; purist, 253–254, 257–260; riots and, 248, 251; styles of, 253–257; themes, 251–253; violence incited by, 255–257

rapatriés, 167, 181n1; compensating, 177; history of, acknowledging, 169; questioning of, 173–174; revalorizing memory of, 173–174. *See also* Haut Comité des rapatriés

rappers: African French, 267–270; *banlieue,* 16, 252; education, 252–253; ethnic origins of, 274n18; legislation aimed at, 276n48; New Right and, 272; prosecution of, 258, 276n48

Rassemblement pour la République (RPR), 173

rebeux, 88n1, 284

reconstruction, 239

refugees, representations of, 52

religion: anti-headscarf legislation and, 190; in France, 267; race and, 53–54; in schools, 189–190; secularism, 189–190; Zidane's, 211–213

religious space, 189–190

religious symbols, ban on, 202n19. *See also* anti-headscarf legislation, 2004

Renaud, 252

rendre français, 130

Renseignements Généraux (RG), 265

réparations/repentance, colonial, 136

representation, 78

Republic of Congo, 154–155; civil war, 156; Elf and exploitation of oil deposits in, 154–156; Oxy and oil deposits in, 155–156. *See also* Africa

Republic of Equality, 280. *See also* equality

Republic of Haiti, 94

republican/republicanism, 91; citizens, 94–96; colonialism and, 92; immigrants adapting to, 91; secular, 58, 192–194; universalism and, 245

la République coloniale, 126

RER. *See Réseau Express Regional* (RER)
Réseau Express Regional (RER), 291
retournement, 5
RG. *See* Renseignements Généraux (RG)
Rhoff (rapper), 257
rhors, 284
Ribéry, Frank, 212–213, 225n14
Right: anti-headscarf legislation and,
    203n27; headscarf affair and, 199
right(s): Algerian, 109; Algerian, FAS
    and, 241; citizen, 12–13, 94, 237; *le
    foulard islamique* and, 204n36; immi-
    grant, social, 72; minority, CRAN
    and, 128–129; *originaires,* 96. *See also*
    civil rights movement; Declaration
    of the Rights of Man and of the
    Citizen
right-of-soil citizenship, 278
rioters, 42–43; hostile stance taken
    toward, 46n72; range of, 34; 2005
    riots, 232
riots/rioting: Africa and *banlieue,* 3–4,
    49; *banlieues,* 3–4, 49; civil rights
    movement, 27, 39; as collective
    action, 23–27; La Courneuve, 1988,
    32; Dammarie-lès-Lys, 1997, 28, 32;
    La Duchère, 1997, 27–28; emotion,
    mobilizing and, 32–37; expression,
    22, 38; French government approach
    to, 6; gain achieved, 39; injustice
    and, 27–32; institutions questioned
    during, 40; logic governing, 41; Los
    Angeles, 1992, 16n1; meaning, 26, 37;
    media and, 36, 44n9; *les Minguettes,*
    1981, 3, 24, 73–74; moral indignation,
    27–32, 35–36; motivation, 34; police
    and, 27–32; policy changes due to,
    38–39; political action and, 25–27, 38;
    poverty and, 41; race and, 59; racism
    and, 11, 42; rap music and, 248, 251;
    "rodeo riots," 73–74; societal state as
    manifested in, 25–26; solidarity, 33;
    spread of, history, 35–36; Toulouse-Le
    Mirail, 1998, 24; U.S., 1960, 27, 39;
    unemployment and, 41; "us" and
    "them" in, 36; Vaulx-en-Velin, 1990,
    24; violence and, 37–42; violence and,
    legitimacy of, 40–41; widespread, 37;
    youth, 3. *See also* 2005 riots

Rocard, Michel, 75, 162
Rocé (rapper), 253, 274n19
"rodeo riots," 73–74
RPR. *See* Rassemblement pour la
    République (RPR)
La Rumeur (music group), 166n31, 253,
    257–259, 268, 273n5, 274n14
Rushdie, Salman, 68
Rwanda, French intervention in, 164n7.
    See also Africa

Les Sages Poètes de la Rue (rap group),
    252
Said, Edward, 213, 253
Saint-Domingue: revolution of, 93–94;
    slaves freed in, 93
Salif (rapper), 257, 274n18, 276n48
Salles, Rudi, 178
sang mêlé, 151
sans papiers, 291
sans-parts, 291; class of, creating, 65; race
    and appearance of, 60–63
"Sarko-ization," 206
Sarkozy, Nicolas, 224n3; Bourokba
    charges pressed by, 258; Dakar
    speech, 208; ethnic stereotypes and,
    259; Ministry of National Identity,
    267–268; National Front Party and,
    267; political agenda of, 264; *racaille*
    and, 5, 85–86, 88n1, 162; 2005 riots
    and, 4, 17n7, 36–37
Sarkozyism, 49
sauvageons, 291
Sauvy, Alfred, 263–264
secular republicanism, 58, 192–194
secular space, 189–190
secularism: anti-headscarf law and,
    187–204; discrimination and,
    194–197; egalitarian, 194–197; French
    culture, 188; identitarian, 194–197;
    libertarian, 191–192; public education
    and, 190–192; racism and, 194–197;
    rational, 189–190; religious, 189–190;
    securitarian, 191–192
segregation: racial, 60; urban questions
    and, 78–81
Senegal: citizenship model, 116; *citoyen-
    neté dans le statut* and, 96; *état-civil*
    in, 118n14; Mali Federation founded

by, 107; nationality acts, 114. *See also* Africa; *Quatre Communes* (Four Communes of Senegal)

Senghor, Léopold Sédar, 63–64, 98–99, 117n7, 152–153; in Assemblée Nationale Constituante, 100

"sensitive areas," 78

September 11, 2001, 197, 264–265

shantytowns, 79

shared experience, 36

Shen, Kool, 249

Shonibare, Yinka, 69

silent demonstrations: symbolism, 33; 2005 riot, 24, 33

slave trade, 49, 142n6; abolition of, 94; French, 49, 61; Sain-Domingue and, 93

Social Action Fund. *See Fonds d'Action Sociale* (FAS) (Social Action Fund)

social exclusionism, 6

social model, 73

social security deficit, 73

society of exclusion, 76–78

Socrate (rapper), 163–164, 166n29, 257–259, 274n18

solidarity, 33–35, 43

SONACOTRAL, 241, 247n14

SOS-Racisme, 291

souche, 287. *See also Français de souche*

South Africa, 60. *See also* Africa

statuts personnels, 133

stereotypes, 11; Algerian, 218; ethnic, 259; racial, 6

Sudan: Mali Federation founded by, 107; nationality acts, 114

suffrage, 102. *See also* voting rights

Suprême NTM (rap group), 252, 254, 257, 259

Tandem (rap group), 166n29, 174n13, 257–259

Taubira, Christiane, 153

"testing," 275n33

Tévanian, Pierre, 14–15, 158, 187–204, 286, 321

Thomas, Dominic, 5, 9, 18n16

Thuram, Lilian, 206, 224n3

Tin, Louis-George, 128–129, 144n21, 285

torture, 169–171, 181n3

totalitarian space, 193

Toulouse-Le Mirail, riots in 1998, 24

Toussaint L'Ouverture, 93

traceurs, 290

transcolonial vector, 5. *See also* colonialism

Traoré, Bouna, 3, 228–229

Le 3ᵉ Oeil (rap group), 252

Truffaut, François, 243

Tunisia, battle of, 173

2Bal (rapper), 257

2005 riots, 9, 229; Aubervilliers, 23–24; Clichy-sous-Bois, 3–4, 21, 28, 35–37; cost of, 22; dismissing of, 22–23; La Duchère, 23–24; *état d'urgence* and, 230–232; government policies in response to, 256–257; initiatives taken after, 121; investigation, 22; Los Angeles riots, 16n1; magnitude, 22; meaning, 24; police and, 28, 35–37; rationale behind, 10–11; response elicited by, 21; rioters, 232; Sarkozy's comments on, 4, 17n7, 36–37; silent demonstrations, 24, 33; spark for, 24; spread of, 24–25, 37, 231; understanding, 19–88; Vaulx-en-Velin, 23. *See also* February 23, 2005 law

UMP. *See* Union pour un Mouvement Populaire (UMP)

underclass, 4. *See also* class

unemployment, 251; immigrant, 73; rates, 271, 274n23; rioting and, 41

UNESCO. *See* Universal Declaration on Cultural Policy (UNESCO)

Union Française, 12

Union pour un Mouvement Populaire (UMP), 181n2; anti-headscarf legislation and, 203n25

Union Soudanaise, 119n45

United States: anti-Americanism, 8; criminalizing sections of population within, 65; ghettos, 53; imperialism, 279; 1992 Los Angeles riots, 16n1; police/African American interactions in, 30; racializing sections of population within, 65; riots, 1960s, 27, 39

Universal Declaration on Cultural Policy (UNESCO), 245

universalism, 7, 57, 196–197; French, 7;
republican model of, 245
UNPI. *See* National Union of Real
Property Owners (UNPI)
urban planning, 79; African immigrants
and, 147; housing development,
238–239
"us" and "them": injustice and, 31–32;
rioting and, 36

Vaulx-en-Velin: policy changes due to
riots of, 38; riots, 1990, 24; 2005
riots, 23
verlan, 86, 284
Vichy collaborationism, 6
Vietnam, *Dien Bien Phu* in, 285–286
de Villepin, Dominique, 17n6, 142n7,
166n24, 275
violence: Algerian-targeted, 96; *bavure
policière* and, 17n4; police, 60, 259–
260, 277; rap music inciting, 255–257;
rioting and, 37–42; urban, 25, 59, 74
voting rights, 278; in *banlieues,* 69; citizen, 94; women's, 95. *See also* right(s)

war on terror: minorities and, 4; race
and, 59
welfare: group interests/representation
in, state, 72; social, 73; state, crisis
of, 81
whiteness, 159–160

women: anti-headscarf legislation, feminist arguments against, 202n20; voting rights of, 95
working class: districts, 78; immigrants
and, 72–73; police and, hostility
between, 29–30; political dependence
of, 41; welfare state and, 71–72
World War I, citizenship and, 96
World War II: colonialism after, 96;
imperialism after, 97

Yamakasi movement, 15, 232–233, 290
Youssoupha (rapper), 252, 274n14
youth: African, marginalization of, 156;
banlieue, 29, 31; male, 43n2

Zidane, Zinédine, 15, 205–226; Algerian
trip, 213–215, 219–220; anger of, 222;
Arab image, 214–215; on Arc de
Triomphe, 209; ethnicity of, 208, 210;
god-like status of, 216; head-butt, 212,
215, 224n12; as hero, 206; identities
of, 205, 217–218; identities of, fusing,
219–220; in media, 206, 209; multinationalism, 207; naturalization, 211;
parents of, 220–221; politicization,
206–207, 221–222; rags-to-riches
story of, 220–221; red cards, 222; religion, 211–213; silence of, 222
Zoxea (rapper), 252
zupiens (ZUP), 88n1, 291